FORENSIC SCIENCE

AUSTRALIA
The Law Book Company Ltd.
Sydney : Melbourne : Brisbane

INDIA
N. M. Tripathi Private Ltd.
Bombay

ISRAEL
Steimatzky's Agency Ltd.
Jerusalem : Tel Aviv : Haifa

MALAYSIA : SINGAPORE : BRUNEI
Malayan Law Journal (Pte) Ltd.
Singapore

NEW ZEALAND
Sweet and Maxwell (N.Z.) Ltd.
Wellington

PAKISTAN
Pakistan Law House
Karachi

U.S.A. AND CANADA
Praeger Publishers Inc.
New York : Washington

FORENSIC SCIENCE

An Introduction to Scientific Crime Detection

By

H. J. WALLS

SECOND EDITION

LONDON
SWEET & MAXWELL
1974

First Edition 1968
Second Impression 1971
Second Edition 1974

Published in 1974 by
Sweet and Maxwell Limited of
11 New Fetter Lane, London
and printed in Great Britain
by Richard Clay (The Chaucer Press) Ltd.,
Bungay, Suffolk

SBN 421 17110 3

PREFACE TO THE FIRST EDITION

At the present time science is expanding at an ever-increasing rate, and forensic science—the application of scientific techniques to provide objective, circumstantial evidence—shares in this process. As a result more and more scientific evidence is being given, is becoming more and more technical and is all too often less and less comprehensible to the non-scientist.

For all those concerned in the administration of justice—lawyers, police officers and others—this is a most unfortunate fact. There seems therefore to be a need for a book such as this—a book in which an honest attempt has been made to explain, assuming the very minimum of scientific background, the processes involved and the significance of the results obtained in producing scientific evidence. There is plenty of technical literature for the working forensic scientist, but much of it is dauntingly incomprehensible to the non-scientist, in that it is addressed to readers who already have a good background of scientific knowledge. There is, as far as the writer is aware, no up-to-date book in English of just the same scope as this one.

The book may also prove of interest to those contemplating forensic science as a career; they should find in it sufficient information about the various branches of the subject to tell them what kind of work they would be doing if they became forensic scientists, or just where their own specialities could be utilised if they are already trained scientists.

The writer has attempted to cover with the same degree of thoroughness both those parts of the subject which have changed little over the years—document examination, or the comparison of instrument marks, for example—and those parts which have changed a great deal. In the latter category he has been at some pains to include the very latest information available at the time of going to press: descriptive information will be found on such subjects as modern instrumental methods of analysis, the application of these to fields such as toxicology, recent advances in fibre identification and the immense strides which have recently been made in forensic blood grouping.

A very large number of people have helped in the writing of this book, and the writer is glad of the opportunity now offered of thanking them publicly.

First, many colleagues, ex-colleagues and friends have given generously of their time and expert knowledge in checking various sections, particularly: Mr. Hamilton G. R. Bantock (firearms); Detective Superintendent Chapman,

Durham County Constabulary (safebreaking and photography); Mr. Brian Culliford (blood grouping and general biology); Dr. Alan Curry (toxicology); the late Dr. Ivor Dunsford (blood grouping); Detective Inspector Forrest, Durham County Constabulary (fingerprints); Mr. W. A. Gliddon (general biology); Dr. Wilson R. Harrison (documents); Mr. J. V. Jackson (toxicology); Mr. N. R. Lee (general biology); Mr. J. McCafferty (firearms); Miss Margaret Pereira (blood grouping); Dr. Ursula Philip (genetics); Detective Chief Superintendent Squires, Metropolitan Police (fingerprints). The writer is also indebted to Mr. N. R. Lee and Mr. E. B. Parkes (Director of the Home Office South Western Forensic Science Laboratory) for details of some illustrative cases.

Secondly, the writer is much indebted to a number of correspondents who have supplied him with information on matters outside his own knowledge: Dr. David A. Black (Los Angeles); Sir Arthur Dixon (formerly Assistant Under Secretary of State, Home Office); Professor Roland Grassberger (Criminological Institute, University of Vienna); Mr. J. Edgar Hoover (Director, Federal Bureau of Investigation); Dr. A. J. Howard (Director, Department of Industrial and Forensic Science, Northern Ireland); Mr. George Maclean (formerly Assistant Chief Constable of Glasgow); Dr. Franz Meinert (formerly Director, Bavarian *Landeskriminalamt*); Professor Giovanni Muzzioli (*Istituto di Patologia del Libro*, Rome); Dr. F. G. Tryhorn (formerly Forensic Science Adviser to the Home Office); the late Dr. H. Ward Smith (formerly Director, Laboratory of the Attorney for the State of Ontario, Toronto); Mr. Stanley Ellis (Leeds University).

Thirdly, the writer is indebted to the Times Publishing Company for permission to use material which first appeared in an article in the *Times Review of the Progress of Science*, to the Focal Press Ltd. for similar permission to use material which appeared in *Perspective* and the *Focal Encyclopaedia of Photography*, and to several of the publishers of the books listed in the bibliography for supplying him with information about them.

The writer would also like to thank the people and organisations without whom it would have been impossible to illustrate this book, and whose names are acknowledged in the captions to the illustrations.

The writer thanks Mrs. M. D. Conway for her professional assistance in the preparation of some of the line illustrations, and his colleagues and former colleagues Detective Superintendent Chapman, Mr. S. Denton and Mr. J. McCafferty for help in the preparation of some of the photographs.

Thanks are also due to several now anonymous persons who gave their permission to use material which, on grounds of economy, was eventually excluded. The writer also, it is perhaps hardly necessary to add, offers his apologies to anyone who should have appeared in the above list but whose name has been omitted through inadvertence or forgetfulness.

PREFACE TO THE SECOND EDITION

The purpose and "slant" of this book is still adequately described by the opening paragraphs of the preface to the first edition. However, in preparing the second, the writer has been influenced by the fact that the first, though primarily addressed to non-scientists concerned with law enforcement, proved more successful than he had dared to expect as an introduction to forensic science for those entering it professionally. In this edition, therefore, he has tried—with what success, others must judge—to combine a complete and scientifically acceptable coverage of the field with sufficient elementary explanation to make this comprehensible by readers without a scientific training.

In the attempt to do this the book has been largely re-written. Much has been added dealing with the important, numerous and in some cases unexpected developments in the field since the first edition appeared. The most noteworthy of these are the introduction and exploitation of new instrumental methods of analysis, and the advances in blood grouping. In order to make as much room as possible for these additions some of the original text has been shortened—without, it is hoped, omitting anything essential—and a few passages which were merely ornamental or which dealt with matter no longer topical have been omitted altogether. The writer has also taken the opportunity to re-arrange and, he hopes, clarify some parts, and to make some changes in emphasis where the relative importance of different methods have proved different from what was anticipated.

As with the first edition, the writing of this book would not have been possible without a great deal of help willingly given. The writer is especially indebted to Mr. E. G. Davies, Forensic Science Adviser to the Home Office, and to the Directors and staffs of the Metropolitan Police and Home Office Laboratories, for opportunities, the value of which cannot be rated too highly, to see what is new in the field and to discuss its problems with those actively engaged in it. Those who have helped in this way are too numerous to name individually; the writer therefore hopes that they will accept collectively this expression of his very genuine gratitude. Many of them, if they read this book, will recognise their contributions; if they remain anonymous here, that is simply because this is not the kind of book which one dare risk making tedious by citing an authority for every statement.

The writer is most grateful to Dr. Barbara Dodd and Dr. P. J. Lincoln of the

London Hospital Medical College for sacrificing some of their valuable time to saving him from error. He also thanks sincerely a number of correspondents who have supplied information or helpful criticism, namely: Mr. Lowell W. Bradford, Director, Laboratory of Criminalistics, Santa Clara County (California); Dr. V. J. Clancey and Dr. K. Gugan of Dr. J. H. Burgoyne and Partners, London; Dr. J. D. J. Harvard, British Medical Association; the late Mr. Edgar J. Hoover, Director, Federal Bureau of Investigation; Mr. Edward J. Kearney, National Committee on Uniform Traffic Laws and Ordinances, Washington, D.C.; Mr. S. S. Kind, Editor of the *Journal of the Forensic Science Society*; Detective Chief Superintendent G. T. C. Lambourne, Metropolitan Police; Dr. D. M. Lucas, Director, the Centre of Forensic Sciences, Toronto; Dr. Daniel R. Morales, Department of Public Health, State of California; Dr. S. K. Niyogi, Thomas Jefferson University, Philadelphia; Mr. Robert Reeder, Northwestern University, Evanston, Illinois; Mr. Keith A. Ritchie, National Safety Council, Chicago; Mr. R. G. Silversides, Fire Research Station, Boreham Wood, Herts.; Professor Kazuo Suzuki, Tokyo Dental College; Mr. Robert Webster, formerly of the Gem Testing Laboratory, London Chamber of Commerce; Mr. Marvin H. Wagner, U.S. Department of Transportation, Washington, D.C.

The following firms have also been kind enough to supply much valuable technical information: AEI Scientific Apparatus Ltd., Manchester (mass spectrometry); Cambridge Scientific Instruments Ltd. (scanning electron microscopy); Finnigan Instruments Ltd., Hemel Hempstead; Lion Laboratories Ltd., Cardiff; Technicon Instruments Co. Ltd., Basingstoke; Technipol International Corporation, Berkeley, California.

Another large group of unpaid assistants, who, from their sheer number, must remain anonymous and be thanked collectively, are those participants in the Sixth International Meeting of Forensic Sciences (Edinburgh, 1972), who have been both generous and helpful in supplying reprints of their contributions.

Lastly, the writer would like to thank the Editorial staff of Sweet and Maxwell for their co-operation at all stages of the preparation of his book.

H. J. WALLS

London
January 1974

CONTENTS

CONTENTS

PLATES

1
INTRODUCTION

This book is almost entirely concerned with the application of science to the detection and prosecution of crime. This is approximately the field which is called "police science" or "criminalistics" in America, "criminalistique" in France and "Kriminalistik" in Germany. The correspondence is not exact, since these terms embrace a certain amount of plain police work with which the British laboratory worker is not concerned. For convenience and the purposes of this book, however, "criminalistics" and "forensic science" will be taken to be synonymous terms.

"Forensic science" means nothing more than the science which is used in the law courts; that is, it is the science behind expert evidence and in everything the forensic scientist does he must bear in mind that he may have to testify as an expert witness. This meaning is now established in Britain by the almost simultaneous founding, slightly over ten years ago, of *The British Academy of Forensic Sciences* and *The Forensic Science Society*. Both of these bodies include scientists, doctors, psychiatrists, pathologists, engineers, technical consultants, lawyers and police officers among their members, and both concern themselves with the whole area over which science, technology, medicine and the law interact. This book deals however with only a part of that area—a part which we shall try in Chapter 2 to delimit more precisely.

The pedigree of forensic science, as it is practised today, is by forensic medicine out of police work. Before about, say, 1900 the policeman could learn, and the doctor was assumed to know, enough science to apply its techniques to the problems encountered as they arose. With the rapid growth of science, however, problems occurred more and more frequently which only the trained scientist was equipped to tackle.

It would not be altogether fanciful to trace the beginning of forensic science to Sherlock Holmes, because his creator Sir Arthur Conan Doyle showed remarkable foresight in making him scientifically trained, and thereby almost certainly helped to publicise the idea that science could be applied to the policeman's problems. Historically and in fact, however, we should start with Hans Gross (1847–1915), professor of Criminology in the University of Prague, whose classic book, *Handbuch für Untersuchungsrichter*, was first published in 1893 and ran through numerous editions; the English translation came out in 1906 as *Criminal Investigation* and has also been revised and reissued many times. The whole craft of detection still bears his stamp, but the particular aspect of his work

which concerns us here is his continual stressing of the help which science
could give to the detective.

Gross, however, was a lawyer rather than a scientist, and did not himself contribute to the development of scientific methods. The greatest contributions in
that field were probably those made or inspired by Edmond Locard, of the
University of Lyons (b. 1877; retired 1951; d. 1966). Many of the methods still
in use can be traced back ultimately to his Institute of Criminalistics, which
began in 1910 as a one-room police laboratory for the Rhône *préfecture* and grew
to be a university department. The first volume of his encyclopaedic *Traité de
Criminalistique* appeared in 1923. Pupils came to him from all over the world,
and many returned to become pioneers of this work in their own countries.

As far as the writer is aware, however, absolute priority among Continental
laboratories must go to that headed by R. A. Reiss, a Swiss-naturalised German
who taught photography in the University of Lausanne, a course which was
changed to one on forensic photography in 1902. Soon afterwards his department
became the Lausanne Institute of Police Science, and since 1909 diplomas in the
subject have been granted by the university.

Similar institutions followed in other countries. A laboratory was started in
Dresden in 1915 by Robert Heindl, who had worked at Lausanne with Reiss; it
foundered on wartime difficulties, and was re-started, this time successfully, as a
national police laboratory in 1919. During the inter-war years, this grew into an
organisation with a central laboratory in Berlin and branches in the larger cities.
Another laboratory was started in Vienna in 1923. Several of the smaller countries such as Sweden, Finland and Holland, had laboratories before 1925; the
Swedish one, under H. Söderman, a pupil of Locard, soon acquired an international reputation.

As has been implied, in the English-speaking countries institutional progress
was slower. The detective there had to turn for help to people, often distinguished
scientists, for some of whom forensic work was a side-line, and the first problem
facing him was the by no means easy one of knowing where to go for the help
he wanted. Well-known names in Britain from that era are those of Dr. Ains-
worth Mitchell, whose work on the identification of inks is still sometimes consulted, and Sir William Willcox, who supervised the toxicological analysis in the
Crippen case.

There are still indeed a number of private consultants in this field, and, even
if they did nothing else, their occasional appearance as witnesses would perform
an invaluable function in keeping the official laboratories on their toes. Nevertheless, even in Britain, with its traditional respect for the amateur, the existence of
capable and distinguished private practitioners could not reverse the inevitable
trend towards channelling this work into official laboratories and by, say, 1930
the need for a forensic science service with a full-time staff was patently obvious
to all who were aware of the problem. In the immediately following years a number of local authorities set up their own small laboratories, and as a result of joint
consultations between the Home Office and the Metropolitan Police, the Metropolitan Police laboratory was started in 1935. About this time, some small local

authority laboratories were also enlarged and transferred to Home Office control, although part of the cost of administration is still paid for by local police authorities.

Development in the U.S.A. was behind that in Europe but somewhat ahead of that in Britain. The Los Angeles forensic science laboratory dates from 1923, but the F.B.I. Laboratory, now the biggest and the best-known in the country, was not started until 1932. In its first full year of operation, it made 963 examinations; in the fiscal year ending in June 1971 it made over 460,000 examinations of 291,008 specimens submitted in over 42,000 cases. A large number of other city and state laboratories were also started immediately before, and since, the Second World War.

In the organisation of a forensic science service there are a number of implicit questions which must be answered, and different countries have produced different answers. Some of these questions are: Is its administration to be the concern of a university or of a government department? Who is to do what—at what points do the scientists take over from technically trained police officers on the one hand and from medical men on the other? Is it better to have a large central laboratory, which can be lavishly equipped but is inevitably remote from most of its police users, or numerous smaller regional laboratories, which are accessible to their users but which cannot each be equipped as lavishly as a central one? Are the laboratories to be responsible to the prosecuting authorities, the courts or some other body? The system which has been adopted in England and Wales is that of a number of regional laboratories, operating independently but considered a common "pool" of expertise. These, with the exception of the Metropolitan Police Laboratory, are all administered directly by the Home Office, and that laboratory is also the regional laboratory for the south-east of England. The provincial laboratories are situated at Aldermaston (near Reading), Birmingham, Bristol, Cardiff, Chorley (near Preston), Harrogate, Newcastle upon Tyne and Nottingham. In addition, there is also at Aldermaston a central laboratory which undertakes fundamental research for the whole service. In Scotland, much of this work was and still is performed by the forensic medicine departments of the universities, Scottish universities having had such departments longer than English ones, but there is also a laboratory, started in 1943, forming part of the Glasgow police establishment. Northern Ireland is served by a laboratory in Belfast administered by the Ministry of Commerce.

The English laboratories are not concerned with the enforcement of food and drugs legislation, nor with the normal business of H.M. Customs and Excise; they also do not concern themselves with fingerprint examinations, which is everywhere the business of specialist police departments. Practically every other aspect of scientific (as opposed to medical) crime detection comes, however, within their province. Medical matters are dealt with by the police surgeons and pathologists. The former are normally general practitioners retained or nominated by the police; the latter are often hospital or university pathologists who are called in as occasion requires, but there is also a number of regional pathologists who are retained by the Home Office but attached to the staffs of universities or hospitals. The normal practice is for the doctor or pathologist to limit himself to the examination of the allegedly intoxicated motorist, living victim of crime or dead body, and to leave to the laboratory all subsequent work arising from the result of his examination.

There is as yet no uniform practice in England for the examination of scenes of crime. This was formerly left to the investigating detective, who called out the scientist when he thought it necessary; there is now, however, an increasing tendency towards the appointment in each area or by each force of "scenes-of-crime officers"; this simultaneously frees the detective to pursue his inquiries and relieves the scientist from a most time-consuming duty. There are also attached to the Metropolitan Police specialist "explosives officers," whose special duty is to deal with all cases involving the illegal use of explosives (see p. 191); this arrangement has not yet, however, been adopted in other parts of the country.

Most of the larger members of the British Commonwealth have also set up laboratories devoted exclusively to this work. In Canada, for example, the Royal Canadian Mounted Police have several well-equipped laboratories in Ottawa, Regina and other centres, and the Attorney-General's Department of Ontario has maintained since 1932 a large and busy laboratory in Toronto. Each of the constituent states of Australia (except the sparsely populated Northern Territory) maintains its own forensic science service, and in New Zealand the service is administered by the Department of Scientific and Industrial Research. In India there are active forensic science laboratories attached to both the central and the various state governments. In the smaller countries of the Commonwealth, and in the few remaining colonies, forensic science is usually the concern either of the Government Chemist's department or of some specialised section of it.

The tendency in most European countries is for the work to be divided between university institutes of forensic medicine and police scientific or technical departments. The former handle not only medical and pathological examinations but also the allied ones in toxicology, blood-alcohol analysis, etc.; the latter deal with everything else. In some of the smaller countries (*e.g.* Norway, Ireland) relatively small police laboratories are maintained to undertake the simpler work, and the more technical and difficult cases are referred to the appropriate department of the nearest university.

The United States presents (perhaps not unexpectedly) a somewhat confused picture. Vast size, a multi-tiered law enforcement system, traditional suspicion of all governments and a huge variation in the size of the police forces (from over 30,000 in New York to under twenty in many rural areas) all combine to prevent the development of any uniform nation-wide practice. The F.B.I. Laboratory has already been mentioned. Its primary function is to assist the federal law-enforcement activities of the F.B.I. itself, but it will also undertake scientific work for any police authority. Originally, some of the universities took a share in this work—the University of California Department of Criminalistics, under the late Professor Paul Kirk, was known throughout the world—but their share has diminished as more of the states and larger cities have set up their own laboratories. There is an apparent preference, especially in the Pacific states, for local independence in this respect, leading to a proliferation of relatively small laboratories, each serving a city or region of, say, half to one million population.

The usual picture in the largest cities, such as New York or Chicago, is for the laboratory to be an integral part of the police machinery. It is often directed and staffed by scientifically trained police officers (although there is a trend towards replacing these by civilian scientists), and it is common for there to be a relatively large body of "evidence technicians" (*i.e.* scenes-of-crime officers) attached to the laboratory. Services such as firearms examination, bomb disposal, fraudulent cheque files and polygraph ("lie detector") operation either come under the laboratory's control or are grouped with it in a technical services section.

By and large, American laboratories handle much less of the marginally medical investigations than British ones do. Many, if not most, of the coroners' or medical examiners' departments of the more populous areas maintain their own laboratory services to deal with toxicological and allied problems.

2

THE WORK OF THE FORENSIC
SCIENCE LABORATORY

I. CRIME

What a forensic science laboratory actually does is determined by three factors:
(1) what is technically capable of being done; (2) the pattern of crime in the area
which it serves; (3) the awareness of police forces served by it of what it can do.
The first of these depends in general upon the progress of science, and, for a
particular laboratory, upon its equipment and the variety of skills possessed by
its staff. The second factor is altogether outside the scientist's control, and, of
course, varies with time and place. He has, on the other hand, considerable
control over the third factor, since the training of the police in the use of scientific
methods must be largely his responsibility.

However, although the work that flows into the laboratory does so because
crimes have been committed, it does not reflect quantitatively the distribution of
these crimes according to the type of offence. With some offences—bigamy, for
example—scientific evidence is never necessary and indeed it is hard to see how it
could be used. With some others it may or may not be useful, depending on
circumstances. And with others again—of which murder itself is the best example
—it has practically always a part to play in their investigation and prosecution.

It must be admitted right away that science can help the detective only in a
minority of the crimes which he has to investigate. The composition of that
minority will naturally vary: there will, for example, be relatively more shootings
in America than in Britain, or more safe-breakings in London than in rural
Wales. In considering any figures, it must be remembered that the great bulk
of "crimes" recorded are trivial offences against road traffic laws and the like.
Two British figures which may help to give perspective are: over 60 per cent.
of *all* offences are road traffic offences; 85 per cent. of indictable crimes are
offences against property. Laboratory returns show that in this country at the
present time scientific assistance is sought in something like 2 per cent. of all
offences recorded. The figure varies from region to region, and could probably
be increased everywhere with profit to society and loss to the lawbreaker, but it
seems unlikely that its optimum would be more than about double the present
figure.

More specifically, the present direction of the forensic scientist's work in this

6

country is illustrated by the figures on page 8 for the laboratories of England and Wales in 1971.

In other parts of the world, of course, where the patterns of crime are different this difference is reflected in the work of the laboratories. In the United States, for example, the examination of firearms constitutes a major task for the laboratories, and for those in the big cities narcotic drug identifications come first by a large margin in their case figures.

II. CRIME AND SCIENCE

The most important function of scientific evidence is to convert suspicion into a reasonable certainty of either guilt or innocence. For example, the blue car which did not stop after the accident was thought to have been a blue Austin, and a blue Austin is traced which must have passed the scene and which bears recent damage (for which the driver may offer some plausible explanation) and, in the damaged area, some fragments of paint of another colour are found. It is the scientist's job to clinch the matter: is or is not the "foreign" paint identical in colour and chemical composition with that of the car damaged in the accident?

Scientific evidence does not often *by itself* convict the lawbreaker. Nevertheless, this does occasionally happen. For example, some years ago several hundred pounds' worth of electrolytic copper strip was stolen from a factory in Wiltshire making electrical machinery, and the local police had no idea at all who might have done it. The only straw at which they could catch was the casual observation by one of their own officers that a certain van had been absent on the night in question from its usual parking place near his house. Nothing was known to them against the owner of the van, who normally used it in his business of selling logs and firewood. When questioned, he denied strongly that he had ever carried copper in it. However, on-the-spot and laboratory investigations revealed that: (1) there was a freshly scraped-off fragment of pure copper on a bolt-head in the tailboard of the van; (2) one of the double doors of the stockroom opened by the thief bore a fragment of paint agreeing in colour and composition with the paint of the van, which had a small recent scrape on its side at the same height from the ground as the fragment on the door; (3) the floor of the van was, naturally, littered with leaves and fragments of bark, and a number of such leaves and fragments, from the same two or three species of trees, were found at the scene of the theft; (4) the stolen strips had been interleaved with paper soaked in a high-boiling British Standard transformer oil, and on the shoulder of the van-owner's jacket there was an oily stain from which about 1 millilitre of a similar oil was extracted. He was convicted of the theft.

The various reasons for which a scientific examination of the evidence may be made can be classified under the heads of the following questions:

(1) Has a crime or tort been committed? For example: was the fire accidental, or was it started maliciously? Was the shooting fatality accidental, suicidal or homicidal?

Type of crime or investigation	Metropolitan Police Laboratory	Provincial laboratories	Total	Per cent. of total	Per cent. of total, excluding drink-and-driving and drug cases
Drink-and-driving cases	20,407	37,360	57,767	59·9	
Drug offences	6,064	8,587	14,651	15·3	
Offences against property (larcencies, breaking offences, etc.)	799	5,377	6,176	6·4	26·4
Road accidents (other than those involving drink)	354	3,227	3,581	3·7	15·3
Forgeries and other cases involving document examinations	502	2,384	2,886	3·0	12·3
Sexual offences	440	1,466	1,906	2·0	8·1
Suicides and unexplained sudden deaths* (mainly toxicological cases)	76	1,651	1,727	1·8	7·4
Crimes of violence (assaults, woundings, robberies, etc.; but excluding rape and murder)	377	1,185	1,562	1·6	6·7
Arson and malicious damage	335	1,176	1,511	1·6	6·4
Firearms examinations†	360	374	734	0·8	3·1
Murder and manslaughter	203	323	526	0·5	2·2
Other offences‡	539	2,267	2,806	2·9	12·0
Cases dealt with by explosives officers	479	—	479		
Totals	30,935	65,377	96,312		

* Different regions show wide variations in the volume of this work submitted to the forensic science laboratories; in some regions but not in others much of it is done by hospital and other competent laboratories.

† Includes examination of firearms coming into the possession of the police, but not connected or believed to be connected with a specific crime.

‡ The incidence of the various types of offences included here varies considerably from time to time. In particular: (a) the number of illegal abortions leading to laboratory examinations has declined to a negligible figure since the passing of the Abortion Act 1967; (b) the number of counterfeit coins examined has increased considerably since the introduction of decimal coinage in 1971, presumably because the new 50p piece, worth four times as much as the old halfcrown, has become worth counterfeiting again.

(2) In some cases, if the answer to question (1) is affirmative, another question follows: how and when was the crime committed? Was the malicious fire simply started with a match, or was petrol used to get it going, and at what time was it started? What type of weapon was used to commit the murder? How did the burglar get into the safe?

(3) What information can in a general way be obtained as to the identity of the perpetrator? This question probably arises most frequently when an article of clothing has been left at the scene of an offence. A proper examination of this may disclose the hair colour, approximate height, occupation, etc., of the wearer. To cite an example, a lady who lived alone in a cottage in Gloucestershire awakened one night a few years ago to see a strange man in her bedroom, naked except for a vest. She gallantly put him to flight armed only with an electric torch, and later, on searching the house, found in the kitchen a pair of trousers which had certainly not been there the previous evening. In the laboratory, some tiny turnings or drillings of a hard grey metal were found in the turnups, and the composition of these as shown by spectrographic analysis strongly suggested a "nimonic" alloy. These are complex heat-resistant nickel alloys used in jet-engine rotors. This suggested to the police a possible suspect who worked as a rotor-blade grinder in an aircraft-engine factory near by. He was subsequently identified by the lady.

(4) The ultimate and most vital question is of course: are the accused man and the person characterised as having committed the crime in fact one and the same person? This question is most commonly answered in one of two ways:

(a) It may be possible to establish a connection between some physical evidence associated with the crime and some personal characteristic of the accused—blood group, hair colour, fingerprints, etc.

(b) It may be possible to show a connection between the scene of the crime and something which is definitely linked with the accused—scratch marks made by his "jemmy," fibres from his jacket caught on a projecting nail, etc.

It is perhaps hardly necessary to point out that the investigation of one single crime may involve the answering of questions under all of these headings.

III. SCIENCE: A CHANGING PICTURE

The case of the stolen copper described on p. 7 also demonstrates that one single case may require the use of a variety of scientific techniques for its elucidation. Traditionally, therefore, the organisation of forensic science laboratories has been based on this. They have usually been—and most commonly indeed still are—divided into sections along the following lines.

(1) The largest section will be a physical-sciences one ("chemistry" or "chemistry and physics") staffed mainly by chemists, and equipped to carry out both the "classical" methods of analysis and the more modern and increasingly important instrumental methods—spectrography, X-ray crystallography, gas and other types of chromatography, infra-red and ultra-violet spectrometry, etc.

The staff of this section must be prepared to analyse and/or identify, probably on a micro-scale, *any* natural or manufactured product. This demands versatility and, in a small laboratory, some familiarity by people probably trained as chemists with the techniques of a variety of sciences—chemistry, physics, pharmacology, metallurgy, geology, bio-assaying and so forth. In a large laboratory there will be greater specialisation; while there will still be plenty of work for the analytical chemist, there are likely also to be separate sections dealing with problems in geology, metallurgy and other sciences. The very specialised branch of chemical analysis which constitutes toxicology has also nowadays developed into an almost completely separate discipline.

(2) There will also be a section dealing with biological problems and occupied mainly, but not exclusively, in the investigation of offences against the person. It will need ample working space, since much of its work will start with a minute search of large numbers of articles of clothing. Technically, it will be much occupied with the identification and grouping of body-fluid stains, the examination of natural and man-made textile fibres, and the identification of animal and plant tissues. This section has commonly been staffed by botanists and zoologists, but the growing importance of serological methods has created more opportunities for those trained in other disciplines, such as micro-biology. Moreover, forensic biologists are increasingly making use of physico-chemical instrumentation and can no longer afford to be pure biologists.

(3) Finally, there are several important facets of the work which no self-respecting science would own, but which the forensic scientist has by tradition dealt with because they demand some "know-how," a scientific attitude of mind and the facilities of a laboratory for their investigation. These are, chiefly: the examination and photography of the types of material described in the next chapter; the examination of firearms; the examination of documents. Again, in large laboratories, these aspects of the work are normally the concern of separate specialised sections.

The organisational framework which I have just described has evolved during the half-century or so since forensic science began, but it is becoming strained and even, some believe, unrealistic because of the greater number of scientific disciplines which can usefully be applied to a single problem and because of the blurring of the boundaries between these disciplines. Forensic science is in fact at present having to meet the problem of reconciling two opposing trends: the increasing need for a polymath's synoptic view of its work, and the specialisation forced on its practitioners by the increasing sophistication of the techniques which they use. The all-round expert competent in a wide field and relying on his own knowledge is disappearing and giving way to specialists supported by highly skilled technicians and relying on codified retrievable information. Some may regret this, partly perhaps for sentimental reasons, but the change is inescapable.

It may also be convenient to mention at this point three particular lines of development which are at present growing in importance. One is the introduction of *automatic*, and therefore time-saving, methods in examinations (to be

Laboratory discipline	Physical fits	Casting	Low-power microscopy	High-power microscopy	Photography	Detector powders	Physical properties	Chemical analysis simple ("wet")	Chemical analysis sophisticated (instrumental)	Metallurgy	Geology	Serology	Botany (Zoology)
Crime													
Theft*	●●	●●	●●		●●	●●●	●●	●●	●●				
Burglary†	●●●	●●●	●●●		●●	●●	●●	●●	●●●		●		●
Road accidents	●●●	●	●●		●●		●●		●●	●●	●	●	
Drink & driving								●●	●●●				
Homicide (other than by shooting)			●	●●	●				●			●●●	●●
Shooting			●●●		●●				●			●●	
Other crimes of violence				●●●					●			●●●	
Sexual offences				●●●								●●●	●●
Poisoning				●				●●	●●				●
Bombs and explosions	●●		●●●	●	●			●●	●●	●●			
Arson and malicious damage					●		●●	●●●	●●●				
Forgery and fraud	●		●●●	●●	●●●		●●	●					
Obtaining by deception			●				●●●	●●●	●●				
Abortion	●		●				●	●	●●				●
Drug offences				●●				●●●	●●●				●●

* *i.e.* Stealing not involving unlawful entry.
† *i.e.* Theft (and other offences) involving forcible entry into a building.

described in due course) requiring the routine performance of large numbers of similar analyses. Secondly, there is the increasing reliance on codified and possibly computerised *data storage and retrieval*. The mass of factual information needed by the working forensic scientist is now so great that, without such assistance, he would be unable, or able only at an unacceptable cost in time, to find just the relevant background data he needs. In this country, it is one of the functions of the Home Office Central Research Establishment to provide this service, and its rapid growth has shown just how valuable it is. Thirdly, there is the growing realisation of the value and importance of *statistical methods*. These can help to define the scientific equivalent of the law's "beyond reasonable doubt." It is obviously—at least to the scientist—an advance when he can replace vague expressions such as "very probable" or "a reasonable inference" by mathematical expressions of the probability of the truth of his conclusions. This point will be briefly discussed in the next chapter (p. 15).

Returning, to end this chapter, to the descriptive classification of the work of a forensic science laboratory, this is bound to be a somewhat arbitrary compromise between (to use the apt American phrases) "mission oriented" and "discipline oriented" views of it. The former is the policeman's, the latter the scientist's. The compromise adopted in this book may not strike the reader as the best which might have been reached; the writer pleads only that it is the outcome of a great deal of thought on his part.

In the table on page 11 (for the idea of which I am indebted to Mr. Lowell Bradford) an attempt has been made to show how types of crime and laboratory disciplines interlock. The number of ●s in each box is a rough indication of the usual comparative importance of the discipline in the investigation of the crime. However, such a table cannot be other than a very approximate guide; *any* discipline may occasionally be required in the investigation of *any* crime.

3

CONTACT TRACES I—MARKS, SCRATCHES AND PHYSICAL FITS

I. INTRODUCTION

Much of a forensic scientist's work consists in providing physical evidence of the presence of a suspect at the scene of a crime, or in showing that an object which can be conclusively linked with him in some other way was used in the commission of the crime. Examples of the former, direct type of link are fingerprints or blood from a cut hand found at the scene. Examples of the latter, indirect type are the finding of paint similar to that of the window frame attacked on a "jemmy" known to be the property of the suspected housebreaker, or of tyre marks indicating that a car owned or used by the suspect was also that used in committing a crime.

Edmond Locard, who was mentioned on p. 2, laid it down as a guiding principle that "every contact leaves a trace." Identification of the trace may thus provide evidence of the contact. Sometimes of course this task is beyond the present resources of science, but it is up to the scientist to reduce whenever he can the category of undetectable traces.

The examination of contact traces, although it may have to be made in connection with almost any type of crime, is most frequently necessary in connection with thefts and breaking offences of all sorts, with assaults in which there has been a person-to-person struggle and with road accidents in which the offending vehicle does not stop.

In this connection, any or all of the following items may have to be examined and, if possible, compared with the sources from which they are suspected of having been derived.

(1) Broken parts showing irregular fractured edges.

(2) Marks on smooth surfaces made by fabrics, footwear soles, tyres, etc.; also fingerprints and palm prints.

(3) Indented impressions left by tyres or feet in mud or snow, by housebreaking implements in woodwork, etc.

(4) Friction marks or scratches left by hard edges scraping over or shearing through a softer material.

(5) (*a*) Fragments or traces of material carried away from the scene of the

crime on the criminal's implement(s) or clothing, or on motor vehicles.

(b) Other materials which may be transferred on to the criminal's person or clothing in various circumstances—ink, wet paint, lipstick, industrial raw materials, etc.

(6) Fibres, tufts of yarn or scraps of cloth caught on projections at the scene of a breaking offence, carried away on motor vehicles or found on other articles of clothing.

(7) (a) Bloodstains.

(b) Stains of other body fluids.

(8) Biological materials of all sorts—hair, feathers, vegetation, etc.

That list includes some items which are usually considered detectives' rather than scientists' work—the taking of tyre-print casts, for example. Fingerprints are also always in this country the business of specialist police departments (see p. 130). In most cases, however, at what point the detective hands over to the scientist is a matter of arrangement and understanding between them. Taking the list as a whole, the laboratory may or should be concerned in the examination of nearly all of the items in it. Items 1–5(a) are considered in this and the next chapter, and the remainder when we have dealt with the various special skills and techniques necessary.

Even for the simpler types of examination, any of the various technical aids with which the laboratory will or should be equipped may be brought into use —casting, photography, low-power magnification, high-power magnification (microscopy), determination of physical properties, chemical analysis. For the last two of these, many extremely complex and sophisticated types of equipment are now available and give us valuable information otherwise unobtainable. However, it should never be forgotten—as highly trained graduates recruited into forensic science are liable to forget—that complexity and sophistication of equipment are useless unless the contact trace has first been found; they can never entirely replace the intelligent use of one's eyes and nose, judgment and common sense. These must always come first.

There are two other preliminary observations to be made. First, a contact trace must always be compared with a *control* of some sort from the place whence it is suspected of having come—for example, paint from the window attacked, or blood from the person believed to have lost the blood. Now, it rarely—probably never—happens that the control and crime materials are completely identical in every conceivable respect. No two scratches made by a tool are exactly the same, if only because its edge is slightly altered every time it is used. A control of soil will show minute random variations according to the precise point from which it is taken. Paint varies slightly in thickness from place to place. A cautious forensic scientist will rarely if ever say that two things are "identical"; he prefers to say that they are "indistinguishable" (by all the tests which he has thought fit or been able to apply). But the more sensitive the techniques of comparison used, the more likely is it that small variations and discrepancies will be detected. He must therefore consider, and possess the background knowledge to judge, whether any difference he detects is within the expected variability of the material, in which case control and crime specimens could have had a common origin, or whether the difference is so great that they could not. As I have heard it put succinctly: "How different is 'different'?"

Making a decision on this point constitutes one of the scientist's most onerous responsibilities, and it is in discharging it that his experience is most valuable. However, as ever more parameters can be measured and as the differences which are detectable become ever more minute, his task becomes ever more difficult. Current thinking on this subject has perhaps scarcely "gelled" as yet, but it seems likely that the idea of "indistinguishability" will be replaced by that of "discriminatory power," giving us the answer to the question: in what proportion of cases would two unrelated specimens, actually of different origins, be found indistinguishable by the group of tests applied? If that answer can be made quantitative, then an objective assessment can be made of the value of the laboratory findings. This is a field the exploration of which has hardly begun, and which will undoubtedly require the mathematician to be co-opted as navigator. J. B. Parker of the Atomic Weapons Research Establishment made some years ago a valuable study, for which he had to devise a new statistical approach, of the evidential value of the trace-element analysis of hair specimens, and this pioneering work probably points the trail which must be followed.

Secondly, the transfer of traces may be, and often is, a two-way process. Traces from the scene may be carried away on the person, clothing or implements of the perpetrator, and, at the same time, traces from all or any of these may be left at the scene. Similarly, in a road accident, traces may be left by the vehicle responsible on the other vehicle, stationary object, pedestrian, etc., involved, and at the same time traces from these may be carried away on the vehicle responsible.

The value as evidence of what is found in the laboratory depends very much on whether such a two-way transference has occurred or not. If, for example, the end of the suspected "jemmy" fits the mark on the window frame, that is a fact to be noted, but there may well be many other instruments which fit the mark unless there is something very unusual about it. If, however, the suspected instrument has on it in addition paint similar to that of the window frame, then, if it was not the instrument used, a most remarkable coincidence has occurred, which may fairly be felt to call for explanation. (In fact, in elementary mathematical terms, if the odds against another jemmy chosen at random fitting the mark are, say, 20 to 1, and if the odds against any jemmy having this sort of paint on it are, say, 50 to 1, then the odds against a jemmy taken at random both fitting the mark and having this paint on it are 20 × 50 to 1—that is, 1,000 to 1.)

It follows that the help which the scientist can give is limited if no one in particular is suspected or if no arrest has been made—that is, if only the scene of the crime is available for examination. Even in this case, however, the detective and the scientist between them, if they make a thorough examination, may be able to discover what size and type of footwear, or what colour and material of clothing, the intruder wore; or of what colour and (if anything is broken off) make and approximate age the "hit-and-run" car was. An intruder who leaves any clothing behind may also thereby leave information about his height and build, hair colour, or (as in the example quoted on p. 9) occupation.

II. MARKS AND SCRATCHES

We come now to the various types of examination mentioned in the previous section. In revising the following paragraphs, I have been much indebted to various published papers on the topics dealt with in them, in particular to those by Dr. Fawcett of the Home Office Forensic Science Laboratory in Nottingham.

Physical fits and broken edges. If anything gets broken in committing a crime, and if one of these parts is found at the scene and the other can be linked with the suspect, then the fitting together of the broken edges may provide the most incontrovertible evidence possible—evidence which needs no scientific training for its appreciation. Many housebreakers have been convicted by an obvious match between a piece of metal found at the scene and a recently broken edge of a tool in their possession.

Any material which breaks with a randomly irregular edge can provide this evidence—cast metal, plastics, wood, glass (see also pp. 34–35) etc. One can easily if necessary justify rationally the quasi-intuitive conviction that two pieces fitting exactly together must have been one before the break. The fracture can be considered as a line showing a number of points of inflection, at each of which it turns through a certain angle to either the right or the left. But at each of these points it might have turned through a different angle, or in the other direction. Suppose for the sake of argument that there are twenty such points of inflection, and consider only the three possibilities at each point: to the left, to the right or straight on. Then the number of possible configurations of the line is 3^{20}, which is over 3,000 million. An actual line of fracture follows of course one general direction, so that configurations making repeated turns in the same direction must be excluded. However, even if we exclude 99 per cent. of the theoretically possible configurations for this reason, we are left with over 30 million practically possible ones. And in most cases the odds against another similar configuration occurring by chance will be much greater even than that, since there are likely to be many more than twenty points of inflection and since we have not considered the precise angle through which the line turns at each point.

Broken lamp glass, broken-off door handles, etc., may also be left at the scene of a road accident, and, if the suspected vehicle still carries the corresponding broken part, no further proof of its having been involved is necessary. If a head-lamp glass is shattered, the patient "jigsawing" of pieces from the roadway and pieces remaining in the lamp may be rewarding. As it is difficult to assemble curved pieces accurately on a flat surface, a useful trick here is to do the jigsawing on a plaster cast of the inside of an identical unbroken glass.

Another type of fit may be presented when a fixture which has been attached to a car or building for a long time is stolen. It is sometimes possible in such a case to link a fixture found in a thief's possession with its original point of attachment by means of a correspondence between broken lugs, bolt heads, etc., and the place whence the fixture has been removed. (See case 3, p. 24.)

Marks on smooth surfaces. These may be on linoleum, polished wood, paper, glass, etc. The actual mark may consist of oil or grease, mud or dust, or it may have been made by the partial removal of a pre-existing film of any of these things from the surface. Glove-fabric patterns will usually be revealed in a routine dusting for fingerprints (p. 132), but rarely show more than the type of gloves worn. Footprints are more often usefully characteristic, and a greater proportion of them than is possibly realised may be of great value to the investigator. It is usually sufficient to photograph them to a known scale, although with a faint mark it may be difficult to secure a negative showing adequate contrast. For a dimensionally accurate record, the negative emulsion and the mark must be parallel and the axis of the lens perpendicular to both; a somewhat frustrating problem is therefore presented by those occasional marks which are clearly visible only when viewed obliquely by specular reflection. A natural-sized photograph of the print is finally compared with a control footprint made with the suspected article of footwear (fig. 1). According to whether the print to be compared is light-on-dark or dark-on-light, the control print is made using a light powder (*e.g.* powdered aluminium) on a dark surface or a dark powder (*e.g.* powdered graphite) on a light surface. The surface may be paper, but the tacky side of one of the modern self-adherent plastic sheet materials is better. The control prints may be preserved as permanent exhibits by covering them with wide, clear sticky tape (if on paper) or clear plastic film (if on a tacky surface). It will finally be possible in the most favourable cases—highly irregular crêpe rubber or similar irregular patterns and/or characteristic damage by wear—to find sufficient points of identity to leave no doubt that the mark was made by that particular article of footwear and no other. For this it is not necessary that the mark shows the whole or even most of the sole or heel in question; valid conclusions can be drawn from quite small fragmentary marks provided that they are sufficiently detailed. With some types of mark—for example, one showing a barred pattern with several defects in the bars—it may be possible to calculate the odds against two items of footwear showing an identical arrangement of defects; the figure may then turn out to be surprisingly large (several millions to one).

Prints not easily photographed can sometimes be "lifted" with the same wide, clear sticky tape or even, at a pinch, by the old "dodge" of using tackily damp photographic printing paper (unexposed and fixed for dark marks, blackened and fixed for light ones).

A new method for showing up footmarks on carpets devised by the Shirley

Institute in Manchester utilises the static charge generated on the areas of contact. If small plastic beads are sprinkled over the carpet before the charge has dissipated, they adhere to these areas and "develop" the marks. The finer details cannot however be revealed in this way.

A rather special type of mark which occasionally occurs is that produced when a smoothly cellulosed car wing or body has hit a pedestrian and shows on its surface the pattern of his clothing fabric. The actual mark may be no more than a pattern of faint abrasions on the glossy surface and will require very nicely adjusted lighting for its photography. In comparing mark and fabric it must not be forgotten that the latter may be distorted in the instant of a severe impact; it may therefore be necessary to make a control mark by simulating the conditions of the collision, even taking such drastic measures as driving the car at speed into a dummy dressed in the clothing in question.

Foot and tyre impressions. Impressions in mud or snow may be photographed to a known scale, and the photograph compared with the suspected footwear or tyre. If some small object such as a matchbox placed beside the mark is included in the photograph, the shadow cast by this will usefully show the direction of lighting. It has also been pointed out that a better photograph of greatly increased contrast is obtained if the mark is lightly sprayed with an aerosol paint, white for marks in dark mud etc., and dark-coloured for marks in snow or other white material. Casts of the impressions may also be made (pp. 21–23), but photography, being non-destructive, should come first. In either case the amount of information obtained will depend on the clarity of the mark (which in turn depends on the material in which it is made) and on the amount of individual characteristic detail on the object which made it.

With footwear, any clear impression will show the sole pattern, and a complete impression will show the size. (The impression may however be a little larger than the sole/heel which made it, due to movement of the foot in putting it down). Wear and random defects may even enable the actual article of footwear to be identified, as discussed in the previous section; however, prints in rough soil can never show the same detail as impressions on a smooth surface. With tyre marks the details of the tread pattern, and of sidewall lettering if present, should indicate the make and type of tyre, which may further indicate the type of vehicle. The way in which the tread is worn may also give some information on this point. It may further be possible to identify an individual tyre by the occurrence of fortuitous cuts or other damage, and by the precise relative disposition of sidewall lettering and tread-pattern elements, the latter being intentionally randomised in manufacture to minimise noise. It has also been pointed out in Germany that heavy-lorry twin-tyre pairs possess an additional identifying characteristic, even although the individual tyres themselves may show no peculiarities, in that the mutual relative positioning of the twin tread patterns is variable, random and hence identifiable. Finally, many laboratories keep indexed collections of footwear and tyre-tread patterns, which may enable one to say how common a certain pattern is.

Indented marks. The use of a jemmy, chisel, screwdriver, etc., to force a door or a window may leave a clear impression of the end of the tool on the woodwork. If it is a new tool of standard type, the mark is obviously of only limited value as evidence. If it is old, worn or broken, the mark will be more characteristic—perhaps even to the extent of indicating that tool and no other.

The tool and the mark may be compared in various ways. There is often none better than the "feel" of an experienced investigator that the tool fits the mark as a hand an old glove. This, however, should *never* be tried by anyone except the expert who is to give evidence; a premature trial might alter the mark, and would, if the mark is on a painted surface, render valueless as evidence the subsequent finding of any paint on the tool. The tool and the mark may also be compared by means of casts (pp. 21–23), or, in some cases, by means of superimposed photographic transparencies.

Valuable characteristic marks may also occasionally occur when the hungry housebreaker bites off a piece of apple, chocolate, cheese, etc., and in doing so leaves a tell-tale impression of his teeth. Since few if any people have completely regular teeth, subsequent comparison, by casting and/or photography, with a control bite made by a suspect may provide good evidence of identity. It has in fact been suggested that such identifications could be made more frequently than they are if investigating officers were more vigilant in collecting discarded apple cores and the like.

Scratch marks. The edge of jemmies, cold chisels, screwdrivers and shearing tools are finished by grinding. Even when they are new, therefore, their microprofiles will show randomly distributed irregularities the pattern of which is unique for each. After they have been used for some time, the edges generally become damaged more or less irregularly, and the fine random pattern of the new edge is gradually replaced by the coarser random pattern of the much used one.

When such an edge slips on a smooth grainless surface (*e.g.* the keeper plate of a lock), or shears through similar material (*e.g.* wire cut by wire-cutters or bolt-croppers), the resulting mark will show striations corresponding in spacing and depth to the spacing and elevation, respectively, of its random projections. If therefore a scratch mark associated with a crime, and a mark made on a suitable surface by a suspected tool, show an identical pattern of striations, one can say that that tool was used to commit the crime. (See fig. 2 and case 4, p. 24.) Spanners have also been linked in this way with nuts and bolt-heads which they have been used to unscrew.

As already mentioned, the crime and test patterns are rarely if ever *completely* identical. However, although any two scratch marks each containing a large number of individual striations will always show a chance correspondence of some of these, a true match, once found, is unmistakable. Even if one simply counts lines, without regard to their relative prominence, it was found in tests made in America about 30 years ago that the correspondence was always less than 25 per cent. in marks made by different tools, but always more than 70 per cent. in two marks made by the same part of the same tool. In addition, in all tool marks some lines (those made by the larger prominences) are always more conspicuous than others, and in a true match the pattern and spacing of the prominent lines is replicated in a way that leaves no room for doubt. Attempts have recently been made, again most successfully in America, to remove the subjective element from scratch-mark comparisons by reducing them to a calculation of probabilities. However, although it is obvious that the odds against a match showing a high degree of coincidence occurring by chance are enormous, it cannot be said that these attempts have so far led to any routinely applicable mathematical procedure.

Much trial and error is necessary in making the comparison: either side of any given edge may have made the scratch; there is rarely any indication which part of an edge has made a scratch often much narrower than the edge, or which part of cutting blades has severed a wire; and there is also no indication of the angle at which the tool which made the scratch was being held, although quite a small change in this angle may alter considerably the characteristics of the scratch. It is necessary therefore to make many control scratches with different parts of the suspected tool held at different angles.

A rather special type of scratch mark is sometimes met with in lead pipe and similar products. These often show clear longitudinal striations (usually, with pipes, most clearly on the inside) produced by irregularities in the cutting faces of the extruding die, the pattern of which is therefore characteristic of a particular batch of material extruded through a certain die within a certain period. On this basis, lead piping, etc., found in the possession of a suspect may be linked with pieces remaining at the scene of a theft; similarly, a piece used as a "cosh" might be linked with other pieces in a suspect's possession.

Lastly, the theft of scrap metal in the form of turnings has more than once been proved against the thief by finding in his possession and at the scene of the theft turnings which show identical patterns of striations—that is, which were turned off by the same tool at about the same time (fig. 5).

The comparison of scratch marks may be made in various ways. The simplest is to photograph all the marks to the same enlarged scale, cut the photographs of one set in half across the striations and compare every possible relative position of the two sets. This requires no elaborate equipment, but is laborious. It is much easier to use some sort of comparator or *comparison microscope* with which identically enlarged images of any part of the marks can be viewed side by side (fig. 3).

The essentials of such an instrument are: spotlights to illuminate obliquely from identical angles the sets of scratches to be compared; paired lenses or objectives focused on the marks; some optical arrangement for bringing the images to be compared into juxtaposition; mechanical stages permitting the marks to be moved or rotated while under the lenses.

A number of such instruments have been produced. The simplest arrangement has parallel cameras separated by a thin septum throwing two images on to a common focusing screen, but at high magnifications the images so produced are uncomfortably dim for visual comparison. In more elaborate instruments the objective lenses are separated by a foot or more, allowing ample working space underneath them, and a system of mirrors or reflecting prisms is used to bring the images into juxtaposition. It is possible to use two ordinary microscopes in this way in conjunction with a bridging comparator head, but complete instruments specially designed for this work are available and preferable. In the well-known (and in western Europe) well-established *Leitz* comparison microscope, and also in the similar American and Japanese instruments, the juxtaposed images are examined through an eyepiece, each occupying half of the circular field. A choice of objectives of different focal lengths and of eyepieces of different powers makes a very wide range of overall magnifications possible. Any selected field can be photographed using a camera mounted vertically above the eyepiece.

Comparison projection microscopes have also been produced in which the two images are viewed side by side on a ground-glass screen. This arrangement is convenient for photography, and has the advantage of allowing more than one viewer to see the images simultaneously. However, such instruments have not really caught on among forensic scientists; possibly the types so far produced have lacked the optical sophistication of the older-established instruments.

In all scratch-mark comparisons there are two recurrent difficulties which no degree of optical refinement can overcome. First, the surface bearing the mark may be part of a large unwieldy object which can neither be positioned conveniently under the microscope nor cut down to a manageable size. Secondly, the comparison, and even more the eventual photography, are more difficult if the substances bearing the marks are very different in colour. Both difficulties can be overcome by comparing, not the original marks, but casts of them. A casting material suitable for this purpose, which will reproduce the minutest striations and is of a convenient colour for both viewing and photography, consists of a mixture of sulphur and finely powdered graphite. (See the following section.)

The very large magnification given by the scanning electron microscope (p. 82) has also been utilised for scratch marks the details of which are too fine for resolution by ordinary optical means. This instrument cannot however be constructed as a comparison one enabling two marks to be examined simultaneously. Its great depth of focus is valuable with marks on irregular surfaces, where the high optical magnifications necessary may make it impossible to have the whole of the mark in focus at the same time.

Lastly, it is also possible to "mechanise" scratch-mark examination by using an instrument in which the up-and-down movement of a lightly loaded stylus drawn across the mark at right angles to the striations is greatly magnified and recorded as an enlarged cross-section of the mark. Instruments of this type have been used successfully in bullet examination (see p. 201), but they have not yet, as far as the writer is aware, been developed for use in the present context.

III. CASTS

Casts have been mentioned several times. They are used fairly extensively to compare footprints and footwear, tyre marks and tyres, tool marks and the instruments that made them, etc.

The ideal casting material should:

(1) be cheap;

(2) be easy to prepare and apply under adverse conditions (*e.g.* in bad weather at a remote outdoor scene of crime);

(3) set rapidly;

(4) reproduce the shape cast faithfully and accurately;

(5) be capable of reproducing fine detail;

(6) be dimensionally stable after setting, without distortion or shrinkage occurring.

Unfortunately, there is no ideal all-purpose casting material. The choice among actual materials must therefore depend on circumstances. For example, when the impressions are numerous or large, as with footprints and tyre marks, the material must be cheap; if very fine details are to be reproduced (as with the scratch marks discussed in the previous section) it must be grainless and very free-flowing when liquid; it must be flexible when set if the mark has re-entrant angles or interior shapes; if it is important not to alter the mark, the casting material must not adhere to it and should preferably not be mechanically stronger

Of the numerous available materials, the most useful can be classified as: (1) plasters—*i.e.* watery mixtures which set by chemical action; (2) thermoplastic materials which are melted or soften by heat and set on cooling; (3) materials which remain flexible when set.

Plasters. The only important material of this type is plaster of Paris. This is finely powdered calcium sulphate hemihydrate; when mixed with water to a slurry, it sets rapidly by the formation of the dihydrate, which is chemically identical with gypsum or alabaster. It is cheap, even in the best ("dental") grades and reproduces detail accurately and permanently. Its use requires no equipment other than water and a basin, together with some means of containing the liquid slurry in the mark. On the other hand, it adheres to many surfaces, cannot be used readily on vertical ones and cannot because of its brittleness be used on re-entrant angles. It is the normal material for casting footprints, etc. (but see also below, p. 23); it may also be used for making positive casts of negative impressions taken in other materials.

Taking good plaster casts demands a certain modicum of skill, chiefly in knowing just how thick to make the slurry and in avoiding entrapped air bubbles. These, if on the surface of the cast, could be mistaken for features of the object being reproduced, but they can be recognised with a little experience. The only other mistake that is likely to be made in plaster casting is succumbing to the temptation to clean off adhering soil, etc. too soon; if the cast is not allowed to get completely hard before this is attempted, its fine detail will be destroyed.

Proprietary materials of this type are also available which claim to set faster and stronger than ordinary plaster of Paris, but they are much more expensive. Other water-setting materials which have been used can now be considered obsolete.

Thermoplastic materials. These can be sub-sivided into:

(*a*) Materials sufficiently fluid to pour when hot. Sulphur has already been mentioned in this connection (p. 21). It can also, surprisingly enough, be used for casting footprints in snow, thanks to its low specific heat and thermal conductivity. In casting with sulphur, it is important to remember that it must be used only just above its melting point, as it becomes viscous at higher temperatures. A mixture of paraffin wax and rosin has been found useful for casting impressions in dry loose sand or soil. There are also a number of proprietary resinous compositions of fairly low melting points.

(*b*) Materials which merely soften on heating. These are obviously of more limited applicability, but are convenient for shallow indented marks in hard surfaces. The dental composition used for mouth impressions is probably the most useful of such materials. It may be softened in hot water and pressed into the mark; it is important to build up a good thickness before it hardens. Well softened plasticine can also give quite good impressions of such marks if no other material is available.

Flexible casting materials. Materials which remain flexible when set yet retain their shape have been known and used for a long time, mainly in preparing cast replicas of parts of the body ("moulage") and in taking casts of the insides of footwear in order to compare the pressure points with the foot of the supposed wearer. "Home-made" compositions based on gelatin have been so used, and a commercial rubbery preparation which emulsified with hot water and set to an elastic gel was formerly available. Both of these suffered from dimensional instability; they shrank as they dried, so that it was necessary to make at once a "positive" cast from them in, for example, plaster or a resin. A much superior type of flexible casting material, using a non-drying silicone base with a catalytic hardener for setting, has now been developed. It does not adhere to most surfaces and the cast, while remaining flexible, is non-shrinking and dimensionally stable.

One other type of casting material that should be mentioned is *fusible alloys*. The best known of these, Wood's metal, is a bismuth/cadmium/lead/tin alloy with a melting-point as low as 70 °C. As it is fairly expensive and not easy to use, it has rather fallen out of favour; however, as it is mechanically strong and gives very sharp casts, it is still likely to prove the best material on some occasions.

A rather special problem in taking casts out of doors is presented by impressions in soft sand, *very* wet mud or snow, with which plaster cannot be used in the normal way. As already mentioned, rosin–wax mixtures may be used in sand. Alternatively, sand or powdery snow can be fixed before casting by spraying with a dilute alcoholic solution of shellac; when it is hard, the shellac film is sprayed with oil. In very wet mud, dry plaster can first be dusted on in sufficient quantity just to absorb the surplus water. The use of sulphur for taking casts in snow had already been mentioned.

IV. SOME EXAMPLES

The techniques so far described, although scientifically primitive, are all capable, if carefully applied, of yielding valuable and even conclusive evidence. They may also prove necessary in the investigation of very many types of crime—many more than it has been possible to describe here. The following examples will illustrate the value of these "proto-scientific" techniques.

(1) The kidnapping of the Lindbergh baby in the U.S.A. by Bruno Hauptmann led to one of the most famous criminal trials of the 1930s. A crucial piece of evidence in this was the fact that the wood of a home-made ladder left at the scene of the crime showed a physical match with boards from the floor of Hauptmann's loft in respect of nail-hole spacing and the striations left by a damaged blade on a multiple-blade rotary cutter.

(2) Ten baited crab pots which had been laid by a south-coast fisherman were stolen, and three days later were found laid about five miles away and identified by the loser. The pots now contained fresh bait, consisting of pieces of fish. In the boat of a man fishing near where the pots had been re-laid there were found a number of pieces of fish one of which showed such an exact physical fit with one of the pieces in the crab pots that there could be no doubt that both pieces had come from the same fish.

(3) A car owner had his battery stolen, and a battery suspected of being the stolen one was found on another car, the owner of which, however, alleged that the battery had always been fitted to his car. The lead terminal posts of this battery bore indented marks left by the clamps of the main leads. Clamps from both cars were sawn in half and compared with one of the terminal posts. Fig 4a shows this comparison with the half clamp from the suspected thief's car; fig. 4b with that from the loser's car. There can be no doubt which clamp was originally fitted to the battery.

(4) The body of a girl was found in a wood. She had been strangled with a thin cheap plastic belt one end of which had been cut off. The cut end showed faint but definite striations left by the blades of the scissors used. A pair of scissors was found in the possession of a suspect, the blades of which when tested with a similar plastic belt produced an identical pattern of striations.

(5) There was a series of burglaries at widely separated places in southern England. A fragment or fragments of metal were found at the scene in each case, obviously broken from the end of the implement used to force doors and locked drawers. A man was eventually arrested for the last of the series, and in his possession was a case-opener the end of which had been broken off. The various fragments and the broken implement all "jig-sawed" together exactly, enabling all of the offences to be attributed to the arrested man.

(6) The owner of a large house in the country made an insurance claim for the alleged burglary from it of valuable pictures, carpets and *objets d'art*. Suspicion was aroused that the claim was fraudulent, that he had "rigged" the break-in and that he had in fact removed the allegedly stolen property to another house he owned elsewhere. Some carpet tacks and fragments of picture-frame moulding

were found in his estate car. In the manufacture of carpet tacks the heads are formed by a mechanical hammer flattening the ends of clamped pieces of soft iron rod. The tacks from the estate car and tacks remaining at the scene of the alleged theft showed on their heads identical random irregular impressed marks, which obviously reproduced the state of the hammer face which made them at the time they were made; that is, all the tacks must have been made on the same machine at about the same time. This suggested that they all came from the same batch, which would have been a most improbable coincidence if there was no connection between those in the estate car and those from the scene.

(7) Some bottled beer was stolen from a public house, and at the scene of the theft there were found some nearly new "crown caps" which bore some rather peculiar marks. A police sergeant investigating the case discovered a man who claimed that he could open beer bottles with his teeth, and, to prove his claim, opened one in the presence of the sergeant. A comparison between the marks on one of the caps found at the scene of the theft and those on the cap removed in the presence of the sergeant showed that both had been made by the same instrument, namely, the suspect's teeth.

4

CONTACT TRACES II—PAINT, GLASS AND SOIL

Among all the materials which may be found as contact traces, three occur so frequently that something approaching a routine can be followed in their examination. They are: paint, glass and soil. The examination of broken glass can also be informative in other ways, which it will be convenient to discuss here also.

I. PAINT

One could almost claim for paint that it keeps the forensic scientist in business. A very high proportion of the surfaces from which traces get removed in committing crimes are painted ones, and paints show a wide variety of identifiable characteristics. "Paint" may be taken in the present context to include also pigmented plastic films such as are used to cover insulated wire and household metal objects, since fragments of such material frequently occur as contact traces.

A hardened paint film is characterised by:

(1) its colour, or, where there are several coats, colours;
(2) its hardness, which depends on its age, and can be assessed roughly with small fragments;
(3) the bonding medium;
(4) the pigment or pigments.

The first step is to note precisely where and in what condition the paint flake or smear was found, then to detach it carefully. It is next examined under a microscope, and the colour, or colours of the several layers, compared with that or those of a control sample from the suspected surface of origin. It may eventually be possible to do this colorimetrically (*i.e.* by measurements of the trichromatic coefficients of the surface), which would have the advantage of recording the colour as a set of numerical retrievable data; however, the eye is so far still the best instrument for the purpose, even though it is difficult to judge accurately the colours of very small fragments. Paints which harden by evaporation of a solvent, such as quick-drying lacquers and the "cellulose" used on cars, fairly soon become so hard that they tend to break off as discrete flakes. Paints which harden by oxidation of the medium (that is, the oil paints normally used for woodwork on buildings) require a long time to become hard enough to flake and consequently, unless they are very old, tend to become detached as smears. With a flake, the order of colours is easily seen by examination of the edge (fig. 6). With a smear, the order can often only be inferred from the appearance of the smear on, say, the end of the "jemmy."

The sequence of colours in a multi-layered fragment is an extremely important identifying characteristic. As many as fifteen or even more layers are sometimes found in fragments from old and frequently repainted woodwork or motor vehicles, but the presence of only a few layers may be valuable. The following elementary calculation may be instructive. If we assume, conservatively, that 50 distinguishable shades of paint may occur as finishing coats, and that 5 shades of primer and 10 of undercoat may be used with each of the 50, then there are 50 × 5 × 10, or 2,500 different possibilities merely for the simple combination of primer: undercoat: finishing coat. With more coats the number of possibilities becomes immense. It is therefore exceedingly improbable that two multi-layer paint fragments from different sources will match, and such a match when it occurs is very strong evidence of an identical origin.

This conclusion was corroborated by a survey recently carried out by the Home Office Central Research Establishment. The pockets and turn-ups of a random selection of 100 suits of clothes were brushed out. From these, 1,077 samples of paint were recovered as fortuitous fragments, and 318 of these were multi-layer. Two three-layer samples matched, but were from different parts of the same suit; no random matches were found when the samples contained four or more layers.

Until fairly recently, there were really only two analytical tests that could usefully be applied to paint fragments: (1) simple but rather crude tests, while examining the fragment under a microscope, of the effect on it of various solvents, gave some information about the bonding medium; (2) spectrographic analysis yielded information about the pigment. Recent developments in analytical techniques have greatly increased the amount of information obtainable.

The bonding medium. This, as implied above, can be of two general types according to whether the paint hardens by evaporation of a solvent or by oxidation to a resinous film. These are easily distinguished by the simple traditional solvent tests: solvents such as acetone or amyl acetate usually soften or dissolve fragments of the first type but do not affect those of the second; solvents such as chloroform or methylene chloride, on the other hand, do not affect the first type, but will usually soften (though seldom actually dissolve) the second.

Oil (*i.e.* oxidation-hardening) paints are nowadays however much more varied in composition than they used to be, when only a limited number of natural drying oils were available to their manufacturers. In modern paints various types of synthetic resins are used, technically known as alkyd, vinyl chloride, acrylic, polyurethane, epoxy and several others. Two methods of identifying these are available.

(1) Their infra-red absorption spectrum (see p. 74) may be characteristic. This can be plotted: (*a*) if the infra-red absorbency of the pigment does not

interfere, by the conventional methods of infra-red spectrometry; the paint is ground up, either with potassium bromide, which is subsequently compressed into a disc, or with pure high-boiling medicinal paraffin; (b) *attentuated total reflection* may be used to record the spectrum without interference from the pigment. This is a technique whereby the beam of radiation to be absorbed is, put crudely, caused to "wobble" in and out of the surface of the paint to a depth of only a few wavelengths, so that after a number of such "wobbles" it has effectively traversed a sufficient depth of the paint medium for the characteristic absorption of this to modify the beam.

(2) The paint fragment may be pyrolysed (*i.e.* decomposed by heat) and the products of pyrolysis characterised by gas chromatography (see p. 67). It is not always possible to identify these products absolutely, but the result will show empirically whether or not two fragments are similar. In any case, the method is a fairly new one and is likely in the future to be improved.

A simple combination of these two methods which, it is claimed, has proved highly successful is to pyrolyse the paint fragment in a small tube so that the vapours condense inside its lip; the condensate is then scraped off and examined by conventional infra-red spectrometry.

Neither infra-red spectrometry nor pyrolysis with gas chromatography will differentiate all of the resin types mentioned above, but luckily one is often effective where the other fails.

The pigment. This was at one time almost always an inorganic compound such as lead chromate (yellow) or Prussian blue (an iron compound), but modern paints increasingly contain a white pigment (often titanium dioxide) to give opacity, plus an organic dye or pigment for the desired colour. Red paints in particular have for a considerable time normally been coloured with a dye. The colouring matter may be identified in several ways:

(1) The simple solvent tests mentioned above may cause the colour, if it is a dye, to "bleed" out of the fragment; it may thereafter be characterised by thin-layer chromatography (p. 64), or, if enough paint is available, by measurement of its absorption spectrum (p. 72).

(2) The metallic and certain other elements present in the inorganic pigment(s) may be identified spectrographically (p. 70). This is the "classic" method of analysing paint fragments in this context. It is primarily qualitative rather than quantitative, but clearly distinguishes main from trace constituents. In any case, since up to 15–20 elements are often detectable in a single paint, out of 30 or more which may be used, the possible number of combinations is immense, and the probability of similar combinations occurring by chance correspondingly small. The method can also be made at least semi-quantitative by ashing the paint fragment and mixing it with a "buffer" containing a suitable internal standard before arc-ing. This must of course be an element not likely to be present in the paint; palladium has been suggested from Sweden.

(3) The main pigment compound present may be identified by means of X-ray diffraction (p. 78).

These last two methods are complementary rather than alternative, since each may afford information that the other does not. Both methods can be used on the same fragment provided that the non-destructive X-ray analysis is done first. Spectrographic analysis is fairly sensitive, and will detect elements present only in traces (possibly from fortuitous contamination of the paint); it does not however tell us how the elements present are combined. X-ray analysis, on the other hand, will not reveal compounds present only as traces, and with complex mixtures produces results very difficult to interpret, but it does give a positive identification of the chief compound(s) present. For example, it would clearly distinguish between the two mixtures (barium chromate + white lead) and (lead chromate + barium sulphate), whereas spectrographically both of these would merely show the presence of barium, chromium and lead. Also, only X-ray analysis will distinguish between different crystalline forms of the same chemical compound—for example, rutile and anatase, both forms of the pigment titanium dioxide. (See fig. 24).

One difficulty with multi-layer paint fragments is that none of the above techniques can be applied separately to the several layers unless they are physically separated. This may be possible if the paint has not hardened completely. It may also be possible to use attenuated total reflection on each of several layers by grinding off one layer at a time. Most commonly, however, we must be content with an "omnibus" analysis of all layers simultaneously. This difficulty may be resolved, as far as the pigments are concerned, by two new techniques coming, or probably soon to come, into use: electron-beam scanning (p. 81), and laser-beam spectrography (p. 71). Either of these can be used to identify the pigment(s) in a pin-point-sized area of paint, and successive layer-by-layer analysis across the edge of a fragment are therefore possible. Other new methods not yet generally used, which may in time enable us to analyse much smaller fragments than we can at present, and therefore give us useful information on more occasions, are mass spectrometry (p. 76) and neutron activation analysis (p. 80).

Even with the techniques at present generally available, however, the examination and analysis of paint fragments can give us remarkably conclusive information. In a survey carried out some years ago by the Home Office Forensic Science Laboratory in Cardiff, 2,000 paint samples of all colours collected at random from buildings were examined. Of these 98 per cent. could be distinguished by simple microscopy and solvent tests, and the remainder, with the exception of two pairs of samples from different sources, by spectrography and pyrolysis with gas chromatography.

Finally, before we leave paint, *putty* should be mentioned. Although this occurs frequently as a contact trace in breaking offences, it has not up till now been a particularly useful one, since it is practically always a simple mixture of linseed oil and ground chalk (whiting, calcium carbonate) without any hitherto demonstrable distinctive characteristics. The advent of the scanning electron microscope (p. 82) has now removed that drawback, since the very high magnifications possible reveal the characteristic shapes of the *coccoliths* in the chalk; these are the calcium carbonate crystals which form the exoskeletons of the fossil micro-organisms in the chalk, and which vary in configuration according to the source of the chalk (see fig. 7).

II. GLASS

Glass, though theoretically a highly super-cooled liquid, is for practical purposes a brittle amorphous solid which breaks with a conchoidal fracture. Obviously, unlike paint or soil, it cannot be transferred as more or less vague smears; on the contrary, when it is broken small fragments fly out. It has in fact been demonstrated that, when a pane is broken by a blow, fragments are ejected on both sides and may travel as much as 10 feet from the side on which the blow was delivered—that is, amply far enough to get on to the breaker's clothing. (See fig. 8). It is these fragments that are of interest to us here. Glass fragments *may* of course occur quite innocently on clothing, and the random survey of 100 suits mentioned above in connection with paint detected them in the pockets and turn-ups of 63; however, most of these were quite minute, and another extensive survey by the same establishment suggests that the odds against a fragment weighing more than one milligram (pin-head size) occurring "innocently" on clothing are several thousand to one.

Ordinary commercial window, headlamp and bottle glass is manufactured from sand, limestone and soda, and is, chemically, a complex sodium calcium silicate of rather indefinite composition containing about 70 per cent. of silica and small amounts of other metallic oxides (alumina, magnesia, etc.) in addition to the sodium and calcium oxides. The magnesium oxide was formerly a fortuitous impurity, but in modern glass up to about 2 per cent. is introduced intentionally. Other types of glass made for special purposes show a wide variety of compositions. Heat-resistant glass (Pyrex, etc.) contains more silica (75–80 per cent.) and up to 15 per cent. boron trioxide, but usually little or no lime (calcium oxide). Optical glass, used for lens making, may contain up to 50 per cent. or even more of barium and/or zinc and/or lead oxides. In some modern optical glasses, even the silica is entirely replaced by other oxides. Colour is usually produced by the presence of metals with strongly coloured ions. Glass containing certain rare-earth oxides (Crookes' Glass) absorbs ultra-violet radiation very completely, and may be encountered in expensive sunglasses.

If, of course, any of these more unusual types of glass are broken in committing a crime, that will be a piece of luck for the forensic scientist. However, since probably at least 99 per cent. of all the broken glass he has to deal with comes from broken windows and car lamps, he must do what he can with ordinary soda-lime glass.

As commercial glass of this type varies little in its gross composition, the ordinary methods of chemical analysis are of little help in characterising it, although certain limited tests—for example, a determination of the sodium/magnesium ratio—are sometimes useful. Also, since modern "float" glass floats on a bath of molten tin during manufacture and therefore bears a trace of this element on its surface, a sensitive "spot" test for tin may be informative. We shall mention later the possible applications in this context of the modern sophisticated instrumental methods of analysis.

With the equipment normally available in all but the most advanced laboratories, however, glass fragments can in most cases be given an identity only by the determination of their physical properties. The problem is therefore to discover properties which are both characteristic through being highly sensitive to small variations in composition and manufacture, and are accurately measurable with very small fragments. There are unfortunately few properties which satisfy both of these conditions.

One will obviously measure the thickness of a fragment which shows both faces of the sheet it came from, but few fragments are large enough to do so. Colour is rarely of any help; although most commercial glass shows a faint colour in the mass, this is quite undetectable in small fragments. It is more useful to examine the fluorescence in ultra-violet radiation, which is occasionally distinctive. Other possibly useful properties which have been suggested are hardness, the coefficient of thermal expansion, and the temperature at which certain constituents of the glass separate as crystals when it is maintained for some time above its softening point (the *liquidus temperature*); none of these however has proved very fruitful.

The only two properties which have so far been used with fairly universal success are *specific gravity* (or *density*) and *refractive index* (see p. 69). Both show considerable variation and both are easily measurable with an accuracy of not less than 1 in 1,000 using small fragments, as long as these are large enough to see and be manipulated. For an ordinary soda-lime glass, the density will probably lie within the range 2·47–2·55 and the refractive index within 1·515–1·535. If we assume that the former can be measured to within ±0·002 and the latter to within ±0·001, then, if these properties were independent, the number of detectably different glasses would be

$$\frac{2\cdot55 - 2\cdot47}{0\cdot002} \times \frac{1\cdot535 - 1\cdot515}{0\cdot001}$$

or 800, giving odds of 800 to 1 against two random pieces of glass matching. Unfortunately the properties are *not* independent; they are in both theory and practice highly associated, one showing only a small variation for a given value of the other (see fig. 9). In fact, in one recent survey using over 300 random samples of glass from buildings, a correlation coefficient as high as 0·93 was found. Hence the actual number of glasses distinguishable by measuring both properties is much less than the figure quoted, and the actual odds against a random match, with measurements of the precision assumed above, are probably something like 100 or 200 to 1.

Obviously, discrimination between glasses could be improved by measuring the properties more precisely. For example, if we could measure them to within ±0·001 and 0·0005 respectively, the odds would be increased four times. In fact, with skill and the proper equipment a precision considerably greater than we have assumed above can be attained. The *useful* increase in precision is how-ever limited by the fact that normal sheets of glass show small variations in their physical properties from place to place within themselves; once we have begun to detect these, greater precision is useless. This limit has in fact been reached with the most precise measurements now possible, made in one of the ways to be described below.

Specific gravity is measured by flotation. If both the test and the control fragments neither sink nor float in a suspending liquid, their densities are identi-cal with that of the liquid and with each other. The test liquid is usually a mixture of bromoform (specific gravity 2·89) and any suitable liquid with a density less than that of glass. The temperatures must be exactly the same for all the fragments, because of the large coefficient of thermal expansion of most liquids. The simplest way of discovering the correct mixture is by simple trial and error in a thermostated specimen tube containing the suspended fragments. This, however, is extremely tedious if it is to be sufficiently accurate. A better method is to suspend the fragments in a mixture in which they just float at room temperature and to warm this up gradually. Since the coefficient of expansion of most organic liquids is around 0·001, and that of glass about 0·000025, the change of density of the glass is negligible compared with that of the liquid, and at some particular temperature the glass becomes denser than the liquid and sinks. If two fragments sink at temperatures within 1 °C. of each other, their densities will be identical within about 1 part in 1,000.

A third method is to use a *gradient density* tube, or set of such tubes. This is a tube perhaps 4–8 millimetres in diameter and 20–30 centimetres long containing a liquid the density of which decreases gradually from bottom to top. If the density range is correctly chosen, a fragment of glass will sink in the liquid until it reaches a level of the same density as its own; the precise level at which it remains suspended is then a measure of its density. The variable-density liquid can be prepared in several ways: by careful stepwise addition of progressively less dense liquid mixtures; by some simple gadgetry which allows both the denser and the less dense liquids to run in simultaneously, but varies the relative rates of addition as the tube fills up; by warming the tube from above with an electric-light bulb, so that the change in density through thermal expansion is greatest at the top and least at the bottom; by warming the tube from outside with a resistance-wire winding. The method of heating from above has the dis-advantage that the rate of change of density with height is greater at the top of the tube than the bottom; by a suitable design of wire winding, on the other hand, this change can be made linear—that is, the change of density for each unit of vertical distance is the same throughout. It is also possible to *automate* the production of a series of tubes with identical density gradients in each.

Whatever method of density measurement is used, the fragments to be com-pared should be of roughly the same order of size, and preferably of roughly similar shapes. They must also be scrupulously clean. Excessively minute frag-ments may not within a reasonable time reach the same equilibrium position as larger ones, and obviously any dirt or an air film on the surface of a fragment will alter its overall density.

It is of course unnecessary to determine the specific gravities absolutely, since we are interested primarily in their comparison. However, the actual figures in a series of cases will form a useful body of reference data.

Refractive index is also measured by an immersion method. A colourless transparent solid (*e.g.* glass) surrounded by a colourless transparent fluid (*e.g.* air or water) is visible only if the refractive indices of the solid and fluid are different. When the indices are the same the solid is invisible, and the index of the fluid is then that of the solid. The simplest technique is to view the fragments under investigation, contained in a small cell, under a microscope by transmitted light; to fill the cell with a liquid having a refractive index near that of the glass (*e.g.* chlorobenzene, refractive index 1·525); and by trial-and-error addition of another miscible liquid with a different refractive index to produce a mixture in which the fragments disappear. Monochromatic (sodium-vapour) light should be used so as to avoid the production of coloured fringes due to the glass and the liquid having different dispersivities (*i.e.* variations of refractive index with wavelength).

That method works, but leads to a lot of frustration in trying to keep the fragments in view under the microscope. A much better method makes use of the fact that the refractive index of liquids, like their density, varies considerably with temperature. One chooses the right liquid, warms it up slowly, and at a certain temperature the fragment disappears. Any liquid whose variation of refractive index covers the right range will do; many laboratories use the proprietary *Cargille liquids*, for which the refractive indices over a range of temperatures have been plotted and can be read off a graph, but a silicone oil is increasingly preferred. The liquid is heated by a microscope hot stage, the proprietary *Mettler* one having proved eminently suitable. The rate of heating of this can be varied between 0·2 and 10 °C. per minute, and by simply pressing a button the temperature at the moment when the fragment disappears can be recorded on a digital print-out device. This avoids the operator having to look away at the crucial moment to read a thermometer.

By whatever method the refractive index of the liquid is varied, the final approach to fragment invisibility is rather critical. Most commonly an optical phenomenon called the *Becke line* is utilised at this stage. When the refractive indices of fragment and liquid are nearly the same, this appears as a dark line adjacent to the fragment boundaries which moves towards the region of higher refractive index as the microscope is focused upwards.

Recent experiments on the *automation* of refractive index determination have also utilised the Becke line, making use of the fact that when this disappears and the refractive indices are identical, the light transmission of the combined glass/liquid field is at a maximum. The Becke line is not, however, the only—or, it has been suggested—the best index to the critical matching point. Among other possible methods, there is a strong case for preferring *phase-contrast* microscopy (see p. 167), which strongly accentuates any refractive-index difference between a transparent object and the surrounding medium. According to a recent American paper, it is possible by using a Mettler hot stage and phase contrast to detect refractive-index differences as small as 0·00004.

As with densities, it is unnecessary to know the absolute value of the refractive index when comparing glass fragments, but again these form a useful body of reference data. The refractive index of the liquid is easily measured with a *refractometer* (p. 69).

A third parameter the measurement of which may help in characterising a glass has already been mentioned above—namely the *dispersivity*. This can be determined by measuring the refractive index in one of the ways just described, but at several wavelengths instead of at only one.

An increasingly severe limitation to the value of glass fragments as trace evidence arises from the increasing uniformity of modern glass. Modern sheet glass production in Great Britain is practically a monopoly of one firm, and is a carefully regulated continuous process employing standardised raw materials and leading to a very uniform product. Hence the variations encountered, and therefore the value of a match when found, are going to diminish as more and more windows are glazed or re-glazed with modern glass. (This difficulty does not arise so acutely with bottle and similar glasses.) It is becoming important, therefore, to find some other property than density and refractive index which gives good discrimination and which can be accurately measured on small fragments. A few have already been suggested (p. 31). *Differential thermal analysis* (p. 68) may also have a future here. However, at present the most hopeful line of research appears to be the identification of the trace elements present. These will differ according to the sources of the raw materials, particularly the sand, since the manufacturer's standardisation does not extend to these differences. If sufficient material is available, trace elements can be identified by *emission spectrography* (p. 70), but this is insufficiently sensitive for very small fragments. For these, the best method is *neutron activation analysis* (p. 80) or *mass spectrometry* (p. 76). The latter seems at the moment to be the more promising, and some encouraging results have been obtained with it, detecting differences between very small otherwise indistinguishable fragments. In one recent English case, for example, it was possible to identify a tiny piece of glass found in a food sample as having come from an electric-light bulb made by a particular manufacturer. *Atomic absorption spectroscopy* (p. 71), which is more generally available, can also be useful if the identity of the diagnostic trace element(s) is known.

III. THE BREAKING OF GLASS

There is still more information to be extracted from broken glass. When a sheet of glass is broken by a blow, primary lines of fracture run out radially from the point of impact (*radial* cracks), and secondary ones (*concentric* cracks) run between the primaries, dividing the broken glass into rough triangles or truncated triangles the apices of which are directed towards the point of impact.

If the edges of pieces are examined, faintly curved linear stress marks will be seen, with their opposite ends nearly asymptotic to one face and nearly perpendicular to the other. It is an invariable rule that in radial cracks the marks are asymptotic to the face on which the blow was delivered and perpendicular to the other; (a convenient mnemonic for this is: Radial—Right angles—Reverse) (fig. 11). In concentric cracks the marks are usually much less clearly developed, but, in so far as they are visible, they nearly always run the other way—that is, they meet the side receiving the blow perpendicularly.

These facts often enable us to say from which side a window was broken, and thus to answer such questions as: Did the intruder break in or break out through a particular window? Was the alleged break-in genuine, or was it "rigged" in order to claim insurance by breaking the window from the inside? To answer these questions, we must of course know the original position in the window of the pieces of glass which we are examining. It is therefore easiest to rely on any pieces still remaining in the frame. Otherwise, it may sometimes be necessary to fit all or most of the pieces together before we can be certain about our reconstruction.

If the blow was struck by a small rapidly moving projectile (stone, bullet, etc.), and particularly if the glass is fairly thick, some glass will be "punched out" at the point of impact, leaving a crater-shaped hole which is invariably wider at the exit side (fig. 10). Hence, as long as the glass is not completely shattered (which rarely happens if the projectile is moving fast enough), we can tell from which side the projectile came. A special case of this phenomenon, which has been known to mystify the policeman on the beat, is sometimes provided by malicious small boys who fire bicycle bearing balls from catapults at plate-glass windows. Such projectiles can puncture the glass without passing through it; the result is a neat circular hole smaller than the projectile, and a smooth cup-shaped crater at the back.

Broken glass can also, of course, by the mere fit of its broken edges, provide absolutely positive linking material, as described on pp. 16–17. This type of connecting link may also, given patience and luck, be provided by quite tiny pieces of glass (perhaps no more than 1–2 mm. across). Moreover, even these tiny pieces often show on a reduced scale linear stress marks of the type described above. Now obviously the stress marks on opposite faces of a single crack correspond in the way that male and female screw threads do; one is an impression of the other, and the opposite faces show complementary hill-and-dale and dale-and-hill configurations. Such a match is clear proof that the two fragments of glass were originally one. It is most easily demonstrated by photography of the two matching edges in very oblique lighting at several times natural size; subsequent reversal of one photograph, both optically to its mirror image, and photographically through an intermediate positive (so that a light-and-shade pattern becomes a shade-and-light one), will then yield two identical matching pictures. (See fig. 12.)

IV. SOIL

Soil, the last of the contact-trace materials we are discussing in this chapter, is, unlike paint and glass, a naturally occurring substance; it is therefore enormously more variable in its characteristics. It is in fact an exceedingly complex substance, and its study constitutes an independent branch of science—**pedology**. Few if any of the pedologist's techniques are, however, useful to the forensic scientist: they are too time-consuming, or require too much material, or relate to properties in which the forensic scientist is not interested.

Paradoxically, the immense variability and universal distribution of soil limit its evidential value as a contact trace. Two samples of soil may be indistinguishable, but that merely means that any differences between them are smaller than can be revealed by the tests applied; the samples *may* have come from quite separate places. Soil examination is most valuable when it can be used to disprove lies. If, for example, a man suspected of burglarious entry over a flower bed says that the mud on his shoes came from the short cut over the allotments, then his defence fails it it can be shown that the mud on his shoes is demonstrably different from that on the path over the allotments although indistinguishable from that of the flower bed.

Another, and in practice severe, limitation on the evidential value of soil is that the mud adhering to clothing or footwear is too rarely a representative sample of the soil from any one single site, with which it could profitably be compared. Very frequently any that may be present from the place in which the police are interested has been overlaid and mixed with further soil picked up later somewhere else.

Surface soil is partly inorganic (mineral) and partly organic in composition. The mineral part consists of particles produced by the weathering of the rock(s) from which the soil was derived, and varying in size from sub-microscopic (clay) to being easily visible to the naked eye. The organic part consists of: complex structureless material known collectively as *humus*; an extensive and varied microbiological population of bacteria, etc.; various species of small invertebrates; and (sometimes) fragmentary and partially decayed but recognisable plant remains. These last four groups of constituents are in general of little help to the forensic scientists. The percentage of humus can be determined chemically by several methods, but experience shows that to do so is rarely very informative. (The characterisation of humus, or an extract of it, by some technique such as infra-red spectrometry *might* be rewarding, but as far as the writer is aware this has not been tried.) Recognisable remains of plants or animals, especially of uncommon ones, will be exceedingly welcome if they occur in sufficient quantity to be characteristic of all the soil from one spot. This happens all too seldom, but a case in which it did is described on p. 178. Some laboratories have also found that the *pollen grains* present in most soils form a useful identifying characteristic. The microflora and microfauna, which would appear to constitute a rewarding line of investigation, have so far proved disappointing as a means of soil identification. (However, this is a field of research in which, in this context, insufficient work has as yet been done.)

In the main, therefore, we must rely purely on the mineral constituents and some simple empirical tests made upon the soil as a whole. Because of this limitation, the category "soil" can be taken here to include also the surface debris from building and demolition sites, outdoor yards, etc.

There is no single sovereign method for the examination and analysis of soil samples. Any of the following list of characteristics may be used for identification; it is unlikely that any one laboratory uses all of them, and indeed there is probably no aspect of forensic science in which the practices of different laboratories differ so widely.

(1) Visual appearance.
(2) Particle-size distribution.
(3) Mineralogical identity of constituent particles.
(4) Particle-density distribution.
(5) Chemical analysis (including the use of modern instrumental methods of analysis).
(6) Nature of the clay present.

It cannot be assumed that identity in respect of all characteristics is proof of a common source, but it will rarely occur that soils from different sources will agree completely in respect of any two or three of the first four characteristics.

Soil samples are first dried thoroughly and broken up if necessary, and any large non-representative lumps of adventitious material removed. At this stage, it is useless to go any further unless the samples *look* alike—that is, have the same colour and texture. A useful empirical test here is to ignite the soils to about 800–900 °C. and compare their colours afterwards; different soils show a wide range of buff to terra-cotta hues (depending largely on their iron and manganese contents).

As already mentioned, soil particles vary enormously in size, and the proportions of different sizes present—the **particle-size** distribution—are highly characteristic. The sizes are by universal agreement classified as follows:

Name of fraction		Particle diameter (mm.)
Gravel		over 2
Sand	Coarse	0·2–2·0
	Fine	0·02–0·2
Silt		0·002–0·02
Clay		Under 0·002

The simplest method of particle-size analysis is by sieving the well-broken-up soil through successively finer sieves, by which process two samples of the same soil identically treated may be expected to give the same proportions of the different fractions. This is not, however, reliable as an absolute method of particle-size analysis, for the simple reason that mere mechanical breaking up will not effectively separate the smallest particles.

More accurate methods of particle-size analysis all use dispersion in a liquid—normally water—and most depend upon *Stokes' Law*. This states that the rate at which a very small particle moves through a liquid under the action of a force such as gravity depends only on its radius and the viscosity of the liquid, and is independent of the relative density of the particle. Therefore, for a given liquid at a constant temperature (since viscosity depends upon temperature) the rate of sinking depends only upon particle size and can be used to measure this.

The measurement can be made in various ways. The soil can be dispersed in the liquid, ensuring (*e.g.* by using ultrasonic vibration) that the dispersion is complete (that is, that the particles are all separate) and allowing the dispersed soil to settle through a fixed distance for a fixed time. Distance and time can be chosen to give any desired particle-size "cut," so that what has settled is larger than, and what is still in suspension smaller than, a particular size. This method is simple but extremely tedious. Quicker but more elaborate methods are: weighing at intervals the sediment settling on to a balance pan suspended in the liquid; pipetting off samples of the suspension from a fixed depth at intervals, and weighing the solids in the samples withdrawn; optical measurement of the turbidity of the suspension at a given depth after various times. A very sophisticated apparatus (the *Coulter counter*) has also been developed which measures particle size by the changing resistance in a slurry of the particles passing between two electrodes. It can be used with very small samples, and its operation can if necessary be automated. It has not however proved as popular or as successful with forensic scientists as might have been expected.

The **mineralogical** examination of the sand and gravel fraction can be considered the most fundamental of all methods of soil examination, in that it is the only one which positively identifies the bedrock(s) from which the soil was derived. As it is a job for the trained geologist it has, not surprisingly, been most used in laboratories which have geologists on their staffs. Many of the constituent minerals can be identified by the geologist on sight under a low-power microscope; the others, the so-called "heavy minerals" (those which sink in bromoform, and therefore have a specific gravity greater than 2·9), may require examination under a polarising microscope (p. 167) for their final identification. Soils from the same place will obviously have the same basic mineral constituents; in addition, soils and debris from urban areas will contain adventitious and possibly characteristic particles of coal, brick, etc.

Since different minerals have different specific gravities, the nature of those constituting the inorganic part of the soil will also determine the **particle-density** distribution. In the opinion of many forensic scientists, this is the most highly diagnostic single soil characteristic, no other revealing small differences so clearly; a sizeable minority, however, have doubts about its value and consider it untrustworthy. In the writer's opinion, for what that is worth, it can form the basis of an extremely useful test, provided that this is used with common sense and in conjunction with other tests.

Particle-density distribution is commonly and most simply determined by using a set of gradient-density tubes (p. 32), one for each specimen of soil to be examined. When a small (say 50 mg.) dry specimen of soil is dropped into a tube, each particle sinks to its own density zone, giving us a density "spectrum" characteristic of the soil (fig. 13). As we are not concerned here with the *rate* of sinking, the tubes should be left for at least 24 hours before examination in order to let the smallest particles reach equilibrium. If bromoform is used for the heavy liquid, as with glass, most but not all of the soil particles will remain suspended. If we wish to include the heavy minerals (see above) in the density spectrum, a liquid of still greater density than bromoform must be used; several are available with densities up to about 4·5, but they tend to be inconveniently expensive and/or unstable. The test can also be refined in several other ways: by preliminary ultrasonic treatment of the soil to ensure complete dispersal of its particles; by "scaling down" so that, it is claimed, as little as 1 mg. of soil is sufficient; by improved methods of preparing the tubes, as with glass.

Chemical analysis. A conventional complete analysis is rarely if ever useful: the similarities and differences which it might reveal are likely to have been obvious from the mere appearance of the soil or from other less time-consuming examinations. Occasionally, however, a single simple specific determination such as acid-soluble calcium (that is, roughly, chalk) can be rewarding. The *acidity* of the soil, a property depending on its chemical composition, may also be a useful characteristic, and can be determined on a slurry or suspension by using a pH meter (see p. 67).

In general, the most useful type of analysis in this context is the detection and/or determination of characteristic *trace elements*. These may be derived from, and peculiar to, the original bedrock, or (especially with urban soils) be adventitious contaminants peculiar to the locality. A case of the latter type is described on p. 45. In another, which occurred in the London area some years ago, a man broke into a colour-photography processing works. One of the strongest pieces of evidence against him was the presence in dried mud on his shoes and in his van of traces of silver. This element is not normally present, or at least detectable, in London soils, but was present in the soil around this works because of years of processing photographic emulsions (that is, silver preparations) in it. In that particular case, the silver was detected by spectrographic analysis (p. 70). This is in general the most useful technique for trace elements in soil. Though it is less sensitive than some other more recent techniques, it is available in most laboratories, and sufficient soil to offset its relative lack of sensitivity is almost always available.

Clay. "Clay"—the mineral part of a soil of sub-microscopic particle size— consists of a group of complex substances, all generically hydrous aluminium silicates, the constitution of which is even now not wholly understood. Broadly speaking, there are about a dozen "clay minerals," of which the most important groups are known as the *kaolinite* and the *montmorillonite*. On the molecular scale, they have a sheet-like crystal structure (which accounts for their ductility when wet). Ions of other metals may replace some of the aluminium in the "sheets," or may be present along with water molecules loosely held between them.

The best the forensic scientist can do with this complexity is to apply such tests as have empirically been found to differentiate clays most clearly. The infra-red absorption, measured on a specimen of clay dispersed in a potassium bromide disc (see p. 74), is sometimes distinctive. Differential thermal analysis (D.T.A.—see p. 68) is a technique holding considerable promise, because the loss of the variously sited water molecules occurring in clay as it is heated produces marked thermal changes. D.T.A. equipment is however rather delicate and its use demands considerable skill. Generally speaking, X-ray diffraction (see p. 78) is for both theoretical and practical reasons the technique most widely used for clay identification: theoretical because it is in their crystal structure that clay minerals differ most fundamentally, and practical because it is a relatively straightforward and well-established technique.

5

OTHER OFFENCES AGAINST
PROPERTY

The two previous chapters have dealt mainly with the types of physical evidence encountered in most investigations of breaking offences. This chapter will tidy up the subject of offences against property in general by dealing with some miscellaneous topics which fall under this heading and about which there is some more to be said.

I. SAFE-BREAKING

There is one type of breaking offence which is rather in a category by itself and deserves special mention. The safe-breaker may be said to be a man at the top of his profession, and his activities set a few special problems for the forensic scientist.

To begin with, it is perhaps not generally realised that the majority of safes in use in Britain today are at least 60 years old. These old safes may be adequate as fireproof document containers, but offer little security against the skilled and determined cracksman. The old safe which has stood in the corner of the office for several generations is probably made of riveted sheet iron. A modern safe is integrally constructed of hardened steel with no joints to offer points of attack, is probably fitted with locking bars which automatically seal the door if explosive is used, and may even have a skin of an alloy which cannot, or can hardly, be cut with a blowpipe. However, just as the unsinkable battleship was never built, there is almost certainly no such thing as the completely burglar-proof safe, given unlimited time. But as time is precious to the cracksman, most of the safes successfully forced are old-fashioned ones.

The traces to be looked for after a safe has been forced depend both on how it was constructed and how it was opened. For obvious reasons, this is not the place for a do-it-yourself course in safe-cracking, but it is giving nothing away to classify the methods used as:

(1) Sheer brute force;
(2) burning open (oxy-acetylene torch or thermic lance);
(3) drilling out a vulnerable part of the door with a high-speed (tungsten carbide) drill;
(4) the use of explosives; (common in Britain; now rare in the U.S.A.).

41

Method (1) is of course possible only with the less adequate safes. This classification does not of course apply to actual strong rooms, which are built structures; burglarious entry to these is liable to leave the same sort of contact traces as any entry involving disturbances of brickwork, concrete, etc. It may perhaps also be added that the expert who opens combination locks with keen ears and sensitive fingers is not encountered outside crime fiction.

The majority of safes are made fireproof by being constructed as two concentric boxes with the space in between filled with an insulating "ballast." This used most commonly to be sawdust, rubble or a mineral insulator such as kieselguhr; a cement aggregate is probably commoner in more modern safes. However, since (as we have just said) older safes are more commonly forced, sawdust is still frequently encountered in this connection. When it is used, it is also often mixed with some salt containing a large amount of water of crystallisation and/or yielding a non-inflammable gas on heating (e.g. ammonium alum). The purpose of this mixture is that, in the event of a fire, the wood and the gases liberated from it form a thermally insulating mass which is fireproofed by the water vapour and other gases from the salt.

When the safe has been opened by brute force, much of the laboratory examination will be of the types we have already discussed in connection with other breaking offences. In addition, however, the damage to the outer casing will allow the ballast to leak out, and this may be carried away on clothing or footwear. The presence on the suspect's clothing or footwear of fragments of wood of the same range of sizes and species as are present in a sawdust safe ballast constitutes valuable evidence; this is even more valuable if crystals of any fireproofing salt present are also found, but the absence of these from the clothing does not vitiate the evidence, since they adhere to fabrics less readily than sawdust particles do. The value of sawdust as evidence is obviously the greater, the more numerous and uncommon the species of woods. It is not unknown, in the case of old safes, to identify 5 or 6 species, some being nowadays quite rare ones. One may in such cases presume that the manufacturer merely used a load of sawdust derived from whatever the nearest sawmill happened to be cutting. The identification of woods will be briefly dealt with in Chapter 13.

With a mineral safe ballast, although discrete particles may be found on the clothing, it will probably be necessary to vacuum-clean this and examine the dust extracted. The examination may be either chemical or microscopic, depending on the nature of the dust, but the best evidence is generally obtained when the ballast consists of kieselguhr. This is also known as infusiorial earth or diatomite, and consists of the siliceous skeletons of diatoms from former geological periods. Several distinctive patterns of diatom skeletons are generally present in any given sample, and the occurrence of the same identifiable patterns in the ballast and the dust from the clothing is clearly almost conclusive. Such cases test the microscopist's skill to the uttermost, since it is generally recognised that the resolution of diatom skeletons represents approximately the possible limits of optical microscopy.

When a safe has been opened by oxy-acetylene cutting, small fused spherules of metal or oxide scale are likely to be carried away on clothing. The full identifi-cation of these may require both visual examination and chemical analysis. Characteristic evidence is also likely to be left if a *thermic lance* is used. This is a modern demolition tool which produces a temperature between 3,000 and 4,000 °C. by the combustion of steel rods in a stream of oxygen under pressure, and will cut through *anything*. Fortunately, it is not generally available to the would-be safe-breaker, and in any case requires more heavy equipment than he could conveniently transport. If the safe is drilled, drillings are of course likely to be carried away as contact traces.

Safe "blowing," or opening safes with explosive, is a skill in which a regrettably large number of people are proficient. Stolen explosives and detonators are a valuable article of commerce in safe-cracking circles. It is therefore desirable to identify the material used whenever possible; it is even more desirable when someone has been arrested for the offence with explosives and/or detonators in his possession, since a large number of types of explosives and detonators are made, each with its distinctive identity. Even when the safe has been successfully blown, a few scraps of explosive will probably have been dropped or have escaped detonation. A careful search of the debris will usually also reveal frag-ments of the detonator casing, together with the attached wires, or portions of these, from electric detonators.

The identification of the numerous different commercial explosives is dealt with briefly on p. 56. Commercial detonators are also made in a number of sizes and types: copper or aluminium cased; plain (obsolescent) or electrically ignited; with copper or iron wire of various standard lengths for the igniting current; with insulation coded in various colours; instantaneous or delayed-firing, the time interval of the delay in the latter varying from milliseconds to seconds; various special types for use in unusual conditions, such as under water. The number of possible combinations of explosive and detonator is therefore very large, and the simultaneous occurrence of any particular com-bination at the scene of a safe blowing and in the possesion of a suspect con-stitutes correspondingly valuable evidence.

II. THE IDENTIFICATION OF STOLEN PROPERTY

When a theft has occurred without force being used to accomplish it, the prob-lems of detection and proof are much harder ones. (Nevertheless, even here there is one type of contact trace that may still be looked for, namely footmarks: whatever else a thief avoids doing, he cannot avoid putting his feet down.)

Apart from proving the presence of the thief at the scene, the problem of proof in cases of larceny or receiving is that of showing that whatever is found in his possession is in fact the stolen property. Broadly speaking, there are three ways of doing this:

(1) Identification beyond dispute by the loser, the stolen article(s) being in some respect unique. This demands no further discussion here.

(2) Restoration of identifying marks or numbers which have been obliterated by the thief.

(3) Demonstration, when the stolen property is part of a larger quantity stored, that that found in possession of the suspect is identical in every conceivable respect with that remaining at the scene.

The forensic scientist may be involved in both the second and third methods of proof. Identifying marks may be of various types. If they were simply painted or printed on, then they may have been completely removed beyond the possibility of restoration; on the other hand such marks may have been merely painted over or otherwise obscured. The scientist will then have to use his judgment and experience in trying to reveal what was obliterated: careful treatment with solvents (as in the cleaning of valuable paintings), infra-red viewing or photography (see p. 222), and fairly soft (that is, diagnostic medical) X-rays are possible lines of attack.

With altered car number plates, if these are of the normal modern pattern with riveted-on figures and letters, the paint of the plate itself may have weathered less where it was protected by these, and the difference in weathering may be revealed by a difference in the specular reflectivity of the surface, or in its fluorescence under ultra-violet radiation.

When the identification mark has been punched into the surface, the likelihood of restoring it depends on the material bearing it. With wood, leather or plastic, the prospects are not very good. When marks in wood have been erased by removal of the surface, it is sometimes possible to restore them by applying strong alkali and/or steam, which cause the fibres to swell. The bruised or broken fibres immediately under the erased punched marks will swell more than undamaged ones, and the marks may reappear as a pattern of swollen fibres. Other fibrous materials such as leather are usually even less rewarding, but erased embossed marks on stolen bags and cases have been restored on a number of occasions. Various methods have been used for this; these may depend on the differential absorbing power of the undisturbed material and that compressed by the embossing, or on revealing residues of oil from paint which has been used to fill the embossed mark and traces of which have soaked into the material. Erased punched marks on plastics can sometimes be restored by treatment with a suitable solvent, since the compressed material under the mark will be less rapidly soluble than the bulk material.

With marks punched into metal, on the other hand, their restoration after erasure is almost a matter of routine, and the experienced examiner must count himself unlucky if he fails. All metals are crystalline, and when an indentation is punched into a metallic surface the large local stress so produced alters the crystal structure immediately around and below the mark. Therefore, even if the surface is filed or ground down until the mark has been obliterated, the new surface thus produced is not in fact uniform although it may appear so—there is an area of altered crystal structure conforming to the outline of the obliterated mark. On application of a suitable etching reagent, this area will be attacked faster or slower (usually faster) than the unaltered metal, and an etched pattern will appear reproducing more or less accurately the outline of the original mark (fig. 17).

Different metals require different etching reagents, and a good deal of "know-how" is required to select the most suitable, according to whether the metal is mild steel, cast iron, brass, aluminium alloy, etc. This sort of restoration is usually undertaken by chemists, but if there is a metallurgist on the laboratory staff it falls naturally into his province. The know-how is important, since etching is a once-and-for-all process in which the mark may appear only fugitively, and since the use of an unsuitable reagent may spoil the chance of success with the right one. A redeveloped mark can usually be preserved for a time by neutralisation of the acid, cleaning, drying thoroughly and applying a clear protective coating; in any case, however, it should always be photographed when it is at its clearest if a permanent record is required.

Magnetic crack detectors have also been used successfully for the restoration of punched numbers in iron and steel. These work on the principle that the immersion of the surface in a suspension of iron particles in oil while a magnetic field is applied will reveal surface discontinuities by the differential adherence of the particles.

If the mark of identification has not been punched but engraved—as on cigarette cases and the like—the chances of successful redevelopment are small, since little force is applied in engraving and there is correspondingly little alteration to the metal crystal structure. Even in this case, however, restoration is worth attempting, either by etching or by utilising the fact that areas which have been heated in electrical engraving may show a difference in reflectivity when the metal surface has been polished.

No useful generalisation can be made about the scientist's function in the third type of identification—exact comparison of the stolen and control materials —since what he does must depend entirely on what the material is, which may be practically *any* natural or manufactured commodity. He must therefore approach the problem with imagination and an open mind. A complete chemical analysis may be necessary. On the other hand, the material may show some unique identifying characteristic. For example, as already mentioned (p. 20), the theft of scrap-metal swarf has been proved by showing, from striation marks left by the cutting tool, that turnings in the stolen metal and those left at the scene must have been turned with the same tool at about the same time.

Another example is provided by an old case which is now a minor classic of its type. A man stole a quantity of potatoes from a field adjoining his garden. When taxed with the theft, he maintained that the potatoes found in his possession came from his own garden; this was a good defence, since he had admittedly grown the same variety of potatoes there. The soils from the field and from his garden turned out to be indistinguishable by practically every test. There seemed therefore to be no prospect of linking the disputed potatoes with one place rather than another. It was discovered, however, that the field but not the garden had been dressed with a superphosphate fertiliser. Chemical analysis showed that the phosphate content of the mud on the potatoes was similar to that of the soil from the field, and very much higher than that of the garden soil.

A special type of stolen material which comes fairly frequently into most forensic science laboratories is electric cable. Heavy cable may show many distinctive characteristics in its various conducting, insulating, waterproofing and armouring layers, and usually carries the manufacturer's name somewhere inside it. In a case recently reported from Australia, the stolen and control cables were matched by neutron-activation analysis (p. 80) both of the copper wire and of the PVC coating; the trace elements present were identical in both lots of cable and different from those in thirteen other random samples of similar cable examined. In another cable case, the writer once took the trouble to analyse spectrographically each of the 37 copper wires contained in both lengths. All of the wires contained just detectable traces of lead and tin, but the lead/tin ratio was higher in some of the wires (A) than in the others (B). Each lot of cable contained 15 A and 22 B wires, and moreover the *arrangement* of the two types of wire was identical in both. The number of possible permutations of 15 As and 22 Bs in a group of 37 is so enormous that the probability of the same arrangement occurring twice by chance is infinitesimal.

There is perhaps a moral to this case and the potatoes one quoted above: namely, the scientist should be prepared to try anything and not give up too easily!

III. DETECTOR POWDERS

Finally, a special type of contact trace should be mentioned: that which is designed to occur. Pilfering, especially of money, is very difficult to detect when the property is not identifiable, and when the pilferer leaves no traces and may in any case have a legitimate excuse for being at the scene of the theft. One way in which the scientist can, and is often asked to, help here is by devising some sort of *detector* (or *tagging*) *powder*, some of which the thief carries away unknowingly on his hands or clothing.

There are several conditions which such a powder must meet:

(1) Its constituents must be uncommon, so that it is not likely to be found by chance on innocent persons.

(2) It must not be poisonous or corrosive.

(3) Enough to mark the thief should not be noticeable when sprinkled on to the property at risk.

(4) Preferably, the thief should not notice if he gets it on himself, but whether he does notice or not it should be as difficult as possible for him to remove from his hands and clothing.

(5) It should be detectable on the thief's hands or clothing by some simple, quick, unambiguous test.

The mere fact that there are almost as many "pet" detector powders as there are forensic chemists shows that the ideal one has never been devised. The most popular have included: a dye which is inconspicuous as a dry powder but which stains the skin indelibly on sweating or trying to wash it off; a brightly fluorescent powder (*e.g.* anthracene) which is colourless and unnoticeable in normal light but reveals itself as glowing specks when the thief's hands or clothing are examined under filtered ultra-violet radiation; a mixture containing some suitable fairly uncommon chemicals (*e.g.* manganese dioxide) which are easily identified by simple tests on hand swabs or dust from clothing; a mixture containing some uncommon particulate material (*e.g.* unusual pollen grains) which is easily identified microscopically. A refinement of the last category which has recently been suggested is an intimate mixture of several different colours of dyed lycopodium powder (club moss spores). These spores have a very characteristic microscopic appearance, and, by varying the proportion of different colours used, a whole range of clearly distinguishable powders may be produced.

6

ROAD ACCIDENTS

Since so much law enforcement in a modern motorised community is concerned with road traffic, a large proportion of the work entering a forensic science laboratory originates in road accidents. Generally speaking, the accidents which concern us here can be classified as:

(1) "Hit-and-Run" accidents, in which the vehicle responsible has not stopped. These may involve:

(a) only damage to other vehicles or property, or
(b) personal injury or death.

(2) Accidents in which the identity of the vehicle(s) involved is known, but in which the succession of events leading up to the accident is in dispute.

I. HIT-AND-RUN ACCIDENTS

In hit-and-run accidents of the first type, not leading to personal injury, it is normally the responsibility of the police to deduce, from the damage caused or sustained in the accident, the sort of damage to be expected on the vehicle responsible; if they find a vehicle which shows this, and which could, or is admitted to, have passed the scene at the right time, then will they submit to the laboratory whatever samples of paint, glass, broken woodwork or fittings, etc., may be necessary to establish a connection with whatever has been found at the scene. What the laboratory does with these has already been described.

When most cars were black, the finding of black paint fragments was of little help, but the position is different now that numerous and varied colours are the rule. An extensive investigation pioneered by C. F. Tippett of the Home Office Forensic Science Laboratory in Cardiff has established that a paint flake showing all the undercoats and the finishing colour is more often than not unique to a particular make and model of car, and even that each precise shade of finishing colour is normally (in this country at least) used by only one manufacturer. The examination of a flake large enough for a proper comparison of its colours will therefore limit the car of origin to a surprisingly small proportion of all the cars on the road in the area—from perhaps 4 per cent. for the commonest cars/colours to less than 0·1 per cent for uncommon ones. Indeed, these statistics will often—perhaps even in the majority of cases—enable the investigator to say that the chance of another car exactly similar to the suspected one having passed

48

the scene of the accident within the relevant times is negligibly small. Resprayed cars must of course count as "mavericks" in this context, but respraying is commonly done with a nitrocellulose paint, whereas most manufacturers nowadays use an alkyd-resin or similar paint.

When a paint flake is large enough, it is usually worthwhile to try and locate the precise spot from which it came; it may then be possible to show by a "jigsaw" fit with paint remaining on the car that it must have come from that spot (cf. p. 16). Also, if such a flake contains all the layers down to the metal, and if the metal from which it was detached bears any scratches or other adventitious marks, these may be reproduced as a "cast" on the underside of the flake, thereby linking flake and original site beyond question.

Apart from the reassembly of headlamp fragments mentioned in a previous chapter (p. 16), broken glass, whether from windscreen or window, or from headlamps, is on the whole a less fruitful source of conclusive evidence than paint. Nevertheless, even if the fragments are very small, they should be examined in the same way as glass fragments from breaking offences (pp. 30–34). Modern sealed-beam headlamps often use Pyrex or a similar heat-resistant glass. A complete collection of commercial headlamp glasses, if available, may also be useful, since the numerous small variations of pattern which they show may enable quite small fragments to be identified as from a particular model.

Many hit-and-run accidents are of course quite trivial ones, but they become serious crimes if they have caused personal injury or death. In these cases, it is or may be the laboratory's job to find links between (1) the vehicle; (2) the scene of the accident; (3) the victim. Normally of course there is no dispute as to where the accident occurred, and the laboratory's job is confined to linking (1) with (2) and (3).

Once a suspected vehicle in a serious case has been traced, it is often advisable for the scientist to examine it himself, since from his examination of the scene, clothing, etc., he is likely to know exactly what he is seeking and what it will look like if he finds it.

The injuries caused are the concern of the doctor or pathologist, but the forensic scientist will see the medical report, and it may also be expedient for him, if the victim is dead, to attend the post mortem and see the injuries for himself; in any case, the clothing of the dead or injured person will be taken to the laboratory. From these sources, and possibly also from an examination of the scene of the accident, the scientist may expect to find any or all of the following: wounds to the body and damage to the clothing, from which it is likely that traces will have been carried away on the vehicle; fragments of paint or glass in the hair or clothing of the victim; paint, glass or broken-off parts of the vehicle at the scene; oil or grease on the body or clothing of the victim (fig. 14); tyre marks at the scene, tyre-tread impressions on the body or clothing of the victim; fabric impressions from the victim's clothing on the cellulose of the car.

When a pedestrian or cyclist is struck by a car, certain types of injury are so frequent that they may almost be considered stock patterns. The nature and position of the victim's injuries are therefore a guide as to which part of the vehicle is most likely to carry evidence of the collision. (See fig. 14.) Control samples of damaged paint and/or broken glass must of course be taken, and also mud from under the wings, if any, which apparently came from the vehicle found at the scene. The finding of any broken parts at the scene will of course direct attention at once to the corresponding position on the vehicle; a matching part there will be a lucky break (in both senses!) for the investigator, but an apparently new part, especially if it is one which does not normally require replacement, is also a matter for suspicion. If the victim's body or clothing bears any oil or grease, the underside of the vehicle must be examined carefully (which, to be done properly, requires a hydraulic ramp or a roomy inspection pit); the bottom of the sump, or any other part projecting underneath, may show recent smearing, scraping or rubbing (fig. 14), in which case this should be photographed and a control sample of the grease/dirt taken. (The identification of oils and greases is dealt with on pp. 57 and 74.) If the victim's clothing was torn, any projecting part of the vehicle which could possibly, from the circumstances of the accident, have struck him must be examined minutely in a good light for fibres or tufts of fabric. Similarly, if the victim received an open wound, a search must be made for blood or whatever tissue may have been derived from the wound. (This is usually skin or other superficial tissue, but the writer has known of actual brain tissue being found on a vehicle which had caused a serious head injury.) If blood has been spilt, the whole of the outside of the vehicle should be examined for it, since it may have spurted well away from the actual point of impact. Hairs should be looked for whether the victim has any actual head injuries or not. All of that, unless the investigator is singularly unlucky, will give him enough material for a good many hours' work in the laboratory, involving possibly most of the various techniques described elsewhere in this book.

II. WHAT CAUSED THE ACCIDENT?

The other type of accident mentioned on p. 48, in which the identities of the driver(s) and vehicle(s) are not in dispute, calls for a different type of examination. It is now the function of scientific examination to provide the objective assessment of the condition of the vehicles, and of the damage found, which will be essential in coming to a decision whether the account of the accident given by the driver suspected of being at fault is, or at least could be, true.

Just where the boundary here should be drawn between science and engineering must depend on circumstances and on the facilities available. A routine examination of general roadworthiness is a job for a trained mechanic or vehicle examiner; he will check, as far as the condition of the vehicle permits, such things as steering backlash, brake efficiency and compensation, the condition of the tyres, the state of the lights and electrical accessories, the condition of important holding bolts, etc.

The particular examinations which are usually, at least in the writer's experience, turned over to the laboratory are those of burst tyres, metal failures and lights. A driver involved in an accident may blame a "blow-out" for his loss of control, and it may therefore be important to decide whether tyre damage found after the accident was the cause or a result of this. The whole subject of **tyres** and their examination has recently been dealt with in detail by R. J. Grogan, and the reader who wishes to pursue it may refer to his publications (see p. 232), upon which the following brief treatment of the topic is largely based. Tyre failure will not normally, contrary to popular belief, cause a driver to lose control of his vehicle unless the tyre is on the outside of the curve while he is cornering; it is probably responsible for only about 1 accident in 150. Whether or not the tyre was inflated at the moment of the accident is a question which is usually answerable. If it was, damage to both tyre *and* wheel rim indicates a very severe impact, since an inflated tyre is an excellent energy absorber. On the other hand, a tyre already flat offers little protection to the rim. It is frequently possible to estimate the rate of deflation from the nature of the damage. In the right combination of circumstances, apparently quite improbable objects can penetrate a tyre, especially if it is wet. (A case is even recorded of an aircraft tyre being punctured by touching down on a hedgehog!) However it is caused—whether by an object in the road or by hitting another vehicle—an impact burst usually shows a clear cut through both outer casing and inner tube (if present) at the point of impact. In a true "blow-out," on the other hand, the hole in the outer casing has a characteristic ragged appearance, with frayed ends of the cord lining protruding through it, and the inner tube if present shows a star-shaped hole, possibly with a roughly circular piece missing completely.

The interpretation of **metal failures** comes into question when a vital part such as a track rod, steering arm or brake pipe is found broken after the accident. If the break caused the accident, it must have happened first, and it can then be assumed that it was due to metal fatigue (unless there is clear evidence of excessive wear due to lack of proper maintenance). If the broken part shows no evidence of this, then it was in all probability broken by the impact, and the accident was the cause. The diagnosis of metal fatigue is a matter for a metallurgist, whose work will be briefly described in the next chapter (p. 59; see also fig. 16).

It may be important to discover whether the **lights** of a vehicle involved in an accident were on or off at the moment of impact. The switch or dipping-switch setting is not of course a reliable guide, since it may have been altered after the accident. The question may be answerable by an examination of the light bulb(s) and its/their remains, bearing in mind the elementary distinction that a lamp filament is cold when "off" but as hot as about 3,000 °C. when "on." There are four possible combinations to be considered here:

(1) Bulb and filament both intact. If the filament is severely distorted, or if there is evidence of a "short" having occurred inside the bulb, the filament was probably hot when the impact occurred. Otherwise, no conclusion is usually possible.

(2) Bulb intact, filament broken. Sharp or jagged ends at the break indicate a

cold fracture; smooth bulbous ends (caused by momentary arc-ing having occurred) indicate a hot fracture.

(3) Bulb broken, filament intact. If the filament was cold, its surface will be clean and bright. If it was hot, its surface will be coloured by oxidation due to access of air to the glowing metal, and minute particles of glass are nearly always found fused on to it. (See fig. 15).

(4) Bulb and filament both broken. A combination of the effects described under (2) and (3) will be found.

It should also be mentioned, before we leave car-light bulbs, that it has on occasion been found possible to link a detached piece of broken filament with the ends remaining in the bulb from which it came by matching the extrusion striations on the filament wire (cf. p. 20). To do this successfully, however, requires a very high magnification, possibly not less than that afforded by the scanning electron microscope (see p. 82).

Finally, a question which has received a good deal of attention, particularly in the U.S.A., is that of the **speed**(s) of the vehicle(s) at the moment of collision. There are in general two ways in which these can be estimated: the extent of the damage can be compared with that sustained in test crashes at known speeds, or calculations can be based on the length and shape of skid marks. Estimates made by the first method, although useful as better than none, are obviously bound to be rough, and the method is limited by the scanty and expensively won control data available. In calculations by the second method, the following data can be used: the measured length of skid marks; the coefficient of friction between tyre and road for various conditions of tyre tread and road surface; the force (calculated from the gravitational constant and the weight of vehicle) between the tyre tread and the road; the radius of curved marks, and the comparison of this with the sharpest possible curve which, taking into account the other factors already mentioned, the vehicle could traverse at any given speed without side slip. Such calculations can be made to give seemingly quite precise results, but this precision will be spurious if, as must usually be the case, the values of the parameters used in them are not and cannot be known other than very roughly.

7

CHEMISTRY AND THE PHYSICAL SCIENCES: SCOPE AND PROBLEMS

Broadly speaking, the principal line of demarcation in the variety of scientific disciplines utilised in forensic science is that between the physical and the biological sciences. We shall be dealing with the latter in the second half of this book, while the previous chapters have been concerned with applications of the former. Of these, chemistry undoubtedly finds the widest use. Probably more forensic scientists were trained in chemistry than in any other science, and chemical analysis enters into practically every branch of the subject. There is less scope for the other physical sciences, though much of the work could be described as elementary physics. However, modern chemical analysis, utilising the various instruments which we shall describe in the next chapter, relies so heavily upon physical measurements that it is unrealistic to try to draw a boundary here between these sciences. In this chapter we shall outline the various applications of the physical sciences, and in the next we shall explain briefly the various methods used.

I. THE CHEMIST'S PROBLEMS

The forensic chemist's work differs in several respects from that of the analyst in other fields. He is liable to meet a greater variety of substances to be analysed. He has little control over the size and condition of the samples he receives— unlike, say, the industrial process-control analyst, who can get samples as large as he needs and taken as he directs. The forensic chemist must do the best he can with what he is given.

In general, chemical operations in this field may be called either "absolute" or "comparative." The object of the former is to establish some qualitative or quantitative property which is significant by itself, of the latter merely to discover whether two or more specimens are identical, or at least indistinguishable (but see p. 15). Although the chemist must sometimes attain the highest possible accuracy, at other times a comparatively rough analysis may suffice to show that superficially similar substances are in fact different.

It is impossible to enumerate every problem which the forensic chemist is liable to encounter, since the unusual and the unexpected will always crop up, but the following headings will cover the bulk of his work.

53

(1) **The analysis of contact traces** (comparative). The materials most commonly encountered in this context have been described in Chapter 4. Numerous others may however occur when, for example, a man who has broken into a factory carries away traces of some characteristic product or raw material, or an assailant is marked with the victim's lipstick or powder.

(2) **The comparison of stolen and control material** (comparative). As mentioned in Chapter 5, this may tax the chemist's skill and ingenuity to the utmost, since *anything* of commercial value may have to be compared and for that purpose accurately analysed.

Some of the materials most commonly encountered under (1) and (2) are listed alphabetically below.

(3) **The proof of fraud or deception.** An absolute analysis is necessary to show that the material offered is what it is and is not what it purports to be. Here again, the materials to be analysed are limited only by the gullibility and misplaced ingenuity of mankind. No clear-cut distinction can be drawn between what is at one extreme criminally fraudulent and what is at the other merely a technical breach of a regulation (for example, the presence of more than the permitted amount of preservative in food). In any case, the distinction is legal rather than scientific, and it lies in practice between what is the concern of the police and goes to the forensic chemist and what is the concern of some other authority and goes to a public analyst.

(4) **Toxicology,** or the isolation and identification of poisons, and the **identification of drugs of addiction,** are dealt with in Chapter 10 (absolute).

(5) **The determination of alcohol in body fluids** in connection with road traffic offences is dealt with in Chapter 9 (absolute).

(6) **The identification of substances used in procuring abortions** (usually absolute, sometimes comparative). Illegal abortion or attempts to procure it used to bring a good deal of work into British forensic science laboratories, but are nowadays rarely encountered in this country since the passing of the Abortion Act 1967. No doubt this type of work is still encountered in countries where abortion has not been legalised. The necessary examinations were usually either: (*a*) the identification by chemical analysis or pharmacognosy of abortifacient or supposedly abortifacient preparations (*e.g.* iron-aloes mixtures; various herbal preparations); or (*b*) the detection of soapy water in instruments such as Higginson's or enema syringes (see *Soap* below).

(7) **The identification of materials used in committing crimes:** for example, in safe-blowing (see *Explosives* below); in malicious damage or injury (*e.g.* household bleach poured over a neighbour's vegetables or corrosive acid thrown at a victim); in fire-raising (see *Petroleum products* below, and Chapter (14) (absolute or comparative).

(8) **The examination of counterfeit coins.** These are most commonly cast in some fusible alloy, and are occasionally nickel-plated as well. Any quick method

of absolute analysis will reveal the general nature of the metal and suffice to show that the coin is counterfeit; an accurate comparative quantitative analysis will, however, be necessary if metal is found in a suspect's possession (see also *Metals* below).

(9) **The examination of writing materials.** See Chapter 16.

Some of the materials most commonly encountered in these contexts (other than those already dealt with in Chapter 4) are listed alphabetically below. The various methods of examination cited will all be described in the next chapter.

Adhesives. These may have to be identified in comparing broken parts with the objects from which they came, or (sometimes) in connecting sealed packages with the suspected senders. Water-based adhesives (gum, paste, glue) must be tested empirically, using methods such as fluorescence or infra-red spectrometry to discover characteristic properties. The more modern non-aqueous adhesives may be characterised by infra-red spectrometry or by pyrolysis and gas chromatography.

Asphalt, bitumen, tar. These may occur as contact traces. Characterisation of such products is difficult, but may be achieved by means of thin-layer chromatography in combination with fluorescence analysis, infra-red spectrometry, spectrofluorimetry or pyrolysis and gas chromatography.

Dusts frequently occur as contact traces. The first step must be examination under the microscope to determine their general nature—whether organic (*e.g.* flour) or inorganic (*e.g.* talcum powder). If available, the scanning electron microscope (p. 82) is likely to be extremely useful here. If the dusts are mixed, a statistical count of their ingredients may provide a useful basis for comparison. Organic dusts will probably be turned over to the biologist for identification. Inorganic dusts will be analysed by the most appropriate technique—possibly spectrography or X-ray diffraction for the dust in bulk, or, for individual particles, X-ray micro-analysis with the electron-beam probe (p. 81) or scanning electron microscope.

Dyes may call for identification for various reasons. A few dyed fibres may have to be compared with their "parent" fabric, or stains of lipstick, shoe polish, etc. with their suspected origin. If the quantity is sufficient there are purely chemical routines for dye analysis, which may have to begin with stripping the dye from the fibres etc., but the quantity available will rarely be sufficient for this. With very small amounts, thin-layer chromatography of the extracted dye will probably yield the most information; with rather larger amounts, a characteristic absorption spectrum may be measurable. If the dye can actually be extracted and crystallised, X-ray diffraction may prove a rewarding technique. (The writer once succeeded by this method in identifying the dye in some pink sugar crystals found beside a stolen safe with the dye in the pink sugar used by an itinerant candy-floss maker suspected of the theft.)

Explosives may be encountered in connection with safe-blowings, or as constituents of parcel bombs, etc. Though the actual handling and transportation of dangerous explosive devices is not the responsibility in this country of the forensic science laboratories, most of these find it necessary on occasion to analyse small quantities of explosive. Most commercial explosives consist essentially of mixtures of nitrocellulose with nitroglycerine or nitroglycol and, usually, ammonium nitrate. Other possible ingredients include: mono- and dinitrotoluenes; aluminium powder; various inorganic salts; fillers such as china clay, oat-husk flour or wood meal. Most explosives are sufficiently distinctive in composition to be readily identifiable from scraps of a few grams as long as these are not too dirty or wet. Successive extractions with the appropriate solvents will separate the soluble ingredients for identification, and the insoluble residue is examined microscopically to identify organic fillers.

Fats. A fat is technically an ester (see Glossary) of glycerol (glycerine) and one or more of certain complex organic acids known collectively as the "higher fatty acids." True fats are always of animal origin. They may occur as contact traces—for example, in a case of theft from a butcher's premises, or as lipstick. There are purely chemical routines for identifying them, but these require larger amounts than are likely to be available; in that case the most useful technique is likely to be hydrolysis to liberate the fatty acid, followed by conversion of this to its methyl ester and identification by gas chromatography. The infra-red absorption spectrum of the whole fat may also be characteristic.

Greases. See *Petroleum products.*

Hand swabs. See *Swabs.*

Inks. See Chapter 16.

Metals usually require identification either (*a*) as the subject of theft, (*b*) in connection with false pretences (for example, if a cheap alloy is passed off as gold), or (*c*) in the form of counterfeit coins (p. 54). For a quick identification, spectrography is undoubtedly the most convenient method. Where the accurate comparison of control and crime specimens is necessary, however, a complete quantitative analysis, requiring both skill and considerable time, may have to be undertaken.

Oils may be either organic (practically all vegetable in origin) or mineral. For the latter see *Petroleum products.* Vegetable oils are of two kinds: (*a*) "essential oils" (*e.g.* oil of lemon; genuine turpentine) of varied and often complex chemical constitutions, always volatile and often having characteristic fragrant odours; (*b*) non-volatile "fatty oils" (*e.g.* olive oil; linseed oil), which are chemically glycerol esters (*cf. fats*) and some of which are "drying oils"—that is, are oxidised by the air to a solid resin. Being esters, fatty oils are distinguishable from most essential and all mineral oils by being *saponifiable*—they react with alkalis to form glycerol and the alkali salts of the fatty acids, which are *soaps* (*q.v.*). Any of these oils may be encountered as contact traces, as the subject of theft or (occasionally) as fire-raising materials. Refractive index and viscosity are useful identifying properties, but for small amounts infra-red spectrometry and gas chromatography are the best techniques. The odours of many essential oils are also very characteristic.

Paper. See Chapter 16.

Petroleum products range from light oils such as petrol or lighter fuel through white spirit (turpentine substitute), diesel fuel, paraffin oil (kerosene) and heavy lubricating oils to semi-solid greases. They may be encountered as the subject of theft, as fire-raising materials, or as contact traces from machinery or motor vehicles. They are always non-saponifiable (*cf. oils*). If sufficient is available, the refractive index, viscosity and boiling range provide approximate identification. Other methods are necessary for smaller quantities and/or more specific identification. With greases and heavy oils, infra-red spectrometry, thin-layer chromatography or high-pressure liquid chromatography (p. 64) of a solution may be helpful, but the newest and probably the best technique here is spectrofluorimetry. With the more volatile products, which are exceedingly complex mixtures of chemically similar compounds, gas chromatography is by far the best method, and is the only way of making a complete identification which will distinguish between, say, two brands of petrol (see fig. 20).

Plastics. Broken fragments of these are frequently encountered as contact traces. There are various routines for their analysis, utilising properties such as the elements present in them and their solubilities in various solvents. With small quantities, they are best identified by infra-red spectrometry, or by pyrolysis and gas chromatography; differential thermal analysis may occasionally be useful.

Rubber may be encountered as a contact trace in road accidents. Its characterisation is difficult, but may be possible using infra-red spectrometry, differential thermal analysis or pyrolysis followed by gas chromatography.

Soap used to be encountered frequently in abortion cases (p. 54). There is no simple really satisfactory test for it. If the quantity is sufficient, the alkalinity of the ash is a guide. As household soaps are the sodium salts of the acids from fats and oils (*q.v.*), the best and most specific test for small quantities consists in the conversion of the separated fatty acids to their volatile methyl esters, which are then characterised by gas chromatography. This method is sensitive enough for very small quantities, and probably specific enough to distinguish between different brands of soap.

Swabs. Swabs from the hands of persons suspected of handling explosives, or of stealing materials from which traces rub off easily (*e.g.* roofing lead), may be submitted for examination. It is usually a fairly simple matter to test them for the presence of the specific material in question.

Tar. See *Asphalt*.

Water. Samples of river or estuarine water may require analysis in such cases as the illegal discharge of oil in navigable waters, or the pollution of a stream following the spillage of a load. As ample material will be available, the absolute identification of a contaminant is normally easy. If it has to be compared with its suspected source, the method used will depend on its nature; infra-red spectrometry will usually give a specific identification of an illegally discharged oil.

Waxes will most commonly be encountered as candle droppings. For their identification, properties such as softening temperature and fluorescence are empirically useful. For a more positive identification, differential thermal analysis is one of the best methods. Infra-red spectrometry may also provide the answer, as in the case illustrated in fig. 22.

II. OTHER PHYSICAL SCIENCES

As has already been mentioned, the measurement of physical properties such as specific gravity, refractive index or viscosity which are utilised in identification is strictly speaking a problem of **physics**. These are, however, well within the capacity of any chemist, and the more advanced and abstruse developments of modern physics have not as yet found application in forensic science.

Geology. The scope for this in the examination of soil has already been mentioned (p. 38). Otherwise, purely geological problems rarely arise; when they do, however, the geologist's expertise is indispensable. He may, for example, be able to indicate a very limited area as that from which a lump of rock used to break a shop window must have come.

The place here of geology may best be illustrated by some examples of cases in which it was applied. In one case, in which a valuable consignment was stolen in transit by air from Denmark to London and the boxes filled up with broken concrete, a geologist was able to identify the stone aggregate in this as Danish rather than English in origin. In a second case, a member of a local authority was accused of corruptly receiving for his private use a quantity of concrete paving slabs, the property of the authority; again, a geologist was able to show that the aggregate in the disputed slabs was identical with that in the authority's, and could not have come from the alleged source in another part of the country. In a third case, a comparatively modern church in Kent was broken into, and the contact traces submitted for examination included some stone dust believed to come from the window openings. This appeared at first to be rather indistinctive and hence not very useful; however, a geologist was able to show, not only that it was identical with the window stone, but that it was quite different from the local Kentish building stone. It turned out that when the church was built the stone for the windows had been specially brought in from a distant part of the country.

In this sphere, the geologist's requirements in the shape of laboratory equipment are comparatively modest. He can do much of his work with a hand-lens, and his most expensive needs are a petrological microscope and equipment for cutting rock sections.

Metallurgy. The forensic metallurgist, as we have already indicated, is most frequently concerned with the examination of broken components in road (and occasionally other) accidents, in order to diagnose or exclude metal fatigue as the cause of the fracture.

Metal fatigue is the condition produced by the birth and slow growth of a crack or cracks. This, or these, begin as a "slippage" in the crystal structure of the metal at or near the surface, and usually at a discontinuity such as a sharp corner or a corrosion pit. The incipient crack, being a point of weakness, grows every time the component bearing it is stressed by a load. At some point in time the crack will have progressed so far that too little sound metal remains to carry the load, and the component breaks. A break due to fatigue will therefore show: (1) an area of progressive crack growth, which is often corroded or discoloured, and usually shows "beach marks," which resemble in appearance growth rings in wood and which represent the stages of growth of the crack; (2) a smaller area of sound metal, the surface of which shows whichever appearance is typical of cleavage or shear in the metal in question (fig. 16). To confirm his diagnosis from this appearance, the metallurgist may also section, polish and examine microscopically the metal in the neighbourhood of the fracture; fatigue will reveal itself as pits and minute cracks filled with corrosion products.

Another occasional task for the metallurgist is the examination of fragments of metal from the site of an explosion. Some metals on disruption by a very rapidly applied violent stress, such as will occur near the actual point of explosion, may show a characteristic dislocation of their crystal structure known as "twinning." In the case of iron or steel, this manifests itself as distinctive parallel dark bands, known as *Neumann bands*, on the metallographic examination of a polished and etched surface.

As already mentioned (p. 45), the restoration of erased identification marks on metal is also a matter for the metallurgist if the laboratory staff includes one.

Gemmology. In fact as well as in fiction precious stones are not infrequently the cause or the subject of crime, the investigation of which may require their examination and identification. Chiefly because of the high value of the material examined—some gemstones may cost as much as £1,000 per carat (that is, nearly £150,000 an ounce!)—gemmology, or the scientific study of gem materials, is a very specialised field of expertise, outside the scope of the average forensic science laboratory. For the sake of completeness, however, a very short and superficial outline of the subject is included here.

In its forensic aspects, gemmology is usually concerned with either (1) distinguishing genuine from artificial or imitation stones, or (2) the precise identification of the species and variety of natural gemstones. As all gems, except for pearls and a few semi-precious materials such as amber, are minerals, the methods of examination are basically those of the mineralogist (*cf.* p. 38), except that obviously only non-destructive tests may be used. Pearls are usually tested by X-raying them.

The gemmologist lays considerable stress on the distinction between *imitation* gems and *synthetic* (that is, artificial or man-made) ones. Imitation gems merely look more or less like genuine ones, and can be made of anything having the correct appearance—possibly glass or even plastic. Such materials will rarely deceive an experienced eye, but more exotic ones have been developed which simulate natural gems very closely. For example, the compounds strontium titanate and yttrium aluminate ("YAG") are clear and colourless, harder than glass, and, having a very high refractive index, show the "fire" characteristic of diamonds. Genuine are distinguished from imitation gems by using a suitable choice of characteristic physical properties: hardness (rarely used); specific gravity (measured as with glass or soil minerals—*cf.* p. 32); refractive index; fluorescence; the mode of light transmission (whether isotropic or birefringent —see Glossary—and whether the spectrum of the transmitted light shows characteristic absorption bands); whether transparent or opaque to X-rays.

Imitation gems always differ from genuine ones in composition; however, it has on the basis of the known compositions of gem minerals proved possible to produce many of them artificially—that is, to fabricate man-made gems chemically identical with their genuine counterparts. This has been done for most of the well-known gemstones, such as emerald (beryllium aluminium silicate), or sapphire and ruby (both aluminium oxide, with traces of other compounds conferring the appropriate colour). Diamonds have also been produced synthetically, but these are suitable only for industrial purposes. The distinction between man-made and genuine gems is obviously therefore more difficult than that between imitation and genuine ones. It most frequently depends on expert examination by low-power microscopy for the presence or absence of certain characteristic inclusions and irregularities of crystal formation. The photomicrographic recording of these may also sometimes be used as a means of "fingerprinting" particular stones.

8
CHEMISTRY: METHODS

A full description of all the methods used by the forensic chemist would fill a library and would be unintelligible to all but the scientifically trained. On the other hand, to omit any description of them at all in a book such as this would be cheating the reader. Whether the compromise here adopted is successful, he must judge.

A chemical analysis has or may have a threefold function. The fundamental question is: what is the nature and composition of this substance? Assuming that it is composite in nature (and practically all the substances encountered by the analyst are) the answer to that question involves in principle: the separation of the constituents, their identification and the measurement of the amount of each.

I. THE ANALYTICAL REVOLUTION

A revolution has overtaken chemical analysis in the last 20–30 years. In the 1930s, "analysis" meant primarily the traditional techniques which had not changed in principle for about 100 years and which, since they depend mainly on handling solutions in laboratory glassware, are nowadays slightly derogatorily referred to as "wet chemistry." Today, the analyst relies heavily and increasingly on so-called "instrumental" methods, which use complex and expensive electrical and optical equipment and which are everywhere replacing the "classical" methods, in spite of their cost. The reason for this is not hard to discover: instrumental methods are, by and large, vastly more sensitive, often much quicker and sometimes more accurate.

However, in spite of the diminishing importance of classical methods, they cannot yet be entirely dismissed or forgotten. There are still occasions when the forensic chemist can discover the answer to his question most quickly and simply with the aid of the test tube. A question such as "Is the white powder sodium bicarbonate or heroin?" would fall into this category. And *accurate* classical methods still have a limited, though admittedly diminishing, field of usefulness.

Classical methods are by long-established usage classified in two ways: one is into qualitative analysis (identifying the substance(s) present) and quantitative analysis (precisely how much?); the other is into the analysis of inorganic compounds (usually salts of metals) and that of organic (*i.e.* carbon) compounds.

It would be out of place here to attempt a detailed description of these. A few general observations may however be helpful. The teaching of analytical chemistry usually starts with inorganic qualitative analysis. This uses the classical "group separations" to separate and identify salts of metals (*e.g.* sodium chloride, copper sulphate, etc.). Although this approach is hallowed by tradition, it is highly artificial, in that it has little relevance to the real problems of analysis; it also tends to obscure the essential distinction between the three stages or functions of analysis mentioned above, since its fundamental operations of observing the formation of, and removing by filtration, insoluble precipitates, perform the functions of separation and identification simultaneously.

Methods of quantitative analysis have always been divided into gravimetric and volumetric ones. The former depend upon the precipitation of an insoluble compound of the constituent sought, and the weighing of this after suitable treatment to ensure that what is weighed is of a known and pre-determinable composition. In the latter, reactions occurring in solution are utilised, and what is measured (by the operation of *titration*) is the volume of reagent required to complete the reaction; the point at which this has occurred is indicated by arranging for a change of colour (or, in some more modern methods, of some electrical property of the solution) to occur at it. Gravimetric methods are the more fundamental, in that all methods depend ultimately upon weighing—gravimetric ones directly, and volumetric ones for the preparation of the necessary solutions of accurately known concentrations. That is why an accurate sensitive balance is the chemist's most important piece of equipment.

The problems of organic chemical analysis are so different that totally different methods are necessary. In one respect only, these are simpler than those of inorganic analysis; separation and identification/determination are almost universally separate operations in fact, as well as separate stages in principle. Apart from that, few or no clear-cut schematic analytical procedures are applicable. Separations are made in various ways—distillation, differential solubilities in various solvents, etc. The identification and/or determination of the separated individual constituents are performed in a variety of ways. It would be unprofitable to detail these here, but it is perhaps worth mentioning the organic chemist's traditional stand-by: the melting-point.

As the determination of this is quick and easy, and as the melting-points of all organic compounds (except for those that decompose before they melt) have been tabulated, it has always been the penultimate test for identity. The ultimate test is a *mixed melting-point*. If the analyst thinks that his unknown X is in fact the compound A, both melting at, say, 124 °C., then his final step is to mix some X intimately with a roughly equal quantity of A and determine the melting-point of the mixture. If X is A, then the mixture will also melt at 124°; if X is not A, then the mixture will have a lower melting point (see eutectics, p. 238).

However, as we have already indicated, classical methods have several severe limitations which restrict their usefulness to the forensic chemist. First, they are relatively insensitive, requiring comparatively large quantities of sample. The forensic chemist would often be unable to extract by these methods the information he seeks from the very small traces of material he receives. Secondly, many of the substances with which he is concerned are complex mixtures of chemically similar compounds, such as petroleum products or foodstuffs, with which classical methods are not really capable of dealing.

The following sections describe briefly the instrumental methods used in a modern forensic science laboratory, grouped somewhat arbitrarily but, the writer hopes, conveniently. The reader must remember, however, that the novelty and expense of some of these methods mean that not every laboratory, especially if it is a small one, will be equipped for all of them. Also, it will be apparent from the previous chapter and from what follows that for many types of material there is not necessarily one prescribed method of analysis preferable to all others; the methods actually used, therefore, may well depend, not only on the equipment available, but on the particular analyst's experience and preferences.

II. METHODS OF SEPARATION

One of the most valuable and widely applicable of all modern analytical techniques is the group of methods of separation known collectively as **chromatography**. The name has no particular connection with colour; it originated in the historical accident that it was coined in 1906 by the Russian botanist Tswett, who used a crude form of the technique for the separation of flower pigments.

The basis of chromatography is that, in the presence of two phases both of which adsorb or dissolve some particular compound, any of that compound present is divided between the phases in a ratio which depends on the relevant partition coefficient. ("Phase," "adsorb" and "partition coefficient" are defined in the Glossary.) If then a mixture to be separated is carried as the *moving phase* in a suitable fluid past a *stationary phase* selected according to the type of mixture in question, its components will be held back to a greater or lesser degree by the stationary phase. Hence, if the distance over which the two phases are in contact is sufficient, the components will be completely separated, those which are least strongly held by the stationary phase being carried furthest along it. In fact, if the process is continued long enough, they will emerge separately from the end of the stationary phase in the reverse order of their affinities for it.

In **adsorption** (or **column**) **chromatography**, the original form of the technique, a solution containing mixed solutes percolates through a column of granular absorbent, frequently either activated alumina or silica gel, and after a time the solutes will be found spaced out down the column with the most strongly adsorbed at the top. The various fractions may then be differentially washed out (*eluted*) using other solvents for which the partition coefficient is such that they remove the solutes from the solid adsorbent.

In its simplest form this technique requires fairly large samples and has few applications in forensic science. It has however been used to identify the mixed dyes in coloured petrol and other commercial products. It can also be considerably refined in various ways: specially chosen more selective adsorbents may be used; *high-pressure liquid chromatography*, in which the liquid is forced through a narrow column of finely divided adsorbent, gives improved separation and is proving increasingly valuable for some purposes; it may even be possible to automate the detection of different components emerging from the column.

Paper and **thin-layer chromatography.** In these more recent (post-war) developments of the principle, separation takes place almost two-dimensionally on a sheet of filter paper or a thin layer of adsorbent coated on an inert support. Since a very small amount of adsorbed solute covers a relatively large area, the methods are valuable for the traces in which the forensic scientist is interested, and microgram amounts can be detected and separated. This is of particular interest to the toxicologist (Chapter 10), a field in which this application was largely pioneered by Dr. A. S. Curry, and is also of assistance in the analysis of inks, dyes, greases and many other mixed products.

To "run" a chromatogram, a few microlitres of the solutions to be analysed (together with, if desired, control solutions of the compounds being sought) are "spotted" at intervals along a line near one shorter edge of the sheet of paper or layer of adsorbent. The sheet or layer is then supported in a closed glass tank so that the spotted edge dips into a trough of the selected solvent with the spots just out of the liquid. The solvent travels up the sheet or layer by capillary action and in doing so carries with it the various constituent compounds of the spots. However, each of these lags behind the solvent front by a distance depending on its partition coefficient in the system being used. For each solvent and compound, in fact, the ratio

$$\frac{\textit{Distance travelled by compound}}{\textit{Distance travelled by solvent front}}$$

is a constant, and is known as the *Rf value*. The first step in an analysis therefore is to let the solvent run nearly the whole length of the paper or layer. The Rf values are then measured or compared with those of the controls run simultaneously. We thus achieve provisional identification as well as separation (see fig. 18).

Paper and thin-layer chromatography (TLC) have so far been considered together, but there are several differences between them both in theory and practice. The main theoretical difference is that TLC is *liquid-solid* chromatography between a liquid moving and a solid stationary phase, whereas paper chromatography is to a large extent *liquid-liquid*, in that the stationary phase is primarily water adsorbed on the paper fibres. However, this difference is not complete, as the nature of the paper does affect the results. The main practical difference is that TLC is much quicker, requiring minutes for a run rather than the hours needed for paper.

Several modifications of paper chromatography, giving better performance in certain circumstances, have also been devised. By supporting the top of the paper in a trough with the rest of the sheet hanging over the edge, the solvent front can be made to travel downwards instead of upwards (*descending* paper chromatography). The run can be speeded up by carrying it out at higher temperatures. In *reversed-phase* paper chromatography, the paper is impregnated with an organic fat immiscible with water and the moving phase is an aqueous solution; this method is useful with some compounds in which the toxicologist is particularly interested.

A finished chromatogram, however produced, consists of a surface bearing a number of spots or small areas arranged linearly above the original starting point and each representing a particular compound present in the original sample. This will be provisionally identified by its Rf value and by the solvent used, since each class of compounds will run with only a limited number of solvents. Spraying the sheet with an appropriate reagent will produce identifying colour reactions in the spots. Colourless spots can often be located by their fluorescence (see p. 74) being either brighter or less bright than that of the paper background. Finally, the located spot may be cut out and the compound eluted from it for identification with whatever technique is appropriate—for example, infra-red spectrometry.

Sometimes the Rf values of the compounds present are too close together to permit of clear separation. If this difficulty cannot be overcome by using another solvent system with which the Rf values are well separated, the answer may be found in *two-dimensional* chromatography: when the first run is finished, the sheet is turned through 90° and a second run carried out with a different solvent system, producing a new line of separated spots perpendicular to the original.

TLC is a newer technique than paper chromatography and is at present displacing it fairly rapidly. Its advantages lie in the already-mentioned greater speed, in the more sharply defined spots which it produces, in the fact that reagents which attack paper can be used on the more inert adsorbent layer and in the easier excision and elution of the spots. However, some toxicologists still prefer paper for certain groups of compounds, claiming that it gives better separation.

Another technique of separation superficially similar to TLC and paper chromatography is **electrophoresis.** This is a process of separating proteins and similar colloids by utilising the fact that their molecules carry electric charges. By applying a fairly high electric potential (say, 100–150 volts) across a wet strip of paper or jelly bearing at one point the mixture to be analysed, the different constituents travel different distances along the strip under the action of the potential, their speed depending on the charges they carry and on how easily their usually large molecules get through the pores of the support. The technique is extensively used in blood-grouping (see Chapter 12), but finds fewer applications among chemists. It can however be combined with paper chromatography, by applying the potential across a suitably modified sheet while the run is in progress, giving a two-dimensional separation in one operation.

Gas (or **gas-liquid**, or **vapour-phase**) **chromatography** (GC, GLC or VPC) is an even newer technique than those we have just been discussing, and has grown even faster; it now has a good claim to be the most versatile and widely applied analytical technique in the whole of forensic science (as the number of references to it in the previous chapter may have testified). The stationary phase is normally an involatile oil or grease, silicone, fatty ester, etc. This phase occupies a large surface in a long column. Most commonly, it is coated on an inert granular support with which the column (several feet in length) is packed; wholly solid (porous) column packings have also recently come into use. Sometimes, however, unpacked capillary columns with the stationary-phase substance coated directly on the inner wall are used. The capillary must be long enough and narrow enough to ensure that every gas molecule hits the wall in traversing it; a typical column consists of 100 feet of stainless steel or cupro-nickel tubing with an internal diameter of 0·01–0·03 inches.

The sample (*i.e.* the moving phase) is injected into the system as a gas or liquid at the beginning of the column. A few microlitres, or even less, are sufficient. For substances liquid at room temperature, the temperature in the column and injector head must be high enough to keep the sample vaporised. The gaseous or vaporised sample is carried into and along the column by a stream of carrier gas. This is the analogue of the solvent in other forms of chromatography, and is commonly hydrogen, argon or nitrogen. Due to the partition effect, each constituent of the sample emerges separately at a definite time after the sample has been injected (fig. 19). Under fixed conditions this *retention time* is constant for a given substance, and constitutes an identifying property.

The separately issuing constituents are detected in the gas stream by some device which converts changes in the composition of the issuing gas into changing electric potentials and these are fed into a recorder, the trace of which thus reveals the composition of the sample. There are several types of detector, and the choice will depend on the type of compound being analysed. The apparatus is normally arranged so that each issuing constituent produces a peak in the recorder trace, the position of the peak on the time axis representing the retention time, and the area under it (or, to a first approximation, its height) being a measure of the amount (fig. 20). For the most accurate quantitative analysis, the area may be measured automatically by an *integrator*. The method can therefore be made to separate, identify and measure simultaneously. This is the method of analysis now used in this country for alcohol in body-fluids (see Chapter 9).

Apart from its versatility, gas chromatography is extraordinarily sensitive. For example, the air from inside a practically dry cigarette lighter could yield a complete analysis of the lighter fuel it had contained. The potentialities of the method can also be extended even further in a number of ways. Compounds which are too involatile to be analysed directly (*e.g.* the fatty acids of soap— see p. 57) may be analysed after conversion into volatile esters. Mixtures the constituents of which vary widely in their properties may be difficult to analyse by "straight" GC, since conditions optimal for some constituents may be un-

PLATES

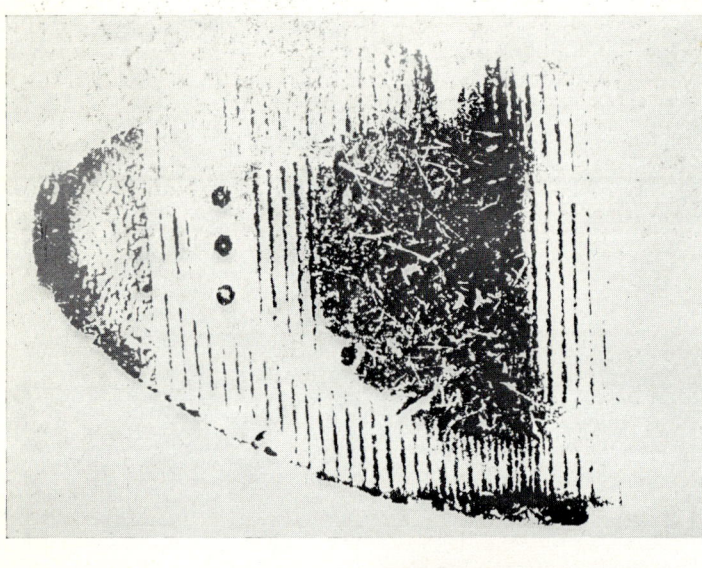

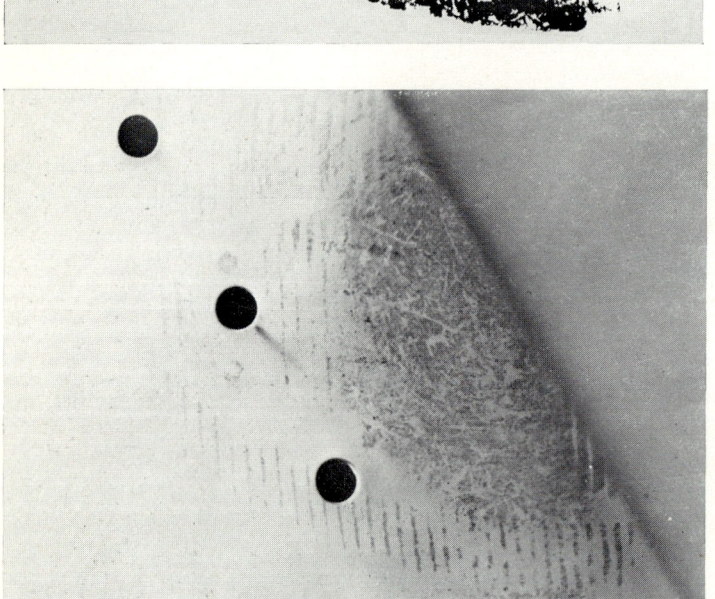

Fig. 1. A FOOTPRINT COMPARISON

The left-hand photograph shows a mark left on a shelf at the scene of a crime, the right-hand a test mark made with the left shoe of a suspect. There can be no doubt that both marks were made by the same shoe; notice especially the exact correspondence of the numerous cuts and other random marks in the central area. (*Crown Copyright. Courtesy of Director, Home Office East Midlands Forensic Science Laboratory.*)

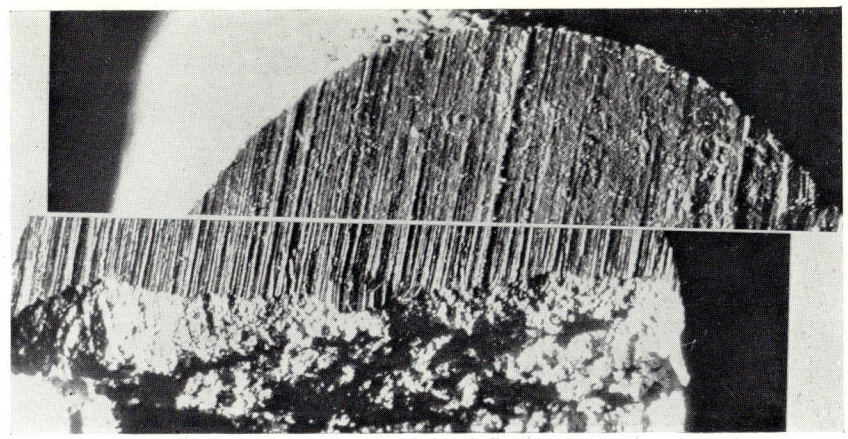

Fig. 2. A SCRATCH-MARK COMPARISON

The segment of a circle at the top is the cut end of a padlock hasp from a breaking offence. The lower part of the picture shows striations made by the bolt-croppers suspected of having been used. The almost complete agreement between the two sets of marks leaves no doubt that both were made by the same instrument. (See p. 19.) (*Crown Copyright. Courtesy of Director, Home Office North-Western Forensic Science Laboratory.*)

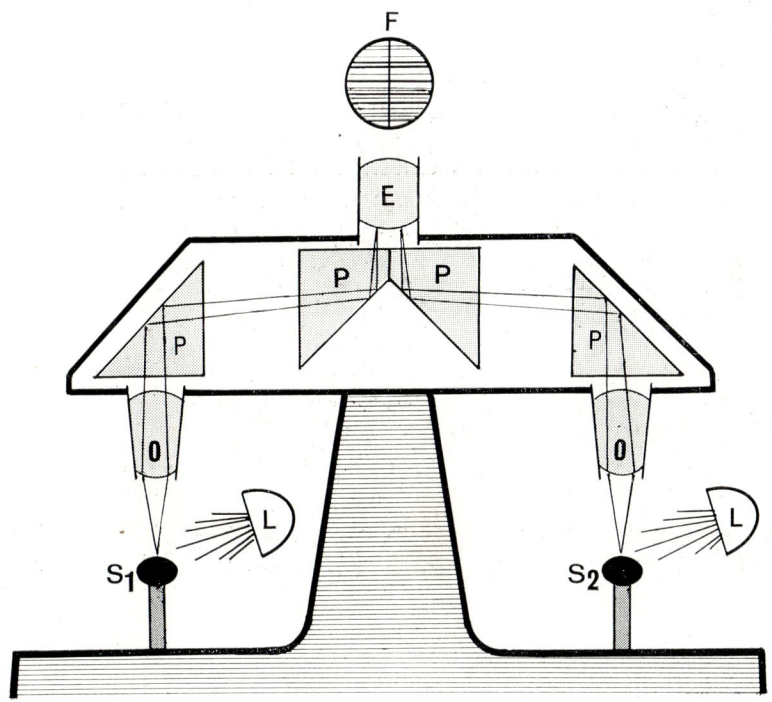

Fig. 3. THE COMPARISON MICROSCOPE

A comparison microscope (text p. 20) is a "Siamese-twin" instrument. The specimens S_1, S_2 (bullets, scratch marks, etc.) are lit by matched light-sources L and examined by separate matched objectives O. The resulting images are brought together (*e.g.*, by a system of reflecting prisms P as in the diagram) in a single eyepiece E. The two sets of marks may then be directly compared side by side in the resulting visual field F.

Fig. 4. INDENTATION MARKS ON BATTERY TERMINALS
(*See text, p. 24.*) (*Crown Copyright.*)

Fig. 5. TURNING STRIATIONS ON SWARF

A comparison, made with a comparison microscope (fig. 3), between the fine striations left by the turning tool on two fragments of swarf—one from a quantity of scrap metal believed stolen, the other from the scene of the theft. The agreement between the two sets of marks leaves no doubt that both fragments were turned by the same tool. (*Crown Copyright. Courtesy of Director, Home Office South-Western Forensic Science Laboratory.*)

Fig. 6. CROSS-SECTION OF A PAINT FLAKE

Flakes of paint detached from structures such as buildings or old cars which have been frequently painted or re-painted show, on microscopic examination of their edges, a characteristic layered structure. This can be an invaluable identifying feature where there are numerous layers of various colours, as in this case. (*Crown Copyright.*)

Fig. 7. COCCOLITHS FROM PUTTY

A specimen of putty can be characterised by the *coccoliths* present in it. These are the skeletons of micro-organisms which lived in the ancient seas from which chalk was deposited. They differ in appearance according to the precise geological horizon from which the chalk used in the putty was quarried. Two different types are shown here in photographs taken with a scanning electron microscope (p. 82). Magnification as reproduced about 6,000 ×. (*Crown Copyright. Courtesy of Director, Home Office West Midlands Forensic Science Laboratory.*)

Fig. 8. FRAGMENTATION FROM BREAKING GLASS

A sheet of glass being broken by a hammer. Notice how the fragments fly out on *both* sides of the sheet. Anyone breaking a window is therefore liable to carry away particles of glass on his clothing. (*Copyright and courtesy, editor and publisher, Journal of the Forensic Science Society.*)

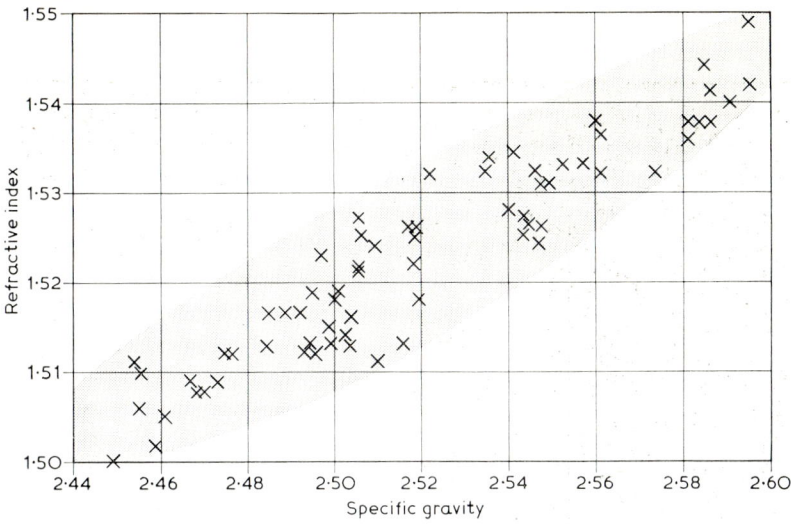

Fig. 9. GRAPH OF PHYSICAL PROPERTIES OF GLASS

The data plotted here are taken from *The Properties of Glass* (George W. Morey, New York, 1954) and show that refractive index and specific gravity are highly associated: that is, a high (or low) value of one property means a high (or low) value of the other. Commercial window and other glass will show an even narrower range of values, since some of the data plotted here relate to glasses not in commercial production.

Fig. 10. BULLET HOLE IN CAR WINDOW

A fast-moving projectile such as a bullet passing through a sheet of glass "punches" a hole with a wide crater on the exit side. The illustration shows a hole in the rear window of a police car made by a ·22 bullet which was fired from in front of the car and entered it through the open front nearside door. (*Courtesy and Copyright of Chief Constable, Durham County Constabulary.*)

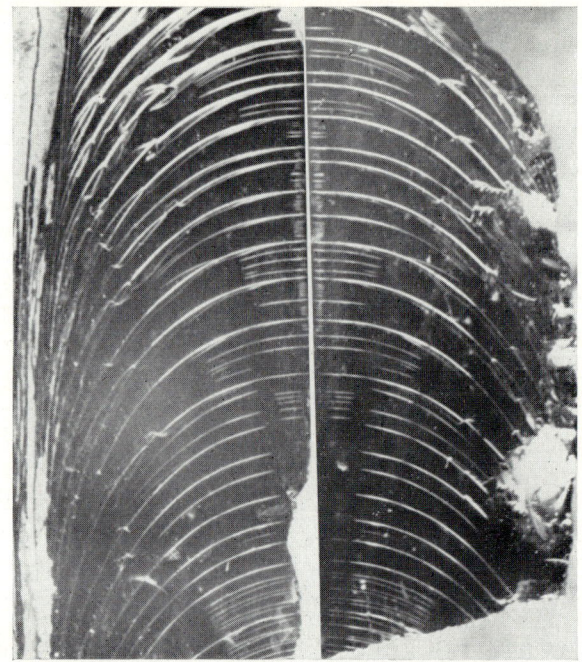

Fig. 12. MICRO STRESS MARKS ON BROKEN EDGES
OF GLASS

Broken edges on quite tiny pieces of glass can be matched,
showing that the two matching pieces were originally one,
by the coincidence of the minute stress cleavage marks on
them. By reversing the marks on one piece as explained in
the text (p. 35), the coincidence can be clearly demonstrated. One of these pieces came from a broken window, the
other from the suspect's clothing. (*Crown Copyright.
Courtesy of Director, Home Office North-Western Forensic
Science Laboratory.*)

Fig. 11. STRESS MARKS
ON BROKEN EDGE OF
GLASS

When a piece of glass is
broken by a blow, the edges of
the pieces normally show
fluted stress marks as described in the text. These may
help in deciding from which
side the glass was broken.
This example of an edge from
a radial crack (edges from
concentric cracks are rarely if
ever so clearly marked) shows
that the blow which broke the
glass came from the side
shown by the arrow.

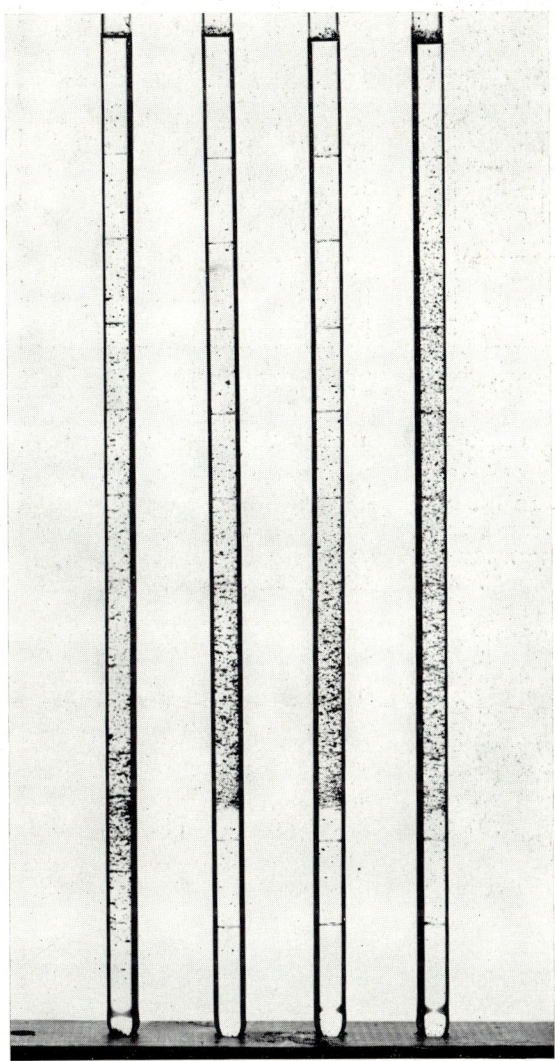

Fig. 13. SOIL COMPARISONS

A set of gradient-density tubes. A 50-mg. sample of dried and roughly dispersed soil was dropped into each of these four tubes. The samples in the two middle tubes came from the same spot, those in the two outer tubes from other localities near-by.

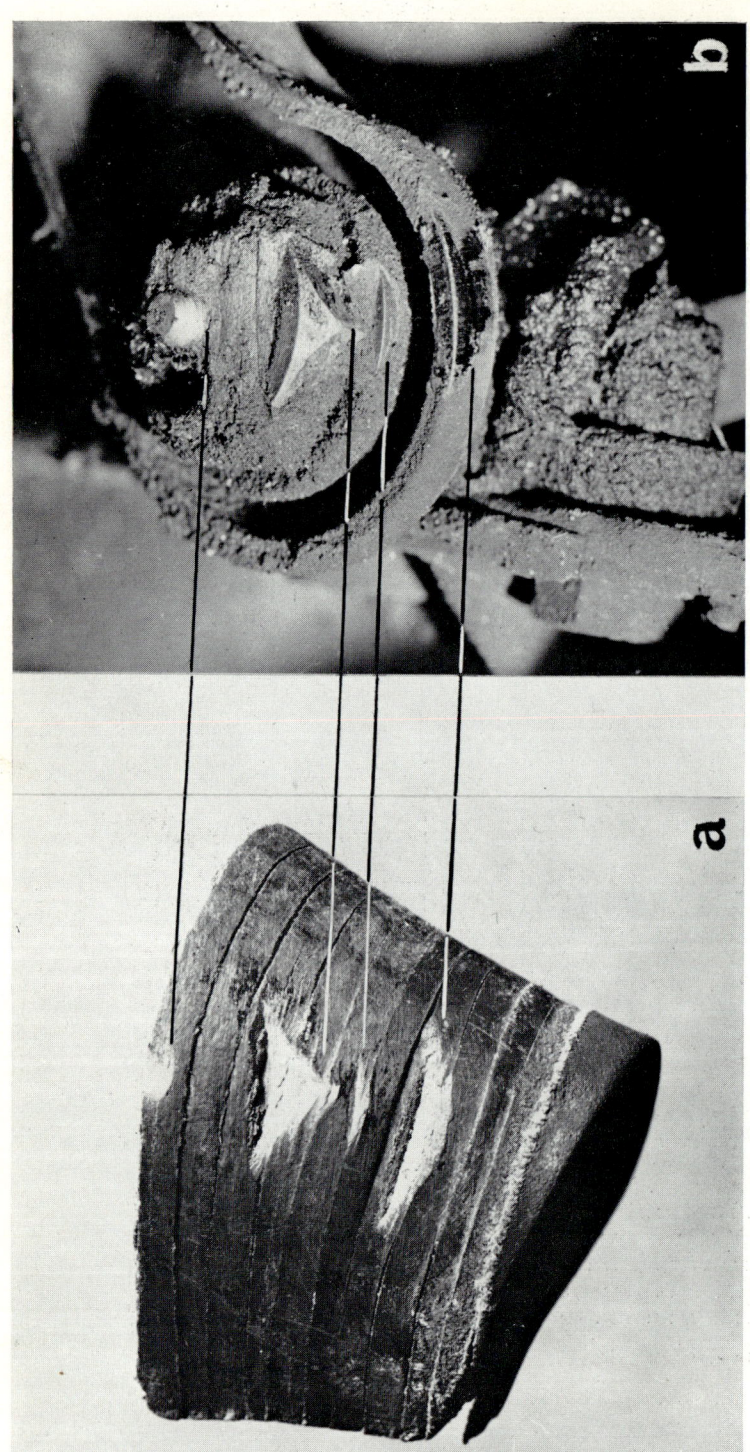

Fig. 14. MATCHING SHOE OF VICTIM AND PART OF CAR CHASSIS

During the examination of a car which was suspected of having knocked down and killed two old women, one of the attachments of the front near-side suspension "wishbone" was found to have been rubbed free of grease and dirt (b). The back of the heel of one of the dead woman's shoes (a) bore some indented marks which formed an exact impression of the suspension component in question. (A trace of dirty grease similar to that on the car was also found in the marks.) ((a) Crown Copyright. (b) Copyright and courtesy of Chief Constable, Durham County Constabulary.)

Fig. 15. CAR-HEADLAMP EVIDENCE

The filament of a car-headlamp bulb which was broken in an accident. The presence of numerous tiny fragments and "blobs" of glass adhering and melted on to the filament shows that this was hot when the glass was broken— *i.e.* that the lamp was alight. (*Copyright and courtesy, editor and publisher, Journal of the Forensic Science Society.*)

Fig. 16 METAL FATIGUE

A fracture in a motor-car crankshaft which failed in service through metal fatigue. The growth from one face of concentric "beach marks" within the original crack is clearly shown, together with a surrounding area showing the characteristic appearance of stress rupture of previously sound metal. (*Crown Copyright. Courtesy of Director, Home Office North-Eastern Forensic Science Laboratory.*)

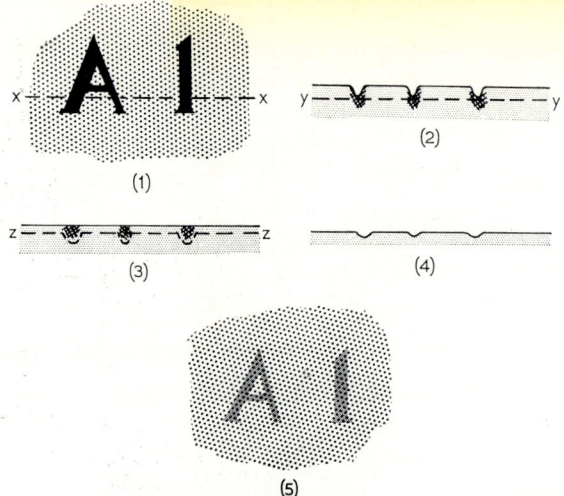

Fig. 17. RESTORATION OF ERASED PUNCHED NUMBERS

When a number is punched in a metal surface (1) a cross-section (*x–x*) of the letters or figures appears as visible indentations (2). Beneath each indentation, there is also an (invisible) area of altered metal crystal structure (shown cross-hatched). Filing the surface down to the level (*y–y*) removes the visible indentations but leaves a surface (3) still bearing areas of altered crystal structure. When this is etched, the altered and the unaltered areas are attacked at different rates, so producing a new surface (*z–z* in 3; also 4) in which the erased figures or letters are visible as "ghosts" (5) of their original shapes.

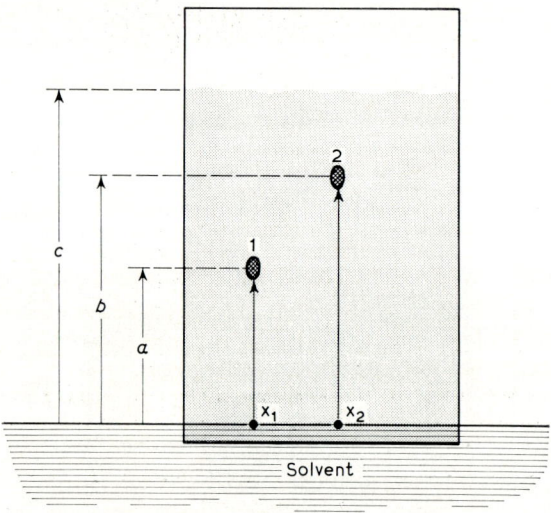

Fig. 18. PRINCIPLES OF PAPER AND THIN-LAYER CHROMATOGRAPHY

The samples to be analysed are spotted on to the paper or adsorbent layer at X, just clear of the solvent surface, and allowed to diffuse upwards by capillary attraction. By the time the solvent front has travelled through some given distance c, the sample compounds will have travelled through smaller distances a and b, forming spots at 1 and 2 respectively. The Rf values characteristic of these compounds are then defined by $\mathrm{Rf}_1 = \dfrac{a}{c}$ and $\mathrm{Rf}_2 = \dfrac{b}{c}$.

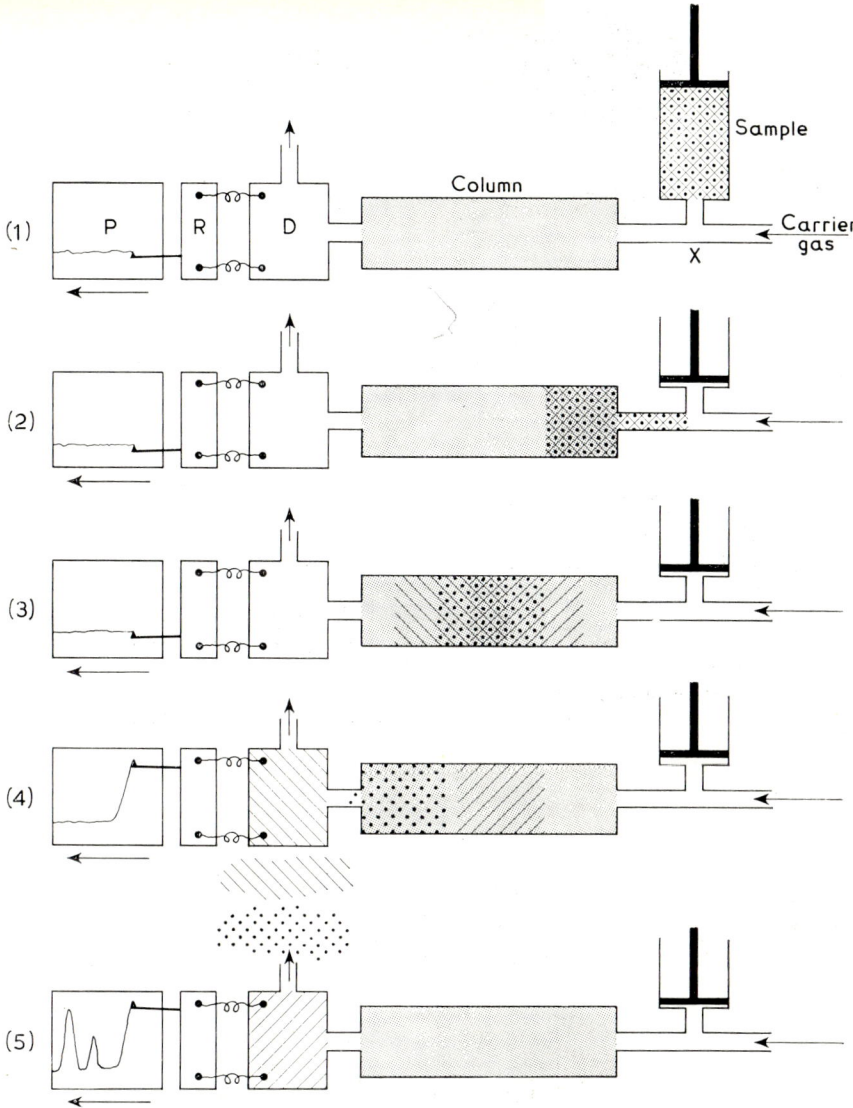

Fig. 19. PRINCIPLES OF GAS CHROMATOGRAPHY

A small volume of the sample to be analysed is injected (1, 2) at X into the stream of carrier gas entering the column containing the adsorbent. The various constituents of the sample are, on account of their different partition coefficients between the gaseous phase and the liquid or solid adsorbent, carried along the column at different rates (3). Hence, provided that the column is long enough, they emerge separately after different times (4). The detector D, through which the issuing gas stream passes, is sensitive to changes in the composition of this, and feeds electrical impulses corresponding to these changes into the recorder R, where they are finally converted into pen motions on a moving paper strip P (5).

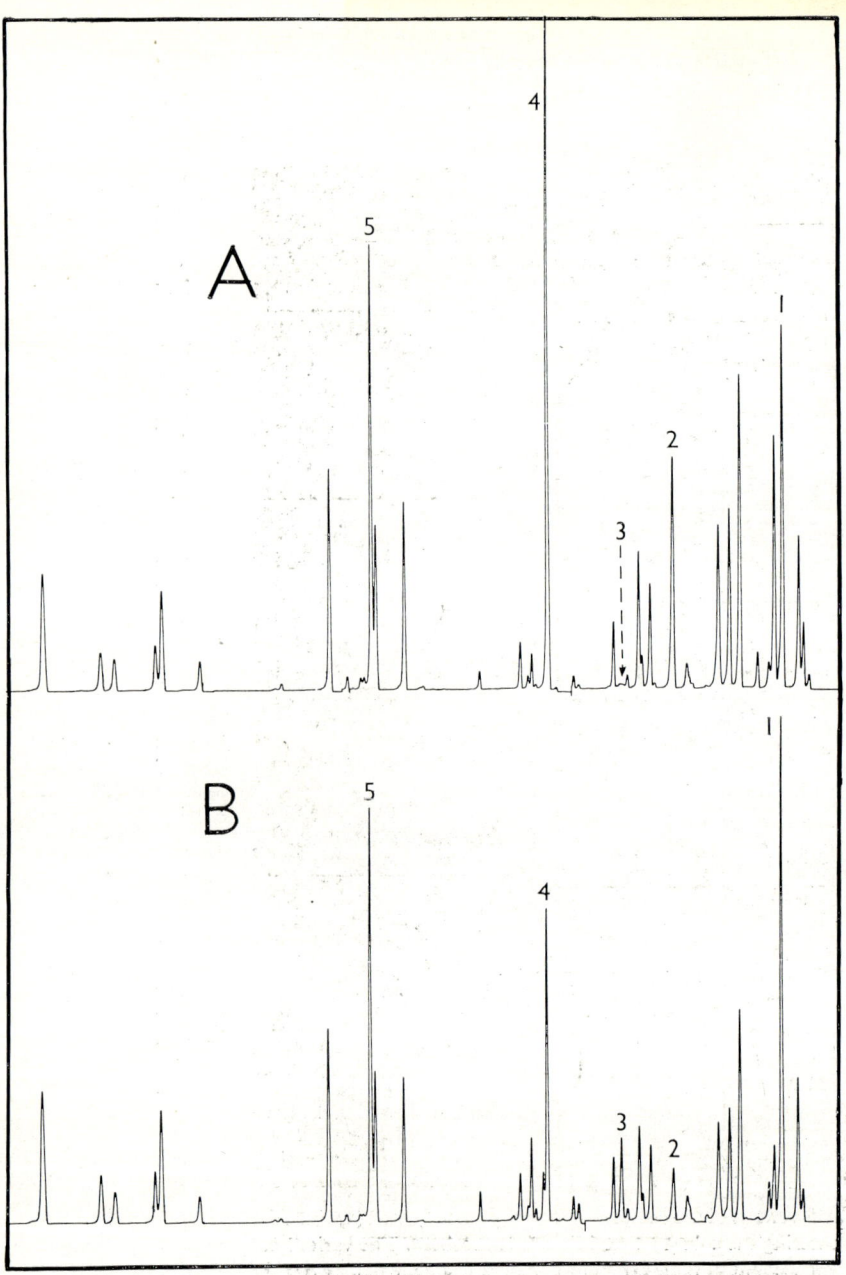

Fig. 20. GAS-CHROMATOGRAPHIC ANALYSIS OF PETROL

As explained in figure 19, each component of a mixture injected into a gas-chromatographic column produces a "peak" on the recorder chart. The two charts shown here are of two brands of 5-star (100–101 octane) petrol. Each contains the same 40 or so individual compounds (as shown by the peaks occurring in the same places, reading from right to left), but in very different proportions. For example: compare the relative heights of the 1, 4 and 5 peaks in A and B (A contains so much of compound 4 that the peak has gone right off the chart); in A, compound 2 is a major component and 3 almost absent, whereas in B there is more 3 than 2. Several other such differences can be found by a detailed comparison of the charts. (*Copyright, Commissioner of Police of the Metropolis. Courtesy of Director, Metropolitan Police Forensic Science Laboratory.*)

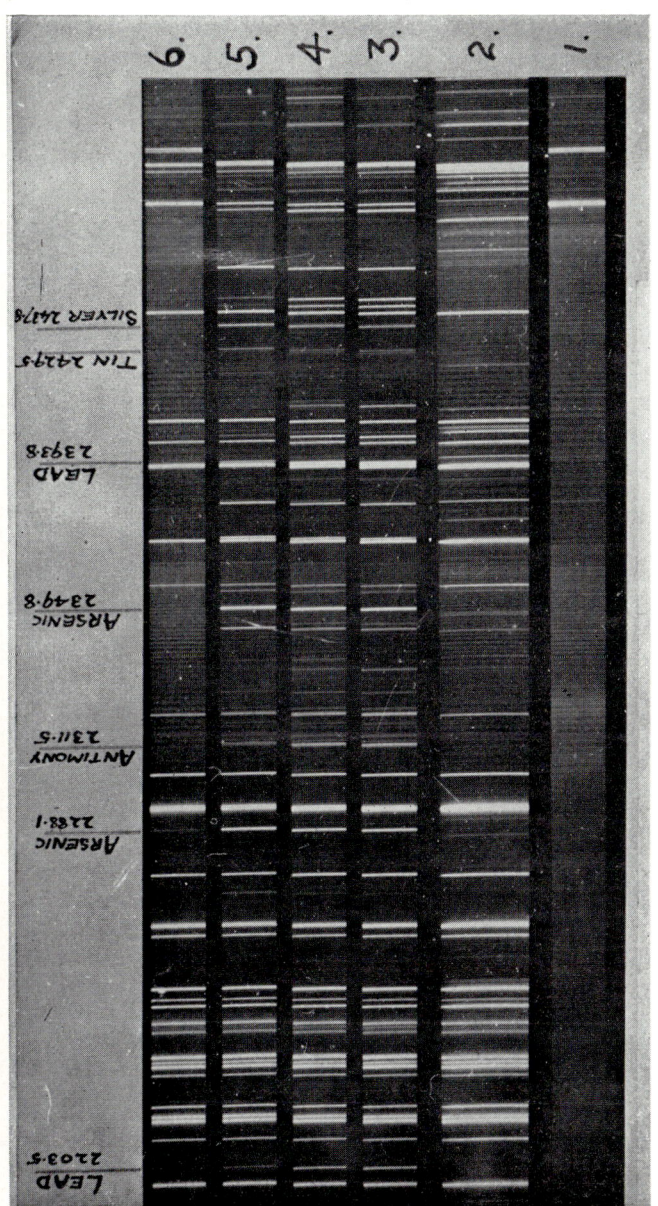

Fig. 21. EXAMPLE OF SPECTROGRAPHIC ANALYSIS

Some lead was stolen from a church roof. It had been fastened down with copper tacks, and this, according to parish records, had happened in 1879. Shortly after the theft, some copper tacks were found in a suspect's lorry. The six spectra here are:

(1) The pure graphite electrodes used to "shoot" the samples. (2) Pure copper.
(3) Tacks from roof. (4) Tacks from suspect's lorry.
(5) Tacks manufactured about 1920. (6) New tacks as sold at time of theft.

Any spectrum lines appearing in 3–6 which do not appear in 2 are due to impurities in the copper of the various tacks. Several of these impurity lines are identified. Note that the impurities present in 3 and 4 are identical, and that commercial copper has become progressively purer since 1879, so that the presence of identical impurities has considerable evidential value. (*Crown Copyright.*)

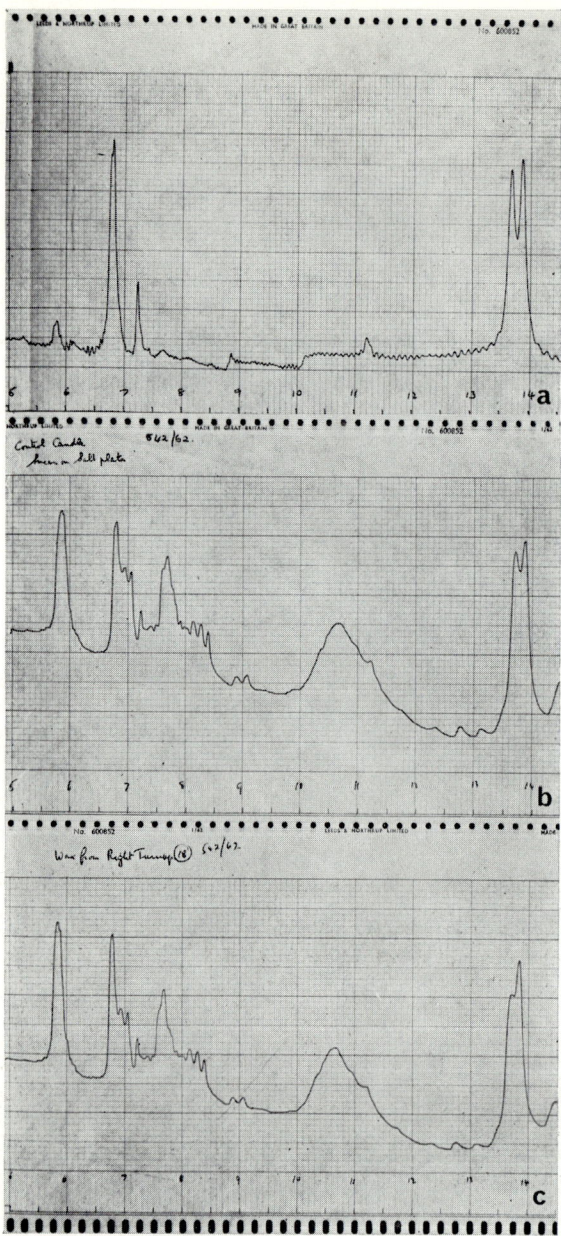

Fig. 22. INFRA-RED ABSORPTION SPECTRA

A gang of youths was suspected of breaking into a church. On the clothing of one of them were found some minute particles of wax. The infra-red spectrum of these (curve b) was identical with that of the wax of the church candles (curve c), but quite different from those of the waxes of all commercial candles tried. (Example shown as curve a.) The extra peaks in the left-hand half of b and c are due to the presence of stearic acid, a compound absent from wax a. The broad peak near the centre of b and c is due to an inorganic filler in the church-candle wax. (*Crown Copyright.*)

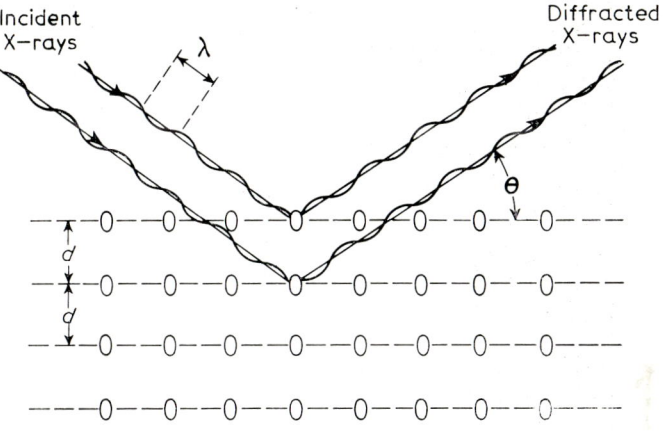

Fig. 23. DIFFRACTION OF X-RAYS

A beam of X-rays of wavelength λ will be diffracted through an angle θ from a crystal lattice in which the distance between the atom planes is d whenever the simple relationship holds that $n\lambda = 2d \sin \theta$ (where n is an integer). Since λ is constant and determined for a given source of appropriately filtered radiation, the measurement of θ enables d to be determined. Each crystalline substance has its own characteristic set of d values, to each of which a separate value of θ corresponds.

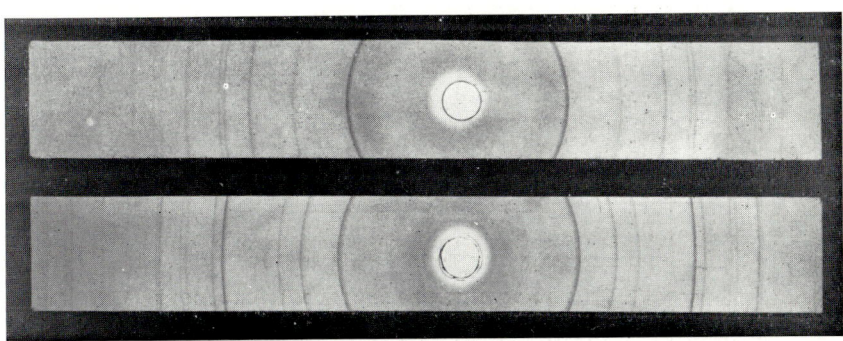

Fig. 24. DIFFRACTION PATTERNS OF TITANIUM OXIDE
PIGMENTS

The X-ray spectra, taken by the powder method described in the text, of (1) *anatase* and (2) *rutile*. These are forms of titanium oxide which differ only in respect of their crystal parameters and are chemically quite indistinguishable. (*Crown Copyright. Courtesy of Director, Home Office Northern Forensic Science Laboratory.*)

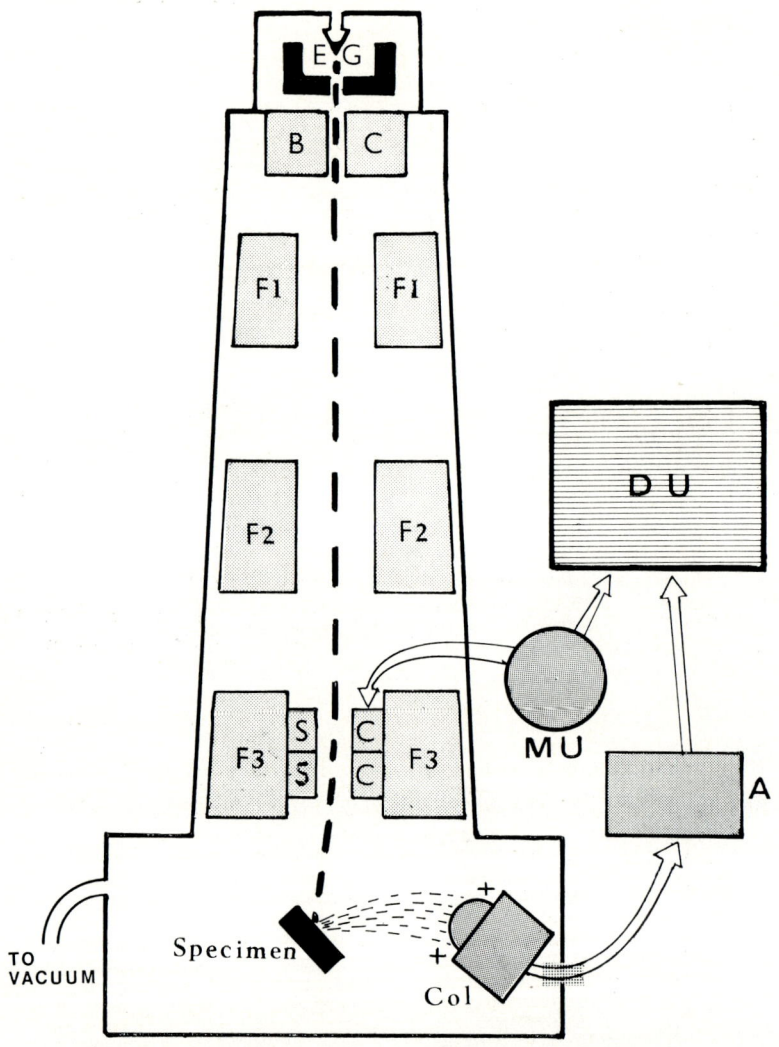

Fig. 25. THE SCANNING ELECTRON MICROSCOPE

Electrons emitted by the electron gun (EG) are collimated into a beam (— — — —), which passes into the highly evacuated body of the instrument through the beam-centring coil BC, and is focused on the specimen by the focusing coils F1, F2 and F3. The scanning coils (SC) cause the point at which the beam strikes the specimen to scan the selected area in a raster pattern. The secondary electrons emitted are collected by the positively charged collector (Col), and the resulting current after amplification at A controls the moving spot in the display unit DU, which is in effect a small television tube. The scanning and display rasters are synchronised by the magnification unit MU. The brightness of each point on the screen is then proportional to the number of secondary electrons emitted by the corresponding point of the specimen; in this way a greatly magnified picture is built up.

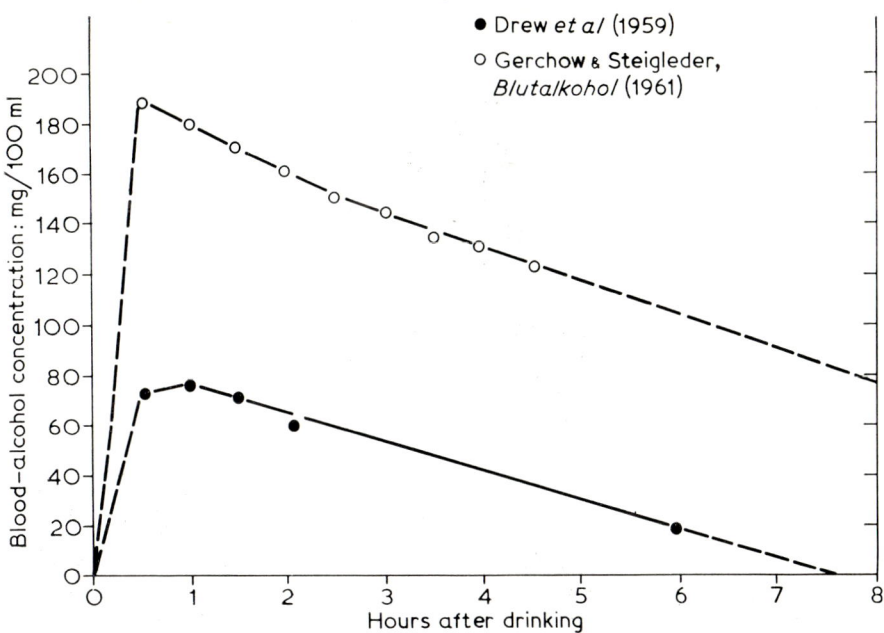

Fig. 26. BLOOD–ALCOHOL CURVES

Two actual blood–alcohol curves, for a large and a small amount of alcohol, based on figures recorded from experiments performed in Germany and Britain respectively.

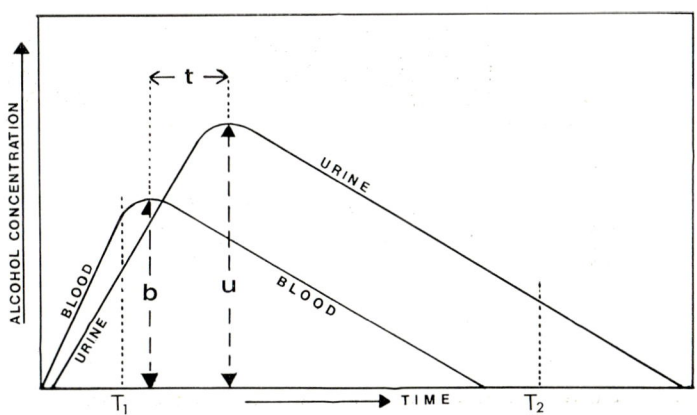

Fig. 27. THE RELATIONSHIP BETWEEN BLOOD AND URINE ALCOHOL CONCENTRATIONS

As explained in the text, the "peak" urine–alcohol concentration is higher than that in the blood but is reached later. The urine peak concentration is about one-third higher (*i.e.* $u/b = 4/3$ approximately) and the time-lag t is usually around $\frac{1}{2}$–1 hour. The figure also shows why the urine concentration is a reliable guide to that in the blood *only* if the specimens are taken at about or shortly after the peak times. For a specimen taken at time T_1, the urine concentration would be *lower* than that in the blood; on the other hand, at time T_2 the blood concentration would have fallen to nothing although alcohol would still be present in the urine.

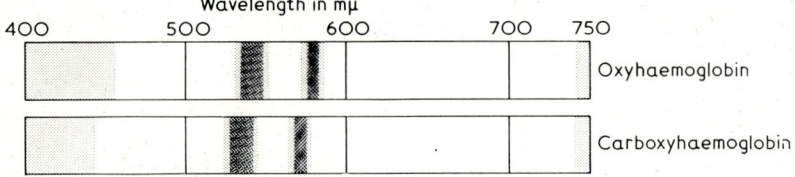

Wavelength in mμ

| 400 | 500 | 600 | 700 | 750 |

Oxyhaemoglobin

Carboxyhaemoglobin

Fig. 28. ABSORPTION SPECTRA OF BLOOD PIGMENTS

The red colour of oxygenated blood is due to two absorption bands in the green/yellow region of the visible spectrum. Carboxyhaemoglobin, formed when haemoglobin takes up carbon monoxide, shows the same two bands, but in a slightly different position. The change of position can be used to measure the percentage saturation of the blood with carbon monoxide (p. 122). A method of measuring the age of a bloodstain is also based on certain features of the haemoglobin bands (p. 147).

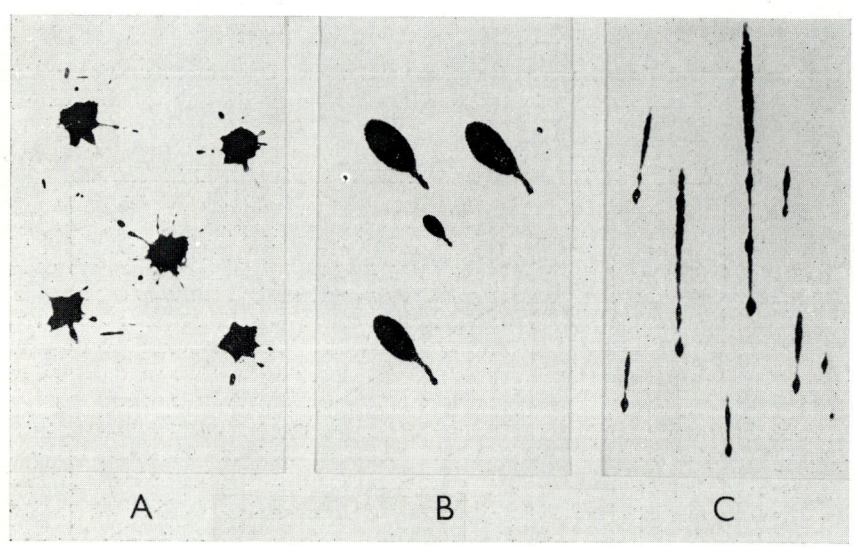

A   B   C

Fig. 29. BLOOD SPLASHES

Drops of dried blood on walls, floors, furniture etc. can tell us by their appearance from which direction they came. At (A) the drops have fallen vertically on to a level surface; at (B) they have splashed obliquely on to a vertical or sloping surface, travelling from upper left to lower right, with the "tails" pointing in the direction they were going; at (C) they were travelling almost vertically downwards when they hit the surface.

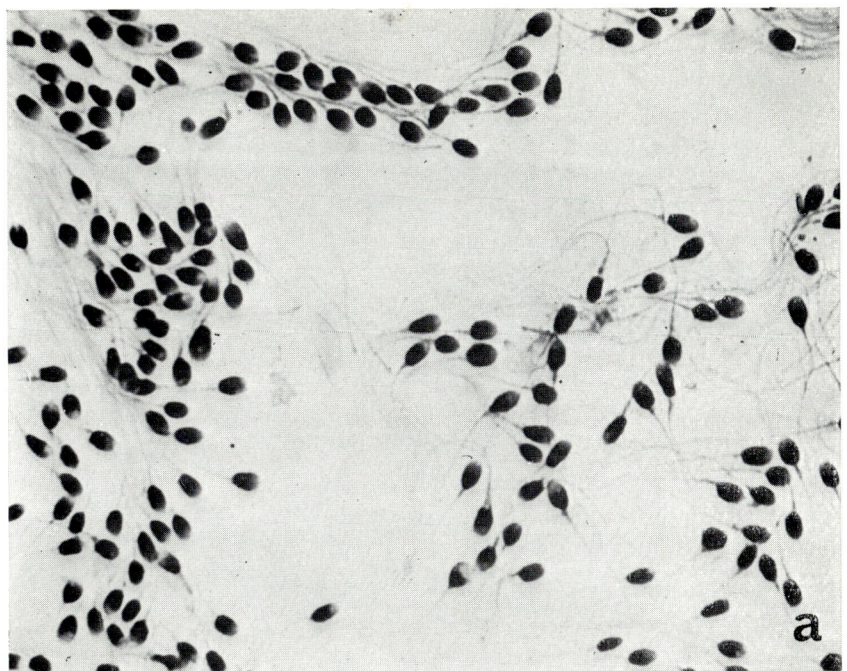

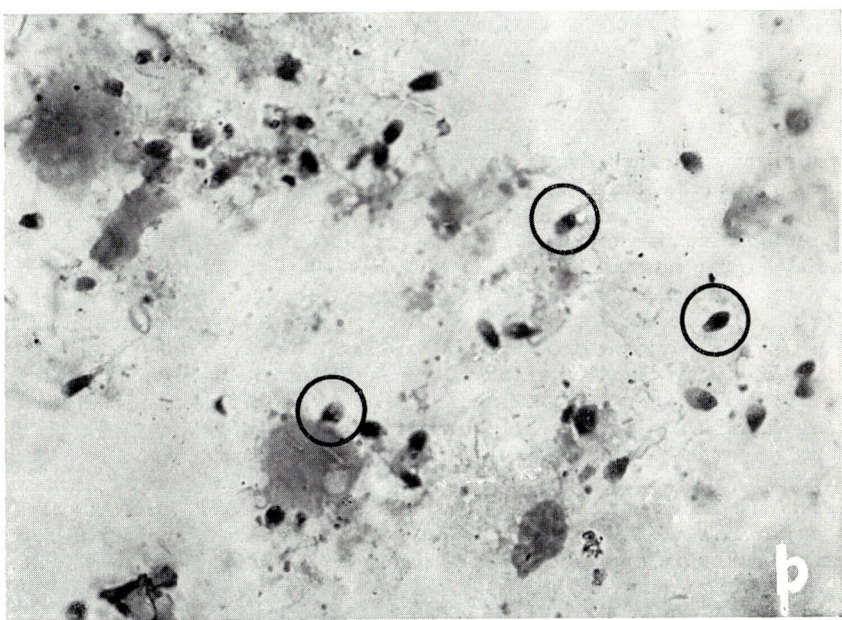

Fig. 30. HUMAN SPERMATOZOA

(*a*) Fixed and stained spermatozoa, magnified about 1,000 times. Note the ovoid heads and the long flagellate tails. It is rare to find spermatozoa as complete as this in an actual case. (*b*) In practice the spermatozoa to be identified have generally lost their tails, and are often mixed with other types of cells and cellular debris. There are about 20 spermatozoal heads in this photograph, of which three have been ringed for identification. (*Crown Copyright.*)

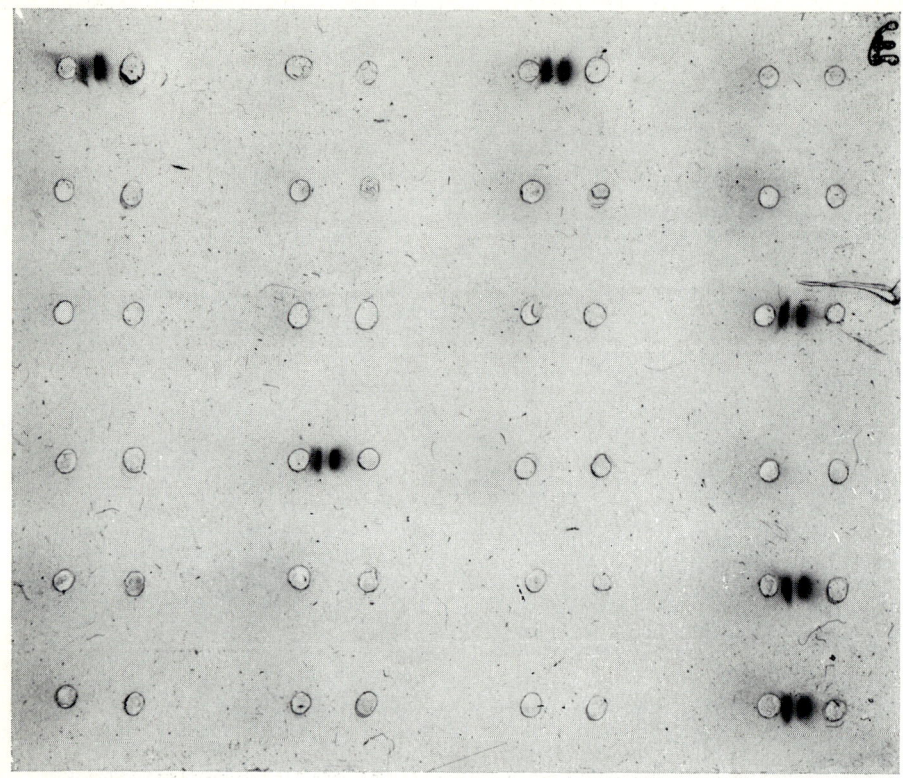

Fig. 31. ELECTROPHORETIC PRECIPITIN TESTING

The 24 pairs of little circles in this photograph are holes punched in a sheet of agar gel as described in the text. Each of the four columns of pairs represents a separate case. In each horizontal line a different anti-serum was used; these were, reading from the top downwards, anti-human, anti-cat, anti-cow, anti-dog, anti-pig and anti-sheep. In each instance the anti-serum is put in one well of the pair, and the stain extract in the other. A reaction after electro-phoresis appears as a cloudy spot in the gel (appearing as diffuse dark areas in the photograph).

Case 1 (left-hand column) shows that a bloodstain suspected of being human was in fact of human origin, the other varieties of animal anti-sera used giving no reaction.

Case 2 (left central column) represents the examination of a bloodstain scraped from a car suspected of killing a pedestrian. The driver said he had hit a dog. The reaction with dog anti-serum confirmed the driver's story.

Case 3 (right central column) represents the investigation of a stain suspected of being human semen. Although no spermatozoa could be detected in it, the result clearly shows it to be human.

Case 4 (right-hand column) is the identification of a bloodstain on a £1 note suspected of being stolen from a butcher's shop. The result shows the presence of cow, pig and sheep blood in the stain. (*Courtesy and Copyright, Shandon Scientific Company Ltd.; also courtesy of Mr. B. J. Culliford and the publishers of Nature.*)

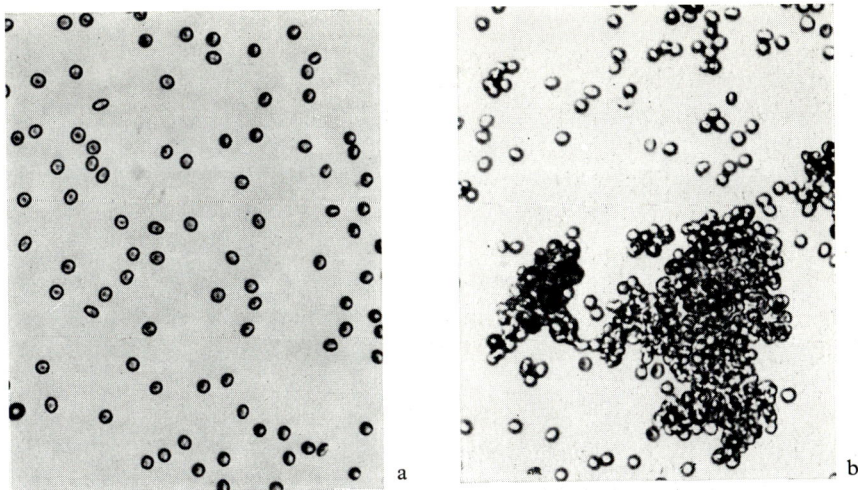

Fig. 32. AGGLUTINATION OF RED BLOOD CELLS

As explained in the text, the reactions used in grouping bloods by systems based on the properties of their erythrocytes (red cells) depend on the *agglutination* of the cells by the action of the appropriate anti-bodies. In these photographs, (*a*) is the appearance under the microscope of normal erythrocytes; (*b*) is what is seen when agglutination has occurred.

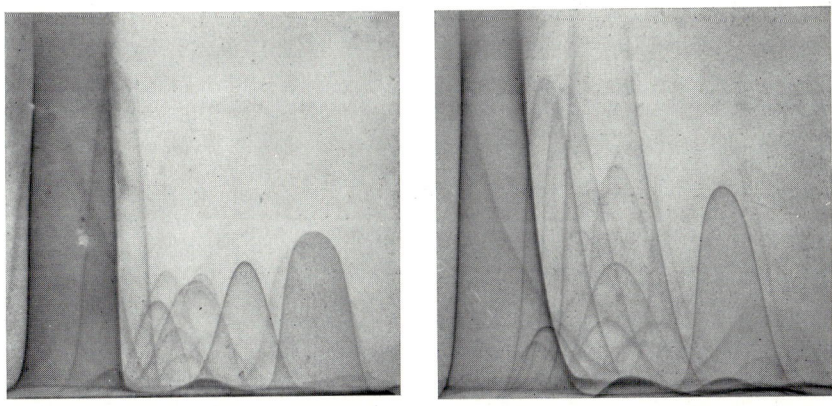

Fig. 33. CROSS-OVER ("LAURELL") ELECTROPHORESIS OF BLOOD PROTEINS

Blood can be characterised by the relative proportions of the various plasma proteins which it contains. As explained in the text (p. 164), this can be graphically demonstrated by two-way electrophoresis. The first electrophoretic separation here was from right to left; turning the electric field through 90° then caused each protein fraction to migrate into a gel containing the appropriate antigen, and the size of each "peak" formed by the zone of precipitation is proportional to the amount of that fraction. The differences between the patterns of the two blood specimens shown here are obvious. (*Crown Copyright. Courtesy of Director, Home Office Central Research Establishment.*)

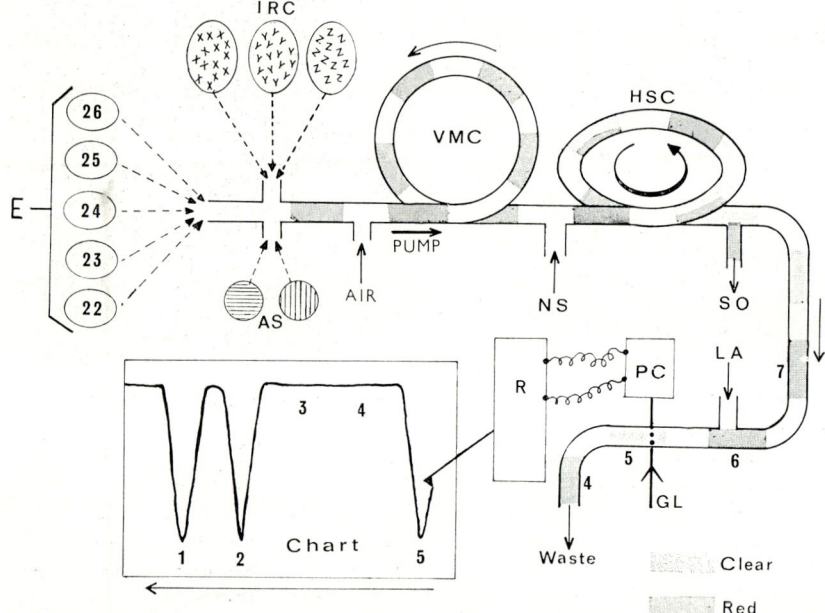

Fig. 34. AUTOMATIC BLOOD GROUPING

Each eluate (E) from a stain to be grouped is mixed with one of several groups of "indicator" red cells (IRC) and certain ancillary substances (AS). Air is injected between each drop of this mixture, and the resulting chain of "slugs" and air bubbles is pumped through vertical mixing coils (VMC) in which mixing is completed; normal saline (NS) is then added, and any agglutinated cells separate as the slugs pass through the horizontal settling coils (HSC). For simplicity, only one of each type of coil is shown here. Agglutinated cells are then sucked out (SO). Finally, after addition of a lysing agent (LA), the transmissivity of each slug to a ray of green light (GL) is measured by a photo-cell (PC) and recorder (R), and recorded on a chart. In the imaginary example shown here, specimens 1, 2 and 5 were agglutinated, but 3, 4 and 6 were not. The next 14 specimens are passing through the apparatus and nos. 22–26 are waiting to be analysed.

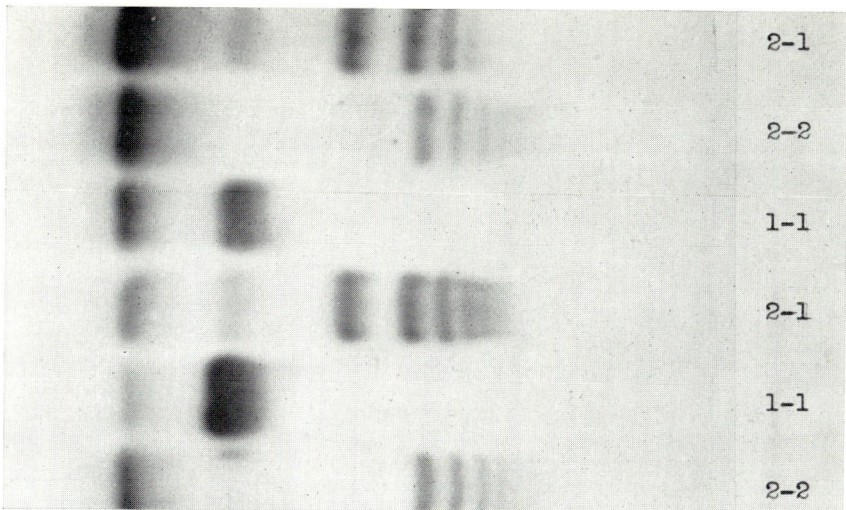

Fig. 35. ELECTROPHORETIC IDENTIFICATION OF BLOOD-PROTEIN TYPES

The blood protein *haptoglobin* occurs in three main types, designated 1–1, 2–1 and 2–2; as explained in the text, these can be identified by electrophoretic separation of their components. This photograph shows the results of starch-gel electrophoresis of 6 specimens of blood sera. Separation has proceeded from right to left. Note how the 2–1 (heterozygous) variety shows some of the characteristics of both the 1–1 and the 2–2 (both homozygous). (*Copyright Commissioner of Police of the Metropolis. Courtesy of Mr. B. J. Culliford and the Director, Metropolitan Police Forensic Science Laboratory.*)

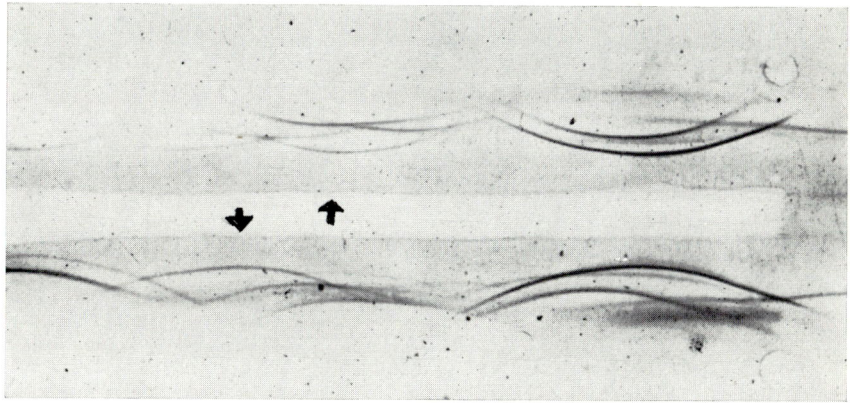

Fig. 36. IMMUNO-ELECTROPHORESIS

The identification of Gc blood groups is shown here. The sera of two blood specimens were placed in the two wells at the right (2–2 Gc in the upper well, 1–1 in the lower) and the anti-serum in the central trough. Under the electrophoretic potential difference, the serum-protein fractions moved from right to left, and produced by sideways diffusion towards the anti-serum the arcuate lines of precipitation shown. Notice the different positions of the components indicated by the arrows. (*Copyright, Commissioner of Police of the Metropolis. Courtesy of Mr. B. J. Culliford and the Director, Metropolitan Police Forensic Science Laboratory.*)

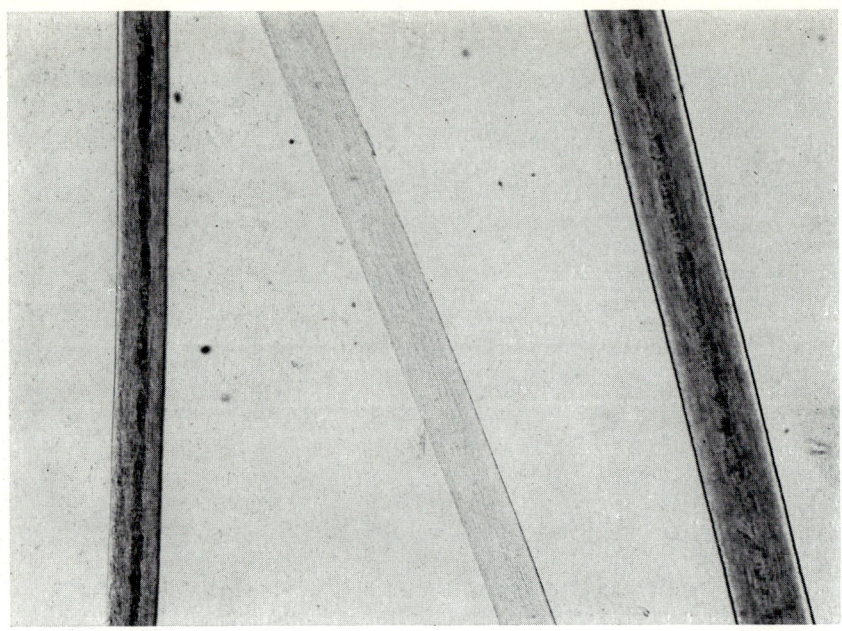

Fig. 37. HUMAN HAIRS

Seen under the microscope, human head hairs vary in respect of their thickness, pigmentation, colour and whether or not they show a medulla. The two outer dark hairs here are medullated; the central fair one is not.

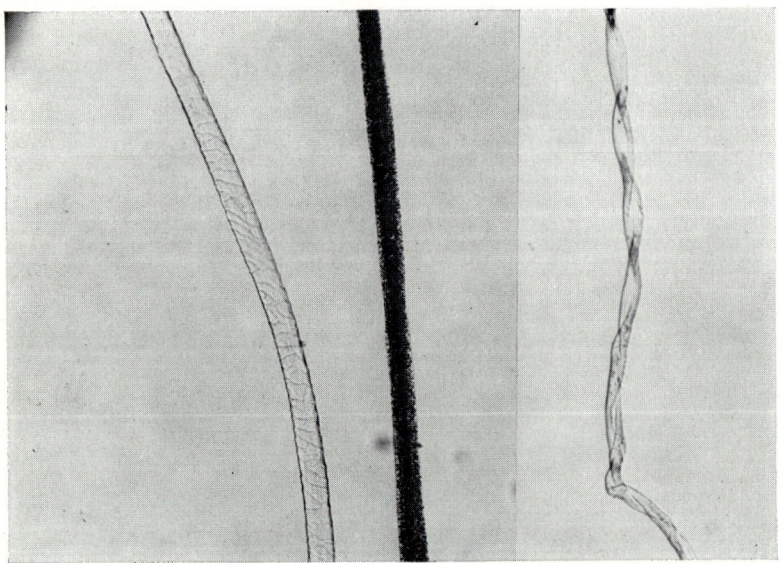

Fig. 38. TEXTILE FIBRES

The most important single identifying characteristic of a textile fibre is its appearance under the microscope. The three shown here are (from left to right): (*a*) Wool (note the characteristic scale pattern): (*b*) A synthetic heavily loaded with an inorganic material ("delustred"): (*c*) Cotton (note the characteristic twist).

Fig. 39. A SEAT OF FIRE

This barn had contained straw, and fire broke out close to the junction of the drainage channel and wall shown near the lower left-hand corner of the picture. Note the damage to the wall and to the roof immediately above the seat of fire. (*Copyright and courtesy, editor and publisher, Journal of the Forensic Science Society. Also courtesy of the Chief Constable, Durham County Constabulary.*)

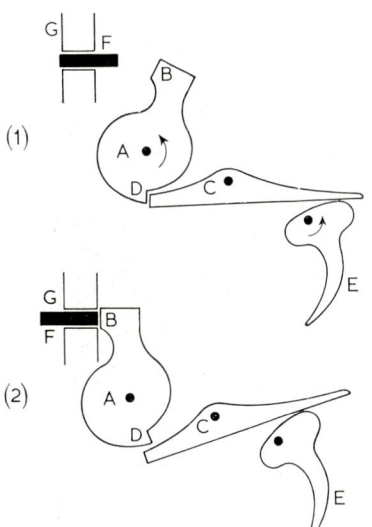

Fig. 40. THE ACTION OF A GUN LOCK

The *tumbler A* rotates on a spindle which also carries the *hammer B*, and is actuated by a strong *main-spring* to rotate in the direction shown by the arrow. When the gun is cocked (1) the tumbler and hammer are held in the position shown by the end of the lever-shaped *sear C* engaging in a notch in the edge of the tumbler (the *bent—D*). Another spring keeps the sear engaged with the bent.

In firing the gun (2), pressure on the trigger *E* disengages the sear from the bent and allows the main-spring to make the hammer strike the *firing pin F*, forcing its point into the chamber *G*, where it detonates the ignition cap and fires the cartridge.

(This diagram is purely schematic; the shapes of actual gun-lock parts may not in the least resemble those shown here.)

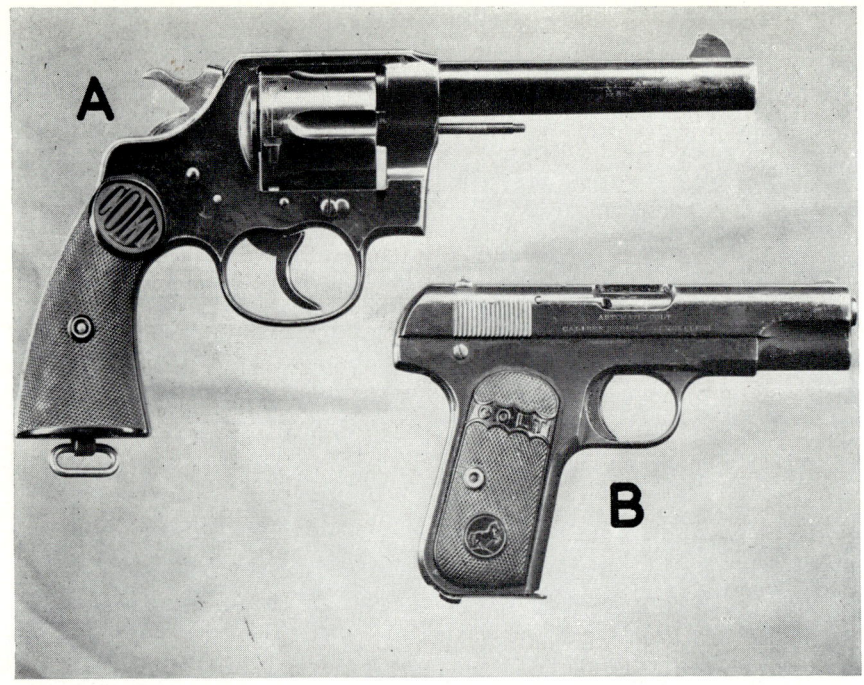

Fig. 41. SMALL ARMS

A—Revolver. *B*—"Automatic" (properly *self-loading*) pistol.

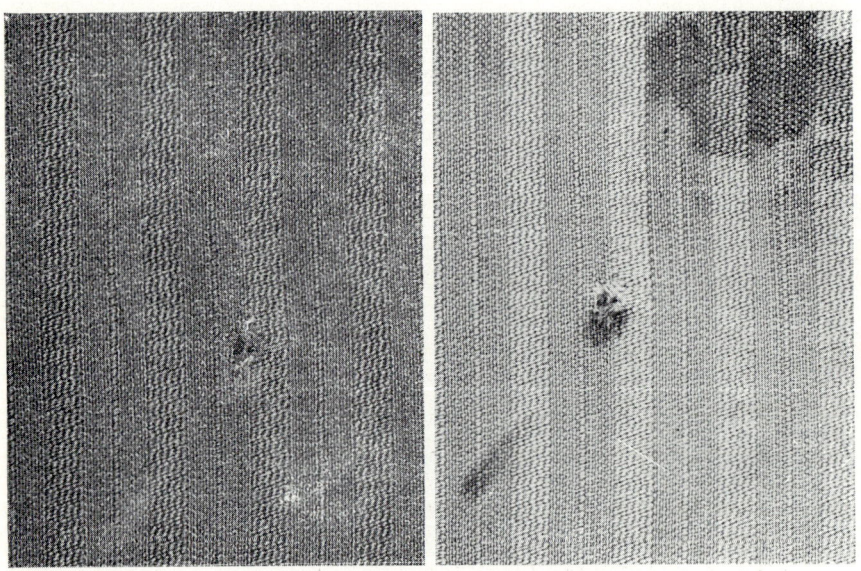

Fig. 42. BULLET HOLE IN DARK FABRIC

On the left is a photograph of the area by ordinary visible light; it affords no useful information. On the right is an infra-red photograph of the same area; note the clear trace left by the oblique entry of the bullet, and the bloodstain in the upper right corner. (*Crown Copyright.*)

Fig. 43. BULLET COMPARISON—OLD STYLE

The traditional and still most generally used method of matching bullets is by means of the fine striations produced by the barrel that fired them. This photograph, taken with a comparison microscope (fig. 3), shows parts of two bullets fired from a ·455 Webley revolver; the test bullet is to the left, the crime bullet to the right. There can be no doubt that both were fired from the same weapon. (*Crown Copyright. Courtesy Mr. George Price and the Director, Home Office East Midlands Forensic Science Laboratory.*)

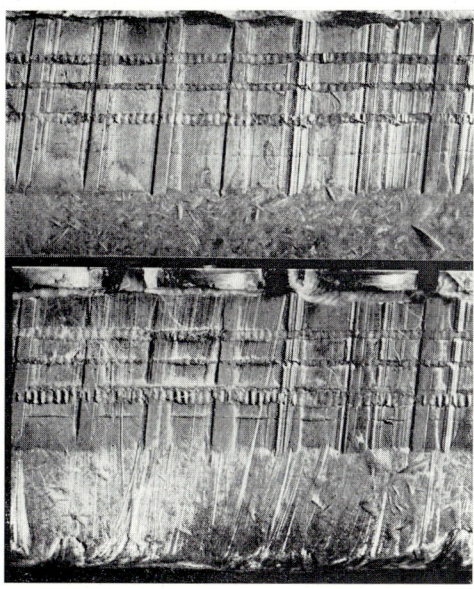

Fig. 44. BULLET COMPARISON USING A PERIPHERY CAMERA

By using a *periphery camera* (p. 201) the whole circumference of a bullet can be shown in one photograph. Two bullets fired from a ·455 Webley revolver and so photographed are shown here —the test bullet above and the crime bullet below. Disregarding the fortuitous scratches on the crime bullet *not* produced by the weapon, the agreement is obvious. (*Crown Copyright. Courtesy Mr. George Price and the Director, Home Office East Midlands Forensic Science Laboratory.*)

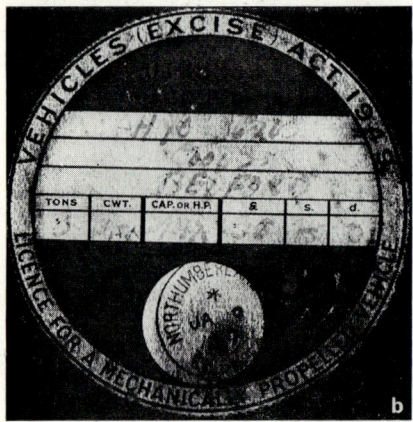

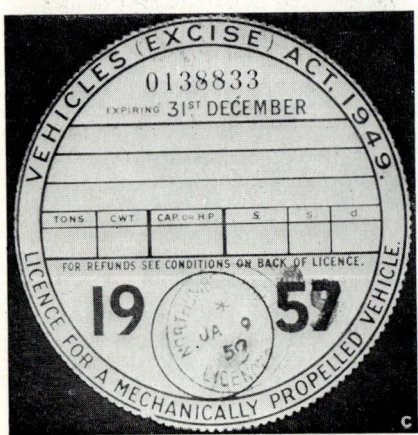

Fig. 45. PHOTOGRAPHY OF A
FORGED DOCUMENT

The road-fund licence shown here attracted the attention of a police officer because it showed no entries in the spaces for particulars of the vehicle (Photograph a). Examination under ultra-violet radiation revealed traces of entries in these spaces, legible by reason of their differential fluorescence (Photograph b). These did not correspond with the vehicle to which the licence was attached, but enquiries showed that they did correspond with the vehicle for which licence no. 0138833 had been issued, and from which the licence had been stolen. Moreover, close examination also showed that there was something amiss with the last figure of the year of issue (Photograph a), and photography by infra-red (Photograph c) revealed clearly that the original "7" had been altered to "9." (*Crown Copyright.*)

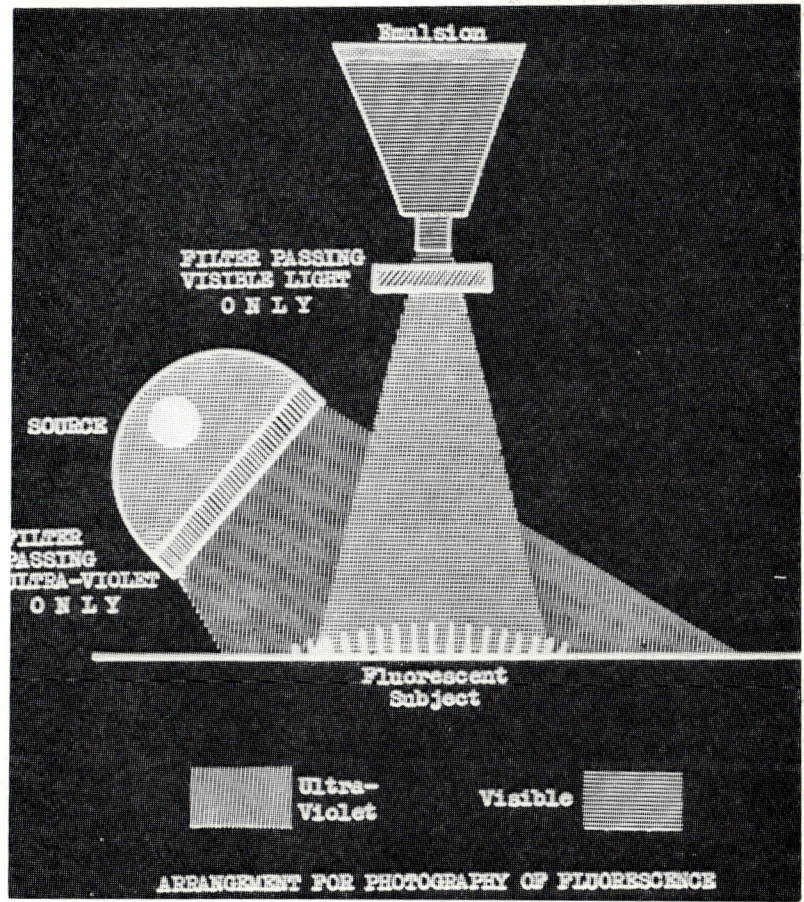

Fig. 46. ARRANGEMENT FOR FLUORESCENCE PHOTOGRAPHY

In photographing fluorescence, it is necessary to ensure that no unchanged exciting radiation reaches the photographic emulsion, and, in order to see the fluorescence in setting up the subject for photography, it is necessary that no visible radiation falls upon the subject. (*Copyright and courtesy, editor and publisher, Journal of the Forensic Science Society.*)

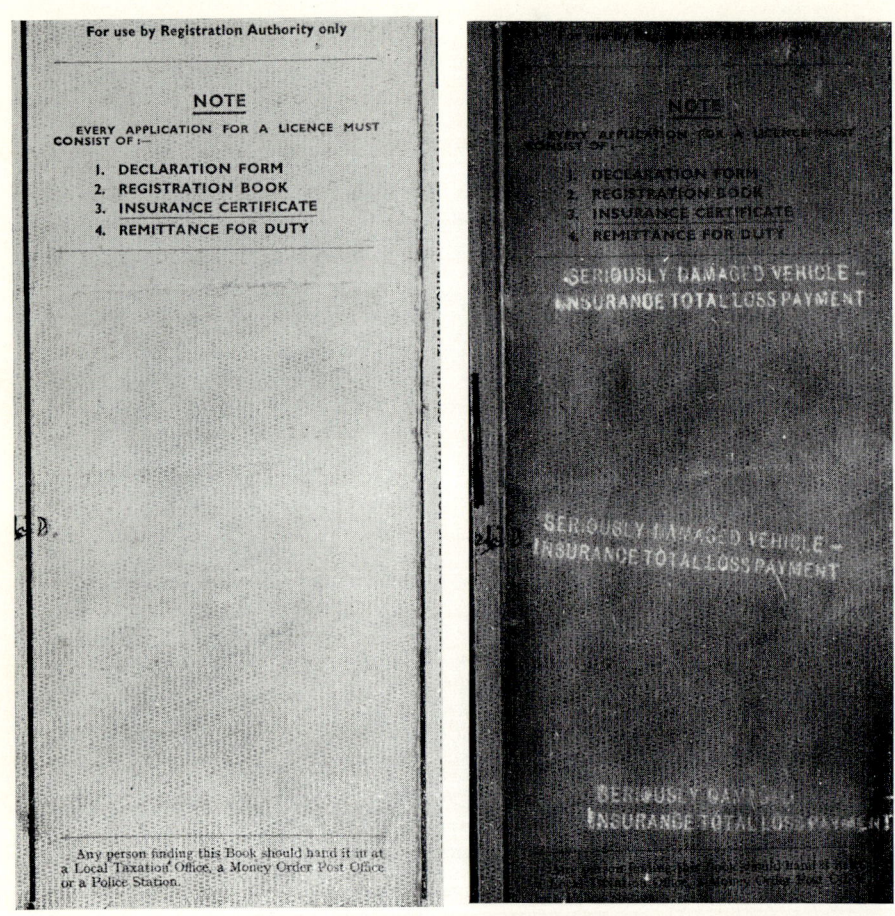

Fig. 47. INFRA-RED LUMINESCENCE

Part of a motor-vehicle registration book from which entries had been removed by chemical erasure. (A) shows the visual appearance, in normal lighting; (B) is the same area photographed by infra-red luminescence. No other technique revealed the erased entries. (*Copyright, Commissioner of Police of the Metropolis. Courtesy of Director, Metropolitan Police Forensic Science Laboratory.*)

suitable for others. This difficulty can be overcome by *temperature* or *pressure programming*, in which the parameter in question is made to vary continuously during a run, thereby maintaining optimal conditions throughout. The value of GC after *pyrolysis* in the identification of paints, plastics, etc. has already been mentioned (pp. 28 and 57). The original experiments on this used a small electrically heated filament, but the results were not very reproducible, chiefly because the rate of heating was inconstant. This problem has been solved, and pyrolysis turned into a routine technique, by the use of *Curie-point* heating. This depends on the existence, for any ferromagnetic material such as iron, of a *Curie temperature* above which it loses its characteristic magnetic properties, and which is a constant for each material lying somewhere between 200 and 1,200 °C. A piece of such a material in a radio-frequency alternating field is heated by the induced currents almost instantaneously (within a few milliseconds) to that temperature precisely but no higher. A convenient pyrolysis unit can therefore be based on this fact, the material being chosen according to the temperature desired. Finally, the latest development (so far) is to link GC with mass spectrometry (p. 76), whereby each constituent emerging from the GC apparatus is automatically identified by the mass spectrometer. This technique has been used in the U.S.A. in toxicology and drug identification, and is also currently under investigation in this country.

III. ELECTROCHEMICAL MEASUREMENTS

It is sometimes important (for example, in soil analysis—p. 39) to know exactly how acid or alkaline a solution is. All aqueous solutions contain hydrogen ions, and the greater the concentration of these the more acid the solution. By convention, this concentration is expressed by a figure which is its negative logarithm, and this figure is known as the **pH**. If it is less than 7, the solution is acid; if more than 7 alkaline; if exactly 7 (or, in practice, between about 6·5 and 7·5), neutral—that is, neither acid nor alkaline.*

The simplest but least accurate and not always practicable method of determining the pH is to use test papers impregnated with a dye or mixture of dyes the colour of which depends upon its value. Litmus, which everyone has heard of, is such a dye. For more accurate determinations a *pH meter* is required. This instrument utilises the fact that the difference in electrical potential between a glass surface and an aqueous solution in contact with it depends upon the pH of the solution. Although glass in bulk is a non-conductor, by making it sufficiently thin it can be incorporated as an extremely fine membrane in an electrical cell with one face in contact with the solution to be measured; the voltage produced by the cell is then proportional to the pH.

Some forensic science laboratories have utilised the **polarograph** as an analytical instrument. It is convenient for the quantitative determination of very low concentrations (or, which comes to the same thing, trace amounts) of

* A few actual values are (very approximately): soapy water 9; saliva 7–8; vinegar 3; gastric juice 2.

metals; it can therefore be used in the analysis of, for example, paint-fragment pigments. It works on the principle that in the electrolysis (see Glossary) of a solution containing metal ions (that is, a solution containing soluble salts of the metals) a certain minimum voltage is required before each species of ion begins to be discharged at the cathode. Below this voltage, no current is carried by the corresponding ions, but above it the current increases rapidly with voltage. When a solution containing several ion species is electrolysed, therefore, a graph of current against voltage will show a series of steps, each representing the discharge of one ion species at its particular voltage. At each step the voltage identifies the ion and the maximum current at that step its concentration in the solution. In practice, there are several complicating factors which make fairly sophisticated equipment necessary; with that proviso, however, polarographic analysis can be both accurate and extremely sensitive.

IV. THERMAL MEASUREMENTS

The thermal properties of many substances may be used to identify them. The simple *melting-point*, already mentioned (p. 62), comes into this category. A more recent technique of identification of this kind is **differential thermal analysis** (DTA). Many substances when they are heated undergo physical or chemical changes (the chemist's "phase transitions") at certain temperatures, and at each change there are energy gains or losses analogous to those which occur when a liquid boils or freezes. These will manifest themselves as discontinuities in the otherwise smoothly rising temperature graph of the substance as heat is applied to it. In a DTA apparatus a small sample of the material under investigation, and one of an inert reference material, are slowly heated together in a small oven or furnace, and their temperatures measured by thermocouples embedded in them. When phase transitions occur in the test sample, the thermocouples will show temperatures differences, and these can be automatically recorded. The temperatures at which they occur then serve to identify the substance under examination. The technique is useful for a great variety of substances—clays, waxes, plastics, etc.

It is frequently possible to use the same equipment for **thermogravimetric analysis**. In this, the sample is heated while suspended from a small recording micro-balance, and characteristic losses of weight at particular temperatures recorded. (For example, the loss of "bound" water from clay minerals—see p. 40).

It has also been found in some recent studies that the luminescent behaviour of glasses and some salts at high temperatures, and of some polymers (man-made films and fibres) as they are oxidised by burning, is characteristic and can be used for identification.

V. OPTICAL METHODS OF ANALYSIS

A large number of analytical methods, however much they differ otherwise, have in common that they utilise light or other radiation. Some are methods of identification, some of quantitative determination, some of both; one, spectrographic analysis (see below), is especially valuable because it can identify numerous component elements simultaneously without preliminary separation.

One physical property the use of which for identification has already been mentioned (glass, p. 31; oils, etc., p. 57) is the **refractive index.** Light travels more slowly in any transparent substance than in a vacuum, and the refractive index of that substance is the ratio

$$\frac{\textit{Speed of light in a vacuum}}{\textit{Speed of light in the substance}}$$

The change in velocity when a ray of light passes from one medium into another of different refractive index has two consequences. First, if the ray crosses the interface obliquely, it is bent (*refracted*) there so that it is more nearly perpendicular to the interface in the denser (more refractile) medium, the deviation being greater, the greater the difference between the refractive indices of the media. (That is why an object under water viewed obliquely appears to lie higher than it would if the water were not there.) The second consequence is: a ray striking the interface from the denser medium, and making more than a certain angle with the perpendicular to the interface, cannot enter the less dense medium at all and is *totally reflected*. (That is why the surface of the water in an aquarium tank seen obliquely from below looks like a mirror.) The particular angle above which this occurs is known as the *critical angle*, which again depends upon the difference between the refractive indices. The determination of this angle therefore constitutes a method of measuring refractive indices. This is the principle of the *Abbé refractometer*, the instrument generally used in forensic science laboratories for this purpose. As the precise value of the refractive index depends on the wavelength of the light (see below), being the greater the shorter the wavelength, accurate measurements must be made by monochromatic (usually sodium-vapour) light.

The remaining optical methods all depend upon wavelength differences. Everybody knows that white light can be dispersed into the familiar colours of the *spectrum,* and most people know that "light" is merely that part of the total range of electromagnetic vibrations which happens to be visible. The wavelengths we are considering here are nowadays expressed in *nanometres*★ (nm), and cover the following ranges:

★ I nanometre $= \dfrac{\text{I}}{\text{I,000,000,000}}$ metre. The same unit was until recently called the *millimicron* (mμ), I micron (μ) being $\dfrac{\text{I}}{\text{I,000}}$ millimetre. See "Metric units" in the Glossary.

Approximate wavelength in nanometres	Type of radiation	Properties and uses
200–400	Ultra-violet (200–250 "far") (350–400 "near")	Invisible. Used in spectrography (below) and in fluorescence analysis (p. 74)
about 400–about 750	Visible light	Colours of the spectrum from deep violet (400) to deep red (750)
about 750–about 1,200	"near" infra-red	Invisible. Used in infrared photography (p. 222)
about 2,500–about 50,000	infra-red	Invisible. Used in infrared spectrometry (p. 74)

Spectrographic analysis (or **emission spectrography**)* is over a century old as an analytical technique and has been used in forensic science for many years. However, it shows no signs of being superseded, and the spectrograph is still one of the forensic scientist's routine tools. The method is one of *elemental* analysis—that is, detection and identification of the elements present in the sample.

Spectrography depends on the facts that:

(1) the radiation from an incandescent gas or vapour is concentrated in certain discrete wavelengths;

(2) what these wavelengths are depends on the emitting element(s) in the gas, and each element emits a unique characteristic pattern of wavelengths—*i.e.* its *emission spectrum*.

The essential parts of a *spectrograph* are (1) a narrow slit to admit the radiation; (2) a prism or grating to disperse it; (3) a system of lenses to collimate the rays and to focus the dispersed images of the slit on to (4) a photographic plate. These images appear as a series of short lines on the developed plate (hence "line spectrum"), each line being an image of the slit formed by radiation of one wavelength (fig. 21).

Spectrographs are made in various sizes and types, but for most purposes in this field a medium-sized quartz-prism instrument dispersing the spectrum from 200 to 1,000 nm is adequate. (Quartz must be used for the prism and lenses, since most of the analytically useful wavelengths lie in a region of the ultraviolet to which glass is opaque.) To make an analysis, the sample is vaporised to incandescence and the radiation from the hot vapour dispersed and recorded in

* Strictly speaking, and by their original meanings, "spectrography" is the photographic or other recording of any spectrum, and "spectroscopy" the viewing by the eye of a spectrum in the visible region. Recent developments, however, have tended to blur this distinction, and "spectroscopy" has acquired a wider connotation than that just defined.

the spectrograph. If, as is normally the case, the sample contains several or even many elements, the spectra of all (or most—see below) of these will be recorded simultaneously. The final stage is then simply the "sorting out" of the resulting complicated sequence of lines. This stage may eventually be automated and computerised.

To vaporise the sample, one may use: (1) a flame; (2) an arc; (3) a spark. Flame excitation is practically limited to the well-known flame tests for the alkali and alkaline-earth metals, with or without the aid of a pocket spectroscope. Spark excitation is useful when (but in this field, only when) the sample is a relatively large metal object which can be used as an electrode. Most forensic analyses are made using arc excitation, for which the sample is "burnt" in an arc between electrodes, using commonly about 5 amps. D.C. at about 200 volts. The electrodes are commonly of specially purified graphite, carbon being particularly suitable in showing very few spectrum lines itself in the region examined, but other electrode materials (copper, for example) are also used. Arc excitation is more sensitive than spark, and will enable all of the metallic elements and several of the non-metallic ones to be detected. It has of course the disadvantage that it destroys the sample.

As we have already mentioned, the particular value of spectrographic analysis lies in its ability to produce quickly in one operation a nearly complete elemental analysis of the sample. Its main use is probably for the analysis of paint pigments, but it can also be used (sometimes after preliminary preparation of the sample) for mineral materials of all kinds, trace elements in dust, traces of "foreign" metals on housebreaking implements and other tools, counterfeit coins, and for several other purposes (fig. 21).

With materials such as paint, 1–2 milligrams of sample are sufficient if this is simply burnt on the surface of the lower electrode, but by incorporating the sample in the tip of the electrode much smaller amounts (perhaps 50 micrograms) can be analysed. This is a high sensitivity compared with classical methods (which is why spectrography was introduced into forensic science), but rather a low one compared with other more modern instrumental methods. It is not in general possible in forensic science to use spectrography quantitatively as is done in, for example, the routine production control of alloys; the variety of materials which have to be analysed is too great for the necessary controls to be prepared and data to be assembled.

A new spectrographic method which appears to have great potentialities is *laser-beam micro-spectrography*. A chosen spot on the sample to be analysed is vaporised by the concentrated energy of a pulsed laser beam, and the spectrographic source proper is a synchronised spark passing through the tiny cloud of vapour so produced. As the spot may be as small as 10 microns (1/100 millimetre) across, it is possible to analyse exceedingly small samples, or to analyse individually (which is impossible with ordinary spectrography) small inclusions, or separate layers in flakes of paint and the like.

Atomic absorption spectroscopy, nowadays increasingly used in forensic science, has as its special function the determination of minute amounts of metals which are known to be present. In a sense, it is emission spectrography in reverse: instead of detecting the presence of an element by the emission from its excited (*i.e.* energised) atoms of radiation having characteristic wavelengths, it measures the amount of an element present by determining how much of this radiation is absorbed by exciting its atoms. (This is the process responsible for the well-known *Fraunhofer lines* in the sun's spectrum, which were discovered about 150 years ago.) The sample is vaporised at a temperature of something over 2,500 °C., either in the flame of a specially hot-burning gaseous mixture or in a small electric furnace, and a beam of radiation of the wavelength of one of the main spectrum lines of the element being determined is passed through the vapour. The beam loses part of its energy in exciting the atoms of that element, so that it emerges with diminished intensity; the amount of this diminution, by comparison with an identical reference beam which has suffered no absorption, is then a measure of how much of the element is present. To supply the radiation, a separate source (*hot-cathode lamp*) emitting the particular wavelength desired is needed for each element to be determined. The method is extremely sensitive, determining accurately less than microgram amounts of the elements for which it can be used. It is also simple and quick to operate, since usually no complicated preliminary treatment of the sample before vaporisation is necessary. Perhaps its most important application is the determination of trace amounts of toxic metals (see Chapter 10), but it can be used with advantage in most cases where the amount of a metallic trace element present is an identifying characteristic.

What can broadly be called **absorption spectrometry** covers a group of methods so useful in forensic science for the identification and determination of a wide variety of compounds that they may be counted indispensable to any adequately equipped laboratory.

One of the simplest physical properties by which a substance can be identified and/or determined is its colour. Many if not most elementary "spot tests" depend on the production of a colour. Many of these tests can also however be made quantitative and *colorimetric analysis* has long been so used. If the sample is subjected to a reaction which converts a particular component into an intensely coloured compound, the intensity of the colour can be used as a measure of the amount of the component. Since a very small quantity of any strongly coloured compound suffices for measurement, the method is of obvious interest in this context.

Colorimetric methods are now available for practically every metallic and acidic ion, and for many organic compounds and radicals. Colorimetry is, however, merely a part of the more general technique of *spectrophotometry* (or nowadays more commonly and shortly *spectrometry*)—in fact, most of its methods are nowadays referred to as spectrometric ones. A coloured substance is one which shows differential absorption in the visible region of the spectrum; one which absorbs blue, but transmits green and red, appears yellow, and so on. This is easily put on a quantitative basis by (1) defining a parameter which shall be a measure of the absorption at any wavelength, and (2) measuring this at a number of wavelengths.

The absorption of a ray of light by an absorbing medium is governed by the *Beer–Lambert Law*, which states that

$$\log_{10} I_0/I = kcd,$$

where I_0 is the initial intensity of the ray, and I is its intensity after passing through a thickness d of a medium containing the concentration c of a substance of which k is the *extinction* (or *absorbency*) *coefficient*.

There are two ways in which this law can be utilised for analysis.

(1) If d and k are known, the absorption (*i.e.* I_0/I) at any wavelength depends upon c, so that the latter is determined by measurement of the former. This is in effect what is done in colorimetric analysis as described above.

(2) A graph of the extinction coefficient plotted against wavelength is an *absorption spectrum*. This may be measured in the ultra-violet, visible or infra-red regions, and is a characteristic property which can be utilised for identification. It is determined by measuring I_0/I at a number of wavelengths in a solution for which d and c are known.

The simplest and crudest way of making a colorimetric analysis is by visual comparison of the sample with known standards. This method may, however, be considered obsolete. The next stage of refinement is the use of a colorimeter in which the light path (*i.e.* d) in the reference solution is varied until the depth of colour matches that of test solution, the two being viewed simultaneously as half-fields through an eyepiece.

In an *absorptiometer* the not altogether reliable human eye is replaced by a photocell, and the colour which this is allowed to "see" is selected by means of a light filter, the colour of which is complementary to that being measured so as to maximise the absorption and hence the sensitivity.

For the complete plotting of an absorption spectrum (case 2 above) more complex equipment is necessary. A *spectrometer* consists essentially of a prism or grating system for dispersing the radiation, means for allowing the dispersed radiation to traverse a known path-length in the specimen being analysed, and a means for measuring absorption at each wavelength in the dispersed radiation. Such an instrument was used to produce the curves shown in fig. 22.

In practice, spectrometers are of two quite distinct types:

1. Instruments covering the *ultra-violet, visible* and near infra-red regions (say 200–1,000 nm). Such instruments can be used both to identify a compound from its absorption spectrum and to determine it by measuring the absorption at a maximum of the spectrum. Although ultra-violet or visible absorption spectra are not usually as individual as infra-red ones (see p. 74), the measurements can be made on smaller quantities than in the infra-red, and some of the compounds of interest to the forensic chemist (*e.g.* the barbiturates—see Chapter 10) do have characteristic ultra-violet spectra. With some also, the identification may

be confirmed by re-plotting the spectrum after alteration of the pH or other treatment and noting whether the new spectrum is that of the compound which would be produced if the original identification was correct. It is obviously useful to be able to make the measurements on very small samples (such as, for example, the dye stripped from tiny shreds of fabric). Cells holding 0·2–0·3 ml. are available with most types of equipment, and a recent paper from East Germany describes a method using less than half a microlitre (about 1/100 of a drop).

2. Instruments covering the *infra-red* region of the spectrum between, say, 2,000 and 25,000 nm (2–25 μ). (In practice radiation in this region is usually designated by its *wave number*, or frequency, which is inversely proportional to the wavelength, rather than by its wavelength.) The value of infra-red spectra rests on the fact that they depend intimately upon the structure of the absorbing molecules, each part of and separate chemical bond in the molecule leading to absorption at a specific wavelength in this region of the spectrum. Therefore, every organic compound shows a characteristic spectrum, usually of such complexity that it forms a unique "fingerprint" of that compound; in addition, the structure of an unknown compound can be deduced from the positions of its absorption maxima. The spectra of thousands of compounds have now been indexed so that any compound on the index can be identified when encountered as an unknown.

Although the principles of spectrometry are the same for all spectral regions, special equipment is necessary for infra-red wavelengths because glass is opaque to them and because special emitters and detectors are necessary. The specimen may be presented in several ways. It may be solid, liquid or even (by using very long absorption cells) gaseous. A common and frequently used technique is to grind the solid or liquid sample with potassium bromide, which is itself transparent over the whole useful spectral region, and fabricate the mass with a powerful press into a transparent plate. Solids may be finely dispersed in medicinal liquid paraffin. When solutions are used, a solvent is naturally chosen which is itself transparent in the region of significant solute absorption. No solvent or dispersing medium is completely transparent over the whole of the useful infra-red range, but this difficulty is overcome by modern instruments being *double-beam* ones; what these actually measure is the difference in absorption between the specimen preparation and a reference cell, plate or the like of the solvent or dispersing medium used.

Infra-red spectrometry is a most versatile tool. Not only can it be used to identify specific compounds, as described above, but it is also useful for characterising empirically a wide variety of substances of indefinite composition such as paint media, greases, asphalts, etc. (fig. 22). Some of its uses have already been mentioned in Chapters 4 and 7; the technique of attenuated total reflection (p. 28) is especially noteworthy.

The remaining optical methods of analysis all depend on the phenomenon of **fluorescence.** In its most familiar form, this is the absorption of ultra-violet radiation and simultaneous emission of visible light. (Emission which occurs after the exciting radiation has been switched off is known as *phosphorescence*.) More generally, however, fluorescence is the absorption of energy at one wavelength and re-emission of part of it at a longer wavelength. This wavelength shift is a consequence of the quantum laws of physics, which state that all radiation is emitted and absorbed in "packets," or *quanta*, and that the energy per quantum is less the longer the wavelength. Hence, as some of the energy absorbed is always dissipated (Second Law of Thermodynamics), that re-emitted is less energetic per quantum, and therefore of greater wavelength.

Since practically all organic materials and many inorganic ones fluoresce, fluorescence has always been valuable to the forensic scientist as a quick provisional identifying characteristic for oils, greases, papers, inks, fabrics and other materials too numerous to mention. The specimen is simply examined under a source of ultra-violet from which all visible light has been filtered out, and the colour of any visible fluorescence noted. The source is always a mercury-vapour quartz discharge tube, which radiates most of its energy at the wavelengths 254 and 365 nm, and the filter material is traditionally *Wood's glass*, which transmits the near ultra-violet. Since however the occurrence and colour of fluorescence depend on the wavelength of the exciting radiation, it is better to have available two lamps with different filters transmitting only the 254 and the 365 wavelengths respectively.

Fluorimetry is a method of quantitative determination based on fluorescence. Many compounds fluoresce brightly in dilute solution (quinine in tonic water and eosin, the dye in red ink, are familiar examples) and at high dilutions the intensity of the fluorescence is proportional to their concentration. In a fluorimeter, therefore, a beam of exciting radiation is passed through a dilute solution of the compound being determined, and the intensity of fluorescence measured by a photocell along a direction perpendicular to the beam. The method is extremely sensitive, and is the best, sometimes the only practicable, one for some compounds of interest to the toxicologist (the drug LSD, for example). A somewhat similar method of potential value for some other drugs of this type is being currently explored; here the parameter measured is the duration, determined with an oscilloscope, of phosphorescence of the compound after irradiation at very low (liquid-air) temperatures.

In **spectrofluorimetry**, the application of which to forensic science has been pioneered largely by Dr. Lloyd of the Birmingham Home Office Laboratory, the intensity of fluorescence is plotted as a function of its wavelength, using an instrument similar in principle to an ultra-violet spectrometer (p. 73). The exciting radiation may be either of a fixed wavelength, or it may be arranged to "trail" behind the emitted by a pre-selected wavelength difference, the conditions being chosen which yield the most useful information. The method has been successfully applied to materials such as oils, greases, car-exhaust soots, bitumens and so forth, which normally rank among the analyst's chief headaches. It is also extremely sensitive, needing as little as 10 micrograms of sample using normal equipment, or 0·1 microgram when working on a micro scale. For example, over 50 different complex and otherwise effectively unidentifiable aromatic (see Glossary) hydrocarbons have been identified in used engine oils, and the analytical differentiation is so precise that the change in composition of the oil after only a few hundred miles of driving can be detected. The possible applications of spectrofluorimetry have barely been explored as yet, but it has already revolutionised the identification of oils and greases occurring as contact traces; it has been demonstrated that the probability of two random specimens of used engine oil being spectrofluorimetrically indistinguishable is negligibly small.

VI. MASS SPECTROMETRY

Another method of analysis which has recently begun to be applied to the problems of forensic science is **mass spectrometry.** This could perhaps claim to be the most versatile of all instrumental methods and to give more information from a minimal quantity of material than any other. It was first developed by F. W. Aston (famous for his pioneer work on isotopes) in this country and by Dempster in the U.S.A. before 1920, but it can be traced in principle to the work of Sir J. J. Thompson (the discoverer of the electron) in the 1890s. Commercial equipment for it has been available since the 1950s.

The principle is fundamentally simple. If a moving charged atomic or sub-atomic particle of mass m and charge (in fundamental electron/proton units) e passes through an electric or magnetic field acting transversely to its line of flight, this line will be deflected, and the amount of deflection depends upon the intensity of the field, the velocity of the particle and the ratio e / m. For any ion species, m is unique and e is always a small integer. Hence, for a given field strength and ion velocity, the deflection depends almost uniquely upon m, and can be used to measure it and so identify the ion.

(The "spectro-" in the name refers to the fact that the range of deflections produced gives a "spectrum" of ion masses. In strict usage, a "mass spectro-meter" measures each mass separately, while a "mass spectrograph" (Aston's original name) records masses present simultaneously. Commonly, however, "mass spectrometer" is used for both types of instrument.)

The essentials of a mass spectrometer are therefore: a means of ionising the specimen; a deflecting field; a receiver for the ion-beam signal and some means of measuring the deflection; a method of recording the results. The whole apparatus, from the start to the finish of the ion flight-path, must also be at a high vacuum, so that there are a minimum number of gas molecules for the ions to collide with.

How the initial ionisation is done depends on the type of specimen being analysed. Organic compounds are usually subjected to electron bombardment, which breaks up their molecules into characteristic and identifiable ion frag-ments. For inorganic compounds, a pulsed high-voltage spark between electrodes into which they have been incorporated, producing the ionised forms of their constituent atoms, is commonly used. (In theory, the method works with either positive or negative ions; in practice, however, positive ions—that is, atoms or molecules which have lost one or more electrons—are always used.)

The ions produced are accelerated by a high potential to pass through a slit into the deflecting field. It is in the design of this part that modern instruments vary most; some use a magnetic field only and some both magnetic and electric fields. In either case a large electromagnet and complex ancillary "hardware" are necessary; a modern mass spectrometer is therefore a large and heavy piece of equipment. Whatever the method of deflection, the essential thing is that all the ions of a given e/m value are brought together at a detector.

There are several ways in which the focused ion beams can be detected and recorded. For a complete qualitative analysis it is convenient to record the whole range of e/m values on a photographic plate; it is also possible to display the spectrum on an oscilloscope screen or convert it into a recorder trace. For a quantitative analysis, it is usual and more accurate to measure the intensity of each ion beam separately, which is normally done by varying the magnetic field to focus each e/m value in turn on a suitable detector of very small electric currents (which beams of moving ions in fact are). However the results are recorded, each ion species is identified by its position in the spectrum and quantitatively determined by the intensity of the signal at that position. (That statement is true only if one assumes that e is always 1. The assumption is not always correct, since multiply charged ions, with e values of 2, 3, ... etc., may have been produced; it is in recognising and allowing for these that mass-spectrometric expertise is necessary.)

As already mentioned, mass spectrometry is an analytical technique of extremely high sensitivity and precision. It will detect and identify the constituents of a specimen weighing less than a microgram, or constituents forming perhaps one part in 1,000 million of larger specimens. The precision is measured in this context by the "resolution"—that is, the smallest detectable difference in ion masses. This can be such that differences in m values of 1 part in 10,000 (*e.g.* values of 100·00 and 100·01) are detectable; with the most sophisticated modern instruments the figure may be as high as 1 in 100,000. However, as sensitivity and resolution are roughly inversely proportional to each other, it may be necessary to work with a low resolution to attain a high sensitivity. In all modern instruments, therefore, the resolution is adjustable according to the sensitivity required.

The technique can be extended in various ways, such as by linking the detection and recording to a computer. The extension of most interest perhaps to the forensic scientist has already been mentioned (p. 67), namely the coupling of mass spectrometry and gas chromatography, making possible the direct "on-line" identification of the constituents emerging from the chromatographic column. The difficulty which has to be overcome here, and for which various solutions have been devised, is to ensure that the carrier gas cannot enter the mass spectrometer, inside which a high vacuum must always be maintained.

The possible applications of mass spectrometry in forensic science are really only beginning to be explored. A few have already been mentioned. It has been used for the identification of minute quantities of toxicological metabolites, ingested drugs and volatile inflammables in lung tissue from fire victims. It will undoubtedly prove itself as useful with other materials (for example, paints and plastics) as it is already doing with glass (p. 34).

VII. METHODS USING X-RAYS AND RADIOACTIVITY

These methods of analysis are grouped together here merely because they all depend on the use or measurement of radiation of very short wavelength, covering the following approximate ranges:

Wavelength range in:		Type of radiation
nm*	Å*	
0·0001–0·01	0·001–0·1	γ (gamma) radiation from radioactive elements
0·01–0·1	0·1–1·0	"Hard" (penetrating) X-rays
0·1–1·0	1·0–10	"Soft" (easily stopped) X-rays

* Å: *Ångström units*, named after the pioneer Swedish spectroscopist Ångström.

$$1\text{Å} = \frac{1}{10{,}000{,}000{,}000} \text{ metre} = \frac{1}{10} \text{ nanometre (nm)}$$

See footnote on p. 69, and "Metric units" in Glossary.

In other respects, the methods differ widely in both theory and practice.

X-rays are produced when atoms are bombarded with electrons, or with more energetic (harder) X-rays, and are the result of the inner electrons of the atoms falling back into the orbits from which they had been displaced. The emitted energy, like radiation in the ultra-violet and visible regions, is largely (though not entirely, for reasons too technical to be explained here) concentrated in particular wavelengths characteristic of the emitting atoms. The resulting spectra, which are much simpler and have fewer lines than those in the other regions mentioned, can therefore be used as a means of elemental analysis; we shall return to this in the next section.

The earliest use of X-rays as an analytical tool, both in pure physics (1912 onwards) and in forensic science (since the last war), was **X-ray crystallography** (or **diffraction**). This depends on the fact that the constituent atoms or ions of a crystal are arranged in a regular three-dimensional lattice, the precise inter-atomic distances in which are characteristic of the compound forming the crystal. The planes of atoms in the lattice reflect a beam of X-rays falling on them, but because of interference effects (diffraction) the reflection occurs only at certain specific angles which depend on the wavelength of the X-rays and the interplanar distances in the lattice.

The parameters involved are connected by the fundamental *Bragg equation*

$$n\lambda = 2d \sin \theta$$

where n is an integer, λ (*lambda*) the wavelength of the X-rays, d the interplanar spacing and θ (*theta*) the angle of diffraction (fig. 23). There are several d-values for each compound, corresponding to the several sets of planes in which, as a matter of geometry, the atoms or ions in its crystals lie. λ having been fixed by choice of X-ray source, and θ being measurable, we can then calculate the values of d. As these values have been measured and tabulated for a large number of compounds, we have thus a means of *identification* applicable to any crystalline solid or compound of which a crystalline solid derivative can be made.

Fundamental theoretical work in X-ray crystallography uses single crystals, but for simple identification the *powder* method is easier. In this the finely powdered specimen is mounted at the centre of a cylindrical box, and continuously rotated while a beam of X-rays of known wavelength (that is, emitted by a selected target metal in the X-ray tube and suitably filtered) is directed upon it. Some of the tiny crystals are then always correctly oriented at each instant for each diffraction angle, each of which is therefore represented by a cone of rays symmetrical about the line of the beam. A strip of X-ray film mounted peripherally inside the box records the position of each cone as a pair of lines (fig. 24); the resulting set of line pairs is sometimes loosely (but incorrectly) known as an "X-ray spectrum." From the distance between each pair of lines, we can calculate the corresponding value of θ, and hence of d. In practice it is often simpler and quicker, not to calculate the d-values, but to compare the unknown pattern directly with those, previously recorded, of the compounds we are likely to encounter.

With the proviso that this technique can be used only for crystalline materials, it is a most useful analytical tool. It is non-destructive, so that the specimen can be recovered for other tests; it can be used with quite small specimens (less than a milligram); it does not require pure materials provided that the impurities are non-crystalline. On the whole, possibly, its most useful applications are in the identification of inorganic and mineral substances—paint pigments, rocks and minerals, corrosion products, etc. With pigments, the necessary initial fine powdering has already been done for us by the paint manufacturer. The following case illustrates the value of the method. A youth was accused of kicking a girl in the face. Her make-up had consisted of anatase (a form of titanium dioxide) in a greasy base. On the youth's shoes there were some flesh-coloured greasy smears the solid part of which was shown by X-ray powder analysis to be anatase. Although it would not have been difficult to identify this as a titanium compound, and it might have been possible to show by other means that it was titanium dioxide, it is certain that only in this way could it have been shown that it was anatase as opposed to rutile, the other crystalline form of this compound (fig. 24).

Although the powder method is the most generally useful, it is not the only possible forensic application of X-ray diffraction. X-rays diffracted through very large angles from metallic surfaces (the "back-reflection" method) can be used to measure the unit crystal dimensions in the metal, which is useful in the identification of some alloys. Synthetic textile fibres (nylon, terylene, etc.) under slight tension also give characteristic diffraction patterns.

The production and identification of the more fundamental true *X-ray spectra* will, as already mentioned, be discussed in the next section.

Lastly in this group of methods we have the use of **radioactivity**. Natural radioactive elements have been known since the Curies' classic discovery of radium in 1898, and artificial ones, with which we are concerned here, since the invention of nuclear reactors during the last war. The distinctive feature of radioactive elements is that their atoms disintegrate spontaneously at a known rate, and in doing so emit several types of penetrating radiation: α (*alpha*)—helium-atom nuclei; β (*beta*)—electrons; γ (*gamma*)—see p. 78. The rate of disintegration is expressed by the *half-life*, which is the time required for half the atoms initially present to have disintegrated, and which varies, according to the element, from a minute fraction of a second to millions of years. The peculiar advantage of utilising radioactivity in analysis is that much smaller numbers of atoms—that is, much less material—can be detected by the radiation they emit than by any other means.

Radio-chemical methods can be used for the determination of very small amounts of a specific element. The specimen is irradiated (see below) to convert this to a radioactive isotope, and a known amount of the ordinary non-radioactive form of the element added and separated by conventional chemical analysis. Since the radio-isotope is chemically identical with the non-radioactive one, both will be separated together; all that then remains is to measure the radioactivity of the separated element and to calculate from the results of this measurement how much of the element is present in its radioactive form—that is, how much was present in the sample before irradiation. This technique can be useful in toxicological analysis (Chapter 10). It was for example the means used some years ago to determine the arsenic content of small sections of an authentic specimen of Napoleon Bonaparte's hair (see p. 109). Another analytical application of radioactivity is mentioned on p. 112.

The best-known and most widely used application of radioactivity in forensic science is **neutron activation** (or simply **activation**) **analysis.** In this, the sample is irradiated with a high neutron flux to convert the elements present in it into their radioactive isotopes; these are then identified by the characteristic energies and rates of decay (inversely proportional to the half-lives) of the γ radiation (p. 78) emitted. To provide the neutron flux, an atomic reactor is necessary, which obviously limits the use of the method to laboratories having access to one. Purely electrical neutron generators have been developed, but few, if any, of these are powerful enough to activate the very small samples in which the forensic scientist is interested.

The radiation is analysed in a *gamma-ray spectrometer*, a complex piece of equipment which records the energies as peaks on a cathode-ray (oscilloscope) trace. By recording a family of curves at different times after irradiation, it is possible to separate the effects of different isotopes having nearly identical γ-ray energies but different half-lives; obviously the peaks representing elements with shorter half-lives will diminish more rapidly than those representing elements with longer ones.

Activation analysis is one of the most sensitive methods yet devised, enabling nanogram, possibly picogram, amounts of trace elements to be determined. However, it is probably fair to say that it has not proved as indispensable a tool to the forensic scientist as seemed likely when it was introduced into the field some years ago. It is relatively time-consuming; the apparatus is costly; and a very high degree of specialised expertise is necessary if the results are to be accurate and reliable. For some of its possible applications, other methods, such as atomic absorption or mass spectrometry, are likely to prove quicker and/or simpler and/or cheaper. Nevertheless it is a versatile analytical tool and can be used to identify and determine the characteristic trace elements in any type of material, including biological ones such as tissues, foods, plant fragments, etc. A great deal of work has been done on its use in characterising hairs by this means (see p. 173). It is on the whole more used on the American continent than in this country. Its uses in the U.S.A. include the identification of natural waters used in illicit distilling. An Australian case was described on p. 46. It has been used to detect otherwise undetectable propellant residues (p. 198).

VIII. CHARACTERISTIC X-RAYS AND THE SCANNING ELECTRON MICROSCOPE

It was mentioned in the previous section that the wavelengths of X-rays are characteristic of the atoms emitting them, and that the resulting true **X-ray spectra** can therefore be used as a means of identification. This, although fundamentally simpler, was in practice a later development than the use of X-ray diffraction. The unknown specimen is made the target either of a beam of fast electrons or of very "hard" (*i.e.* highly energetic) X-rays, and the wavelengths emitted are measured by means again of the Bragg equation on p. 78: by using a standard crystal, for which the *d* values are known, rotating it to the diffraction position, and measuring θ, λ is determinable. The rays emitted may be recorded photographically, but other methods are generally preferred—for example, the use of a movable Geiger counter to scan the whole arc of possible λ angles. It should be emphasised that this is a means, not of measuring crystal parameters, but of identifying the atoms in it; it is therefore a method of elemental analysis and is in that respect similar to emission spectrography (p. 70).

X-ray fluorescence, so-called, which uses hard X-rays for excitation, is a well-known analytical technique, but it has been little if at all used in forensic science because it normally requires fairly large specimens, hence severely limiting its applications in this field. A more recent and for us more useful development is the *electron-beam probe*. This uses for excitation a beam of fast electrons which may be less than a micron in diameter, so that very small specimens, or very small inclusions in a larger specimen, may be examined. For example, the individual layers exposed on the edge of a multi-layer fragment of paint may be analysed, or lead identified on single fibres taken from the edge of a bullet hole in a fabric. It was used in the investigation of the notorious Nudes Murders in London in 1964–65. In that case the bodies of the last four of the six victims all bore very minute spherules of dried paint, obviously derived from paint spraying; these were too small for analysis in any other way, but their analysis by this means established a connection between the bodies and the neighbourhood of certain paint-spraying premises.

Electron beams have also however another, new, mode of use potentially of immense value in forensic science—in the **scanning electron microscope** (SEM—fig. 25). Although this is primarily a technique of examination rather than of analysis, it will be convenient to describe it briefly here.

Electron microscopy stemmed from the development in the 1920s of the branch of mathematical physics known as wave mechanics. This postulated—and the postulate was soon confirmed experimentally—that electrons should behave as waves as well as particles. Their equivalent wavelength is however extremely small—something like 1/10,000 that of visible light. Now, the size of the smallest reproducible detail in a magnified image is limited by the wavelength of the radiation used to form it; the shorter the wavelength, the smaller the detail that can be reproduced ("resolved"). With visible light, this limit is reached at about 1,000 times magnification, greater magnification revealing no more detail; by using electrons to form the image, on the other hand, magnifications up to about 1 million are easily attainable.

On this theoretical basis, and using an arrangement of electric and magnetic fields to focus the image-forming electron beam, the *electron microscope* (or nowadays, to distinguish it from the SEM, "transmission electron microscope") was developed, and was eventually perfected to produce enormously magnified images of great clarity. It has not, however, found many uses in forensic science; the limitations on the types of specimen than can be examined, and the sometimes complicated specimen preparation necessary, have restricted its possible applications here. It has however been used in France for the examination of dust and paint-pigment particles.

The scanning electron microscope, on the other hand, is almost free of these restrictions. It is an extraordinarily ingenious and versatile instrument. Although some pioneer work on its basic idea was done in Germany before the war and in the U.S.A. in the early 1940s, the SEM as we know it today was developed after the war in Cambridge under Professor C. W. Oatley, and the first commercial model, the Cambridge Instrument Company's *Stereoscan*, appeared in 1965. The SEM may be roughly described as a combination of an ordinary electron microscope with closed-circuit television. Its special feature is that the image is formed, not as in the transmission electron microscope by electrons which have passed through the specimen, but by secondary electrons emitted by the specimen where the more energetic electrons of the primary beam strike it. (In certain modes of use reflected primary electrons may be used).

Electrons emitted by a hot tungsten filament or other source (greatly improved ones are now available) are accelerated by a potential of several thousand volts and impinge on the specimen after being electromagnetically focused into the narrowest possible beam; this is at the time of writing about 10 nm—roughly 1/2,500,000 inch—in diameter. At the same time this beam is made to scan the specimen surface in a raster pattern. The emitted electrons are attracted to an adjacent collector, and the greatly amplified signal from this is used to modulate the intensity of the image-forming beam in a cathode-ray tube, this beam being also simultaneously made to scan the tube screen exactly "in step" with the primary beam scanning the specimen. (The design of a sufficiently sensitive collector was the crucial factor in the successful development of the present instrument; the modulating signal is amplified about a million times.) The brightness of each point on the screen is then proportional to the electron emissivity of the corresponding point on the specimen; a picture is thus built up in the same way as on a television screen. It may be added that, because of this complexity, the SEM is inevitably a *large* piece of equipment, taking up most of a medium-sized room.

The resolution obtainable—that is, the size of the smallest visible detail—is limited by the minimum diameter of the primary beam, which, as mentioned above, is currently about 10 nm. The range of overall magnifications in the best instruments is from about 10 to about 100,000 or even 200,000 times. The pictures obtained may represent various properties of the surface examined—topographic (physical shape), electrical, crystallographic, etc. The first of these has obviously been so far found the most useful in forensic science. Almost the only restriction in use is that the specimen surface must be conducting, in order to prevent the impinging electrons building up a stationary charge; this condition is usually met by vacuum sputtering a very thin layer, which can be kept thin enough not to obscure the finest detail, of a suitable metal on to the surface before examination.

The unique property of the SEM, as compared with other types of microscope, is its great *depth of field*. With high-power optical, and even more with transmission electron, microscopy, only a single plane can be in focus at one time, which means that only thin layers can be examined. With the SEM, because of the way in which it produces its image, the whole of an irregular and uneven surface can be in focus simultaneously, and the depth of field is at least 500 times that of an optical microscope at the same magnification. Since the number of secondary electrons generated depends on the angle between the surface and the primary beam, the net effect when the topographic mode of examination is used is to reproduce an irregular surface as if it were strongly lit from one side, thus producing an apparently three-dimensional picture (fig. 7).

Some applications of the SEM have already been mentioned in previous chapters (*e.g.* pp. 21 and 52), and many others will undoubtedly be found when more forensic scientists have acquired and learned to use the instrument. So far it has been used successfully—often where optical microscopy has failed —for organic and mineral dusts of many sorts, for revealing in hitherto impossible detail the structures and surface characteristics of natural and man-made fibres, for the timber-identifying micro-structures in sawdust particles, for lacquered and otherwise treated human hairs, for spermatozoa in semical stains, for difficult striation comparisons and various other purposes.

The SEM has also however another mode of application which promises to be even more useful in forensic science: namely, for *X-ray microanalysis*. By making the primary-beam electrons faster and more energetic, which is done by using a higher potential to accelerate them, they cause the specimen to emit X-rays where they strike. Hence, by switching off the raster scanning, so that the beam is focused on one spot or at most scanned slowly along a chosen line, and attaching an X-ray spectrometer to the specimen chamber, the instrument becomes in effect an electron-beam analyser as mentioned on p. 81. This gives the forensic scientist a very powerful and (which is valuable) non-destructive tool. It can, with certain limitations, be used either to identify the elements present in a small sample, or to map the change in concentration of a given element across a chosen area, or to quantitatively determine selected elements in a small specimen or small area. The limitations are that a few of the lightest elements (*e.g.* lithium) and elements forming less than about 0·1 per cent. of the specimen are not detectable, and that for an accurate quantitative analysis the surface must be, or be made, perfectly flat. Even with these limitations, however, the sensitivity as a method of analysis is fantastic, the lower limit of detection for the major elements being something like 10^{-4} picogram (1/10,000,000,000,000,000 gram).

9

ALCOHOL AND THE DRIVER

It is a commonplace that road traffic in every civilised country today is be-devilled by the problem of the driver who refuses to recognise that drinking and the control of a mechanically propelled vehicle are incompatibles. In practically every state it is a criminal offence to be under the influence of alcohol, or to have more than a prescribed concentration of alcohol in the blood, while driving. We shall in this chapter examine briefly the scientifically ascertainable background facts, how the law deals with these and the forensic chemist's part in enforcing it.

I. PHYSIOLOGY

In the present context, all forms of liquor are simply aqueous solutions of ethanol (*i.e.* ethyl alcohol or, here, just alcohol), the concentration of which (in percentage by volume) varies from, say, 3 for a light beer, through perhaps 9–15 for unfortified (*i.e.* table) wines, up to (in Britain) 40 for spirits. Ethanol being a simple compound of low molecular weight and completely miscible with water, as soon as it has been drunk it begins to enter the blood stream by diffusion unchanged through the walls of the stomach and small intestine (particularly the latter) and from the blood it is subsequently distributed throughout all the body fluids. The initial diffusion is so rapid that alcohol can be detected in the blood almost immediately after it has been swallowed.

A certain amount is excreted unchanged in urine, sweat and expired air after it has passed, again by simple diffusion, through the kidneys, sweat glands and lungs respectively. These, however, are unimportant routes of elimination. From 90 to 95 per cent of the alcohol entering the blood is destroyed by enzymatic oxidation in the liver. Two enzmyes are concerned, each catalysing one stage of the process:

$$CH_3 \cdot CH_2OH \xrightarrow{-2H} CH_3 \cdot CHO \xrightarrow{+O} CH_3 \cdot COOH$$

ETHANOL $\left\{\begin{array}{l}\text{loses 2 hydrogen}\\\text{atoms to become}\end{array}\right\}$ ACETALDEHYDE $\left\{\begin{array}{l}\text{gains 1 oxygen}\\\text{atom to become}\end{array}\right\}$ ACETIC ACID

The acetic acid is finally broken down to carbon dioxide and water in the "main stream" of the body's metabolism. The rate of destruction in the liver is nearly constant—roughly 0·1 gram per kilogram of body weight per hour for man. (This corresponds to about 1 small whisky per hour for the average man.) The rate of elimination may be slightly greater when very large amounts have been taken,

85

or in alcoholics, but the increase is only slight and may be disregarded in the present context.

The alcohol concentration in the blood is therefore the resultant of two opposing processes—absorption from the stomach and intestine, and destruction by the liver. As long as there is an excess present in the alimentary tract the former is the faster process, and the blood concentration therefore rises. However, as the amount present unabsorbed decreases so does the rate of entry into the blood; at some point this rate will become less than the constant rate of destruction, after which the concentration in the blood will fall again, finally reaching zero after a time which depends upon the amount of drink taken in the first place.

The blood–alcohol curve (fig. 26) therefore shows a "peak." The time after drinking at which this is reached depends upon the type of drink taken, on the amount and type of food in the stomach and on how quickly the alcohol passes from the stomach (where it is absorbed relatively slowly) into the duodenum (where it is absorbed very rapidly). With spirits on an empty stomach it may be as little as 15–20 minutes; with beer, or with drink taken with a large meal, it may be as long as $1\frac{1}{2}$–2 hours. An average time for normal circumstances of drinking is probably around $\frac{1}{2}$–1 hour.

II. EFFECTS

It is of course the unchanged alcohol in circulation which intoxicates. There is probably no chemical compound the pharmacology and mode of action of which has been so long and so thoroughly investigated. Contrary to popular belief, it is *not* a stimulant; it is a narcotic. The apparently stimulating effect of drink is due to the facts that drinking is usually done in stimulating company and circumstances, that alcohol affects first those parts of the brain which govern the inhibitions and that its slight anaesthetic action makes the drinker less aware of depression or fatigue. Hence the euphoria felt after a drink or two. The fine edge of neuro-muscular co-ordination is next blunted; hence the slurred consonants and (at a more advanced stage) the staggering gait. At still higher blood concentrations, the respiratory centre is affected; hence the stertorous breathing associated with "sleeping it off," and hence, eventually, death from respiratory paralysis caused by acute alcoholic intoxication.

The grosser symptoms are of course familiar to almost everyone. An immense amount of research, however, has been done, mainly by psychologists, in the attempt to correlate more precisely blood–alcohol concentrations and the effects which they produce. The usual routine is to give the test subject known doses of alcohol, then, after allowing time for absorption, to take blood samples for analysis and to ask the subjects to perform some simple task which requires concentration and precise co-ordination and in which performance can be assessed quantitatively in some way—typing, for example.

All of this work has made it abundantly clear that:

(1) Practically all of the motor and sensory faculties are affected—co-ordina-

tion is impaired, reaction time is increased, the pain threshold is raised, repetitive tasks produce fatigue sooner, etc.

(2) A measurable effect is produced before the subject shows any of the outward signs of intoxication. Also, the more delicate the test the lower the blood-alcohol concentration at which impairment can be detected—that is, there appears to be no threshold concentration below which there is no effect at all.

(3) Although different subjects are differently affected by a given concentration in the blood, this difference is not as great as is often supposed for those who are not habituated to alcohol (see below).

Various methods are used in different countries for expressing blood–alcohol concentrations. Percentage w/v (weight/volume) is used in the U.S.A., and was formerly used in Britain. Most European countries use parts per 1,000 w/v (*i.e.* grams per litre), expressed as parts "pro mille," for which the symbol ‰ is used. Britain now uses milligrams per 100 millilitres (mg./100 ml.), and this usage will be adopted here. It may be convenient to note that 100 mg./100 ml. equals 0·1 per cent. w/v or 1·0 pro mille, and *pro rata* for any other concentration.

Roughly speaking, suitable psychological and other tests will show detectable effects at blood levels around 30–50 mg./100 ml., and at about 60–80 the obvious effects of alcohol may begin to appear and to be felt by the non-drinker or occasional drinker; by about 150–180 he would probably be markedly drunk. At the other extreme, any concentration above about 400 mg./100 ml. is very dangerous and could be fatal; most investigated deaths from acute alcoholic intoxication have shown concentrations in the range 400–700 mg./100 ml.

However, the level at which any particular stage of intoxication appears depends very much on how thoroughly the drinker is habituated to alcohol. Just what the physiological and psychological mechanisms of habituation are, is still not very clear, but their results are empirically well established. The regular toper or problem drinker may well be able to carry over 200 mg./100 ml. without apparent discomfort, and there have been cases recorded of true alcoholics who still appeared passably sober at over 300.

III. DRIVING

There can be no argument that the capacity to perform any precision job is adversely affected by quite small amounts of alcohol. Moreover, because of its social importance, a great deal of research has also been done specifically on how driving is affected. The investigations which have been made are too numerous to be described here. There are in general five ways in which the effects of various blood–alcohol levels on driving skill can be investigated.

(1) The results of psychological tests of the effects of alcohol on such things as perception, dexterity or reaction time can be extrapolated to the particular task of driving. When this has been done, the results are broadly in agreement with the more specific investigations described below.

(2) The subsequently determined levels in arrested drivers can be correlated

with their observed behaviour before arrest and with the results of clinical examination after it. Much useful information has been collected in this way, but is now of mainly historical interest because of more recent and more systematic investigations.

In this connection, it is of interest that the actual blood–alcohol levels of arrested drivers have been surprisingly similar in widely different parts of the world. For example, surveys some years ago in England, western France, West Germany, New York State and California all showed the majority of arrested drivers to have levels between 150 and 250 mg./100 ml., with a most frequent concentration of about 210. One cannot help being struck by the fact that this is approaching half the fatal level!

(3) **The driving-skill method.** Parallel groups of drivers with and without alcohol in their blood may be set tests of car-handling skill under conditions which are safe and which enable their performance to be evaluated quantitatively. The classic investigation of this type was reported from Sweden in 1950, and similar investigations later made elsewhere, chiefly in Canada, have confirmed its results. It was found that quite low levels of alcohol (less than 50 mg./100 ml.) produced statistically significant reductions in the test scores.

A British investigation of this type made some years ago by Professor Cohen of Manchester University is of particular interest, because in it an attempt was made for the first time to evaluate the drivers' willingness to take a risk. The test subjects were skilled bus drivers, who were divided into groups receiving no alcohol, small doses or moderate doses. The highest blood–alcohol level recorded was about 60 mg./100 ml. The drivers were then asked to estimate the minimum width of gap, as marked by a movable pair of vertical posts, through which they thought they could just drive their buses, and after that to make the attempt. The results showed that even the drivers who had received the smaller doses were more rash than when quite sober, and that some were ready with apparent confidence to drive their buses through gaps which were in fact narrower than the vehicles. The value of these results is that they confirmed what was believed but hard to prove—namely, that one of the chief dangers, if not the chief danger, of alcohol is that a little of it leads the driver into taking chances which he would not have taken if completely sober.

(4) **The simulated road test.** In this method there is a dummy "car" with the usual controls, and the test subject at the wheel has to operate these according to the changing picture of "the road" as projected by a moving picture on a screen directly in front of him. There is some more or less elaborate machinery to evaluate the driver's performance in terms of the number of steering errors, etc. Of the several investigations of this type, the most thorough was that made under the aegis of the Medical Research Council by a team headed by Professor C. G. Drew (a psychologist). Its results, which were published in 1959, were subsequently considered by a committee of the British Medical Association, whose conclusions were widely reported in the press at the time. These were,

briefly: with any blood–alcohol level above 50 mg./100 ml. the driver *may* be adversely affected; there is a marked deterioration in safety and performance, even with hard drinkers and experienced drivers, around 100 mg./100 ml., and no one will be safe at the wheel of a car with more than 150 mg./100 ml. These conclusions were of value to prosecuting authorities before the present British fixed-level law was introduced, since, as mentioned above, most drivers prosecuted had blood–alcohol levels well above 150 mg./100 ml. (*Cf.* also the American Medical Association's opinion—see p. 91.)

(5) **The statistical method.** It had often been noted that accident rates, after adjustment to allow for varying traffic densities, rose sharply after "closing time," especially at weekends. This sort of correlation may be made more precise by comparing the blood–alcohol levels of drivers who have been involved in accidents with those of drivers in comparable traffic conditions who have not. The pioneer scientific investigation of this type was that conducted by R. L. Holcomb in Illinois in 1938; others have since been carried out in various parts of the world. The most recent, and certainly the most thorough of these, was that at Grand Rapids, Michigan, the results of which were published in 1964, and were undoubtedly carefully considered in fixing the prescribed level under the Road Safety Act 1967 (see below).

The table on page 90 gives a simplified version of the results of three of these surveys, all from North America.

The Grand Rapids survey showed that there is a clear correlation between drinking and the accident rate for blood–alcohol levels above 80 mg./100 ml., and that above this level the liability to accidents rose much faster than the level—roughly exponentially, in fact, while the level rises linearly.

It must be made quite clear that statistical results of this kind do *not* enable us to predict the effect of any particular blood–alcohol level on any particular driver. (*Cf.* the results described under (4) above.)

IV. THE LAW

Assuming the above factual background, drink-and-driving laws may be of two types. Under the first, it is necessary to prove that driving ability has been impaired *and* that this impairment is due to the consumption of alcohol; it is then the forensic chemist's chief task to demonstrate the presence of alcohol in the driver's body. However, as it is impossible to fix exactly the point at which sobriety gives place to incipient intoxication, or at which a demonstrable impairment of driving ability begins to appear, the offence of drink-impaired driving is difficult to prove unless it is obvious and gross. It is to meet this difficulty that the second type of law has developed. This makes it an offence to drive with more than some prescribed level of alcohol in the blood, whether or not the driving in any particular instance is demonstrably impaired. An analysis of the driver's blood is then critically important, and the analyst's responsibility correspondingly heavy.

Blood–alcohol level (mg./100 ml.)	Illinois 1938	Toronto 1955	Grand Rapids 1964
Nil	(1) 87·9 (2) 53·4 (3) 0·67	(1) 91·3 (2) 77·5 (3) 0·85	(1) 89·0 (2) 83·4 (3) 0·94
Below 50	(1) 5·8 (2) 13·4 (3) 23·2		(1) 7·78 (2) 6·78 (3) 0·87
50–100	(1) 4·42 (2) 7·83 (3) 1·77	(1) 5·4 (2) 7·1 (3) 1·31	(1) 2·47 (2) 3·51 (3) 1·42
100–150	(1) 1·49 (2) 11·56 (3) 7·7	(1) 1·9 (2) 4·0 (3) 2·1	(1) 0·57 (2) 3·10 (3) 5·43
Above 150	(1) 0·42 (2) 13·8 (3) 32·9	(1) 1·4 (2) 11·3 (3) 8·1	(1) 0·18 (2) 3·18 (3) 17·7

Explanation: The first two figures within each set of three give the percentages of drivers falling within that group of blood–alcohol levels. (1) refers to the control (non-accident) group, and (2) to the group involved in accidents. The third figure, in heavy type, is the ratio $\frac{(2)}{(1)}$, and gives for each blood–alcohol level the approximate relative representation of drivers having that level in the accident group.

Within that general framework, there are several ways in which the results of an analysis of a body-fluid for alcohol may be used in a drink-and-driving prosecution.

(1) There may be no legal directive on the point, but a body-fluid specimen may be taken with the consent of the accused, and evidence about its analysis given at the discretion of the courts and the prosecuting authority. This was the position in Britain up to 1962.

(2) The law may direct the courts to take account of the results of the analysis, without however insisting that one shall be made or mentioning any particular blood–alcohol level. This was the position in Britain during the years 1962–67.

(3) The taking and analysis of a body-fluid specimen may be obligatory, or specifically authorised in certain circumstances, without any particular blood-alcohol concentration receiving statutory mention. This is or was until recently the position in several European countries—*e.g.* Denmark and Finland. Some particular upper limit may in practice be adopted by their courts as evidence of driving impairment.

(4) The law, while still making it necessary to prove that driving was impaired as under (1)–(3) above, may lay down a blood–alcohol level to exceed which shall be regarded as prima facie evidence of impairment. This is the position in the

U.S.A.; the laws of every state now make analytical tests compulsory, and prescribe how the results shall be interpreted. (But see also (5) below.) The interpretations are based on a report by a committee of the American Medical Association, which in 1937 recommended that under 0·05 per cent. (*i.e.* 50 mg./100 ml.) of alcohol in the blood should be prima facie evidence of sobriety, over 0·15 per cent. prima facie evidence of unfitness to drive, and intermediate concentrations admissible relevant evidence; a later recommendation by the Association brought the upper limit down to 0·10 per cent. As of July 1972, the level for the presumption of impairment was 0·15 per cent. in five states and the District of Columbia, 0·08 per cent. in two states, and 0·10 per cent. in the remainder. Such legislation would of course be defeated by the driver who refuses to give a specimen; all states except one had therefore by the end of 1971 enacted some form of "implied consent" law, under which consent to the giving of a specimen, when properly demanded, is a necessary condition for obtaining a driving licence.

(5) Finally, an increasing number of countries have now enacted a prescribed-level offence, in proving which, as already mentioned, the analyst carries the main responsibility. In Norway and Sweden it has for several decades been an offence to drive with more than 50 mg./100 ml. in the blood. Several other western European countries now also have such a law, including, as is well known, Great Britain (Road Safety Act 1967 and Road Traffic Act 1972). The permitted level varies: for example, Britain has 80 mg./100 ml., the Irish Republic 125, Austria 80, West Germany 130, Switzerland 80. Several states of the U.S.A. —five by the end of 1971, and the number will probably increase—have adopted similar laws in addition to their impairment ones mentioned above. Canada adopted a federal law similar to the British one in 1969. Some of the Communist countries are even stricter than the Scandinavian ones; they have made it an offence to have any alcohol at all in the blood while driving (although in practice, the writer understands, something like 30 mg./100 ml. is tolerated to allow for analytical error). In both Britain and Canada, however, the older impairment laws also remain in force, so that the driver who is affected by a blood–alcohol level below the permitted maximum has still committed an offence.

It is obviously vital in administering such a law that the analytical results shall be as reliable as is humanly possible. Several countries therefore lay down minimum necessary qualifications for their analysts; Great Britain does so by statute, and in the U.S.A. the National Safety Council has prepared a code of practice which, it is hoped, all states will adopt.

V. ANALYSIS: WHAT?

It will be clear from the above discussion that a decision must be taken on (1) what is to be analysed and (2) how it is to be analysed. The discussion of the first question will occupy the remainder of this section.

The important concentration which it is the purpose of the analysis to discover is that of alcohol in the arterial blood reaching the brain. It is clearly impracticable to analyse this. The question then follows: can we choose some other body fluid and analyse that instead? The answer to that is: yes, we can, but in deciding which fluid, and in assessing the results of its analysis, we must take into account the effects of several complicated interlocking factors.

The choice of fluid must depend on: (a) the relationship between the alcohol concentration in the fluid chosen and that in the blood reaching the brain; (b) the accessibility, in practical terms, of other body fluids than arterial blood. We shall examine these two factors in some detail.

(a) The fundamental consideration here is that, alcohol being (as already stated) a freely diffusible compound completely miscible with water, however it gets into the body it will eventually become distributed throughout all the water in the body. About 50–60 per cent. of the weight of the human body consists of water. (The actual figure in any particular case depends upon sex, age and obesity. The water content is higher in men than in women, in the young than in the old and in the muscular than in the fat.) Hence, when the distribution of the alcohol in the body has reached equilibrium, the alcohol content of any tissue fluid—blood, lymph, cerebro-spinal fluid, saliva, gastric juice, urine, etc.—will be proportional to its water content. About 80–85 per cent. of blood consists of water, the remainder being suspended solids, whereas the other fluids mentioned are practically all water. In addition, since there is free interchange of gases or the vapours of volatile substances between the blood and the air in the lungs, alcohol vapour from the blood will be present in the expired air.

The important qualification in the last paragraph is: when the distribution of alcohol in the body has reached equilibrium. That means, in effect, after the end of the absorptive phase, the period during which excess alcohol is still present in the alimentary tract and is passing into the blood. This is the same as the period during which the blood–alcohol level is rising (see p. 86 and fig. 26). During that period the highest concentration of alcohol will presumably be in the blood which has just absorbed alcohol from the alimentary tract and is flowing thence to the liver, where the oxidative destruction of alcohol takes place (p. 85). Initially, of course, the proportion destroyed during one passage through the liver must be quite small. Furthermore, there is experimental evidence that, during the absorptive phase, the arterial blood–alcohol concentration is slightly higher than the venous, probably because during that period alcohol is still diffusing through the capillary walls into the surrounding tissues. At the same time, it is also diffusing into all the secretions—sweat, saliva, urine, etc. It is only for the last of these that the process has been investigated with any thoroughness.

In fact, however, the physiological complication of the absorptive phase does not in practice affect the use of chemical analysis in law enforcement as much as might at first sight be expected, simply because the period between a driver having stopped drinking and his being examined at a police station is in the majority of cases long enough for his blood alcohol to have reached and passed its peak. Generally therefore we are on reasonably safe ground if we assume that the arrested driver's body alcohol is in a state of equilibrium among his various tissue fluids. In that case, as has already been mentioned above, the alcohol content of any body liquid will be directly proportional to its water content.

(b) Needless to say, the number of other body fluids which can conveniently be taken instead of brain blood for analysis is small, and in practice there are only three: (i) blood from some other part of the body; (ii) urine; (iii) expired breath.

Blood. It is a fairly simple matter either to take a few millilitres of blood from an accessible vein (usually in the arm) or to get a few drops of capillary blood by pricking a finger or the lobe of the ear. As has already been mentioned, once absorptive equilibrium has been reached the concentration from any part of the circulatory system will be nearly enough the same.

The major advantage of blood as a fluid for analysis is that the crucial blood–alcohol figure is obtained directly, without any arithmetical conversion based on the relative water content of blood and the fluid analysed. Its disadvantage is that taking it is a surgical operation, however minor, requiring in Britain at least the attendance of a doctor. Though it was not specifically so stated, it was obviously the intention of the Road Safety Act 1967 that blood should be the preferred fluid for analysis, and it was presumed that this would normally be capillary blood taken by skin puncture. However, as experience has shown, there are disadvantages in the use of capillary blood: the blood may clot; alcohol may be lost during collection; the process is by no means painless; it may be difficult to get enough blood for analysis by both prosecution and defence. The collection of venous blood by syringe has, if skilfully performed, none of these disadvantages, and has therefore in this country replaced the use of capillary blood almost entirely. Also, the analysis of blood for drugs other than alcohol, which is sometimes necessary, requires a larger specimen than can be obtained by skin puncture.

The proper *storage* of blood specimens between collection and analysis is very important. Bacterial contamination can lead to either the loss or the production of alcohol, so that a sufficient concentration of a suitable bactericide must be added to the specimen as soon as it is taken. It has also recently been shown that, if there is a large air space in the container and it is not refrigerated, alcohol may be lost through oxidation, the haemoglobin in the blood acting as an oxygen carrier in this process. This is almost certainly the explanation for the not uncommon finding that specimens which have been stored at normal temperatures for some time before analysis show a significantly lower alcohol content then specimens analysed at once.

Urine. This is a fluid which it is very simple to obtain and which indeed most people who have had a good deal to drink are very willing to supply. It was also, when the older purely chemical methods of analysis were used (see below) the simplest fluid for the analyst to deal with. It was therefore the fluid normally taken in Britain before 1967, and the present law still permits its use if the arrested driver refuses to give blood. It is also the best fluid in which to test for the presence of drugs other than alcohol.

Urine, in spite of its practical convenience, has the disadvantage that the blood–alcohol concentration must be derived from the results of its analysis by a calculation in which several assumptions have to be made, so that the figure is less reliable than that from a direct analysis of blood. The relationship between urine– and blood–alcohol concentrations is fundamentally simple but is complicated by several secondary factors. Since alcohol passes from the blood to the urine in the kidneys by simple diffusion, the ratio of the concentrations in the blood and in the urine leaving the kidneys may be assumed to be as the water contents of the two fluids—say 80:100, or 4:5 (*cf.* p. 92). This simple relationship will not however hold for a specimen of urine analysed; since urine is stored in the bladder and voided in "batches," the alcohol concentration in any batch will depend upon that in the blood while it was being secreted, rather than upon that at the moment when the urine was voided. But the blood concentration, as we have seen (p. 86), is normally either rising or falling and is approximately constant only for a short time around its peak. Hence, while the urine–alcohol curve also shows a peak, this will occur later than the blood–alcohol one (fig. 27). Also, whether or not the ratio of the urine– and blood–alcohol concentrations approximates to the theoretical value mentioned above will depend on whether, during the secretion of the urine, the blood–alcohol concentration was rising rapidly to, or falling slowly from, its peak.

A great deal of experiment and practical experience on the urine:blood ratio when the specimens have been taken simultaneously has shown that: (1) it varies widely and erratically if the urine was secreted while the blood concentration was still rising, so that such specimens of urine are worthless as indicators of this; (2) if the urine was secreted while the blood concentration was falling, the urine:blood ratio is not far from the theoretical figure mentioned above and is approximately 4:3. (This figure is slightly greater than the theoretical 5:4 because the blood concentration is lower at the end of the secretion of a batch than at the beginning, so that its *average* will be higher than at the moment when the urine was voided (fig. 27).)

In practice, most urine specimens will have been secreted from post-peak blood, because the driver will probably have emptied his bladder after drinking and because time will have elapsed between his arrest and the taking of a specimen. However, if urine is to be analysed, in order to ensure that it represents post-peak blood two specimens should be taken at an interval of time (say half an hour) and the first discarded. It was laid down in the Road Safety Act 1967 and the superseding Road Traffic Act 1972, which assumed a 4:3 ratio, that a urine figure of 107 mg./100 ml. should be treated as equivalent to a blood one of 80. They also incorporated the above recommendation about two urine specimens and laid down that they must be taken within one hour of each other.

Urine presents fewer problems of storage than blood. Contamination with stray yeast spores could however lead to the production of "false" alcohol by fermentation of any sugar present (traces may occur even in healthy persons' urine). It is therefore important that a suitable yeast-growth inhibitor should be added to the specimen.

Breath. The value of this as an analytical fluid depends upon simple physics. Alcohol evaporates from the blood passing through the lungs into the air in the alveoli (the tiny sacs in the lungs through the walls of which gases pass in and out of the blood). The concentration of alcohol vapour in the alveolar air depends only upon the vapour pressure of alcohol at the temperature of the body and its concentration in the bood. The usually accepted figure for the blood : alveolar air ratio (based on the pioneer work of Harger and others in America) is 2,100:1— that is, one volume of blood contains at the temperature of the body the same amount of alcohol (in solution) as 2,100 volumes of air (as vapour). The most recent work has suggested that this figure may be slightly too low, but it is still that generally used as a basis for blood–alcohol determination by breath analysis.

The alcohol concentration in expired air may therefore be used as a quick and direct index to the blood–alcohol concentration. It also tells us this at the moment of sampling, not, as with urine, at some earlier time. It has, however, certain disadvantages: it is difficult to make analysis of gases as accurately as that of liquids; the actual blood/breath ratio sometimes turns out, when tested, to be less than the theoretical figure, without any predictable or obvious reason being apparent; it is difficult to transport breath samples, or keep them for later analysis, without some loss of the alcohol in them; finally, the figure found will be too low if the breath tested is not true alveolar air (that is, the "deep breath" from the end of a strong expiration), and will be much too high if any alcohol remains in the mouth from recent drinking.

Breath analysis is used in some countries, particularly in North America, as a direct measure of blood–alcohol concentrations. In this country, however, it is thought insufficiently accurate for the operation of a fixed-level law and is used only as a screening test. The methods of analysis are briefly described in the following section.

VI. ANALYSIS: HOW?

The methods of analysis for liquids (blood or urine) must be quite different from those for a gas (breath). We will consider first together those for blood and urine. Far more than we can even mention here have been proposed and used, but many differ from each other only in detail.

A method for the analysis of any body liquid for alcohol must take into account the fact that it is never possible to analyse the whole liquid directly, since all body liquids contain other substances which would interfere with the reactions of alcohol. In all methods, therefore, advantage is taken of the volatility of alcohol to separate it from interfering substances by evaporation before it is determined.

With that proviso, the methods used may be classified as (1) chemical, (2) bio-chemical and (3) physical.

Chemical methods are the oldest and most numerous. They all derive from the original work of M. Nicloux in the 1890s. They are all ultimately methods for the determination of volatile *reducing* substances, and rest on the normally justified assumption that alcohol is the only such substance present in specimens from impaired or intoxicated but otherwise healthy persons. However, since such substances other than ethanol may be present in certain circumstances (*e.g.* acetone bodies in urine; various products of putrefaction in post-mortem blood), it is usually necessary to prove qualitatively that the reducing substance present is in fact ethanol. It is also important, with urine, to exclude the possibility that "false" alcohol has been produced *in vitro* by fermentation (see p. 94).

In making the quantitative analysis the alcohol separated from the specimen by evaporation is caused to react with a suitable oxidising solution and the analysis consists in determining how much of this is used up by the alcohol from a measured quantity of the specimen. Of the numerous oxidising agents which may be used, the commonest is chromic acid (in practice, an acid solution of potassium dichromate). In most methods using that, the amount used up is determined volumetrically (p. 62), but in some, and in perhaps most methods using other oxidising agents, the amount used up is determined colorimetrically (p. 72); chromic acid and many of the other possible reagents undergo a marked change of colour on reduction.

The chemical methods can be further divided into macro ones (using 1–2 ml. of specimen per analysis) and micro (using 0·1–0·2 ml. or less per analysis). They also differ that in some the evaporation and absorption of the alcohol both take place in one closed vessel at a fairly low temperature while in others the vapour is carried from one vessel by a current of steam or hot air and absorbed in another. In general closed-vessel methods are slower but take up less bench space and may, unlike the others, be left unattended during the evaporation.

The chemical methods which have been most extensively used include:

The original *Widmark* method. (See p. 100.) This is a micro-method in which the alcohol from a very small specimen of blood distils slowly at a low temperature into chromic acid in a small closed vessel.

The *Southgate & Carter* method. This is a macro-method, formerly popular in Britain, in which a stream of air passes through the specimen kept at about 90 °C., the alcohol vapour passing off with the air and being absorbed in hot chromic acid in another vessel.

The *Cavett* method is a modification of the *Widmark* one, being also a micro-method but using a different reagent to absorb the alcohol vapour.

The *Nickolls* method is similar in principle to the *Widmark* one but uses a much larger specimen (1–2 ml.). It was much used in Britain before the fixed-level law came in, and was very successful because it was accurate, convenient for the routine analysis of numbers of specimens and, being a macro-method, avoided incurring unnecessarily the greater difficulties of micro-methods when ample quantities of urine were normally available for analysis.

The *Kozelka & Hine* method. This is a macro-method in which the alcohol is distilled from the specimen in a current of steam, which is condensed after passing through a subsidiary reagent to trap interfering substances. The alcohol in the condensate is oxidised by chromic acid as a separate step, and the amount of oxidant so used up determined either volumetrically (in the original method) or colorimetrically (in modifications). This is possibly the best and probably the most widely used of the chemical methods, the removal of interfering substances making it more specific than others. However, it cannot be used with very small specimens, and is hardly suitable for the routine analysis of large numbers of specimens.

The **biochemical** method of analysis, which was developed in Sweden and Germany in the early 1950s, also depends upon chemical laboratory techniques, but uses as reagent not an oxidant but the enzyme (extracted from liver or yeast) responsible for the first stage of metabolism shown on p. 85. As this reaction is the conversion of ethanol to acetaldehyde by the loss of hydrogen, the method is known as the ADH one (**alcohol dehydrogenase**). It is elegant, in skilled hands at least as accurate as any other, and has the great advantage of being almost specific for ethanol. (The enzyme acts to some extent on certain other alcohols, but these do not normally occur in the blood of living persons.)

The alcohol from a micro-sample of blood or urine is allowed to evaporate at room temperature in a closed vessel into a buffered solution containing the enzyme and other necessary reagents, and the products of the reaction determined colorimetrically. The method can also be scaled down to become a "submicro" one, and can be adapted to automation (see pp. 10 and 98).

By far the most important **physical** method of alcohol determination is *gas chromatography* (p. 65 and fig. 19). It is completely specific for ethanol, and has therefore long been used for identifying this compound in post-mortem blood specimens possibly containing interfering reducing products of putrefaction. It also requires only an extremely minute quantity of specimen per determination. It was not however formerly used in routine traffic-law enforcement, because the apparatus for it is expensive and because it had not proved possible to make it accurately quantitative. The latter disadvantage having now been overcome, its many advantages more than outweigh the former, and it is since 1967 the method used routinely in Great Britain, as being the best method for the analysis of large numbers of very small specimens with the accuracy demanded by a fixed-level law.

The principle of gas chromatography has already been described (p. 66); each compound passing through the apparatus produces a "peak" on a recorder chart and the area beneath each peak is proportional to the amount of the compound producing it. In the procedure now adopted, the specimen is diluted in a fixed ratio, using an accurate mechanical device, with a solution of a suitable *internal standard*, a compound being chosen for this which is chemically suitable and which has a retention time sufficiently different from that of ethanol for the peaks to be clearly separated. A minute volume of the diluted solution is injected into the chromatographic column. An *integrator* automatically measures and prints out the peak areas. The equipment is calibrated at frequent intervals by putting through the analytical procedure ethanol solutions of very accurately known concentrations, the values of these being the ultimate standard on which the accuracy of the analyses depends. Each analysis then (1) identifies ethanol qualitatively by its retention time, and (2) enables it to be quantitatively determined by a simple calculation from the printed-out peak-area figures.

Since any method of analysis is subject to some inherent experimental error, it is important under a fixed-level law to ensure that injustice is not done by the reporting of analytical results which are just above this level and which may be slightly too high. Some correction must therefore be applied to the results. Different countries do this in different ways. In Britain, it is assumed that replicate analyses of the same specimen will show a standard deviation (see Glossary) of 2 per cent. (the actual figure is in fact less); in arriving at the figures which are reported, they are based on at least four determinations which show a "scatter" of less than three standard deviations, and this amount (*i.e.* 6 per cent.) is then subtracted from their mean. The chance of the reported figure being too high is then not greater than 1 in several million.

When large numbers of analyses have to be made routinely, as is commonly the case today, there is obvious scope for **automation** of the process. Automatic ADH analysis has been developed and used successfully in Germany. In Britain, it has proved possible to automate the gas-chromatographic method by using *head-space* analysis. When a solution of a volatile compound such as alcohol is contained in a closed vessel, the concentration of its vapour in the space above the liquid ("head space") depends only on its vapour pressure (see Glossary) and its concentration in the solution. Since vapour pressure depends in turn upon temperature, if the latter is kept constant the concentration in the head space will depend only on, and can be used as a measure of, that in the liquid. In the equipment now being used in Britain, the specimens after dilution are put into small bottles closed with a rubber septum, and a number of these are mounted on a rotating stand immersed in an accurately thermostated water-bath. The apparatus may then be switched on and left to perform the rest of the analyses automatically—withdrawal of a small volume (0·2–0·5 ml.) of head-space air by hypodermic needle, injection of this into the column, and printing out of the ethanol and internal-standard peak areas. It is even possible to link the apparatus to a computer programmed to perform the necessary final calculation and print out the result. There are various possible ways of identifying each printed-out result with the specimen to which it applies. It may also eventually be possible to incorporate the initial dilution step into the automatic sequence.

Breath alcohol. The determination of this is essentially a problem in gas analysis. Various quite sophisticated techniques have been used for research purposes. However, since the main value of breath analysis in law enforcement lies in its speed and directness, most if not all the methods used for this purpose have so far relied on a simple determination of volatile reducing substances in the breath. They differ, however, according to whether the analytical result is to be taken as accurately measuring the blood–alcohol level (as in many parts of North America) or simply (as in this country) as a screening test to show whether a blood or urine analysis should be made.

Several types of apparatus have been devised for the former purpose, ranging from the early *Drunkometer* invented by Professor Harger of Indiana University to the currently best known and most widely used of such instruments, the *Breathalyzer* invented by Professor Borkenstein of the same university (and manufactured under licence in Europe as the *Ethanograph*). This precise and reliable instrument automatically measures a fixed volume of "deep breath" (see p. 95), passes this through a standardised ampoule of dilute chromic acid and measures by an accurate photo-electric device the colour change produced by the reduction of this compound.

A much simpler and cheaper, though less accurate, arrangement suffices for a screening test. That generally adopted passes the breath through a small column of granules impregnated with chromic acid, and measures the breath–alcohol concentration by the length over which reduction of this has changed its colour from yellow to green. The *Alcotest* used in this country (and commonly but inaccurately referred to here as the "breathalyser") is an instrument of this type. It passes approximately 1 litre of breath, measured by the inflation of an inelastic plastic bag, through the column, and bears a graduation mark at the point to which the colour change just reaches when the breath–alcohol level corresponds approximately to a blood level of 80 mg./100 ml.

Apart from the possibility of developing *portable* gas-chromatographic equipment, the preceding paragraphs would, almost up to the time of writing, have embodied the last word on the subject. Very recently, however, two entirely new instruments for measuring breath alcohol have appeared. The first, the American *Intoxilyzer*, has been nominated by many in the U.S.A. qualified to judge as *the* accurate breath–alcohol instrument of the future. It determines the alcohol in a breath sample by measuring the absorbency at the wavelength of the principal ethanol infra-red absorption band (3·9 microns). This method of determining breath alcohol is not new, but it has not hitherto been used outside the laboratory. The whole instrument will work off a car battery and fits inside a case about the size of a portable typewriter and containing the infra-red source and radiation filter, the breath chamber, the detector and associated electricalities and an automatic print-out. The breath chamber is thermostated at 55 °C. to prevent condensation, and a system of mirrors extends the path-length of the radiation inside the chamber to nearly 3 metres, thereby making the accurate measurement of very low alcohol–vapour concentrations possible. The instrument is extremely rapid in operation and uses no expendable chemicals, and a standard deviation (see Glossary) as small as 1 mg./100 ml. blood alcohol is claimed for it.

The other new instrument—the *Alcolyser FCD*—is a British invention and is much more revolutionary in conception. It has been developed primarily as a screening device, but greater accuracy than is needed for that may be attainable. It uses a *fuel cell* (a piece of equipment the successful translation of which from theory to practice is in part a "spin-off" from space-flight technology). This converts directly into electricity the energy liberated by oxidation of the alcohol vapour on a special electrode; the resulting electrical potential is directly proportional to, and therefore a measure of, the alcohol–vapour concentration, and is shown within about 20 seconds on a meter calibrated directly in blood–alcohol figures. The prototype instrument is about the size of a box of chocolates, but a miniaturised version easily fitting into a pocket has also been produced. Again, no expendable chemicals are needed, but the fuel cell has a limited life and requires to be renewed occasionally.

It is still too soon to predict the future of these new devices. The Intoxilyzer is at present the more expensive and more accurate, and requires a minimum of operator training; the Alcolyser FCD is the cheaper and more portable.

VII. HOW MUCH?

Occasionally one wishes to know how much liquor must have been drunk to produce the blood–alcohol level found. This question was investigated by E. Widmark, the Swedish pioneer in this field, who published his results in the years during and after the First World War. He produced the formula:

$$a = c \times p \times r$$

where a is the weight of alcohol ingested, c is the highest concentration reached in the blood, p is the weight of the drinker and r is a factor (usually known simply as the *Widmark factor*) which is actually the ratio of the water content of the entire body to that of the circulating blood. As already mentioned (p. 92), this ratio will depend on sex, age and body habit. Theoretically, it is about 0·7 for men and 0·6 for women. It is then, when we know c and p, easy to calculate a, from which, if we know the alcoholic content of the liquor drunk, we can further calculate how much would have provided this quantity of alcohol.

Such back-calculations of liquor consumed from blood–alcohol levels are however dangerous in that the results may be grossly in error, partly because of unknown and variable personal factors and partly because, if the liquor was beer, the quantities are likely to be seriously underestimated. The calculation is likely to give an approximately correct answer only if the liquor was fairly strong and taken on an empty stomach. Because of this possibility of serious error, the British Medical Association abandoned several years ago the tables of quantities based on such a calculation which it had previously published.

If for any reason it is important to get some sort of estimate of liquor consumed, this qualification must be borne in mind when making the calculation and its results not accepted as other than approximate. The purely empirical Widmark factors of 0·9 (men, beer), 0·6 (men, other liquors) and 0·5 (women, liquors other than beer) may be assumed for the purposes of calculation. The mean body weights of the two sexes are: men, 70 kilograms (155 lb.); women 55 kilograms (120 lb.). Ordinary beers and commercial ciders contain around 12–20 grams of alcohol per pint; table wines 8–10 grams per 4-oz. glass; port, sherry and aperitifs about 10 grams per 2-oz. glass; spirits 7½ grams per "single" (5/6 fl. oz.).

10

TOXICOLOGY AND DRUG
IDENTIFICATION

Toxicology is the science of poisons. If we disregard that aspect of it cultivated by the Borgias, it can be divided into:

(1) *Clinical toxicology:* the recognition of the symptoms of poisoning, and the application of the proper remedial measures;

(2) *Chemical toxicology:* the detection of the poison in stomach washings, blood samples, etc. (if the patient or victim recovers), or in post-mortem material (if he dies).

We shall be concerned here only with chemical toxicology. However, the two divisions of the subject overlap, in that in both it may be necessary to know something of the physiological action of poisons.

Homicidal poisoning is fortunately an uncommon crime in the civilised countries of the temperate zones. However, accidental poisonings are always with us, and suicidal poisoning is relatively frequent. It is generally the business of the forensic toxicologist to investigate *all* fatal cases of poisoning, partly because someone has to do the analysis in order to determine the cause of death, and partly because he himself welcomes the experience gained; *any* death from an uncommon poison, however sad an event, is grist to his mill.

The investigation of a poisoning case involves:

(1) the *separation* of the poison (or, sometimes, its metabolite) from the material submitted;

(2) the *identification* of the poison extracted;

(3) the *estimation* of the total amount present, and comparison of this with the known lethal dose.

It is mainly in the techniques of separation that toxicology is a specialised subject, because of the difficulties which peculiarly beset it of separating what is being sought from a huge excess of matrix material. In its identifications it differs from any other branch of analysis merely in that the amount of material available may be inconveniently small. At the estimation stage we must of course also remember that some poisons (*e.g.* lead) are always present as trace constituents of healthy tissues, and that others (*e.g.* barbiturates) may have been taken therapeutically in small doses.

It will also be convenient in this chapter to deal with the identification of drugs which are controlled or prohibited by law, because the same techniques are used as in the identification of many poisons, and because the same compound may occur either as a drug of addiction or as a fatal poison.

Chemical toxicology is a field which is changing and expanding so rapidly that its study is really a whole-time job. There are two main reasons for this change and expansion: first, the development of new analytical techniques (see Chapter 8) the use of which makes identification quicker and more certain, but which themselves have to be learned; secondly, the present-day flood of new synthetic pharmaceuticals and pesticides. The former, being active drugs, are dangerous in an overdose, and the latter are meant to be poisonous. The "classic" poisons such as arsenic or strychnine have become rarities, and the commonest poisons are now the complex synthetic organic compounds devised by the manufacturers' inventive research staffs. Even in India, it has recently been reported, about 60 per cent. of poisoning cases are now due to synthetic drugs. Finally, it will, I hope, be plain that the subject is now too vast and ramified for a book such as this to contain more than a brief synoptic sketch of it.

It is generally agreed that modern toxicology was started on the right lines by M. J. B. Orfila, a Minorcan who worked in Paris and died in 1853. Before his day, a chemical analysis, if it was conducted at all, was usually confined to the contents of the stomach and (possibly) intestines. However, the inside of the alimentary tract is technically outside the body, and Orfila, realising that poisoning depended on the substance responsible being absorbed into the system, analysed *all* of the various organs, thereby instituting the modern practice. (Some of his experiments even involved boiling down whole bodies in great iron pots, an operation which fortunately is not nowadays considered necessary.) As far as Great Britain is concerned, the spreading of Orfila's ideas here is due mainly to one of his pupils, Sir Robert Christison (d. 1882), professor of Forensic Medicine in Edinburgh. It is only within the last two or three decades, concurrently with the development of modern instrumental methods of analysis, that toxicology has really emerged from the Orfila era.

What the chemist receives from the doctor or pathologist depends, *inter alia*, on how well they have organised their collaboration. Most toxicologists of any experience have at some time received a bucketful of sloshed-in organs and a bald request for "analysis for poisons." These bad old days are, one hopes, gone for ever. Ideally, the toxicologist will receive: (if the victim is alive) samples of blood, urine, possibly vomit and/or faeces, and *all* the stomach washings; (if the victim is dead) all the internal organs including the stomach and intestines with their contents, the brain, and adequate specimens of blood and urine, all separately packed in sealed jars. Stomach contents, although their analysis will not show how much poison has actually been absorbed, will normally yield the greatest amount of unchanged poison for identification, unless the victim has lived for some time after taking it. An analysis of the blood reveals the concentration actually circulating at death. The liver being the organ in which most organic poisons are detoxicated, it normally shows a higher concentration of these than the blood. A separate specimen of bile is nowadays commonly submitted, as certain poisons tend to be concentrated in this fluid. Many drugs are most easily recovered from urine, which is therefore the best fluid for preliminary screening tests.

The toxicologist should also receive a file of papers containing all the relevant available information, and (sometimes) control samples of whatever drugs, pesticides, household chemicals, etc.—the victim is believed to have taken. A type of sample which he also occasionally receives, and dislikes heartily, is food or drink which someone has taken to the police in support of an allegation of poisoning by wife/husband/lodger/etc. Such samples are almost invariably much too small for a proper analysis; yet although the complainant is in most cases merely neurotic, something must be done just in case the allegation is well-founded. Incidentally, the simplest test of a sample of food alleged to be poisoned is to feed a little of it to some laboratory mice and to watch whether they are any the worse for it!

The toxicologist's first action must then be to decide, in the light of the information at his disposal, what has to be done. The information may come from various sources. The background history may show that a large quantity of some poison to which the victim had access is missing. There may even be a suicide note and an empty bottle. The symptoms exhibited before death, especially if a doctor was present to record them, may be highly diagnostic. The post-mortem report may suggest certain types of poison as being likely to account for what the pathologist found. The toxicologist's own eyes or nose may help him: for example; recognisable fragments of a poisonous plant may be present in the stomach; prussic (hydrocyanic) acid has a characteristic smell* (bitter almonds); a yellowish liver is indicative of a small group of poisons which damage that organ. Then, in the light of what is known or discovered, the necessary analysis may be anything from the determination of one specific poison which there is every reason to believe will be found and only the quantity of which is unknown, to a complete examination for every known poison, in the not infrequent case of an unexpected death which was not medically attended and for which the pathologist can find no obvious cause at autopsy.

Assuming that a complete analysis is necessary, it must be systematic; "inspired" guesses mean irretrievable waste if they are wrong. The best modern practice is, first, to make, using the smallest possible amount of material for each, a small number of preliminary screening tests chosen either to detect the commonest poisons (e.g. barbiturates) or, if they are negative, to exclude at once as many poisons as possible. Stomach contents, blood and urine are most commonly taken for these tests. According to the equipment available, they will range from simple colour tests done on a micro scale to gas-chromatographic analysis. In the light of what these tests tell him, the toxicologist will then go on to his main analysis. Finally, to anticipate, his report will say what poison(s) (if any)

* For the majority, at least; 20–30 per cent. of people cannot smell it.

he found and how much; the latter will be expressed either as concentrations in the organs he analysed or as a total in the whole body calculated from these figures. He may from his results be able to suggest the mode of ingestion—orally, by inhalation, by injection, etc. He will or should conclude by comparing the amounts he found with the recorded normal and acutely toxic tissue levels of the compound(s) in question.

II. CLASSIFICATION

To return to the analysis, in order to make the mass of factual information in this field manageable, some system of classification is essential. Poisons were once classified as animal, vegetable or mineral. A more sophisticated method was based on their mode of action—corrosive, irritant, narcotic and so forth. However, whatever their immediate effects, the action of many, if not most, poisons is ultimately the same: whether they affect primarily the heart, or the respiratory centre, or the oxygen capacity of the blood, or the tissue enzymes, their ultimate effect is to withhold from the tissues the oxygen necessary for the continuance of life.

For this reason classification tends nowadays to be severely practical. Modern textbooks of clinical toxicology therefore classify not poisons but symptoms, since it is on the basis of these that the clinician must decide what to do to save his patient. The chemical toxicologist, on the other hand, although as already mentioned he is helped by a knowledge of what the symptoms were, is primarily concerned with methods of analysis. These may be grouped (following Dr. A. S. Curry) according to the type of specimen being analysed, but it has long been customary, and is more illuminating in the present context, rather to group the poisons themselves according to the methods used for their extraction. On that basis there are, broadly speaking, five groups:

(1) Gases and vapours.

(2) Poisons, mostly liquids, separable by distillation or steam-distillation.

(3) Water-soluble substances, mostly anions (see Glossary), which are neither volatile nor soluble in organic solvents but are separable in many cases by dialysis (see Glossary).

(4) Poisonous elements, mainly metallic, not included in (2).

(5) Organic compounds, mostly solids, more soluble in organic solvents than in water and hence separable by extraction with these.

Group (1) is rather the "odd man out," and will be left until we have dealt with the others, which we shall do in the above order. The toxicologist must of course be prepared to encounter *any* poison—and there are hundreds, even thousands, of possible ones—but carbon monoxide from town gas,* aspirin and the barbiturates were for long, in this country at least, at the top of this sinister league table, although the order is now changing.

It is not theoretically impossible to analyse one sample for all of the last four

* See footnote on p. 122.

groups listed above, by performing the separation in the order: steam distillation; dialysis; solvent extraction; analysis for poisonous metals. There are, however, serious practical objections to this: the large amounts of reagents and liquids used in the earlier stages would make the sample inconveniently bulky and dilute in the later ones; also, even although the reagents are (or should be) the purest obtainable, they may contain traces of the very substances which are being sought in subsequent stages.

It is therefore usual to divide each sample into several portions, one for each group of poisons being sought (although it is unobjectionable and sometimes convenient to use for further tests, especially dialysis, a portion which has already been steam-distilled). The first step is to weigh the material. The next, if it is a solid organ, is to reduce it, or an aliquot of it, to a finely comminuted slurry, so that the process of extraction may be rapid and complete. An ordinary mincing machine can be used for this, but a power-driven "blender" is vastly cleaner and more efficient.

The conditions of extraction for groups 2, 3 and 5 above must be adjusted according to whether the poison is neutral (non-ionic), acidic or basic. In general, acids and bases will be present as salts, from which they must be liberated before isolation; control of the pH is therefore important.

Assuming that a complete analysis is necessary, the conventional toxicologist will arrange his work something like this:

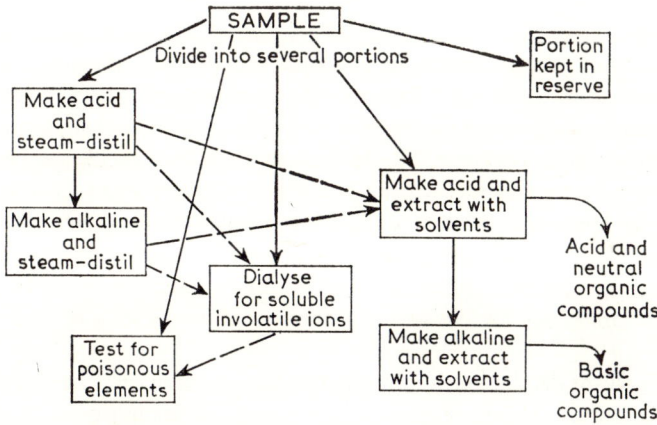

The dotted arrows show possible procedures when economy of the available material is important.

III. VOLATILE AND DIALYSABLE POISONS; POISONOUS ELEMENTS

Volatile poisons. This group comprises a large number of chemically diverse substances, of which some of the most important are:

Hydrocyanic (prussic) acid, and cyanides after liberation of the free acid
Chlorinated organic solvents, such as chloroform, carbon tetrachloride (Thaw-

pit), trichlorethylene, etc. which are used domestically and industrially for cleaning and de-greasing

Benzene, and its industrially important derivatives (*e.g.* nitrobenzene, aniline); these are much more poisonous than is generally realised

Phenols—*e.g.* phenol itself (carbolic acid) and the cresols in lysol; used as disinfectants

Alcohols such as methanol (methyl alcohol, wood alcohol; about five times more poisonous than ethanol), ethylene glycol (anti-freeze), methyl pentynol (the drug Oblivon)

Aldehydes, some of which are used as drugs (*e.g.* chloral, paraldehyde)

Some essential oils—*e.g.* methyl salicylate (oil of wintergreen)

Some agricultural pesticides (*e.g.* Parathion—see p. 117)

Yellow phosphorus (a "classic" poison)

Nicotine (the poisonous alkaloid in tobacco; used in gardeners' pesticides)

The traditional method of separating these and other similar compounds is by steam distillation: they will collect in the water condensed from a current of steam blown through a hot slurry of the material under examination. For chemically neutral compounds, such as alcohols and chlorinated organic solvents, the pH of the slurry is unimportant; to liberate acid compounds such as hydrocyanic acid or phenols, the slurry must be acidified with a non-volatile acid such as sulphuric or tartaric; for basic compounds such as nicotine it must be made alkaline.

The amount of poison recoverable by distillation depends of course on how it was ingested and on its toxicity. Compounds such as benzene or the chlorinated hydrocarbons are likely to be recovered in this way in identifiable quantities only if the liquid has been swallowed; in the commoner case of accidental poisoning by their vapours, the analysis will be as for poisoning by a gas (p. 120). And, obviously, the more toxic the compound the less is likely to be present and therefore recoverable. The toxicities of the above substances vary widely, the probable lethal dose ranging from more than 50 grams for the least poisonous to as little as about 60 milligrams for the very poisonous such as nicotine or hydrocyanic acid.

Although steam distillation is still often necessary, or at least used, for many of these compounds there are now sensitive tests employing quicker and less cumbrous procedures. For a simple screening test, diffusion of the vapour at room temperature inside a closed vessel into a suitable reagent will be adequate. And the modern toxicologist will certainly make use of gas chromatography (p. 65); he may steam-distil first, or he may simply use air withdrawn from above the specimen in a closed vessel, or he may even inject a sample of urine directly on to the GC column. However used, GC will both separate the poison and identify it by its retention time (p. 66) when using a particular column and operating conditions.

Phosphorus presents rather a special case. It is one of the few solid poisons separable by distillation. It was formerly (but is no longer) freely available in this country as a constituent of a popular rat poison, and was used in several rather notorious homicidal poisonings. It is extremely poisonous, a lethal dose being possibly as little as 100 milligrams. However, as it is rapidly oxidised by contact with air to phosphate, and as phosphates are normal constituents of the body, it is effectively undetectable once it has become oxidised. Special precautions, such as distillation in a current of inert gas, may therefore be necessary in looking for it. It is most simply detected by the old *Mischterlich* test: steam in which it is present becomes luminous in contact with air. For quantitative determination, it is collected in the distillate and determined after oxidation to phosphate. Somewhat similar methods are also used for the phosphorus compound zinc phosphide, a rodenticide.

A few special points in connection with other volatile poisons are mentioned on p. 119.

Dialysable poisons. Most poisonous anions are neither volatile in steam nor soluble in organic solvents, and must be isolated by dialysis. They include: bromate (used in hair tinting), chlorate (used as a weed killer), chromate, fluoracetate (a deadly rodenticide), fluoride, nitrite (used in meat curing), oxalate. Dialysis is most conveniently performed through a cellophane bag kept rotating in distilled water. It is usual to dialyse first from neutral solution, as the salts of most of these anions are soluble, then to acidify in order to liberate the anions from insoluble salts, and dialyse again.

Apart from fluoracetates, which are extremely poisonous, none of the anions in the above list is a particularly potent poison, but soluble fluorides and oxalates are both dangerous; anything over 1–2 grams of the former or 3–5 grams of the latter is likely to be fatal.

Iron salts may also be included in this group, in the unfortunately too frequent case of a young child having swallowed iron-tonic tablets. The resemblance of these to sweets gives them a dangerous fascination, and the iron salts they contain act as a powerful irritant poison to young children. In such a case, iron will probably be separable by dialysis from acidified stomach or intestinal contents.

Another anion which should be included in this group, although it is not normally separable by dialysis, is borate. Boric acid and borates, although not very toxic, are more so than is commonly realised, and fatal poisoning of children by the former is not unknown. There are several specific tests for boron compounds; they are most simply determined after ashing the sample in presence of excess alkali. This latter technique is also convenient for some of the other anions considered here (*e.g.* fluoride).

Poisonous elements. The elements which are inherently poisonous in any soluble state of combination are practically all metals or metalloids, and the whole group is therefore commonly referred to simply as "the heavy metals." Its most poisonous members are: antimony, arsenic, barium, beryllium, cadmium, lead, mercury and thallium. Soluble salts of several other metals can also however cause poisoning: for example, bismuth, copper, manganese, silver, tin and zinc.

Compounds of these elements which are completely insoluble, such as calomel (mercurous chloride) and barium sulphate (given as a "barium meal") are usually however non-poisonous.

The detection of most of these elements is the simplest problem of toxicology. A useful "omnibus" test which is commonly performed first is the *Reinsch* test. A piece of clean copper foil is boiled in a hydrochloric-acid slurry of the specimen; if arsenic, antimony, bismuth, mercury or silver are present, they will be deposited on it as a black or grey stain, and can be identified by several methods. The next step is the complete destruction of all the organic matter so as to leave a solution containing only salts of the metals present. Various methods for doing so have been used, but the oldest and probably still the most popular is to use a boiling mixture of concentrated nitric and sulphuric acids ("wet combustion"). If volatile elements such as mercury are known to be absent, the tedium of watching a wet combustion in case it boils over can be avoided simply by ashing the material and extracting the ash with acid. A modern method of doing so, which minimises the risk of losses, is to use radio-frequency heating at a low temperature in an atmosphere of pure oxygen.

The identification and determination of the metals present in the final solution is a matter of straightforward chemical analysis, and can be done in various ways. A series of the appropriate spot tests may be done. The Reinsch test may have indicated what is to be looked for. Conventional inorganic analysis, precipitating many of the metals as their sulphides, may be used. The sulphuric acid left from the wet combustion may be fumed down to a small volume and converted into ammonium sulphate, which is then examined spectrographically. All of the poisonous metals can be separated by paper chromatography. The method used for their determination when identified will depend on the metal, but the most popular and convenient nowadays is atomic absorption spectroscopy (p. 71). If the equipment for this is not available, the toxicologist will probably make use of that versatile reagent diphenylthiocarbazone ("dithizone"). This, although it offers traps for the unwary and demands care and skill in its use, can be used for the spectrophotometric determination of a number of different metals by adjustment of the pH.

Arsenic, and to a lesser degree lead, are of course classic poisons. (Perhaps, after a recent sensational English case, thallium should be added to these!) The notorious *aqua Tofana* from Sicily is believed to have been based on arsenic. The poisonous properties of lead have also been known for a very long time; when Pope Clement II died in 1047 A.D. contemporary rumour had it that he had been poisoned, and a recent German analysis of portions of bone from his mummified body has somewhat belatedly justified the rumour by showing that he almost certainly died of lead poisoning. Both arsenic and lead when administered over a long period are deposited in particular parts of the body—arsenic in the hair and nails and lead in the bones; the toxicologist may therefore demand specimens of these in addition to the usual viscera etc.

Many methods for the detection and estimation of arsenic have been developed, of which the *Marsh* (or *Marsh-Bezelius*) and the *Gutzeit* tests are the best known. The former is a favourite of detective-story writers, but is hardly ever used now, since the latter is less troublesome and even more sensitive, being able to detect less than a microgram. Both tests utilise the reduction of the arsenic to arsine (AsH_3) by nascent hydrogen, and in the *Gutzeit* the arsine is passed through a reagent-impregnated filter paper to produce a stain the depth of which is proportional to the amount of arsenic. Small amounts of arsenic can also be conveniently determined colorimetrically.

The deposition of arsenic in the hair mentioned above can form the basis of a useful "calendar" in chronic poisoning; if we can discover how far along the hair the arsenic has reached, we can know when it was taken, since hair grows at a fairly constant and uniform rate ($\frac{1}{3}$ to $\frac{1}{2}$ an inch a month). This can be done by the analysis of successive short (say half-inch) lengths from a bundle of hairs aligned with their roots together. If purely chemical methods are used for this, several thousand hairs are necessary, the alignment of which is extremely tedious, even if that number is available. This task has now been made much easier by radio-chemical activation analysis (p. 80), with which 50–100 hairs are enough. This was the method used in the analysis some years ago of Napoleon I's hair which showed that its arsenic content was about thirteen times the normal average and thereby supported the theory, formed on other grounds, that he had in fact died of arsenical poisoning and not, as had been supposed, of cancer. Activation can also be used rather elegantly to locate the arsenic in a specimen consisting of only one or two hairs, by auto-radiography of the irradiated hair with a piece of photographic or X-ray film, the section containing the arsenic printing much darker than the rest.

Lead is practically never encountered nowadays as a homicidal poison, and lead poisoning is usually either a non-fatal occupational hazard or an accident. The paint-gnawing habits of young children are particularly dangerous, and children have died of lead poisoning after eating the supposedly lead-free paint off their cot sides.

IV. INVOLATILE ORGANIC POISONS

This group is nowadays by far the largest and most important, and presents the toxicologist with the most various and complex problems. These arise in four ways:

(1) In the extraction of the poisonous compound;

(2) In the identification of this among the enormous number of compounds which may be encountered;

(3) Because the metabolism of the poison may mean that the compound extracted is not that which was taken;

(4) Because of the natural occurrence in post-mortem material of compounds chemically similar to those which the toxicologist is seeking.

The third and fourth of these heads will be considered in the next section; we shall consider briefly now the first and second.

(1) **Extraction procedures** depend on the fact that the compounds sought are, or can be made to be by a suitable choice of pH, more soluble in some organic solvent than in water. No other method of extraction is possible; drastic methods of destroying the tissue material cannot be used, since they would also destroy the organic poison.

The ideal method would extract *all* of the poison and *none* of the natural tissue constituents. No existing methods do this. A method which recovers more than 80 per cent. of the poison present must be accounted a good one. Also, while it is always possible to purify an extracted poison from co-extracted tissue constituents, some of the poison will almost certainly be lost in this process; a balance must therefore be struck between the most efficient extraction of both poison and impurity and their most effective separation.

A very large number of procedures have been devised. They may be classified as follows (for which the writer is much indebted to a recent critical survey by Dr. S. K. Niyogi):

(*a*) The classical *Stas-Otto* method (now over 100 years old) and its modifications. In this the minced organ is mixed and warmed with the extracting solvent, usually hot acidified alcohol, in which most organic poisons are readily soluble but fats, proteins and other tissue constituents comparatively insoluble. Other extractants have also however been tried. This method is now rarely used; it is extremely tedious, and elaborate subsequent purification is necessary. It appears to be generally agreed that the method will extract an identifiable amount of practically any organic poison but that extraction is never complete.

(*b*) Methods depending on *precipitation* and removal by filtration of the tissue proteins, with subsequent extraction of the poison from the aqueous filtrate. Many precipitants have been tried, of which trichloracetic acid, ammonium sulphate (*Nickolls-Daubney*), tungstic acid (*Valov*) and aluminium chloride are probably the most successful. Extraction may be done either by repeated shaking with the chosen solvent at the appropriate pH, or in a continuous-extraction apparatus as in (*c*) below.

(*c*) *Direct-extraction* methods. It is a standard procedure to solvent-extract blood specimens directly for screening tests, and direct *continuous* extraction methods for minced organs have also been devised. These recycle the distilled and condensed extracting solvent through the material under examination, whereby the poison is gradually removed from this and concentrated in the boiling solvent. This may also be done under reduced pressure (*Curry*), thereby lowering the boiling point of the solvent and minimising the risk of destroying heat-labile poisons. Continuous extraction can also be applied, using an immiscible solvent such as chloroform, to an aqueous extract prepared as in (*b*) above.

(*d*) *Adsorption* methods. In these the poison is preferentially removed from urine or an aqueous solution by a suitable adsorbent (for example, activated charcoal, fuller's earth or an ion-exchange resin) and subsequently re-extracted from this by solvent elution. These methods have not however proved very successful.

(e) *Dry-extraction* methods. In these the water is removed by freezing the material in liquid air or by grinding it with a dehydrant such as plaster of Paris or anhydrous sodium sulphate; the frozen or ground-up mass is then pulverised and solvent-extracted.

The toxicologist will choose whichever method seems to him most suitable for whatever he is examining, but the most frequently used methods are probably those classifiable under (b) or (c).

Some success has also been achieved in the *automation* of the extraction stage. Automatic equipment which will work unattended for long periods has been developed for the routine screening of large numbers of urine specimens for a variety of drugs. Using the principles of extraction described above, it will detect, for example, the barbiturates excreted by persons on maintenance therapeutic doses, or the morphine excreted by addicts. The extracted compounds can subsequently be identified and determined non-automatically, or, if their identity is known, determined automatically as part of the process.

At all extraction and separation stages control of the pH is vital. This is because most organic compounds are more soluble in organic solvents than in water, whereas if they are acids or bases their salts are more soluble in water. The standard procedure, therefore, assuming an aqueous solution to start with, is: make the solution acid, and extract with a suitable solvent (*e.g.* ether), which removes acid and neutral compounds but leaves basic ones in the water layer as salts; extract the solvent with aqueous solutions, first of a weak alkali (sodium bicarbonate) to remove strong acids, and then of a strong alkali (sodium hydroxide) to remove weak acids, the neutral compounds remaining in the solvent; finally, make the original aqueous solution alkaline (usually with ammonia) and solvent-extract bases from it. If the extracted poison is a solid, it may finally be purified after evaporation of the solvent by the old but still useful technique of sublimation in a vacuum on to a cooled surface.

(2) For the **identification** and **determination** of the extracted poison it used to be necessary to extract at least a visible quantity for testing; this, thanks to the various modern methods of analysis described in Chapter 8, is no longer the case. Their use also means that time can be saved by working with smaller quantities of material.

Needless to say, when in a fatal poisoning case there are available tablets or the like which the deceased is believed to have taken, the toxicologist's first task must be to identify these. Chemically, this should be a simple task, since sufficient pure material will normally be available, but the enormous number of pharmaceutical preparations on the market may make it quite a difficult one. This topic will be dealt with briefly on p. 125.

How the isolated poison is identified will depend on what it is, the experience and preferences of the toxicologist and the equipment available to him. Traditionally, he used colour spot tests, micro-crystalline forms and melting-point determinations; nowadays, though he may use some or all of these, he will probably rely routinely on infra-red or ultra-violet spectrometry, gas chromatography or thin-layer chromatography followed by colour tests on the spots. For the final step, the determination of the amount of the poison, he used frequently to purify and weigh it; now he will probably use quantitative colorimetric or spectrophotometric measurements.

At the time of writing, however, this part of toxicology is in a state of incipient revolution because of the new methods which have arrived or seem about to do so or are looming over the horizon. Mass spectrometry (p. 76) is making a take-over bid that will be hard to resist. Some new analytical methods take advantage of the high specificity and sensitivity of enzyme assays. Some rather esoteric research techniques such as electron-spin resonance are finding toxicological application. Possibly the most revolutionary development, however, is *radio-immuno assay*. This makes use of the very great specificity of immunological reactions (see p. 134) in what has hitherto been the chemist's undisputed domain. Its general principle is as follows. A specific antibody to the drug, or (if the drug itself is not antigenic) to a compound of the drug with a suitable antigen, is first prepared by animal injection. A measured small amount of serum containing the antibody is then reacted with a radioactively labelled preparation of the drug (that is, one in which one of the constituent atoms has been replaced by an artificial radioactive isotope) and the amount of radioactivity so bound by the antigen-antibody reaction is measured by the intensity of the radiation emitted. The test is then repeated using a mixture of the radioactive drug and the toxicological extract; if the normal (non-radioactive) form of the drug is contained in this, it will compete with the radioactive for antibody reacting sites. The intensity of the bound radioactivity will then be reduced if the drug is present in the extract, and the amount by which it is reduced measures the amount of the drug. The method has proved valuable for drugs difficult or impossible to identify by purely chemical means, a few examples of which will be mentioned in their places.

Organic poisons used to be classified by toxicologists as acid, neutral and basic, according to their conditions of extraction, as described above. However, as this is not a textbook of toxicology, it will probably be more informative to deal briefly with them here grouped according to their origins and uses.

Analgesics. The most important member of this class, aspirin (acetyl salicylic acid), is the most extensively used drug in the whole pharmacopoeia, and was for long, after the barbiturates, the most commonly encountered organic poison. It is also the only strongly acid compound likely to occur. The lethal dose for an adult is very large—perhaps 30–60 5-grain tablets—but it is much more dangerous to children, who are fatally poisoned by it with distressing frequency. Its identification in fatal cases will be easy, because its low toxicity means that plenty will be recovered. However, after ingestion it quickly loses the acetyl part of its molecule, so that part or even most of that ingested will be recovered as the simpler parent compound salicylic acid.

Other analgesics sometimes encountered include paracetamol (*N*-acetyl-*p*-

aminophenol; weakly acid, but extraction complicated by protein-binding—see p. 119) and phenacetin (neutral). Their toxicity is about the same as that of aspirin. Phenacetin has however been shown to cause kidney damage if taken regularly, and is therefore much less used than formerly.

Hypnotics and sedatives. By far the most important members of this group, and in fact the most important single class of poisons at the present time, are the barbiturates (weak acids). Although obtainable only on prescription, they are dispensed in vast quantities as "sleeping pills" in our nerve-ridden age (several hundred tons per annum in Great Britain alone, for example). The minimum fatal dose is probably around 10–15 times the therapeutic dose, but suicides are commonly found to have taken much more.

The parent compound, barbituric acid, has the chemical formula

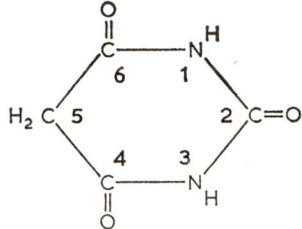

the numbers inside the ring referring to the positions at which other chemical groupings (radicals) may be added to the molecule. The barbiturates are a group of drugs formed by "ringing the changes" on that molecule. In a few, one of the hydrogen atoms at positions 1 or 3 is replaced by something else, and in the thiobarbiturates (mainly used as intravenous anaesthetics) the oxygen atom at position 2 is replaced by sulphur. However, in all of the common barbiturates used as ordinary soporifics, the two hydrogen atoms at position 5 have simply been replaced by the same or different radicals. In the original barbiturate, barbitone or Veronal, now seldom encountered, the substituents were two ethyl radicals. Among the commonest in Britain today are:

(1) phenobarbitone (Luminal) one ethyl, one phenyl radical
(2) amylobarbitone (Amytal) one ethyl, one *iso*-amyl radical
(3) butobarbitone (Soneryl) one ethyl, one *n*-butyl radical
(4) pentobarbitone (Nembutal) one ethyl, one methyl-butyl radical
(5) quinalbarbitone (Seconal) one methyl-butyl, one allyl radical.

In American usage the name ending "-al" is used instead of "-one": phenobarbital, amylobarbital, etc.

Barbitone and phenobarbitone act and are metabolised slowly and are excreted unchanged (barbitone) or largely unchanged (phenobarbitone); pentobarbitone and quinalbarbitone act and are metabolised quickly; amylobarbitone and butobarbitone are intermediate in both respects. In a death from a rapid-acting barbiturate, therefore, especially if the deceased had lived for some time after taking it, very little of the unchanged compound may be left in the body.

We are still more ignorant than we would like of the full details of barbiturate metabolism, but it is known that the first stage is hydroxylation (replacement of hydrogen atoms by –OH groups); although the resultant hydroxy-substituted compounds are in themselves easily identifiable, they are much more soluble in water than the parent compounds, hence may not be extracted completely or at all by the usual solvents.

However, with the barbiturates more is known than with most other drugs about the significance of the tissue levels found. The probable lethal levels for the different types are well established, and in non-fatal cases the time for which the victim will remain in a coma can be predicted from the blood level. As the liver is the site of barbiturate breakdown and detoxication, the highest concentration is normally found in that organ. It has also been shown that in many cases the magnitude of the ratio $\dfrac{\text{liver concentration}}{\text{blood concentration}}$ is a guide to the length of time between ingestion and death. The danger of taking alcohol and a barbiturate together is (or should be) well known. In many fatal cases, less than individually lethal amounts of either are found, and they may even potentiate each other's action. Some recently reported Canadian animal experiments suggest that alcohol may inhibit barbiturate metabolism.

Numerous analytical tests for barbiturates have been proposed and used. Their behaviour in paper and thin-layer chromatography is well documented. They are perhaps most commonly identified today by their retention times on a heated gas-chromatographic column and/or the characteristic changes in their ultra-violet absorption spectra as the pH of the solution is changed from alkaline to acid. The absorbency at the ultra-violet peak is also used for quantitative determination.

Apart from the morphine derivatives and substitutes which may be used as hypnotics (see p. 124), most of the other hypnotics and sedatives will be present in the neutral extract. These are less toxic than the barbiturates, but a sufficient overdose of any can kill. They include: chloral hydrate (an old but still used sedative; lethal dose perhaps about, say, 10 grams); bromvaletone and carbromal (both among the relatively few organic drugs which are bromine compounds; about as toxic as chloral hydrate); glutethamide (sold under about a dozen proprietary names throughout the world). The more recently introduced methaqualone will, unlike those just mentioned, be extracted from alkaline solution; it is the most important ingredient of the proprietary *Mandrax*, and as such a fairly common drug of abuse.

Tranquillisers, Anti-depressants and Anti-histamines. These are all types of synthetic drugs which have proliferated enormously in recent years and are now freely prescribed; many of the first two types are used in psychiatry. Though none is highly toxic, all can be dangerous and some lethal in an overdose. The danger is also well known of taking certain anti-depressants with some other drugs, or with foods such as cheese rich in the amino-acid tyramine.

With the exception of the tranquilliser meprobamate, which is a neutral carbamate (one of a class of compounds related to urea), most of these compounds are basic, and many are derivatives of the compound phenothiazine:

Phenothiazine derivatives are a notorious headache to the toxicologist, being rather firmly bound to tissue protein and therefore difficult or impossible to extract by the usual methods (see p. 119). The nomenclature of these types of compounds is also rather a jungle. The following are those probably most commonly encountered in Britain.

Type of drug	"Trivial" (i.e. accepted pharmaceutical) name	Full chemical name of base	Some proprietary names
tranquilliser	chlorpromazine	2-chloro-10-(3-dimethylamino-propyl)phenothiazine	Largactil (U.K.) Thorazine (U.S.A.)
tranquilliser	chlordiazoepoxide	7-chloro-2-methylamino-5-phenyl 3H-1,4-benzodiazepine 4-oxide	Librium
tranquilliser	diazepam	7-chloro-2,3-dihydro-1-methyl-5-phenyl-1H-1,4-benzodiazepine-2-one	Valium
anti-depressant	imipramine	1-(3-dimethylaminopropyl)-4,5-dihydro-2,3:6,7-dibenzazepine	Tofranil
anti-depressant	amitriptyline	3-(3-dimethylaminopropylidene)-1,2:4,5-dibenzocyclohepta-1,4-diene	Triptafen (U.K.) Elavil (U.S.A.)
anti-depressant	phenelzine	phenylethylhydrazine	Nardil
anti-histamine	promezathine	10-(2-dimethylaminopropyl)-phenothiazine	Phenergan
anti-histamine	antazoline	2-(N-benzylanilinomethyl)-imidazoline	Antistin

Several different types of drugs may loosely be classified as **stimulants**. The most important in the present context are amphetamine and its isomers and derivatives (all basic). Amphetamine itself is the racemic form of an optically active compound (see Glossary), but only the *dextro* isomer is physiologically active; hence this by itself (dexamphetamine) is twice as potent as amphetamine.

They are very rarely encountered as lethal poisons, but are notoriously abused drugs (see p. 124) and may therefore be sought in urine specimens. They are most simply identified by thin-layer or gas chromatography, if necessary after conversion into suitable derivatives.

Another stimulant which may be mentioned is nikethamide (*Coramine*), used as a respiratory stimulant. It is a neutral compound, but may also be extracted as a basic one. No fatal poisonings by it have been recorded, but it may be extracted and have to be identified by the toxicologist if it had been administered shortly before death in an attempt to save life.

Alkaloids are complex basic nitrogenous compounds occurring naturally in plants and fungi. They are the "classic" organic poisons, being almost the only ones likely to be encountered before the days of synthetic drugs. Many hundreds have been isolated; a few of the best known are: *morphine* and *codeine* from opium; *strychnine* from *nux vomica* (the seeds of an East Indian tree); *nicotine* from tobacco; *quinine* from the South American cinchona bark; *cocaine* from the leaves of another South American tree; *atropine* from belladonna (deadly nightshade); *coniine* from hemlock (Socrates' poison); *aconitine* from monkshood root; *ergotoxine* and several other related alkaloids from ergot (a fungus parasitic on rye). Nicotine and coniine, unlike nearly all other alkaloids, are liquids (see p. 106).

All alkaloids are physiologically active and some are intensely poisonous. Even quinine, taken in large doses as an anti-malarial, can be lethal; deaths have been caused by women taking large doses of it (several grams) in an attempt to abort. At the other extreme, the fatal dose of strychnine may be as low as 30–60 milligrams, and of aconitine (possible the most deadly natural poison known) 2–5 milligrams.

The high toxicity of many alkaloids means that the amounts extracted in a poisoning case will be very small. Traditionally, the toxicologist looking for an alkaloid did a Stas-Otto extraction (p. 110) and tested his purified extract, first using a series of reagents known to produce colours or precipitates with all alkaloids, and secondly with specific reagents giving characteristic colours with individual alkaloids. Nowadays alkaloids will usually be identified by paper or thin-layer (sometimes even gas) chromatography, followed by colour tests or infra-red spectrometry.

Morphine is rather a special case, if only because opium has acquired such an extensive literature, from classical times down to de Quincey and Wilkie Collins. It is still, unlike most formerly popular vegetable drugs, used extensively in medicine in treating pain, although heroin (diamorphine—p. 124) is even more effective in this respect. It is chemically almost unique among the alkaloids in that its molecule contains a weakly acid phenolic group as well as a basic nitrogenous one; it is not therefore extractable from strongly alkaline solution, which is why a weak alkali (ammonia) is used in the routine extraction of basic compounds (p. 111). It also appears to be concentrated during excretion in the bile, which is why that fluid may be submitted for analysis (p. 103).

Glycosides are also a class of naturally occurring plant substances, in which a sugar is linked with another, usually alcoholic or phenolic, compound. They are themselves mostly rather insoluble, but are easily hydrolysed by enzymes also present in the plants to liberate the non-sugar parts of their molecules, many of which are rather poisonous. For example, plum and other soft-fruit kernels contain the glycoside amygdalin, from which hydrocyanic acid among other products is liberated. The glycosides most likely to be encountered by the toxicologist are however those of digitalis (foxglove) used as heart stimulants. The principle glycoside in digitalis itself is called digitoxin; the less toxic and more commonly used digoxin comes from a closely allied species. They are potent drugs, and an overdose can be lethal, especially to children. They are best sought as neutral compounds in the urine. They are not however easy to identify chemically; a bio-assay may help, but a recently developed method of radio-immuno assaying (p. 112) is likely to prove the best yet.

Pesticides have been encountered as accidental, suicidal and homicidal poisons. In the present context their only common feature is toxicity; chemically they are a most diverse group. Phosphorus and the fluoracetates have already been mentioned (pp. 106, 107). The organic pesticides (all extractable as neutral compounds) may be divided into: coumarin derivatives used as rat poison (*Warfarin*) and medicinally as anti-coagulants; chlorinated benzene derivatives such as dicophane (DDT), aldrin, dieldrin, benzene hexachloride (*Gammexane*), paraquat, etc., few highly toxic to Man but some (*e.g.* paraquat) liable to kill; the extremely poisonous organo-phosphorus insecticides. Chemically the last are esters of substituted phosphoric acids. *Parathion* (O, O-diethyl-O-*p*-nitrophenyl thiophosphate), the most poisonous, may be taken as a type of the whole class; it is said that one drop of the pure compound on the skin could be fatal unless promptly washed off. As already mentioned (p. 106), it may be separated by steam distillation.

However, Parathion and similar compounds may be difficult or impossible to detect after a death caused by a minimal quantity, and the toxicologist must then utilise as a test their physiological action—namely, cholinesterase inhibition. In the living body, traces of the compound acetylcholine are produced at muscle-nerve junctions, and destroyed as fast as they are produced by the enzyme cholinesterase. As acetylcholine is toxic and as organo-phosphorus esters inhibit cholinesterase, their effect is to produce acetylcholine poisoning. An exceptionally low cholinesterase activity of the victim's blood or tissue is therefore presumptive evidence of poisoning by one of these compounds. The activity is measured by measuring the rate at which an acetylcholine substrate is decomposed.

Of the possible organic poisons which do not fall into the above categories we shall mention only one—insulin. This, being a secretion of the pancreas, is a natural constituent of the healthy body, and being a protein it is chemically undetectable. However, the injection of a sufficient amount can kill by drastically reducing the blood-sugar level, and at least two detected murders have been committed in this way, one in this country in 1957 and one in California in 1968. Its detection in the former resulted from what was probably up till then the most elaborate toxicological investigation ever made; after several months' work by a team of specialists it was established that an extract from the neighbourhood of some injection marks on the victim's body had the biological properties, as demonstrated by bio-assays and animal experiments, of insulin and of no other known substance. A radio-immuno assay method (p. 112) for insulin has now been developed which makes its detection much less laborious.

Finally, a rather specialised field of organic-compound toxicology is the investigation of racehorse and dog doping. The detection of trace amounts of drugs in samples of saliva, urine, blood or droppings leads to problems which differ from those of routine toxicology in two respects: the compounds sought— those given to the animal to improve or impair its performance—will be present in minimal quantities, detectable only by a highly skilled analyst; they may occasionally not be "drugs" or "poisons" at all as normally understood, and may in fact be normal body constituents such as steroids (*e.g.* testosterone), which are very difficult to detect or identify.

V. DIFFICULTIES AND SPECIAL CASES

The preceding sections have not, it is to be hoped, created by their inevitable brevity the impression that toxicology consists of the routine application of cut-and-dried procedures. No one knows better than the experienced toxicologist that it is beset with difficulties and possibilities of error. These are broadly speaking of two kinds: those which may lead to a poison present remaining un-detected and those which may produce false positive results.

The first kind crops up in various ways. For a few poisons there just are no chemical tests. One of these—insulin—has already been mentioned. The toxin from the fungus *Amanita phalloides* ("Death Cap") used also to be in this class; there is now a chemical test for it, but this is unlikely to be applied unless there was circumstantial evidence of the fungus having been eaten or remains of it were found in the alimentary tract. There are also a number of substances for which, although chemical tests do exist, physiological ones or bio-assays may be more specific and/or sensitive. For example: traces of atropine may be recognised by their action in dilating the pupils of a cat's eye; cantharides ("Spanish fly"— the poison in a case of homicide in London some years ago) can be presumptively identified by its blistering action on the skin; traces of the cardiac glycosides (p. 117) may be most easily identified by electro-cardiography of an experimental animal to which they have been administered. The water flea (*Daphnia sp.*) has also been suggested as a biological test subject; if its water is poisoned it stops swimming, and it also appears to concentrate certain poisons in its body, which might form the basis of a useful technique of separation.

Some other poisons disappear fairly rapidly from the body and become un-detectable for that reason. The example of phosphorus has already been men-tioned (p. 107). A similar difficulty may arise with the extremely poisonous fluorine compounds used as pesticides; they are metabolised to fluorides in the body, and the lethal dose is so small that the fluoride normally present in all tissues is not increased by a significant amount.

The metabolic fate of poisons is in general a matter of some concern to toxicologists. Many poisons are metabolised to compounds which, though neither body constituents nor undetectable, do not have the same properties as their parent substances and hence are not detected by tests for these. The barbiturate metabolites have already been mentioned (p. 114). To take another, though uncharacteristically simple, example, ethylene glycol (p. 106) is oxidised to oxalic acid, which is itself quite toxic (though for quite different physiological reasons) but requires totally different methods of extraction and detection. However, we still know too little of the metabolic pathways of even the commoner drugs and poisons, and even less of those of the unceasing flood of new ones. In general, the body's method for dealing with harmful substances appears to consist in converting them into more soluble and more rapidly excreted compounds. The first stage in this is often oxidation (*e.g.* ethylene glycol) or hydroxylation (*e.g.* the barbiturates). Many of the more complex poisons, however, are dealt with by *conjugation*—that is, combination with a fairly large, very soluble molecule such as glucose—so that in analysis of urine one must seek the conjugated rather than the original compound. What toxicologists would like to have is a "reference library" of metabolites and their properties, but to establish this a great deal more research is necessary.

The last obstacle to detection that we shall mention is *protein binding*. Many physiologically active compounds (particularly phenothiazine derivatives—p. 115) attach themselves so tightly to blood-plasma and other body proteins that the standard processes of solvent extraction do not remove them. To do so, fairly drastic treatment such as hydrolysis with hot hydrochloric acid is necessary, but this may destroy some other compounds that are being sought. This difficulty can in some cases be avoided by destroying the protein with a suitable enzyme, but it has no universal solution.

The second kind of difficulty—false positives—does not occur in so many guises, but does constitute a trap for the inexperienced. A positive result in a toxicological analysis should mean unambiguously that such-and-such a poison was present and that it was taken by or administered to the victim. Yet, for example, bacterial action in decomposing tissue can produce amounts of cyanide comparable with those found in cases of genuine cyanide poisoning. Another example is a historical one. In a once notorious trial for murder with arsenic, the prosecution's case failed because, although lethal amounts of that element were found in an exhumed body, no one had thought to analyse the soil from around the coffin. When the defence produced evidence that this was highly arsenical (the burial was in an area where this was not unexpected), it could not be excluded as a possible source of the arsenic in the body, and a charge of murder failed. It is nowadays therefore an invariable parctice in any exhumation to take control samples of soil from above, beside and below the coffin.

The analysis of organs from an exhumed body presents indeed several possible sources of confusion. Not only must precautions against misleading contamination be taken, but also the length of time after burial for which a poison will remain detectable varies greatly with the poison and the circumstances. Poisons such as arsenic or lead will persist practically indefinitely in dry conditions (although it is not impossible that water might leach them out). Some organic poisons may disappear within months or even weeks, while others (*e.g.* strychnine) are very stable and may remain detectable for years. Even as easily destructible a poison as phosphorus may remain detectable for quite a lengthy period in organs which protect it from oxidation. In a poison murder in the north of England some years ago, for example, lethal amounts of it were detected in two bodies which had been buried for three and two months respectively.

However, what is perhaps the greatest difficulty here, particularly when the victim has been dead some time, is caused by the production during putrefaction of a variety of compounds which are extracted in the routine search for poisonous ones. Substances such as *p*-hydroxybenzaldehyde and related compounds— derived whence no one yet knows—may be found in the weak acid (barbiturate etc.) fraction. Many basic nitrogenous compounds are also formed by the decomposition of proteins. Some of these were formerly known by the now obsolete name "ptomaines," and they were liable to be mistaken for alkaloids when using the comparatively imprecise tests which formerly had to be relied upon. However, this mistake should never now occur, better tests being available and the properties of these bases having been thoroughly investigated.

VI. GASES AND VAPOURS

Poisoning may also occur by inhalation of a gas or of the vapour of a volatile liquid; examples of the latter were given on pp. 105–106. In either case, none of the methods of analysis so far described is applicable. Deaths occur in industry from the accidental liberation of gases such as chlorine or ammonia. Poisoning by hydrogen sulphide (H_2S, sulphuretted hydrogen) is an occupational hazard of sewer workers. (H_2S is a much more poisonous gas than is commonly realised; it is stated that 0·1 per cent. in air will cause rapid unconsciousness and be fatal unless the victim is treated at once.) Accidental, suicidal or even homicidal poisonings with anaesthetics and the vapours of dry-cleaning agents, paint thinners, industrial solvents, etc. are also always liable to be encountered. Of all the compounds in these classes, the most important are possibly the chlorinated hydrocarbons—chloroform, carbon tetrachloride (Thawpit), trichlorethylene and several others.

Toxic doses of some of these compounds produce characteristic post-mortem effects—for example, chlorine produces pulmonary oedema and H_2S alters the blood haemoglobin—and the appearance of such effects may be diagnostic. However, until the development of gas chromatography the toxicological detection of an inhaled poison was a problem which was at least formidable and too often insoluble. Now, thanks to that powerful tool it presents no special difficulties. It may be sufficient to inject into the gas-chromatographic column a few millilitres of air withdrawn from a closed vessel containing blood, brain or (if available) lungs. The test is made more sensitive (*Curry*) if the blood is saturated with potassium carbonate and warmed. Mass spectrometry (p. 76) appears also to have considerable potentialities here.

What is possibly still the commonest gaseous poison is carbon monoxide, CO. It was for long the commonest poison of any type, but (as far at least as Great Britain is concerned) the introduction of non-poisonous natural North Sea gas ⋆ is greatly reducing the number of accidental poisonings and making gas-oven suicides impossible. Carbon monoxide is not excessively poisonous as poisonous gases go; it is dangerous because it is insidious and odourless. It owes its toxicity to the fact that its affinity for haemoglobin (the oxygen-carrying pigment of the blood) is about 250–300 times greater than that of oxygen. Hence the continued breathing of air containing more than a very small concentration of CO will convert so much of the haemoglobin to carboxyhaemoglobin that the blood can no longer carry enough oxygen to support life, and death from anoxia results.

The amount of CO in blood is generally expressed as a "percentage" (more accurately, a percentage saturation), the figure signifying the extent to which the available haemoglobin has been converted to carboxyhaemoglobin. Under 5–10 per cent. will be unnoticeable in a normally fit person and a figure of this order may be found in a heavy smoker; 25–30 per cent. may prove fatal to a person who is old, weak or has heart trouble; a healthy young adult might survive up to about 70–80 per cent. The final percentage saturation reached (which may take some time with low CO concentrations) will then determine the effect of any given concentration, and any concentration will be dangerous the breathing of which ultimately produces a percentage saturation seriously affecting the individual in question.

(An interesting fact which has recently been discovered by D. J. Blackmore at the Home Office Central Research Establishment is that CO is apparently taken up more readily by some red cells than by others; at low saturations a few cells initially contain all the carboxyhaemoglobin, and as the saturation increases so does the proportion of carboxylated cells. Once absorption has ceased, however, the CO is then gradually redistributed among all the cells.)

The toxicity of air containing carbon monoxide therefore depends on how long it is breathed, the CO concentration and (as mentioned above) the individual breathing it. As far as the first two factors are concerned, approximate figures for an average healthy adult are shown in the table on page 122.

In fact, the relationship holds roughly that, for a given degree of poisoning to be produced:

$$\text{concentration} \times \text{time of exposure} = \text{constant}$$

For the effect to be just lethal, if the concentration is expressed in parts per million and the time in hours, the constant in the above equation will be about 2,000. (This will not apply with very low concentrations breathable almost indefinitely without serious effects, or for very high, very quickly fatal, concentra-

⋆ See footnote on p. 122.

tions.) A knowledge of figures such as these may be of practical importance in the investigation of poisoning or suspected poisoning by CO produced in incomplete combustion (see below).

Carbon monoxide forms up to about 10–20 per cent. of manufactured town gas,* up to 6 per cent. of car exhaust gases, and is produced in small amounts when any carbon compound (coke, town gas, Calor gas, paraffin) burns with an inadequate supply of air. This may happen when, for example: there is an inadequate flue in a bathroom geyser; a gas or paraffin heater is allowed to burn for a long time in a small unventilated space; a sleepy smoker accidentally sets his bedding or the upholstery of his chair on fire, and this smoulders for a long time (possibly hours).

Proportion of Carbon monoxide in air		
Per cent	Parts per million	Effect
0·01	100	None appreciable in several hours.
0·1	1,000	Unpleasant symptoms after 1 hour; possibly fatal overnight.
0·2	2,000	Dangerous after 1 hour; fatal in several hours.
0·4	4,000	Fatal in less than 1 hour.
1·0 or over	10,000	Immediate unconsciousness and death within a few minutes.

Carbon-monoxide poisoning by town gas or exhaust gases may be accidental, suicidal or homicidal, but that through incomplete combustion is nearly always accidental. Its investigation requires (1) the detection and determination of CO in the victim's blood, and, when it is due or thought to be due to incomplete combustion, (2) experimental confirmation if possible that CO has been produced and determination of the concentration.

The methods which have been used for the determination of carbon monoxide in blood would fill a book. Some are accurate only in the hands of those with much practice in them, and some do not work with old or partially decomposed blood. The most useful may be broadly classified as optical, chemical or a combination of the two. The optical methods utilise the fact that the absorption spectra of both oxyhaemoglobin and carboxyhaemoglobin show similar sharp bands in the yellow/green about the same distance apart, but that these lie nearer the blue end of the spectrum in the carboxy than in the oxy spectrum (fig. 28). (That is why carboxy- is markedly pink compared with oxyhaemoglobin.) The distance by which the bands are displaced from the oxy position depends nearly linearly on the percentage carboxy saturation, and forms therefore a convenient means of measuring this. In the *Hartridge reversion spectroscope* an ingenious

* "Town gas" is a better term than "coal gas," since much of the gas still manufactured is not produced by the direct gasification of coal. The present tendency is for the figure quoted to be reduced, even in manufactured gas; it will of course drop to nothing when only natural (North Sea, in the case of this country) gas is used everywhere.

optical device shows the two spectra side by side, one reversed with respect to the other, and the displacement necessary to bring them into coincidence is a measure of the percentage saturation. It is a quick and convenient instrument, but measurements by it are not accurate to better than about ± 5–10 per cent. saturation, and it may be considered almost obsolete. The difference between the oxy- and the carboxyhaemoglobin absorbencies at particular wavelengths may also be utilised.

Chemical methods rely mostly on liberation of the CO from a measured volume of blood by a suitable reagent, and determination of this, either purely chemically with a reagent such as palladium chloride, or by gas chromatography. To enable the percentage saturation to be calculated, the amount so found must be related to the haemoglobin content of the blood determined by a separate operation. Other methods have utilised the fact that carboxyhaemoglobin is coagulated by heat at a slightly lower temperature than oxy-.

The combined chemical–optical methods, which many laboratories think the best and most accurate, depend on the fact that the chemically more stable carboxyhaemoglobin is unchanged by reagents which act on the oxy-; the proportion of the total haemoglobin which has been so acted on (or not acted on), and hence the proportion originally present as oxy- or carboxyhaemoglobin, can then be measured spectrophotometrically.

When the source of the carbon monoxide is incomplete combustion, experimental investigation of this may or may not be possible. The conditions in a fire or produced by smouldering upholstery cannot of course be exactly duplicated experimentally; on the other hand, the effects of burning a paraffin or gas heater in a small unventilated room can be easily checked. It is only necessary to reproduce the appropriate conditions as closely as possible and to analyse samples of air from within the room, withdrawn without opening it by whatever means is suitable. Repeated analyses over several hours will immediately show whether a potentially lethal concentration of CO is building up. The actual analysis is most conveniently performed by an apparatus in which a pre-determined volume of air is aspirated through a reagent for carbon monoxide—usually a palladium-chloride preparation.

In cases of carbon monoxide poisoning by incomplete combustion, it is sometimes found on investigation that the actual CO concentration has been less than would have been expected from the duration of the exposure and the effect on the victim. (See table opposite.) This anomaly has been explained by Machata of Vienna, who also supported his explanation by some animal experiments. In such cases, a high concentration of carbon dioxide (CO_2) is also always present; as CO_2 is a respiratory stimulant, the victim will have been breathing deeply during exposure to the CO, and will therefore have absorbed this more quickly than if he had been breathing normally, so that the equilibrium saturation in his blood will have been reached sooner.

VII. DRUG IDENTIFICATION

The identification of **drugs of addiction** (or, to use the currently more correct term, of **dependence**) constitutes for all laboratories today, especially those serving large conurbations, a formidably growing part of their case load. The work involved may be considered a branch of toxicology, since the same techniques of identification are used and since the same compounds may be encountered as fatal poisons or as drugs of dependence. This identification in drug cases is nearly always necessary even if illegal possession is admitted, since the addict customers are sometimes the victims of fraud or mistake, and the seized "drugs" may prove to be some harmless substance the possession of which is no offence.

What particular drugs or types of drugs arrive for identification depends mainly on what the law of the country currently prohibits, but also to some extent on fashions among drug users. The laws of most countries make some distinction between "hard" and "soft" drugs. The former, of which the best known is heroin, cause true *physical* dependence—that is, their continued use makes the user effectively unable to do without them, and on deprivation of them he suffers genuine physical withdrawal effects. The latter, of which the best-known are perhaps cannabis, the amphetamines ("pep pills") and lysergide (LSD), produce (like the more familiar alcohol and tobacco) *psychological* dependence—that is, although no physical withdrawal effects can be proved, the user is unwilling to face the impoverishment of life without them.

British legal attempts to control drug misuse were formerly embodied in the various Dangerous Drugs Acts and regulations made under them, and in the Drugs (Prevention of Misuse) Act 1964. Because of the former, the term "dangerous drug" is still used in this country for the hard drugs—morphine, heroin, cocaine, etc. In the U.S.A. these are generally known as "narcotics," and "dangerous drug," having no legal connotation, may be used loosely for any habit-forming drug. British law has now however been consolidated in the Misuse of Drugs Act 1971, which repeals the other Acts mentioned.

This Act names in an appended three-part Schedule the drugs to which it applies, grouped according to the degree of danger which their misuse is believed to present, and with maximum penalties for production, supplying, possessing etc. adjusted accordingly. Part I (the most dangerous) lists 99 drugs or classes of drugs. These include: *opium*; *morphine*; *diamorphine* (heroin); synthetic morphine substitutes such as *Pethidine* ("*Demerol*" in the U.S.A.) and *Methadone*; the exceedingly potent recently discovered morphine derivatives such as *etorphine*; *cocaine*; *cannabinol* (a constituent of cannabis); *lysergide* (LSD); *mescaline* (made famous by Aldous Huxley). Part II lists 13 drugs, including *cannabis* and *cannabis resin*, and the *amphetamines* (p. 115). Part III (the least dangerous) lists 10 drugs, including *methaqualone* (p. 114).

The framing of the definitions in such lists is incidentally a matter requiring considerable scientific knowledge. They must neither be so lax that harmless substances fall within the letter of the law, nor so restrictive that they can be interpreted as excluding substances which were included by intention. In this country it is one of the duties of the Government Chemist's Laboratory to assist the legislators in this matter.

Other types of drugs the misuse of which may lead to the necessity for their identification by the laboratory include the barbiturates (the availability of which is already restricted by other laws) and the various intoxicating and narcotic solvents to which "glue-sniffers" become addicted. Should an addiction of the latter type lead to death (an all too possible eventuality) the analysis will of course be for a vapour, as described in the previous section.

Apart from cannabis or opium (see below), the drugs to be identified are most frequently in the form of tablets or capsules. Every laboratory will therefore keep as large a reference collection as possible of those likely to be encountered. (This may also be useful in "pure" toxicology—see p. 111.) An adequate collection represents a great deal of work; throughout the western world several hundred thousand different pharmaceutical tablets and capsules are produced, and a working collection must contain several thousand items. They must be classified in some way—usually on the basis of shape, colour(s), size and markings if any. Different laboratories have evolved different systems of identification using such a classified collection; a "peek-a-boo" punched card index is probably as quick and certain as any. Final identification must of course depend on simple analytical identification of the active constituent(s), for which infra-red spectrometry is usually the best method.

Some problems of drug identification are however more difficult than those presented by commercial tablets or capsules. Hallucinogens such as lysergide or "STP," the doses of which are minute (of the order of 50 micrograms) may come absorbed in sugar cubes or blotting paper, in tiny foil wrappings, in minute and easily concealed "micro-dots" and in various other ways. Spectro-fluorimetry (p. 75) may be used for identification. Heroin, which is totally prohibited in most countries other than Britain, is almost certain to be of illicit origin. Its identification as a simple morphine derivative is not difficult (p. 116), but it is likely to be adulterated. The nature of the adulterant may of course form a useful guide to the origin of a particular sample, as may also the extent to which the diacetylation of the parent morphine—the essential step in preparing the drug—is complete.

Opium is rarely encountered in this country, but its identification is not difficult. Any resinous material which looks, smells and burns like opium can be assumed to be opium if it contains both morphine and meconic acid (the latter being a harmless but characteristic constituent of poppy juice). It may however be legally necessary to prove that a sample of "opium" was in fact derived from the opium poppy, *Papaver somniferum*, and not from some other species of poppy; in that case a full identification of all the allaloids present in genuine opium from *Papaver somniferum* may be necessary. The United Nations chemists have also done much valuable work on the identification of the origin of opium by means of the detailed and painstaking analysis of its constituents. Activation analysis (p. 80) has also been used in this connection.

More research has probably been done on the identification of cannabis than of any other drug. The chemistry of its constituents has been minutely researched, and its microscopic morphology compared with that of a large number of allied botanical genera. It is a drug of world-wide use (or misuse). No other drug has so many names in so many languages: the United Nations list of internationally controlled narcotics gives no fewer than 251 synonyms, of which the most familiar to us are Indian hemp, "pot," hashish ("hash"), marijuana and bhang. Cannabis itself, which is the dried flowering or fruiting tops of any species of the genus *Cannabis*, is commonly smoked in cigarettes ("reefers") with or without the admixture of tobacco. The active constituents, which are contained in the resin secreted by the plant, are a number of complex phenolic compounds—cannabinol and several others—all derivatives of methyl-3-(4-pentyl-*nor*-orcinol)-4-isopropyl benzene. These may be identified by colour tests and, more specifically, by thin-layer and gas chromatography.

Research has been going on in several countries for several years, with varying success, on the problem of identifying the illicit drug user. With cannabis the difficulty was that the amount of the active constituents absorbed was very small and their chemistry imperfectly known. Now however that the latter difficulty has been overcome, the application of the most sensitive instrumental techniques has made it possible to detect cannabis constituents in the urine, on the fingers and even in the breath, of users. It has also recently been found possible to detect lysergide in the urine after it has been taken, infinitesimal though the amount present must be, by means of radio-immuno assay (p. 112); the development of this method required some extremely sophisticated chemistry to confer the necessary antigenic properties on the drug.

The routine examination of large numbers of suspected drug samples has become so onerous a task to forensic chemists everywhere that necessity has given birth to invention, and two ways of easing the work have been developed. One (mainly in the U.S.A.) is the design of field-testing kits intended for use by police officers, with which most of the commonly abused drugs can be identified by a carefully chosen series of simple spot tests. The other is the automation of the testing under laboratory conditions, most successfully by using a combination of gas chromatography and mass spectrometry, possibly computerised as well.

11

PERSONAL IDENTIFICATION

I. THE PROBLEM

The question of personal identity is of course a crucial one in the detection and prosecution of crime. In proving this, the law has always relied a good deal on the testimony of eye witnesses; however, there are the notorious cases of Adolf Beck and Oscar Slater to remind us that this testimony may be disastrously unreliable.

The proof of identity can be regarded from two quite different standpoints. From one, the problem is to describe, measure and classify physical bodily characteristics with such exactitude that, if the same data apply to A—— B—— and C—— D——, they must be the same person. From the other, the problem is to identify an individual from personal traces which he has left behind at the scene of the crime.

The chief personal characteristics which can be used for identification are: (1) hair colour; (2) voice; (3) general appearance; (4) the shapes, sizes and arrangement of the teeth and bones; (5) fingerprints; (6) blood groups. (Hair colour is separated here from general appearance because a man can leave his hairs behind, but not the shape of his ears.) Any or all of these categories may be invoked in proving identity from the first standpoint described above; obviously, however, only (1), (4) sometimes, (5) and (6) can be used to identify a person by the traces he leaves behind him.

II. PERSONAL APPEARANCE, HAIR, BONES, TEETH, ETC.

Each of us probably knows several hundreds or even thousands of other people by sight, but few of us could give a description of any one of them so exact that it would make possible certain recognition by a stranger. Nevertheless that is just what the police would like to have; it would be immensely valuable if a published description could lead to the arrest of the right man in a place where no one has ever seen him before.

Most if not all police forces train their men to describe personal appearance in precise and recognisable terms. Under headings such as "build," "complexion," "nose," "gait," etc. etc. lists of standard descriptive terms are prescribed— perhaps a dozen or so under each heading. Obviously such a system will achieve a certain amount of serviceable communication of personal impressions of appearance; equally obviously, it can never be other than a rough guide, since, for example, one policeman might classify a complexion as "ruddy," another the same complexion as "weather-beaten."

In a refinement along these lines, the witness and a competent quick artist are closeted together. The artist first of all draws a face which seems to him to be as nearly as possible what the witness is trying to describe; the witness then corrects the first impression—"the nose is too long," "the cheeks should be more sunken," etc.—and by gradual trial and error a picture is produced which the witness finally pronounces to be the face he remembers. A modern development of this idea, the *Identikit*, employs a series of over 800 transparent outline drawings of the different possible shapes for the several features; various permutations of these in combination are tried until the witness is satisfied, and the final result can be photographed for circulation. Several million permutations are possible, and many wanted men have been traced with this device. Another modification of this idea which has recently been suggested uses a small number of basic face outlines, and varies the overall shape of this by combining one half of the outline itself with the other half reflected in a movable mirror.

Another, once very famous, system of identification was invented about 90 years ago by Alphonse Bertillon, a clerk in the Paris *préfecture* who had studied medicine. He devised a system based on eleven "key" measurements, namely: height; span of arms; length from waist to shoulder; height and width of head; length and width of right ear; lengths of left foot, left middle finger, left little finger, left forearm. The system scored some notable successes in fixing identities and made its creator's reputation. Its heyday may be said to have been the decade 1890–1900. However, it has now been dead for over half a century. It required greater precision of measurement than was possible in routine police work, and the uncritical application of its methods led to some catastrophic mistakes. Its final death blow came with the arrival of fingerprinting (introduced at New Scotland Yard in 1901).

However, identification by bone dimensions, upon which *bertillonage* fundamentally rested, has taken on a new lease of life since X-radiography became a commonplace. Numerous cases have now been reported, from both sides of the Atlantic, in which human remains have been identified by agreement of their skeletal conformation with that of the presumed deceased as revealed by X-ray photographs taken during life. The precise shapes of almost every part of the skeleton, from skull sinuses to ankle bones, as well as old fractures, have been used for this. It is, however, a matter for the forensic pathologist, and as such outside the scope of this book.

It is also fundamentally a matter of anatomy that it has sometimes been found possible to link a well-worn article of footwear with its owner by showing agreement of foot shape, pressure points, lines of flexure, etc.

It is probable that no two persons' teeth are precisely identical in size, shape and disposition, and the value of tooth marks has been mentioned on p. 19. The teeth are probably the most indestructible part of the body, and identification by means of them and of what the dentist has done to them, after aircraft crashes, fire disasters and so forth is now a well-established branch of forensic medicine (*forensic odontology*). Bite marks on victims' bodies have also on many occasions been matched with assailants' teeth. These matters are also, however, outside the scope of this book.

The colour and length of the hair is also, of course, a distinctive personal characteristic, which has the additional value that it can sometimes be discovered *in absentia*. Unfortunately, it is a very imprecise means of identification. Not only do many people have similar hair, but several quite different hairs can come from the same head, especially when it is going grey or is of the common medium-brown type. Nevertheless, when hairs are found in connection with a crime they must be made to yield such information as they can; we shall deal with this in Chapter 13. Also, although head and hair cannot, in the present state of our knowledge, be precisely "mated," and although the length of a hair is nowadays no guide to sex, it is always possible to draw a few firm conclusions, such as, for example, that a short curly negroid hair is not likely to have come from the head of an ash blonde.

In the case of the other extruded dead tissue, fingernails, it has been found that the striations on these which become increasingly prominent with age appear to remain constant for long periods at least. This means—though the fact is unlikely to be often of practical assistance—that nail clippings could be matched with the hand they came from by the methods described in Chapter 3.

Some other possible methods of identification by bodily characteristics are still matters of speculation. It was suggested some years ago in Germany that the bacterial population of the skin probably varies from one person to another, and that the culture of the bacteria from collars or cuff edges might form a basis for identification. The possibly individual bacterial flora of faeces have also been suggested in this connection. Again, it is known that the trace elements present in the blood vary from person to person and from time to time; we shall return to the possible utilisation of this on p. 137.

Finally, an entirely different method of identification—by "voice prints"—was proposed some years ago by L. G. Kersta in the U.S.A. He found that plotting on a time base-line all the frequencies produced by the utterance of even a single syllable gave an "acoustic spectrogram" (or *sonogram*) which appeared to be uniquely characteristic of the speaker, and that voices (or recorded voices) could be identified in this way with considerable certainty. Evidence of identity obtained by this technique has been given both in the U.S.A. and this country. The value of the method is not, however, universally admitted: the equipment for it is expensive, and it has been alleged that it does no better than a trained ear, that it cannot distinguish between a voice and a good mimic's imitation, and that it is defeated by the changes inevitably produced by emotion, telephone transmission, etc.

III. FINGERPRINTS

Everyone knows that fingerprinting constitutes the most certain—in fact, the only *certain*—means of identification ever discovered. The subject is not (in this country at least) dealt with by the forensic science laboratories, simply because it was an established branch of police work long before science was fully mobilised in that field. Since an even approximately complete treatment of the recording and classification of fingerprints would not be within the writer's competence in any case, only the barest sketch of the subject can be attempted here.

Fingerprints are impressions of the random patterns formed by the papillary ridges of the palms of the hand, and particularly of the fingertip. (The soles of the feet and the toes bear similar patterns, which have also on occasion been used to prove identity.*) It has been known for over a century that these patterns vary from person to person. To establish the full value of fingerprinting, however, it was necessary to show that each person's patterns are both *unique* and *unchanging* throughout life. This was done in the latter decades of last century, mainly by Sir William Herschel (an Indian civil servant) and Sir Francis Galton (the creator of eugenics). (Much of the credit for the early development of fingerprint identification has also been claimed for a medical missionary called Henry Faulds, but his claim to priority is not generally accepted.) Since then, several millions of people have been fingerprinted, but no two single prints have ever been found to be the same. Even the most identical of identical twins have always shown fingerprint differences.

Obviously, if the matter rested there, the utility of fingerprinting would be limited to the comparison of prints found at a scene with those of a known suspect. Fingerprint evidence of this kind was first given in this country at the Central Criminal Court in 1902, and even earlier (*c.* 1900) in Argentina. However, for the checking of prints found against the thousands or even millions recorded, as is done today, some system of classification is clearly quite essential. That most widely used was devised by Mr. (later Sir) Edward Henry, an Inspector General of Police in Bengal who was appointed Assistant Commissioner of the Metropolitan Police and very soon after that, in 1901, introduced the system at New Scotland Yard.

Henry started with the observed fact that all fingerprint patterns can be assigned to one of four basic types—*arches*, *loops*, *whorls* and *composites*, of which loops and whorls are by far the most common. In classification, the ten digits are first divided into two groups of five. (The original Henry system, still used by New Scotland Yard in a greatly extended form, did not use a simple right-hand/left-hand division; some other fingerprint bureaus now do so, however, and that method of division will be assumed here for simplicity of description.) To each digit is assigned the number 0 if its pattern is an arch or loop, and a number which depends on its position in the group (hand) if it is a whorl or composite. The latter number is 16 for the first digit (thumb), 8 for the second

---

* Lip prints, although they do not show papillary ridges, may also, it is said, be characteristic, and there is even a case on record of an ear print having been used.

(forefinger), 4 for the third, 2 for the fourth and 1 for the fifth. The primary classification of a set of fingerprints is then expressed as the "fraction"

$$\frac{\text{Sum of digit classification numbers for right hand} + 1}{\text{Sum of digit classification numbers for left hand} + 1}$$

The peculiar beauty of this system is that, first, each numerical value corresponds uniquely to a particular distribution of pattern types among the digits, and, secondly, that it gives us at once no less than 1,024 (*i.e.* 32^2) primary classes ranging from $\frac{1}{1}$ (all digits arches or loops) to $\frac{32}{32}$ (all digits whorls or composites; $16 + 8 + 4 + 2 + 1 + 1 = 32$). For example, putting A for arch or loop and W for whorl or composite, the following pairs of hands

Right	A	W	A	A	A
Left	A	A	W	W	A

Right	A	A	W	A	A
Left	W	A	A	A	W

would have the classifications

$$\frac{0 + 8 + 0 + 0 + 0 + 1}{0 + 0 + 4 + 2 + 0 + 1} = \frac{9}{7} \qquad \frac{0 + 0 + 4 + 0 + 0 + 1}{16 + 0 + 0 + 0 + 1 + 1} = \frac{5}{18}$$

Conversely, a set of prints classified as, say, $\frac{9}{22}$ could *only* be

A	W	A	A	A
W	A	W	A	W

That, however, is only a beginning. Quite clearly, with a large collection of fingerprints (New Scotland Yard has those of over $2\frac{1}{2}$ million people), further subdivision is essential if time spent on searching is to be kept within reasonable limits. This is particularly the case with the $\frac{1}{1}$ class—a very large one, since loops are the commonest of all the four basic types. The secondary and tertiary classifications are based on (1) the occurrence of sub-varieties of the four types, and (2) the positions where these occur.

Arches may be simple or *tented*. Loops may be inclined either towards the centre line of the body (*radial* loops) or away from it (*ulnar* loops). Whorls may be simple closed curves, closed curves with a central island, clockwise spirals or anti-clockwise spirals. Also, in all patterns except arches there are points where ridges bifurcate, known as *deltas*; loops have one each and whirls and composites two or more. Deltas provide further classifying characteristics which depend on the number of ridges lying between the delta(s) and the *core* of the pattern.

It is impossible to enter here into the details of secondary and tertiary classifications. For quicker searching, the codes assigned to each sub-group are arranged in a rigidly prescribed order, so that the full code for a set of prints leads the searching officer as quickly as possible to a relatively limited group.

Criminals, however, are rarely considerate enough to leave full sets of prints, and the Henry system cannot help in the case where only one or two individual prints are found. Various systems of classifying single prints have been devised to meet this difficulty, and that used in this country was invented in the 1920s by Superintendent Battley of the Metropolitan Police. A separate collection for each digit is made from the reference prints, and each of these ten collections is divided into nine groups based on the Henry types; these are then further subdivided according to the ridge arrangement at the core, the absolute distance of the delta(s) from the core, ridge counts, etc. As a print may contain about 100 classifiable characteristics, the amount of information which it carries is obviously enormous. Search is therefore limited to one, or at least a very few, of several hundred sub-groups. The searcher must know or guess which digit made the print he is trying to match, but experience usually enables him to do this correctly.

It will be obvious that, even for the experienced officer, fingerprint searching can be extremely laborious. It is common knowledge that research into the computerisation of this task has been going on for some years; the difficulties are, however, formidable, and eventually a different system of classification may prove more suitable for this purpose.

Fingerprints at a scene of crime may occasionally be made in blood, dirty grease, or the like, but more often than not they are *latent*. A latent fingerprint is an invisible or barely visible impression left on a smooth surface by traces of sweat exuding from the pores which lie along the papillary ridges. It may be "developed"—*i.e.* rendered visible and hence photographable—in several ways. The commonest method, which is used as routine on non-porous surfaces such as glass or polished wood, is dusting with an adherent powder. From long experience "grey powder" (finely divided mercury in chalk) was formerly used for dark surfaces and lamp black or fine powdered graphite for light ones. Nowadays, however, proprietary mixtures are increasingly replacing grey powder. Prints on glass may sometimes be developed by etching with hydrofluoric acid vapour. Prints on porous materials such as paper used to offer great and too often insurmountable difficulty, but this has now been overcome by the use of *ninhydrin* (triketone-hydrindene hydrate). This is a compound first used by biochemists for the paper-chromatographic detection of amino-acids, with as little as a few micrograms of which it produces a purple colour. As sweat contains amino-acids, the same reagent will therefore successfully develop fingerprints on paper and other porous materials. (This application of the ninhydrin reaction has been patented.)

Finally, two quite different methods have recently been devised which show some promise for prints on fabrics and other difficult surfaces. The first depends on the fact that sulphur dioxide (a gas) is preferentially absorbed by lipids (fatty compounds) from the skin present in the print; this can therefore be developed by treatment with sulphur dioxide "labelled" with radioactive sulphur and subsequent autoradiography (see Glossary). In the other new method, metal (gold followed by cadmium) is deposited on the print by vacuum sputtering, and defines it by adhering only to the spaces in between the ridge lines.

The identification of dead bodies by means of their fingerprints has frequently to be attempted and is sometimes successful. It is neither an easy nor a pleasant task if the body is badly decomposed, and various means have been tried of getting over this difficulty: these include injections to inflate wrinkled fingertips, hardening of pulpy epidermis with formaldehyde before printing, taking prints from the sloughed epidermis of the fingertips, and utilising the identical but fainter patterns in the underlying dermis.

To return to the living, if the prints at the scene match those of the suspect or are found in the collection, the last stage is the convincing demonstration of this fact for the court of trial. This is invariably done by using enlarged photographs of the scene-of-crime and known prints, with indications on them of the various *characteristics* which establish the identity. A characteristic is any identifiable peculiarity in a certain position—a bifurcation, the end of a ridge, an "island," a delta, etc. If eight characteristics match, it is for all practical purposes certain that the same finger made both impressions. However, in this country at least, in order to safeguard the utter certainty of fingerprint identification, evidence about it is not given unless at least 16 matching characteristics can be found. (With two or more prints, 10 per print are considered sufficient.)

Various estimates have been made of the odds against two persons having prints identical to this degree. The figure is certainly many thousands of millions, or even millions of millions, to one, and is in any case a much larger number than the entire population of the world.

IV. BLOOD GROUPS

It was discovered in 1900 in Vienna by Karl Landsteiner (who subsequently received a Nobel prize for his work), and has since been amply confirmed by work all over the world, that the blood of all human beings falls into one or other of four main types, and that these arise from the presence or absence in or on their red blood cells of two *antigens*. Since each antigen is quite sharply either present or absent, that fact constitutes an identifiable characteristic for each individual.

These antigens are now universally called A and B.* The four types (or groups) of blood are therefore:

Group O: Antigens A and B both absent
Group A: Antigen A present, B absent
Group B: Antigen B present, A absent
Group AB: Antigens A and B both present.

* Later work has shown that many antigens are not single entities, but complexes which may show wide difference in antigenic reactivity (see below). For example, several subgroups of A have been described, of which two are common enough to warrant mention here; these are A_1 (strong reactors) and A_2 (weak reactors). This gives us six blood groups instead of four, namely: O, A_1, A_2, B, A_1B, A_2B. For the sake of simplicity, however, this subdivision will be ignored here.

An antigen is a very broad term meaning any substance which, when introduced into an organism to which it is foreign, stimulates the production by the organism of an *antibody*. Each antibody is specific for a particular antigen, and will neutralise or react with, or possibly in some cases even destroy, any of that antigen subsequently introduced. This is of course the basis of vaccination and similar methods of conferring immunity to infectious diseases, the antigen being in each case a substance produced by or associated with the infecting virus or micro-organism.

In the case of the A and B blood-group antigens, however, the unusual situation exists that the antibodies to them occur naturally; all bloods from healthy human beings over the age of six months contain in their plasma all of the A–B antibodies which do *not* react with their own cells. Thus, group-O serum contains anti-A and anti-B, A contains anti-B, B contains anti-A, and AB serum contains neither antibody. The chemical constitution of antigens and antibodies need not concern us here, although some of the former have been isolated and identified.

Blood groups are of vital importance in clinical medicine, since the mixing in the body (by transfusion) of incompatible bloods leads to an antigen-antibody reaction which can be dangerous or even fatal for the recipient. That fact does not, however, concern us here; what does concern us is that in isolated blood samples the presence of the antibody causes the antigenic red cells to stick together firmly in clumps instead of floating freely separate. This is called *agglutination*. (Hence the blood-group antigens are also known as *agglutinogens*, and the antibodies as *agglutinins*.)

An unknown sample of blood is therefore grouped by noting which known sera agglutinate its cells and/or which known cells are agglutinated by its serum. The facts already given enable us to construct a table which can be used for such experiments.

Group of cells	Serum from blood of group			
	O	A	B	AB
O	−	−	−	−
A	+	−	+	−
B	+	+	−	−
AB	+	+	+	−
Antibodies present	Anti-A Anti-B	Anti-B	Anti-A	None

+ Agglutination   − No agglutination

The techniques actually used in forensic science will be described in the next chapter.

We have started this section with a brief description of the ABO blood groups, because they form a usefully simple introduction to the whole subject of blood types and because of their historical importance. In fact, however, they are only the beginning of the story, and are now merely one of several independent means by which a characteristic identity can be assigned to a sample of blood.

There are several quite distinct and unrelated types of difference between the bloods of different individuals.

(1) They may differ in respect of the **erythrocyte** (red-cell) **antigens,** which are located on the cell walls. Three systems of this type are now forensically useful: the *ABO,* the *MNS* and the *Rhesus.* However, numerous others are known to exist. The ABO system is the most familiar and was until a few years ago the only one detectable in dried bloodstains and hence usable in forensic science. The M and N antigens were discovered in 1927; one or other or both are always present. (The associated antigen, S, is not yet but may soon be used forensically.) The Rhesus groups were discovered in 1940. (Their discovery—and naming—came from the surprising observation that the antibody produced by rabbits immunised with rhesus-monkey blood also agglutinated the blood cells of 85 per cent. of the white population of New York.) Their importance in obstetrics is well known, but for us they form the newest and possibly most useful forensic blood-group system: new because the difficulty of determining them in dried stains has only recently been overcome, and useful because the large number of groups within the system makes it particularly valuable in individualising blood.

The nomenclature of the Rh groups is complex and can be confusing, and not less so because more than one method has been used. The original terms "Rh-positive" and "Rh-negative" referred simply to bloods in which the anti-rhesus rabbit serum did or did not produce agglutination. It is now known, however, that this effect depends on several genetically controlled factors (see p. 140), and the disentangling of their relationships has required a vast amount of research. Very briefly, the Rh group is determined by a set of three antigenic factors which occur together and each of which may be present in one of two alternative forms (or *alleles*—see p. 141). These, which are designated *C, c, D, d, E* and *e* respectively, can therefore be assembled in eight different ways: CDE, CDe, CdE, Cde, cDE, cDe, cdE and cde. (The capitals refer to the factors present in Rh-positive blood, the small letters to those present in Rh-negative.) Rare variants to most of these alleles have also been discovered, but only one, C^w, allelic to C and c, need be mentioned here. Each of these antigens, except d, can produce its own specific antibody. In addition, as the antigenic make-up of every individual contains a contribution from each of his/her parents (see p. 141), a full description of an Rh group contains all six specifying letters: for example, cde/cde, CDe/cdE, etc. (These may also be written, as in the table on p. 139, ccddee, CcDdeE, etc.) Counting the contribution of the C^w allele, over fifty such groupings are possible; some of these are vanishingly rare, but about fifteen have been found among western Europeans, of which seven or eight are common enough to form useful identifying characteristics.

The numerous other red-cell antigenic systems which are known to exist have been discovered during and since the last war. Most are named after the family in which they were first found (*Lewis, Kell, Duffy, Kidd, Lutheran,*

Diego, etc.). All appear to be quite independent both of the systems already mentioned and of each other. Some of these antigens are so common that nearly everyone has them; others are exceedingly rare. None has yet proved useful in forensic science, partly because it has not yet been found possible to detect it in dried stains, and partly because very common or very rare antigens are in any case of limited value (see p. 138). However, further research may overcome the difficulties of detecting some, at least; at present the Kell system seems the likeliest candidate for success.

All of these systems, from the MN onwards, are distinguished from the ABO by the fact that the antibodies do not regularly occur in human plasma. The antigens can be identified therefore only by using antisera in which the antibodies have been produced artificially. For the MN and some other systems, this can be done by the injection of animals with the appropriate antigenic cells. The remainder, apart from a few which occasionally occur in Man as irregular natural antibodies, are produced in persons who have been sensitised to the various antigens by pregnancy or blood transfusion.

(2) People can be divided into **secretors** and **non-secretors** according to whether or not they secrete a soluble form of the ABO antigens in their various secretions—in a high concentration in saliva, semen, vaginal secretion and gastric juice, and a rather lower in sweat, tears and urine. This characteristic is independent of the blood group in the ABO and all other antigenic systems (except the Lewis, with which it is linked). In addition, all secretors, even group-O ones, secrete another red-cell antigen known as H (which is now known to be the parent substance from which the A and B antigens arise). Between 75 and 80 per cent. of the white populations of western Europe and North America are secretors.

(3) A more recent, still expanding and immensely valuable addition to the blood-grouper's armoury is **blood protein** and **enzyme polymorphism** (that is, the existence of several different forms of a particular protein or enzyme).

(*a*) The proteins utilised, which can also be identified by their antigenic properties (see p. 134) are mostly those in the blood plasma. Plasma proteins (following the usual somewhat unattractive nomenclature) are divided broadly into the albumins and the globulins; the latter are subdivided into the α, β and γ globulins, and the α and β globulins are further divided into the α_1, α_2, β_1, β_2 etc. types. The polymorphic proteins which have proved most useful are:

Haptoglobin, an α_2 globulin which has the special physiological function of "mopping up" the residues from ageing and degenerate haemoglobin. It occurs in either homogeneous or heterogeneous combinations of two forms, so that three types are possible, known as 1–1, 2–1 and 2–2. They can be identified either in liquid blood or dried stains.

The α_2 globulin *Gc*, which also occurs in 1–1, 2–1 and 2–2 forms. It is not as yet, though may soon be, capable of being identified in dried stains.

Haemoglobin, present unlike the others within the red cells. Its varieties are racially linked, so we shall deal with them in the next section, after we have discussed heredity.

The globulin *Gm*, which has been more investigated on the Continent than in this country. This occurs in so many variants that it is potentially the most useful polymorphic protein, but the routine detection of these in dried stains has not so far been possible, largely because of the lack of suitable reagents.

(*b*) The numerous polymorphic enzymes catalysing vital biochemical reactions (mainly those involved in the breakdown and utilisation of glucose) are mostly contained in the red cells. As the full name of each, which refers to the particular reaction catalysed, is rather long, it is usually contracted to its initials for convenience. The biochemical functions of these enzymes do not concern us here, but those which in the present context are most likely to be useful or which have been most investigated are:

PGM (phospho-gluco-mutase)
EAP (erythrocyte acid phosphatase)
GPT (glutamate-pyruvate transaminase)
ADA (adenosine deaminase)
AK (adenylate kinase)
6PGD (6-phospho-gluconate dehydrogenase)
G-6-PD (gluco-6-phosphate dehydrogenase)
PCE (pseudo-cholinesterase)*

Several of these, like the polymorphic proteins, occur as 1–1, 2–1 and 2–2 types; the others are more complex (see table on p. 139).

The methods used for identifying the protein and enzyme groups are described briefly on pp. 161–164.

(4) Yet another method of characterising blood may eventually be possible—the use of *continuously variable parameters*. The blood groups we have been discussing are all qualitative properties—a blood simply belongs to one or another particular group within each system. However, some blood properties vary continuously over a wide range and are quantifiable, and it may therefore be that the precise magnitude of these parameters could form another identifying characteristic. A good deal of work has been done on measuring the relative proportions of *all* the numerous plasma proteins, in order to discover how far these proportions could be used to characterise a blood; we shall return to this on p. 164. Another method which has been suggested (notably by B. J. Culliford of the Metropolitan Police Laboratory) is still as yet in the stage of speculation: it is the quantitative determination of the trace elements present. Blood contains small, possibly fortuitous, traces of numerous elements, probably derived from the diet and some probably inessential. Accurate determination of these in very small samples is possible using atomic absorption spectroscopy (p. 71). It has yet to be established, however, which elements show the greatest variation in concentration (necessary if the measurements are to be useful) and how far it

* The "pseudo-" in this name refers to the fact that this enzyme, which unlike the others is present in the plasma, though it will hydrolyse acetylcholine, shows some differences from the true cholinesterase found at muscle-nerve junctions (see p. 117) and within the red cells.

may be possible to circumvent the effects of accidental contamination after the blood has been shed.

To return to the blood-group systems described under (1)–(3) above, the important thing about them in the present context is that they are completely *independent* of each other; there is no known association between the group in one system and that in another. To illustrate this point by a simple analogy, if the only known characteristic of a wanted man were his height, a large number of people would fit his description, whereas the addition of other independent characteristics such as hair colour, shape of ears, build etc. greatly reduces this number, and the more characteristics are described the fewer the men to which their totality would apply.

As mentioned above, very common or very rare blood groups are of little value in practice: the former for obvious reasons, and the latter because they will so seldom be encountered that the labour of looking for them is unproductive. In general, blood grouping will be most valuable when as many systems as possible are used and when the groups are roughly equally distributed within each system. In elementary mathematical terms, if a systems each contain b equally distributed groups, each combination of groups will occur in $\frac{1}{b^a}$ of the population. The most effective way of making this fraction as small as possible is to make a as large as possible. In the long run, this will afford more valuable information than will the occasional occurrence of rare groups within a small number of systems. Even if each system contained only two equally distributed groups, ten systems ($a = 10$) would suffice to identify a set of people forming only about 1/1,000 of the population, and twenty systems ($a = 20$) a set forming about 1/1,000,000—that is, in the latter case, about 50 people in the whole of Great Britain.

The usefulness of a particular system can also be assessed according to its power of *discrimination*. This is measured by the proportion of occasions on which the use of that system will distinguish between two unrelated samples of blood. This will obviously be the greater the more groups which the system contains, and will again be greatest when these are evenly distributed within the system (*cf.* p. 15).

The table on page 139 gives the percentage frequencies for the population of Great Britain* of the various groups, in their accepted notations, within the most useful of the systems we have mentioned.

The discriminatory power, as defined above, of the systems in the above table varies from about 80 per cent. for Rh and 60 per cent. for ABO to between 15 and 20 per cent. for ADA and AK. Taking all of the systems in the table, but neglecting secretor status, the commonest group in every system will occur in only (46·7 per cent. of 33·8 per cent. of 49·8 per cent. of . . . etc.)—that is, rather less than 1 per cent.—of the population. At the other extreme, and con-

---

* Since groups are genetically determined (see next section), the figures for other races may be, and often are, quite different. Those for the white population of North America are, however, very similar.

ABO	Rh*	MN	Haptoglobin (Hp)	PGM	EAP	ADA	AK
O 46·7	CcD ee 33·8	MN 49·8	2–1 52·6	1–1 58·2	Type BA 42·7	1–1 90·4	1–1 91·2
A 41·7	CCD ee 17·4	M 28·8	2–2 32·0	2–1 35·7	Type B 35·4	2–1 9·4	2–1 8·7
B 8·6	ccddee 15·1	N 21·4	1–1 13·8	2–2 5·5	Type A 12·9	2–2 Very rare	2–2 Very rare
AB 3·0	CcD Ee 12·9		Rare variants 1·6	Rare variants 0·6	Type CB 5·5		
	ccD Ee 11·7				Type CA 3·3		
	ccD EE 2·3				Type C Very rare		
	ccD ee 2·1						
	Others: all very rare						

	Secretor status	
	Secretor	Non-secretor
London	76·9	23·1
U.S. Students	75·9	24·1

* It will be noticed that the d antigen is specified in only one of the groups mentioned here. This is because, as anti-d does not exist (p. 135), there is no way of testing directly for d. If D is present, we cannot know whether or not d is also present—that is, whether the total description of the group should contain DD or Dd. Hence dd can be inferred only if D is totally absent.

The other systems mentioned on p. 137 but not in the above table are less useful. PCE has been exhaustively investigated, but the results from old stains are unreliable. In addition, in the cases of both PCE and 6PGD, over 95 per cent. of the population belong to the commonest groups, so that the systems are of very limited usefulness. The G-6-PD and GPT systems have not yet been sufficiently investigated to know whether their routine use with dried stains is useful or possible.

sidering only groups the incidence of which is over 2 per cent., a combination such as, for instance: AB; ccD ee; N; Hp 1–1; PGM 2–2 should statistically be found in only about 1 person in a million. The figure for the rarest groups in all the systems works out at less than 1 person in the whole world—which means that, practically speaking, it will never be found, and reinforces the point made above that, in the practical long run, it is more useful to use numerous systems than to hope that rare groups will crop up. It is then not too optimistic to look forward to the day when every individual person's blood can be shown to be unique. However, in the routine work of a forensic science laboratory is it impracticable and usually unnecessary, for reasons to which we shall return on p. 164, to group every bloodstain by every system.

V. A NOTE ON HEREDITY

It was suggested in 1908 and proved in 1910 that the ABO blood groups are inherited, and it is now known that this is also true of all blood groups, both the red-cell antigen ones and those due to polymorphic variants. They belong in fact to the small number of characteristics the incidence of which is known to be governed by simple Mendelian inheritance. Before we mention the consequences of this fact, a very short explanation of the principles involved may not be out of place.

The transmission of hereditary characteristics from generation to generation depends on exceedingly minute rod-like structures in the cell nucleus known as *chromosomes*. These appear to be identical in character and number in practically every nucleated cell of every normal individual of any given species. They are always, in normal individuals, present in pairs, although neither the separate nor the paired chromosomes can be distinguished in the resting (*i.e.* non-dividing) cell. Man, *Homo sapiens*, has 46 chromosomes grouped in 23 pairs. The operative units of the transmission code are called *genes*. Until a few years ago we knew no more about them than that they also acted in pairs and occupied specific positions (*loci*) on the chromosomes. We now actually know something about genes, thanks to the recent discoveries in molecular biology, but that does not concern us here. It is assumed with apparent justification that each hereditary characteristic is controlled by one or more pairs of genes; in dachshunds, for example, there is a gene for short legs.

In multi-cellular organisms growth occurs by their cells dividing and increasing in number. In normal cell division (*mitosis*), each chromosome splits lengthways into two halves, so that each daughter cell receives a full set of chromosomes resembling those of the parent cell, and the two generations of cells are genetically identical. However, in the reproductive organs which produce the *ovum* (egg) in the female and the *spermatozoon* in the male, cell division takes place in such a way that one chromosome from each pair goes to each of the two daughter cells. These have therefore half the normal number of unpaired chromosomes; the human ovum and spermatozoon, for example, have 23 chromosomes each. In the fertilised egg-cell (or *zygote*) which is the beginning of a new individual, the

chromosomes carried by the ovum are paired with those carried by the spermatozoon, and the zygote therefore starts all over again with its normal complement
of paired chromosomes. Since half of these come from one parent and half from
the other, both parents contribute equally to the genetic make-up of the offspring.

This blending of hereditary characteristics manifests itself in one of two ways.
In one, the characteristic in the offspring is an intermediate form between characteristics of the parents; for example, a hybrid between a white and a red antir-
rhinum is pink. In the other, one parent's characteristic appears in the first-
generation offspring apparently unmodified, and is said to be *dominant*, while the
other parent's is "masked" and apparently disappears, and is said to be *recessive*.
The classical example of this is Mendel's original experiment on peas, in which
tallness was dominant to dwarfness; first-generation hybrids between tall and
dwarf were all tall.

This brings us to the conception of *genotypes* and *phenotypes*. A genotype
describes an individual in terms of its fundamental genetical make-up, a phenotype in terms of its outwardly manifest hereditary characteristics. The symbolism
will be obvious if we say that a pure tall pea has the phenotype T and the
genotype TT, and a pure dwarf the phenotype D and the genotype dd. (This is
not the symbolism used by geneticists, but it is used here for the sake of clarity.)
A tall first-generation hybrid will also have the phenotype T, but its genotype
will be Td. There are in fact in this instance three genotypes (TT, Td and dd),
but only two phenotypes (T and D). Genotypes having two identical genes are
known as *homozygous*, those having two unlike genes as *heterozygous*, for the
particular genes referred to.

The heterozygous first generation of peas, although tall, is no longer a pure
breed, and carries the genes for both tallness and dwarfness. Hence from the
second generation onwards the chance combinations of the genes will cause both
talls and dwarfs to appear. In the ideally simple case, the second-generation
descendants of one pure tall (TT) parent and one pure dwarf (dd) parent will be
25 per cent. pure tall (TT), 50 per cent. tall (Td) phenotypes and 25 per cent.
dwarfs. Thus:

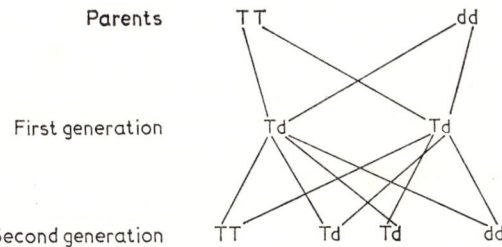

Alternative genes occupying a particular locus on a chromosome are known
as *alleles*, and the alternative forms of the corresponding characteristic as
allelomorphs. In the simplest case there are two alternative genes, giving tallness–

dwarfness, whiteness–redness and so forth. In more complicated cases, of which blood groups are one, more than two genes may be concerned.

We can now return to blood groups. In the ABO system both the A and the B characteristics behave as dominants, O being recessive. However, both the A and the B genes may occur together (*viz.* in group AB); as both characteristics then appear, A and B are said to be *co-dominant*. The four ABO blood groups are in fact three allelomorphs which are produced by one recessive and two co-dominant genes. The genotype of a group-A phenotype may therefore be either a homozygous AA or a heterozygous AO, and similarly with group B. The group-O phenotype can only be an OO genotype. The secretor characteristic (p. 136) is also dominant over non-secretor.

There are two other points we should also note here. First, the gene distribution in any human population is the resultant of many generations of mating and crossing, and is in fact analogous to the second and subsequent generation of the peas discussed above. Secondly, ordinary blood-grouping techniques can in the ABO groups reveal only phenotypes; the genotypes can be discovered only by deductive reasoning from tests on several generations. For example, if parents who are A and B respectively have an O child, they must both be able to pass on an O gene, and their genotypes must therefore be AO and BO.

Facts of that kind form the basis of the well-known blood group tests for paternity. It should be emphasised that such tests can never *prove* paternity; they can merely prove non-paternity, that is, *exclude* those men who could not be the father. The discussion on pp. 138–140 should also make it clear that the more systems are employed in such tests, the greater the chances of a conclusive result and the greater the chance of a man who is not the father being positively excluded. However, to discuss this subject here in the light of all the blood-group systems which might be used would occupy too much space. We shall therefore limit ourselves to the ABO system, using it as an example.

The table on page 143 shows the phenotypes which result from all of the possible parental ABO gene combinations; within each box the genotypes and their corresponding phenotypes appear thus: AO (*A*). The table also shows us which parent–child phenotype combinations are possible and which impossible. For example: two group-O parents can only have a group-O child; the group-A child of a group-B mother must have a father of groups A or AB; if the child is group AB neither parent can be group O.

Although we cannot discuss the use in this connection of the other systems, the general rule in all cases is: any blood-group factor which the child possesses must be present in one or both of the parents; a factor which is absent in the mother must therefore be present in the father, and any man in whom this factor is absent is therefore excluded from paternity. The chance of exclusion in any particular case depends on the groups concerned and systems used. Overall, however, a western European falsely accused of paternity has about a 1 in 6 chance of proving his innocence by ABO blood-group tests, and the figure rises to about 3 in 4 using all the antigenic blood-group systems; it can even be as high as about 8 in 9 if the enzyme systems can also be used. If, of course, the blood of the alleged father showed one of the extremely rare combinations of serological types, and if tests showed that he could be the father, then he probably was if his brothers can be ruled out, since several million other men might have to be tested before another with the same total blood-group characteristics was encountered.

Second Parent		First Parent						Pheno-type
Pheno-type	Geno-types	O	A		B		AB	Geno-types
		OO	AA	AO	BB	BO	AB	
AB	AB	AO(A)	AA(A)	AA AO }(A)	BB(B)	AO(A)	AA(A)	
		BO(B)	AB(AB)	BO(B)	AB(AB)	BB BO }(B)	BB(B)	
				AB(AB)		AB(AB)	AB(AB)	
B	BO	OO(O) BO(B)	AO(A) AB(AB)	OO(O) AO(A) BO(B) AB(AB)	BO BB }(B)	OO(O) BO BB }(B)		
	BB	BO(B)	AB(AB)	BO(B) AB(AB)	BB(B)			
A	AO	OO(O) AO(A)	AO AA }(A)	OO(O) AO AA }(A)				
	AA	AO(A)	AA(A)					
O	OO	OO(O)						

Paternity tests are usually a matter for civil litigation, and they are *not* in this country done for this purpose in the Home Office and Metropolitan Police Laboratories. Their use in this country has now been given legal status by the Family Law Reform Act 1969. Under Part III of this Act, a court may, on application by any party to the proceedings, direct that grouping tests be made. No penalty is prescribed for failure to obey such a direction, but, in the words of the Act, in the event of such a failure "the court may draw such inferences, if any, from that fact as appear proper in the circumstances." A list of approved testers of established skill and reputation is kept by the Home Office. Paternity tests could also in certain circumstances be important in criminal proceedings—for example, a prosecution for incest as a result of which a child has been born, by providing proof of innocence or corroboration of guilt. Blood-group tests may also help to settle the identity of babies where there is an allegation of theft or of accidental interchange in a maternity ward.

Blood-group distributions also show pronounced regional and racial differences. For example, in the ABO system both the A and the B genes are, as far as the world's pure-bred aboriginal populations are concerned, confined to certain areas and absent from others. Hence old inbred isolated groups—"remnant populations"—show distributions very different from those of western Europeans and white North Americans. Such differences also persist through a good deal of racial migration and mixing. Even in as small and racially thoroughly mixed an area as the British Isles differences are detectable; for example, the incidence of the O gene is much higher in Inverness than in London.

Facts such as these are of immense importance in anthropological studies, but scarcely concern us here; if the blood on a broken window is of group A, the detective will not be greatly helped by the knowledge that the burglar who cut his hand in breaking it cannot have been an aborigine from a certain area in Upper Burma where the A gene is totally absent. If, however, we go outside the ABO system, some racial differences emerge which can be of practical assistance. The most important is connected with the haemoglobin groups already mentioned on p. 136.

At least four forms of haemoglobin can be distinguished, namely:

A: the normal type in white adults
F: the foetal type
S: found in 10–15 per cent. of Negroes
C: found in about 3 per cent. of Negroes

S is by itself a harmful variant, and an individual unfortunate enough to be genetically of the homozygous SS genotype (see p. 141) is likely to die young of sickle-cell anaemia. However, the S characteristic is recessive to the A, so that homozygous AA and heterozygous AS haemoglobins are phenotypically indistinguishable as far as any outward symptoms are concerned. They can, however, be distinguished by certain tests (see Chapter 12), and this can be of value in forensic work. There have been several cases in London where the bloods of coloured men involved in affrays could be distinguished by, and only by, the presence or absence of haemoglobin S.

Racial differences are also found in connection with several of the more recently discovered red-cell antigenic blood-group system. For example, the Kell antigen is virtually confined to the white races, whereas one of the Duffy phenotypes (which may now be identifiable even in dried stains) is found in 90 per cent. of West African Negroes but practically never in the white races.

Some animals other than Man have also been found to possess their own genetically controlled blood-group systems. The investigation of these has naturally been confined in the main to species of interest to the stock-breeder, particularly cattle. They are unlikely to be often of forensic interest, and only a very few veterinary laboratories can undertake to identify them. However, cases have occurred in which they have been used to prove thefts of calves, and one can imagine that they might be utilised in a case of, say, malicious injury to a valuable bull.

12

BIOLOGY I—BLOOD AND OTHER BODY FLUIDS

We will consider in this chapter the problems connected with the various body fluids which may have to be identified in the investigation of a crime (usually, of course, as dry stains). The most important of these is of course blood. The chief questions which the forensic biologist has to answer are: What sort of fluid is it? If it is blood, is it human? If it is human, to what groups does it belong? As will be seen, the third (and to some extent the second) of these questions can also usually be asked and answered for other fluids than blood.

I. IS IT BLOOD?

This will be dealt with first, because of its importance in this context. Whenever blood has or may have been shed, the identification of bloodstains is obviously of primary importance. The occasion usually arises from personal violence, but may also arise from, for example, sheep-worrying, the illegal slaughtering of animals or the burglar cutting himself.

The first step in the investigation is to distinguish bloodstains from others due to rust, boot polish, fruit juices, jam, chemicals, paint, etc. At the same time, blood must be looked for in places where it has not been seen but where the circumstances of the case suggest that it may be found—for example, in the welt of a boot which has been roughly wiped clean, or in the crevices of a folding knife which has been rinsed. In a murder case in London some years ago, crucial evidence was the finding of a trace of blood of the victim's type in the bottom of the murderer's car-door map pocket, into which he had dropped the knife used when he drove off in a hurry.

Where actual stains, smears or splashes are seen, and if, to anticipate, these have been shown to be in fact due to blood, their appearance and distribution are of great evidential value. Spots and splashes are produced by drops of liquid blood. If these hit a surface perpendicularly they produce a stellate splash, whereas if they hit it obliquely they produce a characteristic "tailed" splash, with the tail pointing away from the direction of impact (fig. 29). A number of such splashes distributed over an area will serve to locate the position of shedding; this may be important knowledge in, for example, the investigation of a murder indoors. In another London case, blood splashes were found on the wall of a room in which a protection-racket victim had been beaten up; their directions corroborated in detail his account of the sequence of events in the beating. A boot which has inflicted serious injury may also show a characteristic distribution of fine blood spots radiating from the toe. If the blood on the front of an assailant's clothing is from an injured victim, its distribution will be different from that which it would show if it came from a bleeding nose or head injury of the assailant himself. Smears of blood indicate rubbing contact with a bloody surface, and are, for example, commonly found inside cuffs when the hand has been bloodstained.

Stains can be proved to be blood in several ways. Microscopic recognition of the characteristically shaped red cells would be conclusive, but is impossible with dried stains. With these, other tests have to be used, and all laboratories now use one or more of them for routine searching and checking. These tests are of two types: those utilising the *peroxidase* activity which is fundamental to the blood's role in tissue oxygenation, and which is preformed by the haemoglobin molecule; and those depending on the direct identification of blood pigments (that is, haemoglobin and its derivatives). The former are highly sensitive and can be used in the routine localisation of bloodstains, but are not completely specific; the latter, though inherently more specific, are less sensitive and can be applied only to detected and visible stains.

Peroxidase tests depend on the fact that these enzymes will also catalyse certain other oxidations. The reagent used contains: a suitable peroxide (most simply and most usually hydrogen peroxide); a colourless reduced compound which gives an intensely coloured oxidation product; acid or alkali to adjust the pH to that suitable to the reaction. A variety of reduced compounds may be used. In acid solution, benzidine, *o*-tolidine or 2:4-dichloroindophenol produce an intense blue, and leuco-malachite green the strongly coloured malachite green; in alkaline solution phenolphthalin produces pink phenolphthalein (*Kastle-Meyer* test). Benzidine and *o*-tolidine are the most sensitive of these reagents and give the most clear-cut positive result. Unfortunately they are now known to be carcinogenic; the laboratory must therefore choose between the extra trouble of the special precautions required if they are used, and the routine use of a slightly less sensitive reagent.

The simplest method of performing the test is to rub a filter paper on the suspected stain, or area where blood is being sought, and then to wet it with a reagent containing all of the ingredients mentioned above: a positive result is then shown by the immediate spreading of an intense colour from around the rubbed-off trace. Any of these reagents will give a strong reaction with traces of blood too small to be seen. The peroxidases of blood are also extremely stable, and can be detected in stains which are very old or have been quite strongly heated.

Unfortunately, though a negative result from a peroxidase test is complete proof of the absence of blood, the test when performed as just described will also give positive results with certain chemicals (either oxidants or catalysts for the reaction) and some plant juices (which also contain peroxidases). It has been suggested, therefore, that no reliance can be placed on positive results. However, if the test is suitably modified and intelligently used the risk of false positives is minimal. The modification consists in applying the benzidine etc. solution, and the peroxide, separately; a reaction due to chemical oxidants will then appear before the peroxide is applied, and one due to chemical catalysts will have a different appearance easily distinguished by experience. If plant peroxidases are present, a green vegetable smearing will generally be observable on the area being tested, the reaction is much less intense and usually disappears when the stain is a few days old, and the peroxidases, unlike those of blood, are easily destroyed by heat. Finally, if any doubt still remains, it can be resolved by electrophoresis (p. 162) of an extract of the stain, in which all plant peroxidases behave differently from haemoglobin.

If the article being examined gives a positive peroxidase reaction but shows no visible bloodstaining, the identification cannot be carried any further. With visible stains, however, the more specific tests for blood pigments can be made. Haemoglobin and also the various other compounds into which it is converted by age or chemical treatment (haematin, methaemoglobin, etc.) all have highly characteristic absorption spectra. These can be seen using a microscope fitted with a direct-vision micro-spectroscope in place of the normal eyepiece, but their recognition in this way is not easy. There are also several quite simple purely chemical tests for haem compounds; the best of these is probably the haemochromogen (*Takayama*) test, in which reduction of haemoglobin in the presence of pyridine produces characteristic salmon-pink crystals, readily identifiable microscopically, of pyridine haemochromogen.

A stain having been identified as blood, and assuming it to be human (see pp. 151–155), two other questions may then be asked: how old is it, and from which sex did it come? We shall defer dealing with *sexing* until the next chapter (p. 179). The *age* of a bloodstain may obviously be a matter of great importance. Dried blood changes colour from red to brown with the passage of time, and with an old stain the peroxidase-test colouration develops more slowly and is less intense than one would expect from a similar fresh stain. However, this change is affected so much by factors other than time (conditions of storage, material bearing the stain, etc.) that it is quite unreliable as a guide to absolute age. The differential solubilities of aged haemoglobin in various solvents may afford rather more reliable information. At best, however, tests such as these merely enable an experienced worker to hazard an opinion that the stain is, as the case may be, days, months or years old.

Recently, however, a spectrophotometric technique has been devised which marks a great advance in this field. The change with age in the absorption spectrum of certain haemoglobin derivatives appears to occur fairly independently of factors other than time, and work by Kind, Patterson and others suggests that a reliable objective method may soon be available for routine use. As mentioned on p. 122, haemoglobin shows two absorption bands in the visible region of the spectrum at 540 and 578 nm. respectively, with an intermediate position of minimum absorption at 560 nm. (fig. 28). The height and precise wavelength of the "α-peak" at 578 nm. changes as the stain ages, and these workers have found a way of measuring this change. By plotting the absorption curve of the pigment dissolved from the stain by dilute ammonia, and using a geometrical construction based on certain features of this curve, they derive a parameter (the "α-ratio") which is independent of all factors other than the age of the stain and hence can be used as a measure of this. Using micro-techniques, the method is applicable to exceedingly minute amounts of blood.

Lastly, it may be important to decide whether or not a stain is of *menstrual* blood. We shall return to this point on p. 163.

II. OTHER BODY FLUIDS

Before we discuss the species identification and grouping of bloodstains, it will be convenient to deal with the examination of other body fluids, since certain techniques to be described later are applicable to these as well as to blood.

The identification of *semen* is important in practically every sexual case. In most assaults it will be found on the clothing of one or both parties; when full penetration and intercourse have occurred (rape, incest, etc.) it will be found on vaginal swabs if these are taken in time; in cases of buggery, it could be found in anal swabs taken from the catamite.

The localisation of seminal stains and their provisional identification as such used to rest on properties such as appearance and texture, and on the fact that dried semen is strongly fluorescent. Identification in these ways was, however, uncertain (since many food and other stains have similar appearance and fluorescence), was nothing more than a localisation of possible sites, was laborious if a large quantity of clothing or bedding had to be examined and was sometimes nugatory if the articles were themselves, from the laundering process used on them, strongly fluorescent.

Luckily, these methods of examination are now largely obsolete since the development of satisfactory chemical methods of testing. That now in general use depends on the fact that human semen contains an (as far as is known) uniquely high concentration of an enzyme, derived from the prostate gland, which catalyses in acid conditions the hydrolysis of phosphoric esters (*acid phosphatase*). In the usual and simplest form of this ("AP") test, filter paper damped with distilled water is pressed on to the areas being examined to extract some of the enzyme, and is then treated with a reagent buffered to a slightly acid pH and containing the phosphoric ester of a reactive phenol and a suitable "coupler" (that is, dyestuff intermediate). The hitherto most popular ester and coupler, respectively, are probably sodium α-naphthyl phosphate (an ester of the phenol α-naphthol) and Brentamine Fast Blue (or Black) B salt, which give an intense purple (or black). However, as the Brentamine coupler may be carcinogenic, some laboratories now use 4-methyl umbelliferyl phosphate as a test reagent: simple hydrolysis of this by the AP liberates the intensely fluorescent compound umbelliferone, which is detected by examination of the paper under filtered ultra-violet radiation.

The particular value of the AP test is that it is the only test for semen which can be used to localise stains as well as to identify them; other tests can be applied only to stains already seen. Unfortunately, though a positive AP result is strongly suggestive of the presence of semen, it is not conclusive because the test is not entirely specific. Some plant juices (*e.g.* from gaillardia flowers and cauliflower) contain acid phosphatase (though some of these are scarcely likely to occur in some of the places where semen is being sought!). More importantly, both vaginal secretions, especially of young girls, and certain chemicals used in contraceptive jellies give a positive reaction. It is therefore essential that a provisional identification in this way be confirmed. There are several ways of doing this; the normal one, which is absolutely conclusive but not always possible (see below) is the microscopical identification of spermatozoa ("sperm"), which occur *only* in the male ejaculate.

The human spermatozoon has an ovoid head about 4 microns long and a thin flagellate tail 40–50 microns long (fig. 30a). A good microscope is therefore necessary for its identification. This is normally done on a dried and stained preparation of a scraping or extract from the stain, or of a smear from a vaginal or other swab. However, if sperms are scarce and hard to find, they may be concentrated by shaking them off the stained area into water with ultra-sonic vibration, then collecting them at the bottom of the water by centrifuging. Staining is practically essential, mainly because, unless the stain is a fresh one, the sperms will probably have lost their tails by the time they reach the microscope slide (fig. 30b), and isolated heads are easily confused with, for example, stray yeast cells. If these are numerous enough to make the sperm heads hard to distinguish under the microscope, fluorescence microscopy after staining with acridine orange may help, since the nuclear material of the reproductive sperm cells fluoresces a different colour from non-reproductive cells such as yeast.

A seminal stain does not necessarily both give an AP test and contain spermatozoa. It is possible by washing a stained garment in detergent to remove all the enzyme but leave some of the sperms; in such cases these may still be found if the worker is persistent and looks in the right places. On the other hand, sperms are not always detectable in known seminal stains. The semen of some men, although they are potent and capable of ejaculation, contains few or none—conditions known as oligospermia and azoospermia respectively. It is also nowadays increasingly possible that the man may be artificially azoospermic through having had a vasectomy (though men who are socially responsible enough to have done so are perhaps unlikely to commit sex crimes). In such cases one must use other methods of confirming the presence of semen.

Other characteristic constituents of semen which may be tested for are the bases choline (not specifically seminal) and spermine. The *Florence* test for choline (the formation of needles of choline iodide) has been used since long before the AP test was introduced. If necessary both bases may be isolated by paper or thin-layer chromatography, and their occurrence together is strongly diagnostic of semen. The suggestion has also come from India that the preferential growth of certain moulds on seminal stains in hot humid conditions might

even be used for identification! Another (and perhaps more useful) Indian discovery is that the AP test can be made more specific by applying it to a stain
extract containing *laevo*-tartaric acid, which inhibits the action of most phos-
phatases except the seminal (prostatic) one. Unfortunately, one other phosphatase that it does not inhibit is that present in vaginal secretion. However, it
has recently been shown that this crucial distinction can be made using an
electrophoretic technique, which may be either "straight" or "crossed-over"
(see pp. 162–164). Finally, an immunological method may be practicable. By
using human semen as an antigen (p. 134), it is possible to prepare by animal
injection an *anti-human-semen* anti-serum containing antibodies specific to the
human seminal proteins. This may be used to test for human semen by the
techniques described in Section V. This method is in theory the most specific
and conclusive of any, other than the actual identification of spermatozoa; unfortunately, in practice the preparation of a completely specific and adequately
potent anti-serum presents considerable difficulty.

Once semen has been identified, its position and condition become facts of
importance. Seminal staining on a man's trousers or underpants is obviously of
comparatively little evidential value. Spermatozoa can be detected in urine
passed after ejaculation or even sexual excitement, a fact which may be significant
if a suspect denies any sexual activity. When spermatozoa are found on the
clothing or bedding of a woman who alleges that she has been sexually assaulted,
its significance will clearly depend very much on whether she is or is not having
regular sexual intercourse, was or was not a virgin, is chaste or promiscuous, is
clean or dirty in her personal habits. Spermatozoa may disappear from the
vagina within a few hours after coitus, and will be undetectable after some
days, at the very most; therefore if a woman alleges rape and also says, credibly,
that she has not otherwise had intercourse for more than a week, the detection
of semen on a vaginal swab will be corroboration of her story.

There is as yet no known way of measuring the age of a seminal stain, but its
colour and texture enable an experienced worker to make a fair estimate of
whether it is recent (days) or old (weeks or months).

The other secretions or excretions with which the biologist has to deal may be
more briefly mentioned. It may be necessary to identify *saliva*; for example, the
teeth may have been used in a struggle, leaving saliva in clothing. Saliva stains
usually contain squamous epithelial cells, since the lining of the mouth is one of
the few places where these occur. However, it is usually more easily and more
positively identified by the presence of ptyalin, the amylase (starch-hydrolysing
enzyme) which it contains. It is a well-known test for starch that it gives an
intensely blue colour with iodine; if a portion of starch solution no longer gives
this test after incubation at 37 °C. with an extract of the area under test, while
another portion similarly incubated with an extract of a control area does, then
the test area contains starch-reducing enzymes. There are also now available
commercially tablets containing an insoluble dyed starch polymer; in the presence of amylase this is dissolved and the dye released into solution. Other
tests (sensitive, but rather unspecific) which have been suggested are based on

the detection of, respectively, the reducing sugars formed by the hydrolysis of starch, and vitamin C (ascorbic acid), which is present in saliva.

It is not often necessary to identify *urine* stains, but it is not difficult to do so. Urine contains 2·0–2·5 per cent. of urea and about 1 per cent. of sodium chloride, and its dry stain shows a characteristic whitish fluorescence. The chloride ion is easily identified by a simple spot test, and urea by simple qualitative tests after extraction of the stain with acetone. A more sophisticated test for urea is to treat the moistened stain or an extract of it with urease (an enzyme present in certain species of beans and acting specifically on urea); if urea is present, ammonia will be liberated.

Staining due to *faeces* has sometimes to be identified—in investigating cases of buggery, for example. Microscopically, vegetable residues and, occasionally, muscle fibres from meat can be identified; chemically, bile pigments or their degradation products can be tested for. In a case of rape and murder reported some years ago from Norway, in which the identification of faeces was particularly important, intestinal bacteria in the stain were also identified by their species and strain, but this degree of refinement is rarely necessary. Intestinal worms, or recognisable fragments of them, or (more often) worm eggs, have also been used for identification.

III. SPECIES IDENTIFICATION

The nature of a stain having been identified, it is important if it is a bloodstain (and, occasionally, if it is of some other fluid) to discover what species of animal it came from. This most commonly means in practice answering the question: is it human blood? However, other species than Man have sometimes to be identified—for example, if a dog is suspected of sheep-worrying, or if a suspect claims that blood on his clothing is from an animal or bird which he shot.

With liquid blood, the microscopic appearance of the red cells is characteristic for a very few species, but, as has been mentioned, the blood to be tested is rarely liquid. In any case, this is a most unreliable method of identification; the writer knows of an instance in which identification by this means in a hospital laboratory of a pool of blood as human started some feverish police activity, which was called off smartly when a more skilled re-examination of the blood showed it to be dog's!

Reliable methods of species identification go back to the beginning of this century. The blood of each animal species is unique in the precise properties of its serum proteins, and the now almost universally used *precipitin* test depends upon this fact. It is an application of the antigen-antibody reaction already mentioned in connection with blood groups (p. 134). When a small quantity of the blood of one species is injected into the body of another, the injected animal reacts self-protectively by producing an antibody to the proteins of the foreign blood. As this is specific for the injected blood (but see p. 153 below) it can therefore be used in species identification. In practice, specimens of all the bloods which may have to be identified are injected into a series of experimental animals, each receiving blood from a different species. Rabbits are commonly used, except for rabbit blood itself, for which sheep may be used. After a suitable time, the animals are bled, and their blood sera separated; each batch of serum then constitutes a reagent for the type of blood that was injected into the animal from which that serum came. Because the experimental animals are *immunised*, the whole subject is known as immunology.

Such anti-sera are available commercially, and all laboratories carry stocks adequate to test for all of the bloods likely to be encountered—in this country, say, Man, dog, cat, horse, sheep, ox, pig, rabbit, fowl. The need for some unusual anti-serum might of course arise at any time; for example, if a man was accused of maliciously injuring a rare animal in a zoo.

In performing the test, a filtered isotonic-saline extract of the stain is allowed to come into contact with the anti-serum; a reaction between the two is then shown by the formation of a cloudy precipitate at the line or plane of contact. This test always used to be, and in many laboratories still is, done by layering the extract above the anti-serum in a small tube; a positive result is shown by an opalescent layer appearing at the interface between the layers after the tube has stood for about half-an-hour at room temperature. This method, although quite reliable, has the disadvantage that it is not always easy or even possible to get the *perfectly* clear extract which is essential for it, and that comparatively large amounts of expensive anti-sera are used. Both of these disadvantages are avoided in the better electrophoretic method, in which minute amounts of extract and of anti-serum are dropped into small cavities punched a few millimetres apart in a wet gel layer, and a potential applied to the layer in such a manner that the stain proteins and the antibodies, which carry opposite electric charges, migrate in opposite directions towards each other. (*Cf.* pp. 65 and 162.) They finally meet somewhere between the cavities, and a positive result is shown by a line of opalescence developing at this point (fig. 31); the line may if necessary be rendered more distinct by staining. This method can be used even with extracts which are not perfectly clear, since whatever causes the turbidity will not migrate through the gel.

Various control tests must be made to check the result. A new batch of anti-serum should be tested with known material to ensure that it is correctly labelled and fully potent. An unstained area of the material bearing the stain must be used as a control, in case anything extracted from the material itself is giving a false positive. Especially if the reaction is performed in tubes, a preliminary treatment of the stain may also be necessary to remove contaminants which interfere with the test—for example, fat or soap. Several different anti-sera must also be used in the test, to ensure that any reaction observed is not a non-specific one.

In practice, then, a precipitin test is carried out in the following manner. Suppose that we are testing a bloodstain, thought to be human, on the cuff of a jacket. Two saline extracts will be made, one of the stain, the other of an equal area of clean fabric from another part of the jacket. Some workers also run a further control of the fluids used. A block of tubes is then set out, or of cavities in a gel prepared, in which the two extracts (and control if used) are tested with several anti-sera, these including both the species we are testing for and several other species the blood of which the stain might be. The result might then be like this:

Serum	Anti-human	Anti-dog	Anti-cow	Anti-pig
Jacket, stain	X	○	○	○
Jacket, control area	○	○	○	○

X = Precipitation   ○ = No Precipitation

Such a result would be clear proof that the bloodstain which we have tested is human.

An elegant variation of the method involves the use of fluorescent antibodies. By chemically "tagging" the antibodies in the anti-serum used with a fluorescent dye very small fragments of tissue and even individual cells can be species identified by observing, under a microscope and using ultra-violet illumination, which of a series of such fluorescent specific anti-sera they bind, such binding being obvious by the whole fragment, cell, etc. becoming brightly fluorescent.

The most recent method was published only a few months before this was written (*Cayser, Whitehead and Pereira*). Final judgment of its value would be premature, but at least it seems to hold very great promise indeed. A saline extract of the bloodstain is mixed with a dilute suspension of latex particles sensitised with anti-serum; a positive reaction is then shown by agglutination (*cf.* p. 134) of the particles into clumps. The test requires only a drop of each solution and the very minimum of equipment, and the result can be read with the naked eye. The method is also at least as sensitive (especially for human blood) and specific as any other. Though the saline extraction may require up to several hours for very old stains, the actual test can be made in five minutes.

The precipitin test suffers in theory—though not greatly in practice—from the fact that anti-sera prepared as briefly described above are not fully specific. The antibodies formed in the bodies of the injected animals react not only with the proteins of the species from which the injected blood came, but also with those of closely related species. For example, anti-human will react with ape blood, anti-sheep with goat, anti-horse with zebra and donkey, and so on. (Facts such as these are used in the study of evolutionary relationships.)

There are in theory at least two ways in which anti-serum specificity can be increased. One is to treat the anti-serum with serum proteins of all of the species of bloods with which it reacts except for the one for which it is to be fully specific, and in this way to remove the interfering antibodies. For example, if anti-horse/zebra/donkey anti-serum is treated with zebra and donkey serum proteins, the zebra and donkey antibodies will be precipitated and the anti-serum will then be anti-horse only. The other way is to prepare the anti-serum in the first instance in an animal closely related to that from which the blood injected was taken; for example, an anti-serum prepared by injecting a goat with sheep's blood will be anti-sheep but not, obviously, anti-goat.

Anti-sera prepared in either of these ways are, however, of such low potency that they are almost useless in practice. In any case, the incomplete specificity of ordinary anti-sera is normally of no practical significance; the fact that a blood identified as human could have come from an ape is unimportant in the temperate zones. Occasions do arise, however, in which greater specificity is needed—for example, in the case in which the owner of a dog suspected of sheep-worrying claimed that the blood on its muzzle came from the goat's flesh on which he fed it. The distinction between human and monkey blood is also important in many tropical countries, especially India, and a good deal of work has been done on that subject there. An unambiguous answer may be obtainable if the reactions with the allied species disappear first as the anti-serum is progressively diluted (cf. serum titre—p. 156), so that at a sufficiently high dilution only the homologous (i.e. "proper") species reacts at all. However, what is probably a better method in expert hands is to surround a cavity in a gel layer containing the anti-serum with a ring of cavities containing bloods or sera from all of the species to be differentiated; the zone of precipitation between the central and the homologous-species cavities will then differ in appearance from the corresponding zones for all of the allied species.

Lastly, the precipitin reaction is not limited to the identification of blood-stains only. It can be used equally with extracts of any tissue. The serous exudate from a wound, traces of skin and superficial flesh adhering to a vehicle after an accident and even dandruff scales can all be species identified in this way. It is also reported that the method can be modified to species-identify hairs (even single ones) and small fragments of bone.

Although a precipitin reaction is the most popular and probably the simplest and most certain method of species identification, it is not the only possible method. It is possible to use the mixed-agglutination blood-grouping technique described on p. 157 as a method of species identification by using anti-sera specific for, and the red cells of, several species including that which is to be identified. Other tests make use of incomplete antibodies. These are antibodies which, although they react with red-cell antigens, do not cause agglutination. The most important of these tests in the present context is the anti-human-globulin test (often known as the Coombs test). If an anti-serum from an experimental animal which has been injected with human serum is treated with well-washed human red cells, the anti-species agglutinating antibody will be removed, but an anti-globulin remains which reacts specifically with human serum globulin. ("Globulin" is defined on p. 136.) The treated anti-serum will therefore agglutinate well-washed human red cells if, but only if, these have previously absorbed an incomplete antibody that is itself a globulin; it will, however, no longer do so if it has first been allowed to react with human serum, since the globulin in this will have removed the anti-globulin in the anti-serum. This rather complicated series of reactions can form the basis of a specific test for human serum.

IV. THE IDENTIFICATION OF RED-CELL ANTIGENIC BLOOD GROUPS

All blood-group determinations within the red-cell antigenic systems described on pp. 135–136 depend ultimately on whether or not agglutination of the cells from bloods of known groups is seen to occur in predetermined conditions. Known bloods must therefore be available. These can be obtained from, say, a blood-transfusion centre, but are more simply stored "on the hoof"—that is, in the bodies of colleagues and staff members who have been reliably grouped and who are willing to furnish a few drops of blood whenever it is required (though this is not likely to be possible for the rarer groups in a small laboratory). Agglutination can be looked for in a number of ways—in small tubes, on a white tile with the naked eye or a hand lens, or in cavity slides under the microscope (fig. 32). Generally speaking, most of these ways can be used in most methods of grouping, but which is used in any particular case depends on the technique employed and on the personal preference of the worker. On the whole, most experienced workers prefer to use a microscope since slight agglutination might otherwise not be detected.

Normally, the only samples of liquid blood which the laboratory will receive for grouping are those taken from the victims of crime, when it is important to know their blood groups before testing stains on a weapon, suspect's clothing, etc. Suspects themselves will sometimes offer samples for elimination purposes. The ABO grouping of such bloods simply requires centrifuging them to separate cells and plasma, and cross-testing both along the lines of the simple table on p. 134; for other systems, of course, only the separated cells can be used.

Most of the laboratory's blood grouping will, however, be on dry stains. These are most commonly of blood, but stains of other body fluids may provide valuable evidence if they came from a secretor. In general, having regard to the facts that only ABO antibodies occur naturally, and that, of the antigens described on pp. 135–136, only the ABO are secreted, the grouping of dried stains may be considered under three heads:

(1) The ABO grouping of blood.
(2) The grouping of blood by other systems.
(3) The ABO (*i.e.* ABH) grouping of secretions.

Although the A and B agglutinins (antibodies) occur naturally, they are unstable and soon become undetectable on drying. They can however be detected in fresh stains, and this is the basis of the old, but still occasionally useful, *Lattes* method of ABO grouping. Unlike the other methods to be described, it requires a stain dense enough for crusts of dried blood to be detachable. Its principle, whether in its original form or as modified by Outteridge and others, is that three small crusts of the unknown blood are immersed in dilute suspensions of A, B and O cells, well washed free of the agglutinins of the bloods from which they came. On gentle agitation, the test cells will be agglutinated by the agglutinins dissolving out of the crusts. Thus group-O crusts will agglutinate both A and B; group-A will agglutinate B only; group-B will agglutinate A only; group-AB will agglutinate neither. The O cells are used to exclude false results due to agglutination by substances other than the anti-A and anti-B agglutinins. A weakness of the method is that, if neither A nor B are agglutinated, we do not know whether the blood is AB or whether the test is just not working for some reason.

All other methods of grouping depend upon identification of the relatively stable agglutinogens by means of suitable anti-sera. In this connection, a crucially important concept is the serum *titre*. This expresses the extent to which the serum retains its activity on dilution. The primary results are rarely of the simple form agglutination/no agglutination, and it is therefore important to be able to express the degree of agglutination as a quantity—the titre. This is determined by preparing successive dilutions (*e.g.* undiluted, 1:2, 1:4, 1:8, ...) of the serum, and noting the greatest dilution which will agglutinate the corresponding cells. The results are usually recorded by designating complete agglutination in large (naked-eye visible) clumps as $++++$, and the least degree of definitely identifiable agglutination (small clumps with many free cells) as $+$. Tests on two sera might then yield results like this:

Serum dilution	Undiluted	1:2	1:4	1:8	1:16	1:32	1:64	1:128
Serum 1	$++++$	$++++$	$++++$	$++++$	$++++$	$+++$	$++$	$+$
Serum 2	$++++$	$++++$	$++++$	$+++$	$++$	$+$	$-$	$-$

Serum 1 would then be said to have a high, and serum 2 a low titre. Most anti-sera now used are, however, prepared centrally and distributed, and have a standardised titre.

Up to the present, three methods of grouping by the identification of agglutinogens have been developed. We will consider first their application to ABO grouping.

(1) Absorption-inhibition. This, the "classical" method, appears to have been invented in Italy about 50 years ago. It can be used only with ABO grouping, and is much less sensitive than the more modern methods to be described. The blood or other stain is allowed to react with anti-A and anti-B sera for a sufficient time to complete the reaction, and the titres of these determined before and after. At the end of the test the agglutinogens in the stain will have absorbed the agglutinins from the corresponding anti-serum, and the titre of this will therefore be very much reduced. The anti-sera used should have a fairly low titre to begin with or be well diluted, so as to maximise the effect. If the blood to be tested has soaked into a fabric and cannot be detached, then small pieces of stained fabric must be used for the tests; in that case it is essential to run parallel tests on similar-sized control pieces of unstained fabric, since some fabrics absorb agglutinins strongly but unspecifically.

The results of such an experiment might run something like this:

Dilution		1:2	1:4	1:8	1:16	1:32
Untreated serum	Anti-A	++++	++++	+++	++	—
	Anti-B	++++	++++	+++	++	—
Serum after absorption on fabric control	Anti-A	++++	++++	+++	++	—
	Anti-B	++++	++++	+++	++	—
Serum after absorption on stain	Anti-A	++++	++++	+++	++	+
	Anti-B	+	—	—	—	—

Such a result would be clear positive evidence that the stain tested was of group B, if blood, or came from a group-B secretor, if some other fluid. Any reduction of titre by the stain only of more than 2–3 dilutions can be considered a good positive test. If the control fabric shows strong absorption, then the stain cannot be grouped unless an actual crust is detachable. For the sake of simplicity, the above table omits the anti-H tests which are always now also done.

Absorption-inhibition grouping performed as just described has two disadvantages. Since a group-O stain contains no A and B agglutinogens, neither the anti-A nor the anti-B antibodies will be absorbed, and the serum titres will be unaltered. With blood, this result will be indistinguishable from that obtained if the test has failed altogether for some reason. With a secretion stain, one would not know whether it is group-O, whether it came from a non-secretor of any group or whether again the test has failed. However, as mentioned on p. 136, group-O bloods and secretions of all groups contain the *H antigen*, and luckily for the blood-grouper anti-H antibodies have been discovered. They occur in some rather unexpected places such as eel blood, but the best source found so far is the seeds of the common gorse (*Ulex europaeus*). A water extract of these agglutinates O and A_2 cells (see footnote on p. 133) strongly and A_1 and B cells scarcely at all, and reacts strongly with the H antigens in secretors' secretions. This makes a satisfactory *positive* test for group-O bloods and secretions.

The other disadvantage of absorption-inhibition grouping, its comparative insensitivity, is insurmountable; by using only the antibody which has *not* reacted, it depends on a *difference* in anti-serum titres, and a relatively large amount of blood is therefore necessary if this difference is to be significant when using the smallest practicable quantity of anti-serum. It would obviously be better, therefore, to detect directly if possible the anti-body which *has* reacted, and this is precisely what is done in the other methods of grouping.

(2) **Mixed agglutination.** This method, which owes its name to having been based on some research in a rather different branch of serology, was introduced in 1961 by R. R. A. Coombs (Cambridge) and Barbara Dodd (London Hospital). It offered an immense increase in sensitivity, enabling the blood on a few milli-

metres of a single thread to be grouped easily and with certainty. The stained fabric is teased out under a microscope, and the fibres are treated to fix the blood coagulum firmly and to ensure that any adherent cells are haemolysed (that is, have lost all recognisable structure). The treated fibres are incubated with anti-A, anti-B and anti-H anti-sera, thoroughly washed, and flooded with suspensions of A, B and O cells (which may have been pre-treated—see p. 159). Then, on microscopic examination, a positive result is shown by each fibre being coated with an adherent layer of cells, a negative by cell-free fibres and any cells present being distributed at random. (This is of course why the original stain must contain no unhaemolysed free cells.) The method marked a great advance when it was introduced, but is admittedly somewhat tedious and complicated.

(3) **Absorption-elution.** In this, after antibody and antigen have reacted and excess antibody has been washed away, the absorbed antibody is *eluted* and subsequently identified. Such a method was suggested several decades ago, but credit for its successful practical development (1960) should go to S. S. Kind of the Home Office forensic science service. Very briefly, he "fixed" small portions of stain by heat, treated them separately with anti-A and anti-B anti-sera, washed off the excess and eluted in A and B red-cell suspensions at 50–60 °C.

Since then, many variations on the absorption-elution theme have appeared. The most successful is probably that published in 1962 by Miss Pereira and L. C. Nickolls of the Metropolitan Police Laboratory and derived in part from both the Coombs–Dodd and the Kind methods. In this, the blood is held throughout the test in small pieces of thread a few millimetres long—either threads from the stained fabric or clean pieces with which stains on other surfaces have been soaked up. These are soaked for several hours in the anti-sera at 4 °C. and rinsed well with chilled saline; the absorbed antibodies are then eluted into dilute (pale pink) suspensions of indicator cells in bovine albumin solution (which preserves the cells whole); finally the results are read after half-an-hour's gentle agitation at room temperature.

Originally the stained threads had to be handled loose and teased out, which was "fiddly," but in a later modification they are lightly cemented at one end to cellulose acetate sheets, to which they remain attached during the whole sequence of operations, teasing being unnecessary and handling easier. Pairs of stain and control threads are used for each test, thus:

Thread pair:	1	2	3
Anti-serum:	anti-A	anti-B	anti-H
Indicator cells:	A	B	O

(In the current form of the test, 5 thread pairs are in fact used, the fourth and fifth being treated with an anti(A + B) anti-serum and with A and B indicator cells, respectively. This helps to eliminate certain possible sources of error.)

In all of these "positive" methods the final results are the reverse of the "negative" ones given by absorption-inhibition: the stain is of the same group as the cells which *are* agglutinated. Thus:

A and B cells both agglutinated: Stain is group AB

A cells agglutinated ⎫
B cells not agglutinated⎭   Stain is group A

A cells not agglutinated⎫
B cells agglutinated   ⎭   Stain is group B

O cells agglutinated by anti-H ⎫
Neither A nor B cells agglutinated⎭   Stain is group O

Practically speaking, grouping within the other antigenic systems mentioned on pp. 135–136 is possible only by absorption-elution. Using the appropriate anti-sera and indicator cells, the principles are the same as for ABO grouping, but for each other system there are various differences in detail into which we have not space to enter here. For the MN grouping of dried stains, success in which was first announced by Miss Pereira in 1963, very careful selection of the rabbit anti-sera is quite essential for reliable results. Rhesus-system tests, to the development of which, because of their potential value (p. 135), numerous workers have contributed, are inherently less sensitive than ABO and require more stained material, because the concentration of antigen on the cells is much lower; rather different techniques are therefore necessary. Anti-C, anti-c, anti-D, anti-E, anti-e and anti-C^w anti-sera are all available, though some are more potent than others.

In general, in all of this grouping work the fresher the stain the better. However, provided that it has dried fairly quickly and remains dry, the A and B antigens seem to persist almost indefinitely. The M and N antigens, on the other hand, are usually undetectable after perhaps 6–12 weeks, though the M antigen is more stable than the N. The Rhesus antigens appear to be less stable than the ABH but more stable than the MN.

In some of these grouping techniques greater sensitivity can be achieved by using indicator cells which have been *pre-treated* with a suitable enzyme to remove the outermost layer of their cell walls. This treatment is belived to expose more reactive antigenic sites than were originally present on the outside of the cells.

The most recent advance in red-cell antigenic grouping is its **automation**. The manual performance of all the operations in grouping large numbers of samples by the techniques described above becomes a very onerous task in a busy laboratory, especially when working with multi-group systems such as the Rhesus. It is therefore a considerable advantage to have as much as possible of the work performed automatically. Automatic blood grouping was pioneered by Technicon Scientific Instruments Ltd., and has been used for some time in hospitals, but its use in forensic science is a recent development. There are theoretically several ways in which it could be done, but the method at present used is in outline as follows. (See fig. 34.)

(1) Manually-prepared eluates of the stain under investigation are put into the apparatus in small tubes, one for each agglutination reaction required.

(2) A selector device withdraws a small volume from each tube, and to each the appropriate indicator red cells—one "shot" for each group in the system being used—are added automatically, together with a pre-treating enzyme (p. 159) and other ancillary substances.

(3) The resulting "slugs" of liquid are pushed along a fine tube by a pump, and in between each a bubble of air is introduced. Thereafter the resulting "chain" of alternate slugs and bubbles passes through the apparatus with its sequence unchanged, so that the separate identity of each eluate volume is maintained.

(4) The chain passes through vertically disposed spiral mixing coils in which the agglutination process, which began as soon as the indicator cells were added, is completed.

(5) As each slug emerges from the last spiral, a relatively large volume of normal saline is added to it to neutralise the effect of certain of the substances added in stage (2).

(6) The slugs pass through two consecutive horizontally disposed spiral settling coils, in which clumps of agglutinated cells sink into the lower half of the tube, and are sucked out as each slug emerges from each coil. (Two coils are necessary to ensure *complete* removal of agglutinates.)

(7) Each slug is now either clear and colourless, or red, according to whether or not the cells added to it in stage (2) have been agglutinated and removed. A lysing agent is now added to disperse the cell contents throughout the liquid.

(8) Finally, the transparency of each slug to a ray of green light is automatically measured photo-electrically, and the resulting impulses recorded as a continuous line on a roll of paper. Red slugs (those in which there has been no agglutination) do not transmit the light, red and green being complementary colours, and no impulse is recorded; colourless slugs (those in which agglutination has occurred) pass the light, and the resulting impulse is recorded as a marked "peak" in the line.

(9) The sequence of peaks is matched with the order in which the original eluates were introduced in stage (1), thereby obtaining the fundamental agglutination/no agglutination results of the grouping operations.

Secretion stains. As already mentioned, these may be examined to determine whether they came from a secretor, and ABO grouped if they did. It is possible to group, for example, seminal stains on the clothing of a victim of a sexual assault, saliva on cigarette stubs or stamp gum and envelope closures, sweat on underclothes left at a scene, etc. There is however a risk of false reactions in using only dried stains to determine secretor status; it is therefore preferable to use for this whenever possible a specimen of fresh saliva, which contains a higher concentration of A and B antigens than does blood itself. The saliva is heated for 10 minutes to inactivate its enzymes, and is then grouped—commonly by absorption-inhibition, which is found to give the most reliable results in this case.

In grouping of blood and other stains the possibility must always of course be borne in mind that mixed stains may be present to complicate the investigation.

Blood or seminal stains on a sweaty garment may for example contain agglutinogens both from the stain and from the wearer's sweat, if he or she is a secretor. How far it is possible positively to sort out identities in cases like this will depend on whether or not the parties are of the same group, on the circumstances of the case, on the nature and position of the stains and on the blood groups concerned. In the most favourable case, it is even possible by using a combination of absorption-inhibition and absorption-elution methods, to group the semen on a vaginal swab, although this is naturally saturated with vaginal secretion. If the woman is a non-secretor, any agglutinogen in the swab must have come from the semen; if she is a secretor, any agglutinogen which is in the swab and which she herself does not possess must similarly come from the semen.

The ABO grouping of solid tissue such as muscle or skin, simply treating it as one would a piece of bloodstained material, is possible and sometimes necessary. Much work has also been done on the grouping of hair. Although this undoubtedly contains the A and B antigens, and although there have been several reports from Japan of the successful grouping of both hairs and small bone fragments, the general opinion in the West is that hair grouping is not yet possible as a reliable routine.

Finally, it should perhaps be emphasised that forensic grouping of this type is not as simple and easy as the abbreviated account of it in the preceding pages may have suggested. Success in the recently introduced systems admittedly demands great expertise, but even in ABO grouping there are numerous possible snags and complications which we have not had space to mention. To take only one example, a spurious B antigen can be produced in several ways, including bacterial activity, and this might well mislead the inexperienced. It is safe to say that there is no aspect of forensic science which demands a higher, or even an as high, degree of skill as blood grouping.

Recent progress in this field has been so rapid that fresh developments are bound to come quite soon—though to say from what direction would be rather a crystal-ball exercise. The use of antibodies "labelled" with artificial radioisotopes or with fluorescent compounds is attractive in theory. (Cf. species identification by fluorescence microscopy—p. 153.) Such a method should be the most sensitive yet, and it would be unnecessary to use indicator red cells, since the antigen-antibody complexes could be detected directly by their radioactivity, or by fluorescence microscopy, as the case might be. So far, however, experiments here have been rather unfruitful. Another potential method being investigated is similar to that also described on p. 153 for species identification: by using suitable particles (e.g. latex or sheep erythrocytes) coated with antibody, it may be possible to observe directly their absorption on the antigen sites.

V. POLYMORPHIC PROTEIN AND ENZYME SYSTEMS

These have been described on pp. 136–137, and it is in utilising them that some of the most striking recent advances in blood typing have been made. Most of the work has been done on this side of the Atlantic, and the name of B. J. Culliford of the Metropolitan Police Laboratory has become well known in this field.

The techniques used are quite different from those which we have been describing, and cell agglutination plays no part in them. It would fill this book to describe them all in detail, but they all depend on *electrophoresis* (p. 65). The various protein and enzyme blood constituents are all or nearly all colloidal in nature, and, as their large molecules are electrically charged, their polymorphic varieties can be separated according to their mobilities and the magnitudes of the charge carried. Electrophoresis can be done on wet filter paper, but this is not very satisfactory, and a starch, agar or cellulose acetate gel is always used nowadays. Many conditions must be just right if the operation is to be successful. The most important of these is the pH, since this determines the sign of the charges on the molecules and therefore the direction in which they travel. As the separated constituents are invisible in the minute quantities employed, they must be revealed in some way; this requires a second operation, the details of which depend on the protein or enzyme in question.

At present, four different electrophoretic techniques are in use.

(1) **"Straight" electrophoresis.** The bloodstain extract is positioned near one end of the gel layer, usually on a slip of filter paper inserted into a small slot, and a fairly high voltage, commonly of the order of 5 volts/centimetre, applied across the layer. Migration is allowed to proceed until the various components of the extract are well separated, which usually requires some hours (fig. 35). One difficulty which must be overcome is that small molecules tend also to diffuse sideways across the gel, which if unchecked would prevent clean separation. Electrophoresis is therefore usually carried out at a low temperature, at which diffusion is very slow; either the whole equipment is kept in a refrigerator or cold room at 4 °C., or alternatively the gel holder may be mounted on a refrigerated surface.

(2) **Electrophoresis with "molecular sieving."** By using a gel layer the pore size of which decreases continuously along its length, electrophoretic migration of molecules through it stops at the point at which the pores are too small for molecules above a certain size to pass through; a band of such molecules is then built up at this distance from the starting point. Constituents are thus separated according to the sizes of their molecules. For this method a vertical gel layer (usually of acrylamide) in a thin flat vertical tank is used, with the pore size decreasing downwards.

(3) **Immuno-electrophoresis.** This can be used for any potentially antigenic substances—normally in this context proteins. In its original and simplest form, electrophoresis is performed as in (1), but with the addition of a small trough a few centimetres long in the gel layer, adjacent and parallel to the line of electrophoretic separation. When this is complete, the trough is filled with anti-serum; this on diffusing out sideways from the trough reacts with each protein con-

stituent along an arc-shaped line in the gel where antigen and antibody meet. The resulting pattern of arcs (fig. 36) may be rather complex and its interpretation requires considerable expertise. In a more recent modification of this method, instead of relying of diffusion through the gel to bring the antigen and antibody together, after the first electrophoretic separation a second is applied at right angles to it, as in method (4), below. Immuno-electrophoresis can also be used, as has already been mentioned (p. 150), for purposes other than blood typing.

The *haptoglobin* type of a blood can be determined by any of the first three methods above, but with dried stains, unless they are very fresh (a few days), the second (molecular sieving) is by far the most successful. (This method was indeed introduced into forensic blood typing specifically for this purpose.) The positions of the various components after separation can be revealed by utilising the fact that haptoglobin binds haemoglobin and will migrate as a haptoglobin/haemoglobin complex; one therefore simply ensures that some haemoglobin is present (which is easy with a bloodstain) and "develops" the bands with a peroxidase reagent (p. 146).

For *haemoglobin* typing (p. 144) straight electrophoresis followed by peroxidase development is normally used.

For most of the *enzyme* systems (except PCE) straight electrophoresis is used. Normally each system requires its own particular conditions, but some success has been achieved in devising an "omnibus" technique by which several enzyme systems can be run simultaneously in the same gel layer. Development is by means of a reagent so formulated that the enzyme in question catalyses a reaction producing an intensely coloured product. Most of the enzymes examined are blood ones, but PGM occurs also in vaginal secretion. None of the enzymes remains stable after drying, so that stains used for any of these systems should be as fresh as possible, and certainly not more than a few weeks old. The AK system, however, appears to be "hardier" than the others and to be detectable up to about six months.

The plasma enzyme PCE can also be typed electrophoretically, but other, better, methods are available for it. All of its polymorphic forms hydrolyse cholinesterase, but this reaction is inhibited by certain compounds in the case of one but not of the other of the two commonest forms. The *rate* of the hydrolysis reaction in the presence of an inhibitor can therefore be used to identify the type of PCE present. This rate may be measured in several ways, of which the most direct is to measure spectrophotometrically (p. 73) the rate of change of the absorbency at a suitable wavelength of the reaction mixture.

The often important question whether a bloodstain is *menstrual* in origin, though not one of blood typing, is conveniently mentioned here because it is best answered by using immuno-electrophoresis. Menstrual blood does not clot because it contains a factor which inhibits the clotting reaction—the conversion of soluble fibrinogen into insoluble fibrin. Though it cannot be said that a universally applicable method of identification has yet been found, good results have been obtained by the use of an anti-fibrinogen anti-serum in immuno-electrophoresis, followed by a calculation of the ratio $\frac{\text{fibrinogen}}{\text{total protein}}$ for the stain in question.

(4) **"Crossed-over"** (*Laurell*) **electrophoresis.** This is a further development of immuno-electrophoresis which holds considerable promise, though it is not yet, as far as the writer is aware, used anywhere routinely in forensic science. The whole "spectrum" of plasma proteins, of which there are at least thirty, in a blood sample is separated by a first electrophoresis, then caused by a second at right angles to the first to migrate "laterally" into a gel layer containing a "blunderbuss" anti-serum containing antibodies to all of the proteins. The movement of each protein fraction stops when it has all reacted with the appropriate antibody. The final result is then a series of arcuate lines of precipitation (fig. 33), the distance from the starting point to the centre of each arc being determined by the mobility of the corresponding protein, and the height of each arc by the amount of that protein present.

In theory, this technique is a most attractive one for characterising a blood, since the relative proportions of the various proteins may vary quite widely and constitute therefore a *continuously variable parameter* (p. 137). However, the considerable practical difficulties are still unsurmounted. It has not yet proved possible to obtain exactly reproducible results. The method is also in a sense *too* sensitive, in that it gives different results for the same person's blood taken at different times. Of the various possible causes for these differences, diet is probably the most important; one, however, in the case of a woman, is due to whether or not she is "on the pill."

VI. CONCLUSION

It will be clear from the preceding pages that blood typing has become an extremely complex subject. The grouping of every stain or blood sample by every system would therefore be a Herculean task. Indeed, this would often be impossible; fortunately, as we have already mentioned, it is usually unnecessary. What systems are actually used in any given case will depend upon several factors, namely:

(1) In the case of a stain, its size. As each additional system requires a fresh portion of material, if the stain is very small the grouper will naturally turn first to a system which (a) requires the least amount of stain, and/or (b) offers the best prospect of discrimination (see (4) below).

(2) Also in the case of a stain, its age. As already mentioned, grouping within certain systems is possible only if the stain is fairly fresh.

(3) The availability of the requisite anti-sera. Most of these are expensive, and some are difficult to obtain; obviously, therefore, the inessential use of the latter will be avoided.

(4) The circumstances of the case. To obtain the maximum information about a totally unknown blood, the grouper would normally start with the ABO

system, which is the easiest and requires the least material, and proceed thereafter to as many systems as the above factors permit, choosing first those systems which, from the distribution of groups within them, offer the best chance of discrimination. Frequently, however, one starts with *some* prior knowledge on the basis of which the most useful system(s) can be selected. For example, if it is a question of deciding whether a known and an unknown blood are the same or different, one would use first the system within which the known belongs to the rarest group, so that, if they are different, the chance of excluding the unknown by one grouping operation is greatest. Again, if one wishes to assign a stain to one or other of two bloods (say, victim and assailant), one would obviously start with a system within which these belong to different groups; if there are several such systems, one would use that in which grouping is most certain, quickest and cheapest.

13

BIOLOGY II—MAINLY MICROSCOPY

I. EQUIPMENT

The rest of the forensic biologist's work can be broadly summed up in two words: visual identification. His chief tools, other than his eyes, are therefore instruments of magnification, ranging from low-power illuminating magnifiers to the most advanced microscopes obtainable. Expertise in microscopy is therefore a prime requisite.

Until very recently, the words "optical microscopes" would have been used in the previous paragraph—that is, microscopes using light, with which the greatest possible magnification, both in theory and in practice (see p. 82), is about 1,000 diameters. Now however the scanning electron microscope has vastly extended the possibilities here. The instrument has already been briefly described (Chapter 8). It is too soon to say how it will eventually be most profitably used in forensic science as an instrument of magnification, but a few possible applications will be mentioned in this chapter. Otherwise, however, "microscope," unless qualified, should be taken here to mean optical microscope.

The reader is assumed to be familiar with the elementary principle of the microscope. There is of course much more to microscopy than merely magnifying the object with a combination of lenses. For example, the microscopist must know how to get "critical" illumination of his preparation (light source imaged by substage condenser on microscope image plane). Indeed, it needs technical know-how and some knowledge of optics to obtain the best possible resolution at high magnifications.

All microscopists are well aware that there is a limit to the increase in magnification obtainable simply by reducing the focal length of the objective, when this is used in air. This limit is set by the fact that, if shorter objective focal lengths are used in air, marginal rays will enter the objective so obliquely that a prohibitive loss of light will occur. The highest-powered (oil-immersion) objectives are therefore designed to be used with the space between them and the object filled with a liquid having a refractive index near that of glass, reflection losses being thus minimised. With really high magnifications it may also be necessary to use an auxiliary condenser to get sufficiently brilliant illumination over the very small field embraced by a high-power objective. *Köhler illumination* is a refinement of this arrangement in which the optical components are so disposed that all the light is concentrated in the field of vision, and none goes to produce a distracting glare by illuminating the surrounding parts of the object.

Various advanced techniques of microscopy may be used. Several applications of *fluorescence* microscopy have already been mentioned, and it is also useful in the examination of dyed textile fibres (p. 171). In this, the object is illuminated by ultra-violet radiation, using a quartz substage condenser, and the rest of the instrument is a conventional optical one.

Many of the specimens to be examined are too transparent, or apparently too structureless, to show much detail when viewed in the normal way with ordinary transmitted light. It is to overcome just this difficulty that the histologist stains his specimens, but that is sometimes impracticable here. In *dark-ground* illumination, a substage condenser of short focal length has an annular diaphragm passing only marginal rays; these then emerge so obliquely that none enter the objective unless they have been deflected by something lying in the object plane; a specimen examined in this way appears self-luminous on a dark background, with great contrast and clarity of detail.

A *polarising microscope* has a Nicol prism or polarising screen (nowadays usually the latter) between the light source and the condenser, and another between the objective and the eyepiece. Any birefringent object (*e.g.* most fibres) then shows intense colours changing as the polariser (plane of polarisation) is rotated. Some micro-anatomical structures are thus seen with a colour as well as an intensity contrast which makes them more easily distinguishable. Polarising microscopy is also used in rock identification (p. 58).

Phase-contrast and *interference* microscopy are particularly adapted to distinguishing details in structures (*e.g.* living cells) where the differences in optical density are too slight for these to be seen by conventional means. Both methods utilise the fact that different parts of the structure under examination have slightly different refractive indices, so that initially homogeneous rays passing through them emerge out-of-phase. The optical system of a phase-contrast microscope, by producing interference between these phase differences, converts them into considerable intensity differences. An interference microscope is, so to speak, a hybrid between a phase-contrast and a polarising one; the extent of the interference between the two beams produced by the doubly-refracting polariser is governed by the phase change which one of them suffers on passing through the specimen, the final result of this being that faint otherwise indistinguishable details are seen in bright contrasting colours.

For certain purposes, especially the comparison of fibre colours, it is almost essential to use a *comparison microscope*. The type of instrument described on pp. 20–21 can be made to serve here, but, ideally, the biologist's comparison microscope should be designed with his particular requirements in view. He does not need the mechanical refinements necessary for the proper comparison of scratch marks etc.; on the other hand, he does need more elaborate optical arrangements. His instrument should provide for the highest magnifications, and should incorporate provision for fluorescence, polarisation and incident-light microscopy. For colour comparison, it is obviously essential that both halves of the field are illuminated by light of exactly the same colour.

Besides having good microscopes, the forensic biologist must be equipped with reference collections, as complete as he can make them, of the types of material he may have to identify. Textile and other fibres, woods of different species and plant seeds are essential; the enthusiast will add to these whatever else he thinks likely to be useful—animal hairs, fish scales and cattle foods, to name only three possible examples.

II. TEXTILE FIBRES

The examination and identification of these, although not strictly speaking a biological problem, is normally part of the forensic biologist's work, partly because the traditional fibres are biological in origin, and (more realistically) because he has the necessary microscopical expertise.

In the normal run of criminal investigation, textile fibres probably indeed require identification more often than any other class of material with which the biologist has to deal. Since clothes are normally worn in our climate, and since textiles are also used for carpets and upholstery, there will be some transference of fibres in practically every crime involving either assailant/victim contact or entry into a normally furnished house. Fibres from brushes, cordage and the like may also occur as contact traces.

The material to be examined may be of three types. First, when there has been rubbing contact between a relatively smooth surface and the textile (as when a car has struck a pedestrian, or when an intruder has rubbed past a door jamb or shuffled over a carpet) there will be many tiny fibre fragments left on the surface. The collection of these by separate picking off may be virtually impossible, in which case they may be picked up by pressing sticky tape on the surface, subsequently freeing them from the tape with a suitable solvent. (One of the proprietary tapes can be used, but these tend to be *too* sticky and to pick up more than the transferred fibres; a slightly less sticky tape specially made for the present purpose is better.) Secondly, quite long fibres may be transferred in a person-to-person struggle, or from carpets and rugs on to footwear. As far as clothing is concerned, the most desirable case from the laboratory's point of view is when the two sets are both loose-textured and of quite different colours. Thirdly, quite long tufts or even whole pieces torn out may be found on a car which has struck a pedestrian or on a projecting nail or splinter past which an intruder has pushed.

If an actual fragment of cloth is found, it may of course be matched with its parent garment by a number of characteristics—pattern, weave, colour or colours of both warp and weft, types of constituent fibres, etc. It may even be possible to fit the fragment into the hole it left; that sort of comparison, however, belongs rather to the work described in Chapter 3 than to that now being considered.

More commonly, only a few fibres are available for comparison, and these will have to be characterised solely by their material and their colour.

Material. The forensic biologist must nowadays be prepared to encounter more and more uses of man-made fibres, not only in clothing and upholstery but also in ropes etc. Considering both these and the natural fibres, the majority of textile fibres in use can be classified thus:

(1) *Animal hairs.* The most important is of course wool, but there are others— mohair (Angora goat), camel, etc.

(2) *Vegetable fibres.*

(*a*) Seed hairs: cotton, kapok.

(*b*) Bast and structural fibres: flax (linen), jute (hessian, sacking). In this category we may also include fibres used for paper-making (see. p. 207), those used for rope and cordage (hemp, sisal, etc.) and some used in brush making.

(3) Fibres produced by the *solidification of a liquid extruded through a fine orifice.*

(*a*) Natural: silk.

(*b*) Artificial (man-made):

(*i*) Those made from animal or vegetable raw materials: regenerated cellulose (Rayon); cellulose esters, usually the acetate (Tricel, Arnel, Trilon); alginates (from seaweed); regenerated proteins (casein, etc.).

(*ii*) Purely synthetic fibres: polyolefines (polyethylene, etc.); polyamides (Nylon, Brilon); polyesters (*e.g.* Terylene—Dacron in the U.S.A.— polyethylene terephthalate); the acrylics, mostly acrylonitrile polymers (Orlon, Acrilan, Courtelle, etc.); vinyl chloride and vinylidene chloride polymers (Vinyon, Saran, etc.).

(4) *Miscellaneous fibres.* Natural mineral fibres (asbestos); decorative glass, metal, etc., fibres (*e.g.* Lurex).

Most of the natural fibres of classes 1 and 2 have characteristic microscopic appearances (fig. 38) and their recognition is one of the first things that the forensic microscopist learns. However, the second thing that he learns is that the job is not always as easy as he may at first have imagined. For example, although wool, being an animal hair, shows when new a clear surface-scale pattern (fig. 38), in shoddy (reconstituted wool) this is often absent through the scales having been lost in the processing. Again, many of the fibres used for cordage and coarse fabrics—the hemp, etc., group—are not easy to distinguish from each other. Silk and the man-made fibres are, as a natural consequence of the way in which they are made, internally structureless and hence very similar in appearance. Man-made fibres may however be *de-lustred* by the incorporation of a mineral pigment (fig. 38).

There is no single simple analytical routine which can be used for the identification of man-made fibres, and the tests actually used must depend on the nature of the fibre and how much of it is available. Obviously, any test which is to be useful in the present context must require the minimum of material— preferably a single short length of the fibre under the microscope—and destructive tests, if they must be used, must be made last. The following are the means of identification which have on the whole proved most useful.

Physical characteristics

(1) *Shape.* Most if not all extruded man-made fibres show longitudinal striations due to shrinkage as the fibre hardens, and the precise appearance of these gives each type of fibre a characteristic shape. This is best seen in cross-section (to prepare and mount which is not difficult, thanks to various simple "dodges"), and may be circular, irregular, dumb-bell-shaped, trilobal, etc. If circular or approximately so the diameter is also characteristic. The longitudinal striations themselves are easily seen under a good microscope, and are particularly well shown up with a scanning electron microscope (p. 82) if this instrument is available.

(2) Most man-made fibre materials *fluoresce,* though this property will of course be modified if they are dyed, as they most commonly are.

(3) The *refractive index* can be measured by an immersion method, using the Becke line (*cf.* p. 33). The degree of *birefringence* (see Glossary), which is measurable as a difference in refractive indices at different settings of a polarising microscope, is even more distinctive, and is possibly the most useful single identifying property for a man-made fibre.

(4) The *specific gravity* varies from less than 1·0 for polyethylene to over 1·5 for rayon, and is measurable by flotation (*cf.* Chapter 4). This test is of course vitiated if the fibre has been de-lustred.

(5) *X-rays.* The particular molecular structure of each polymer produces, when an X-ray beam impinges on the slightly tensioned fibre, a characteristic diffraction pattern. (*Cf.* p. 79).

(6) *Staining tests.* A number of mixed stains have been developed which differentially dye the several types distinctive colours. Fibres already dyed must of course be decolourised before testing, and this treatment may affect their subsequent behaviour in the strain. Rayons may also be differentiated by a technique known as skin staining.

Destructive physical tests

(7) *Solvents.* The differential solubilities in a suitable selection of organic solvents will generally identify the chemical group to which a fibre belongs. For example, cellulose acetate but not other fibres is soluble in acetone, and nylon is soluble in hot xylene.

(8) The effect of *heat,* which is easily observable on a hot-stage under the microscope, is characteristic. The fibre may or may not shrink when heated, and it will either have a specific melting-point or decompose without melting.

Destructive chemical tests

(9) The *infra-red absorption spectrum,* measured on a fibre dispersed in a potassium bromide disc or by other suitable means (p. 74), is characteristic and is particularly useful for acrylics.

(10) Nylons can be characterised by *thin-layer chromatography* after hydrolysis in hot dilute acid.

(11) For most materials *pyrolysis* and *gas chromatography* are valuable, especially if temperature programming (p. 67) can be used.

Colour and its significance. The majority of textiles are dyed, and therefore the colours of the fibres examined are extremely important. The primary method of comparison is of course by eye with a comparison microscope (see p. 167). Provided that the lighting in both halves of the field is exactly identical, this is an extremely sensitive method; the human eye can distinguish very small differences in *hue*. One must of course allow for the fact that identical fibres identically dyed may show differences in the *depth* of their colours, either because of small local variations in the amount of dye taken up or because a thicker fibre will in any case appear darker.

However, identity of colour is not necessarily proof that chemically identical dyes were used, and an apparent match should always be confirmed if possible. It is useful to examine the fibres by a suitably chosen monochromatic light as well as by white, and as already mentioned their fluorescence is likely to be characteristic. The dye can also be stripped from the fibre by a suitable solvent and examined separately. It is of course unlikely that enough will be available to use one of the standard dye-identification routines (p. 55), but the dye will probably not be a single chemical compound, and the separation of its constituents by thin-layer chromatography is likely to prove informative. It is not difficult to do this with the dye from a few millimetres of a single fibre.

The evidential value of a coloured fibre match may of course vary enormously. At one extreme, an undyed cotton fibre is normally worthless as evidence, since this material is of such universal occurrence. At the other, the occurrence together of several colours, especially if they are of one of the less common materials, may be so exceedingly improbable as a random event that such a match may well amount to proof of contact. Fabrics of even as common a colour as navy blue may show obvious differences when their constituent fibres are examined. Some apparently uniformly coloured fabrics such as khaki can provide valuable contact traces, since the individual fibres composing their yarns often show a wide range of different colours.

When numerous colours are present in each of two lots of fibres, a few random matches are always likely to be found, but if a sizeable proportion match this will be very significant. For example, in a case of murder some years ago a young woman was strangled with a piece of string in which were entangled 18 dyed woollen fibres of 10 distinguishable colours. The string might have come from either a suspect's pocket (in which case he was probably the murderer) or from a certain kitchen drawer (in which case he was exonerated). Both these places contained a very large number of differently coloured woollen fibres. It turned out that 10 of the 18 fibres could be matched exactly with fibres from the pocket, but only 1 with fibres from the drawer.

It is easy to show mathematically that the odds against a match such as this occurring by random chance are very great, but reliable data on which to base such a calculation are rarely available. The evaluation of the significance of fibre-matching evidence must still depend largely on the expert's judgment. There have been several attempts to evaluate statistically the probability of an apparent match occurring by chance—the probability, that is, that a particular fibre or specified group of fibres could have been derived from some other garment than the control one examined—but the admittedly tentative results of these are inconclusive and conflicting. The difficulty is that these calculations are unrealistic owing to the number of unknown factors involved, these including both annual changes in fashion and the local distribution of mass-produced articles of clothing.

III. HAIRS

The examination of human hairs is obviously important in the investigation of many crimes of violence, or in trying to gain some information about the owner of a hat left behind. Animal hairs are less commonly important, but they may occur as contact traces on a variety of occasions—for example, when there are domestic animals, especially if these are of unusual breeds, at the scene of a crime; when furs have been stolen in a smash-and-grab raid; in the investigation of bestiality and malicious injury of farm animals; if a crime is committed in a zoo. Hair from otherwise uncommon animals (*e.g.* skunk, bear, etc.) is also used in making brushes, and may therefore come up for identification.

In a hair, three parts can be distinguished—the *cuticle*, the *cortex* and the *medulla*. The cuticle, or outer "skin," bears a pattern of fine scales, each species of animal, including Man, having a characteristic combination of scale shape and pattern. Several schemes for the classification of these patterns, in which they are grouped into 7 or 8 basic types, have been proposed. The examination of scale patterns is referred to below. The cortex is the substance of the hair and normally contains any pigment present. The medulla is a central canal or sub-divided space lying along the axis of the hair. It may be, or appear to be, absent, but if present appears dark in normal microscopy, on account of the refractive effect produced by the air with which its spaces are filled. The appearance in cross-section is also an identifying characteristic of hairs. There are various simple techniques for cutting and examining hair cross-sections.

Human hairs. These normally have a rather faint surface-scale pattern, of which an impression can if necessary be made (see p. 174). The medulla is either continuous and uniform, irregularly interrupted or totally absent (see fig. 37) and its diameter relative to that of the whole hair is variable. A hair can be characterised to some extent by its colour and general appearance, but, as already mentioned (p. 129), these can never tie it to a particular individual.

Head hairs are smooth and regular, circular in cross-section if straight, elliptical if wavy. Recent cutting, singeing, bleaching, dyeing and the old-fashioned methods of permanent waving all produce characteristic recognisable alterations. Hair which has been lacquered shows characteristic adherent "blobs" of dried lacquer. If enough is available this may be dissolved off and characterised by infra-red spectrometry (p. 74). Beard and moustache hairs, as well as being fairly thick, are occasionally roughly triangular in cross-section. Eyebrow hairs and eyelashes have long fine curved tapering tips. (More than one assailant who has kicked his victim in the face has been convicted by eyebrow hairs wedged into the toe of his boot.) Body hairs (pubic and axillar) are, as well as being short, coarse and curly, practically always elliptical in cross-section and usually medullated. The comparison of pubic hairs is of course important in the investigation of many sexual offences.

Any good optical microscope is adequate for hair examination, but some features, especially the surface scales and dried lacquer "blobs," are more clearly revealed by the scanning electron microscope (p. 82). The possibility of sexing hairs is discussed on pp. 179–180.

The characterisation of hair by means of the trace elements it contains has attracted considerable interest in recent years. This obviously requires an exceedingly sensitive method of analysis, and during the last decade there has been much research in several countries (mainly Canada, Belgium and Great Britain) into the use of neutron activation analysis (p. 80) for this purpose; it had already, however, been so used in France during the 1950s in connection with the notorious Besnard murder case. Mass spectrometry (p. 76) has also recently been used for this purpose. The earlier results, particularly those reported from Canada by Jervis, led to the much too optimistic belief that it was possible in this way to "tie" a hair conclusively to the head it came from, but later researches, particularly those carried out in Belgium and those in this country by the Atomic Weapons Research Establishment on behalf of the Home Office, have not confirmed this belief.

The present position may be briefly summarised as follows. Hair contains a variety of trace elements (zinc, gold, copper, manganese, mercury, arsenic, chlorine, bromine, etc.) apparently derived mainly from the diet but also to some extent from shampoos, rinses, etc. It is not technically difficult to determine accurately the concentrations of these present in quite small specimens. These concentrations vary between one person and another, but also, though to a lesser degree, between different parts of the same head. They also, however, change with time in one individual. The hair of persons sharing the same diet and environment tends to show less variation than that of the population at large, Some elements show a much greater range of concentrations than others.

On the whole, two specimens of hair from the same head taken at about the same time are likely to resemble each other in composition more than either resembles a random specimen from another head. The differences in the latter case may range from negligible to very great, depending on the elements considered. Knowing the distributions of all these elements in a large population. it is possible to calculate mathematically the probability that two specimens of hair did not come from the same head if the element concentrations in them differ by more than some particular amounts, and a statistical procedure specifically for this purpose has been developed by J. B. Parker of the Atomic Weapons Research Establishment. One final difficulty is that the analysis cannot distin-

guish between diagnostically useful elements actually incorporated in the substance of the hair and those present as adventitious superficial contamination.
Washing will remove the latter but may also leach out some of the former. The
procedure generally adopted is to adhere rigidly with all specimens to an arbitrarily chosen washing routine in a suitable solvent.

Animal hairs. The problem in the identification of these is most commonly
the relatively easy one of deciding whether or not the hairs under examination
could have come from a certain known animal or group of animals. The complete
species identification of a quite unknown hair is much more difficult, may be
impossible and will certainly demand patience and access to a good reference
collection. (But see p. 154.) Most animals also have two quite different sorts of
hairs—short fine *wool* hairs forming the "undercoat" which keeps the animal
warm, and long coarse *guard* hairs. The latter, if from a dark animal, are often so
deeply pigmented that they appear quite structureless under the microscope and
have to be bleached before any useful examination can be made.

An animal hair will be identified by its surface-scale pattern, its medullar
structure and its cross-section. In order to see the scale pattern, it is often sufficient simply to examine the hair at a magnification of a few hundred diameters,
focusing on its surface. If, however, the pattern is very faint, or if the hair is so
heavily pigmented as to be opaque, then a cast of the surface must be made. This
can be done simply by pressing the hair into a tacky plastic surface (*e.g.* half-dry
nail varnish) and removing it when the surface is hard. Surprisingly clear and
detailed casts of scale patterns can be made in this way. In many species (*e.g.* cat,
rabbit, mouse) the medullas show characteristic regular repetitive patterns of
little spaces or thickenings. The guard hairs also show a variety of shapes in
cross-section—for example, dumb-bell-shaped in the rabbit, kidney-shaped in
the guinea-pig, cigar-shaped in the seal, variously irregular in deer and ante-
lopes.

IV. OTHER BIOLOGICAL MATERIAL

The remaining types of material which the biologist may have to examine are so
various that a complete description of their identification would be almost an
adequate course of reading for a double honours degree in taxonomic botany and
zoology. It will therefore not be attempted here.

Vegetable material. Anyone committing a crime out of doors is likely to get
plant material on his clothing, and the identification of this may therefore link
him with the scene. The burglar pushing past the damp wall or fall pipe may get
smears of green algae; the over-excitable rural Lothario will probably carry away
fragments of vegetation from the lane in which his passions got the better of him.
A particular case of the latter type, from the north of England, may be quoted.
A girl was raped in a field in which two species of chickweed were growing, and
the biologist subsequently examining the suspect's clothing found on it some

fragments of chickweed. Chickweed is a common plant, but in this case it proved impossible to decide to which of the species it should be assigned; it appeared to lie between the two in its characteristics. The biologist visited the field for himself and found growing a patch of a chickweed hybrid which resembled exactly that on the suspect's clothing. The girl was later asked to point out independently where the crime had occurred, and she identified the precise spot where the hybrid chickweed was growing.

Comparison of vegetable material may also be important in cases of larceny. It will be important, for example, to show that grain found in the possession of the poultry-food thief is of the same species and variety as that stolen. If both samples also contain the same adventitious variety of weed seeds, the evidence for a common origin is strong. The writer was once concerned in a case in which a large wad of stolen £1 notes could be identified because the stolen money had been exposed to damp, and fragments left at the scene of the theft as well as notes in posession of the thief all bore growths of black mould of the same cellulose-destroying genus *Chaetomium*. In another, more recent case some bits of vegetation found at the scene of a theft were identified as barley-malt sprouts; the suspects were known to have bought from a brewery some second-hand sacks which had contained sprouting malt.

There are various other miscellaneous circumstances in which material of plant origin may come up for examination. The presence of starch grains may serve to identify an amorphous mass as a food residue, and the presence of a high proportion in a sample of dust would be highly significant if a crime had been committed in a bakery or by a baker. All starch grains show a highly characteristic "hot-cross-bun" appearance in polarised light, and in addition the starches from different cereals and vegetables are morphologically distinctive. Cases have occurred in which honey sold as "pure English" has been found to contain pollen grains from Eucalyptus species not found outside Australia. The identification and differential counting of fossil pollen grains in a sample of coal also enable its origin (formation, pit or even seam) to be determined. (It is only fair to say, however, that this technique would probably not be used to prove the theft of a bucketful of coal, since it requires several weeks' work.)

The biologist must therefore be prepared to identify almost anything which the vegetable kingdom can produce. He must be a good enough microscopist and botanist to recognise small superficially unidentifiable fragments for what they are—parts of roots, stem, leaf, seed-case, etc., as the case may be. He must further be able to identify the species or at least genus; however, as no one man can know the whole vegetable kingdom well enough, the forensic biologist, unless he is one of a large team, may in some cases have to consult outside experts in the more specialised fields of mosses, lichens, algae, moulds, fungi, etc. Finally, he must know, after he has identified his species, whether it is a common one which might have been picked up almost anywhere and the occurrence of which is therefore of limited value as evidence, or whether it is rare and therefore of great value (as in the case of the chickweed quoted above, where the hybrid was rare although the hybridising species were each common).

Wood. This special type of vegetable tissue deserves a section to itself, simply because wood fragments occur so frequently, either as constituents of safe ballast (see Chapter 5) or because small fragments of wood have been carried away in the commission of breaking offences. The value of wood identification in the latter case is of course limited by the fact that only a few species of fairly common woods are normally used in building construction. When burnt matches are found at a scene, the identification of the wood of their sticks may sometimes be useful; although these are generally of poplar, other woods are sometimes used, especially in foreign matches.

The woods of all species of trees have certain basic structural features in common. The microscopic tissue elements present can be divided into four types (although not all are present in all woods): *parenchyma* (used mainly for storage of photosynthesised organic foodstuffs), *fibres*, *tracheids* and *vessels*. The fibres and tracheids confer strength, and the tracheids and vessels are used for the transport of water and of inorganic foods. Most of these are arranged longitudinally in the tree trunk or branch; there are always present, however, sheets or flattened lines of parenchymatous cells, sometimes supplemented by tracheids, which run outwards from the axis of growth towards the surface (*rays*).

In each species the microscopic arrangement of the elements present, both those arranged longitudinally and those in the rays, is characteristic. The sum of the microscopic features used for identification also includes a number of secondary ones: several types of pits (conducting passages between cells), cell-wall thickenings, various types of crystals deposited intracellularly, resinous masses, etc.

We have just, however, mentioned the fact that not all types of structural elements are found in all species of wood. All woods are broadly divisible into *softwoods* and *hardwoods*. (These names do not necessarily refer to the actual properties of the wood; some softwoods—*e.g.* yew—are very hard, and some hardwoods—*e.g.* balsa—are very soft.) Softwoods come from coniferous trees (an order of the gymnosperms). Many of them are in common use as constructional timbers under names such as "deal." Micro-anatomically, they consist mainly of tracheids, with some parenchyma; neither true fibres nor vessels are ever present. Hardwoods come from trees which are, botanically, dicotyledons (a sub-phylum of the angiosperms). All of the common broad-leaved trees—oak, ash, elm, beech, chestnut, etc.—are of this class. Micro-anatomically, they contain all four types of elements; the vessels in particular are generally large and prominent.

Many of the characteristics by which timber in the mass can be identified (for example, differential colouration of heartwood and sapwood) are not available to the forensic biologist dealing with fragments, and he must therefore depend entirely on microscopy. In the standard method of identifying a wood in this way, sections are cut along three mutually perpendicular planes: *transverse* (perpendicularly across the grain of the wood); *radial* (in the plane defined by the axis of the stem and a ray); *tangential* (perpendicular to a ray). From the information gained by examining these three sections (two may be sufficient) after staining and noting the various characteristic structures seen in each, the wood can be identified. Identification in this way has in fact been highly systematised, and punched-card indexes are available which, given considerable experience in their use, make it largely a matter of patience and routine.

Unfortunately, in this field the pieces of wood are often too small to be sectioned. In that case, all that can be done is to clear the fragments (for example, by soaking in chloral hydrate solution or dilute household bleach), stain them and mount and examine as many as possible. If a sufficiently large representative collection of the individual elements (cells) is present, it may be possible to recognise all of their various identifying characteristics.

The case of a murder which was committed some years ago in one of the Channel Islands affords an excellent illustration of how even tiny pieces of wood can provide vital evidence. The naked body of a girl was found in a field. She had been violated and strangled, and had last been seen alive some days previously. It was clear that the crime had not been committed where the body was found. Suspicion fell on a local butcher's assistant. On the body there were some fragments of sawdust identifiable as *Pinus radiata* (a coniferous species). The same species was present in the sawdust on the floor of the butcher's shop, and probably nowhere else on the island; it was not normally imported there, but one single consignment had been imported to make mushroom boxes, and the butcher had had a load of sawdust taken from the hopper at the sawmill just at the time when it was being sawn up. Some other sawdust fragments on the victim's body were also identified as another species of wood used for the butcher's chopping block, which had been repaired very shortly before she disappeared.

Animal material. Among the biologist's samples, if we except the hairs and textile fibres discussed earlier in this chapter, the animal kingdom is on the whole represented less frequently than the vegetable. He must nevertheless be prepared to identify almost any animal material. It may be important not only to show that a fragment of tissue adhering to a car is human (Chapters 6 and 12), but also to identify histologically the part of the body from which it came. A fish-gutter's knife, which can form a very effective offensive weapon, always has fish scales in its interstices, and fish scales are species-identifiable, which could be useful knowledge if a suspect is known to have been gutting a particular kind of fish. Fowl feathers or parts of them may form an important contact trace in an offence committed on a farm. Down feathers from related species of birds were formerly considered indistinguishable; however, it has recently been demonstrated, in a case received by the Metropolitan Police Laboratory in which a man accused of stealing chickens said that the fragments of feathers on his clothing were from ducks, that significant differences in their fine structures can be discovered by using scanning electron microscopy. Stolen poultry may be connected with the scene of the theft by a comparison of the contents of their gizzards with the poultry food used by the loser. Trout have been connected in a similar way with a particular fish farm. Some of these numerous types of material (*e.g.* human tissue) would be identifiable "by the book"; others would require the *ad hoc* collection of the appropriate control samples.

Because of the universal presence of insects, a knowledge of *entomology* is sometimes valuable. In one case, some valuable equipment was stolen in transit from West Africa to England, and the cases filled up with earth. It was important to know where this substitution had taken place. The earth itself might have come from either country, but on careful separation of every fragment of organic matter in it some termite heads were found. These were of a species local to the place of origin of the consignment—and of course there are no termites in England. In another case, some bank notes believed to have formed part of a sum of money stolen were found in the possession of a suspect. Traces of what was identified as insect excreta were adhering to them. Later the sale of a suit-case to the suspect was traced, and this was found to have been attacked inside by the Brown House Moth. In the excreta on the notes there were found identifiable fragments of strawboard and paper, materials with which the suitcase was lined, and blue and yellow rayon and green nylon, all of which could be matched from garments which had been kept in the suitcase and which had been eaten through by the moth larvae.

A specialised but occasionally important application of entomology is its use to estimate how long a body has been lying where it was found. Bodies, especially in the open, attract a variety of insects: first the diptera (flies, bluebottles, greenbottles, flesh flies, etc.), the larvae of which are maggots; some months later the burying beetles; still later a variety of species attracted by the products of advanced decomposition; after about a year various species of mites; lastly, still other species when desiccation is complete. The most important of all these are normally the maggot-producing flies. Each species has its own time-cycle of development; bluebottle eggs, for example, will be laid within a day or two and in summer hatch within a day; the maggot undergoes several moults before pupation, and the fully developed fly emerges in, usually, about three weeks. The identification of the species and stage of development of maggots may therefore provide valuable dating information. (It may be necessary to breed them to the live flies before species identification is possible.) Evidence of more than one generation of flies having bred may also be found. This method was used successfully in the investigation of the famous Ruxton case about 40 years ago and gave an approximate date for the deposition of the remains which agreed pretty well with that on which the women whose remains they were believed to be were last seen.

Micro-biology (bacteriology etc.) has not as yet found many useful applications in forensic science. Apart from the possible uses already mentioned (faeces, skin bacteria, p. 149), it has occasionally been found helpful to identify the bacteria in decomposing blood samples, or in saliva specimens which gave atypical and unexpected grouping reactions. It may be that this is a field in which more research by an imaginative micro-biologist would be rewarding.

V. SEXING

It would obviously be immensely valuable if biological specimens such as blood or hair could be *sexed*. This is a subject in which, though its problems are by no means all solved, considerable progress has been made since the first edition of this book appeared.

There were some early attempts to sex hairs using the apparent sex differences in such properties as the refractive indices of the cuticles and the differential solubilities of the root bulbs in strong alkali. However, these differences, even if they are real, are insufficiently clear-cut for the sexing of a single unknown specimen. The more recent methods, which are applicable to any sort of tissue, are all development of *nuclear sexing*.

As mentioned on p. 140, in every normal human cell nucleus, other than those of the spermatozoa and ova, there are 23 pairs of chromosomes. The substance of these is known generically as *chromatin*. In 22 of the pairs the two chromosomes are similar in both sexes; in the 23rd, the pair which determines sex, they are similar in women but dissimilar in men, and are conventionally designated XX and XY respectively. The Y chromosome is smaller than the X. These facts form the basis of nuclear sexing.

A high magnification under a good microscope is obviously essential for this. Moreover, the sexually diagnostic chromatin characteristics are visible only during certain phases of the cell's growth cycle. Therefore, given a number of nucleated cells in a specimen, only a proportion of these will at any given time show sex characteristics. At first (late 1940s onwards) diagnosis was based on the presence or absence of the relatively extra large chromatin masses of the XX chromosome pair, which could be made visible by differential staining. They are known after their discoverer as *Barr bodies*; in leucocytes (white blood cells) they may actually project from the nuclei—the so-called "drum-stick" projections. Therefore, if a sufficient number (say 100) of the cells are examined, they can be pronounced female if a significant proportion (say one third) show Barr bodies or drum-sticks, and male if none do so.

This method of sexing has not however proved on the whole sufficiently certain or reliable to be more than occasionally useful with the kind of specimens encountered in a forensic science laboratory, since in these circumstances a sufficient number of serviceable nuclei can rarely be observed. More recent work has therefore been directed at identifying rather the male Y chromosomes. This has been made possible by the discovery in the late 1960s that treatment with certain metallic salts (magnesium chloride is generally used) causes a molecular change in the chromatin substance, as a result of which the Y chromosomes will take up a fluorescent stain and can be detected by fluorescence microscopy. Up to 90 per cent. correct results in blind trials have been obtained with this method.

Nevertheless the problem of sexing cannot yet be said to be completely solved. The methods just described usually fail with specimens more than a few days old. Either method, taken alone, has the disadvantage that it gives a positive result for only one sex; with a negative result, one is uncertain whether the specimen is of the other sex or whether the test has failed for some reason. Ideally, therefore, it should be possible to use two complementary methods giving between them positive results for both sexes. (This could be particularly important if any of the rare chromosomal abnormalities, with extra or missing sex chromosomes, are encountered.)

Recent progress does however seem to promise routine sexing in the not too distant future. It might be applied to tissue fragments or to bloodstains, using the nucleated leucocytes in the latter. Suitable epithelial (mucous-membrane) cells are also normally present in saliva and vaginal secretion: the former might be utilised to discover which sex smoked a cigarette stub or licked the gum on the envelope of an anonymous letter; the latter to distinguish between a pure seminal and a mixed seminal/vaginal stain. These methods have also been used to settle the somewhat embarrassing disputes about the sex of Olympic athletes.

The sexing of hairs remains rather a special problem. It does not appear to be possible to do so using the Y chromosomes, but there have been numerous reports of success here using XX chromatin bodies in the root follicles. Both human and animal hairs have been sexed in this way; it has been used, for example, in America, in cases of illegal deer hunting. In any case, it seems at present that only XX sexing is possible with the lower animals, since fluorescent Y chromosomes appear to occur only in Man and the higher apes.

The correlation which has apparently been established between certain chromosomal abnormalities and criminal behaviour is a matter for the criminologist, and will not be discussed here.

14

FIRES AND EXPLOSIONS

Within our present terms of reference, the investigation of fires is important primarily because arson is a serious crime. However, both the field of investigation and the laboratory's function in it tend to spread beyond this restricted area, for which tendency there are two reasons. First, it is often not known whether the fire was started maliciously or not until an investigation has been made, and in any case the interests of the police overlap with those of fire prevention officers, whose concern it is to determine the causes, and of insurance companies, who are naturally interested in determining liability. Secondly, the scientific part of the investigation cannot here be sharply separated from pure detective work; the expert must take together as his *corpus* of relevant data, the statements of witnesses, the observations of police and fire officers, his own observations at the scene after the fire (an examination that is nearly always essential for him to make, and that as soon as possible), and the results of any subsequent laboratory tests he may find necessary. Expertise in this subject demands common sense and judgment moulded by experience first, and scientific knowledge second. The fact that a successful crime of arson destroys its own evidence does not, it is hardly necessary to say, make its investigation any easier.

The investigation of a fire is therefore directed at answering these questions:

(1) Where was the fire started?

(2) How was it started?

(3) Was it started accidentally or maliciously?

(4) If it was started maliciously, is there any evidence pointing to the method used by, and/or the identity of, the perpetrator?

For an uncontrolled fire which consumes a building, just as for a controlled fire in a grate, five things are necessary:

(*a*) A source of energy (heat) to ignite it.

(*b*) Readily inflammable material (kindling) close to the energy source.

(*c*) A bulk supply of fuel.

(*d*) Free access of oxygen.

In addition to these four material necessities, there is also a condition which must at all times be fulfilled if the fire is to maintain itself, namely:

(e) The rate of production of heat must not be less than the rate of loss by conduction (to the solid boundaries of the space in which the fire is burning), convection (by the hot gases rising from the fire), and radiation. In a steadily burning fire, the rates of production of heat by combustion, and of loss by the means stated, are equal. If the former rate is less, the fire will diminish in size and eventually go out.

In a maliciously started fire, the source of ignition is in most cases simply an applied flame, less commonly some electrical device to produce local heating, still less commonly some sort of gadgetry with acids, spontaneously inflammable chemicals, etc. An accidental fire may be due to any one of an immense variety of causes: a dropped light; an unextinguished cigarette; an electrical short-circuit; live embers falling from the grate; fabrics too near an electric fire; a blowtorch left burning; dry woodwork too near a hot stovepipe; sparks struck from metal on metal or metal on stone; an overheating bearing; focusing of the sun's rays through bottles of liquid, etc., acting as lenses; static electrical sparks from industrial processes; highly exothermic chemical reactions such as the slaking of lime; the spontaneous oxidation of rags soaked in a drying oil; etc. etc. (The whole topic of spontaneous combustion will be discussed briefly later—see p. 186.) Whatever the initial cause, the initial effect is the same—the local heating of a small part of the available fuel to its ignition temperature.*

The temperature at which a combustible will ignite is not a precisely determinable figure, since it depends upon its condition, how the heat is applied and so forth, but for most dry combustibles (paper, wood, inflammable plastics, etc.) it is usually somewhere round about 400–500 °C. (A dull red heat is about 600 °C.) We must remember here that heat and temperature are not the same thing. The temperature of a match flame is far above the ignition temperature of wood, but we cannot kindle a large block of wood with a match because the large solid mass of fuel has too great a heat capacity—it "mops up" the heat, so that its temperature nowhere rises very much.

Consideration of the next stage demands a few words of explanation. In the first place, there are for our present purpose two types of combustion—smouldering and free burning. Smouldering is what chemists call a solid-phase reaction: it occurs at the surface of the fuel (that is, at the fuel/air interface), occurs without free flame, and is (for combustion) rather cool and very slow. The Fire Research Station has shown for example that it may propagate itself in sawdust without going out at speeds as low as 1–2 inches/hour. (That figure is actually for beech sawdust in still air; with other materials it is slightly higher, and with any material it will naturally rise if there is a draught.) The burning of a cigarette is typical smouldering. It is important in practice as an initial phase of some

---

* The ignition temperature should not be confused with the *flash point*, which is the precisely determinable temperature at which the space above an inflammable liquid contains the lowest concentration of vapour which will just permit a flame to propagate itself. The precise values of flash points, though legally important in framing regulations for the storage of inflammable liquids, are rarely a matter of concern in fire investigations.

accidental fires, because its slowness and coolness mean that the fire may burn for quite a long time, possibly hours, without being noticed. Fire may begin in this way with, for example, a cigarette end discarded among old papers, dust, upholstery stuffing and the like.

In what we have called here free burning, although a solid-phase reaction may be occurring (in a bed of burning coke, for example), there is also always a gas-phase reaction occurring. This is fire with production of flame—fire in the usual sense of the word. What is happening is that the heat of the fire is decomposing the unburnt fuel with production of inflammable gas, and this reacts with oxygen with production of heat and light—that is, as a flame.

Now, mixtures of air or oxygen and a combustible gas will burn only if their composition is within certain limits. The mixture will not burn if there is either too little gas or too little oxygen. Both the lower and the upper limits depend on what the gas is; some figures are given on p. 192. A flame cannot be produced until the concentration within it of inflammable gas produced by the decomposition of the fuel is greater than the lower limit quoted there—that is, for the fuels we are concerned with, somewhere between about $1\frac{1}{4}$ and 5 per cent.

If this condition is fulfilled before the source of ignition is applied—as may be the case, for example, in a building filled with petrol vapour—then the spread is for all practical purposes instantaneous, and an explosion results. (See p. 192. Attempts to start fires with the help of a volatile accelerant such as petrol not infrequently have this result, sometimes with unfortunate consequences for the arsonist.) However, in the normal case of a fire involving solid fuel, the initial stages are more complex. The source of ignition first heats a small volume of fuel with a low heat capacity (*i.e.* kindling) to a temperature sufficient to de-compose it with the production of inflammable gas, and as soon as the concen-tration of this is locally sufficient a flame begins. This then heats more kindling, which ignites, producing more heat and more flame, and the fire spreads, slowly at first then gradually more rapidly. It is in fact a typical *chain reaction*. At some point a stage will be reached at which the concentration of inflammable gas produced exceeds its lower combustion limit throughout the whole space occu-pied by the fuel, and the fire will then fill this space. It then continues to burn at a steady rate determined by the rate of decomposition of the available fuel, and continues to do so either until it is put out, or until the fuel is exhausted.

These stages are familiar to anyone who has ever lit a coal fire with the tradi-tional paper and sticks—the initial slow growth, followed by a rapid build-up to a fire filling the grate, leading to a steady fire. The same stages occur in a fire in a building. In this case, however, the transition from the slow kindling stage to the steadily burning state is usually much more rapid and more obvious, because the walls of the building enclose the space more completely than a fire-grate does, and hence make it easier for the critical lower inflammability limit to be reached. This transition is what is known to firemen as the "flash-over." It often occurs with terrifying suddenness; there have been innumerable instances of loss of life in fires where an apparently small and controllable fire has in a matter of minutes or even seconds developed into a large and uncontrollable one. The most rapid and destructive flash-overs occur when the sudden opening or destruction of a door, window or other obstacle allows access of air to a confined space in which a fire has been burning with an inadequate air supply, and in which a high concentration of inflammable gas may have built up.

II. THE EXPERT AT THE SCENE

The expert called to the scene of a fire will first try, from witnesses' statements and from his own examination, to discover where and when it started. Witnesses' statements, even if made in good faith, are not always trustworthy, but they are the only source of some necessary information. When was smoke first seen coming from the building? What colour was it? (This may give a clue as to what was burning, which may or may not be what the building is supposed to have contained.) If the building was empty, when did the last occupant leave? From what direction was the wind? When was the fire call received? What was the state of the fire when the firemen arrived?

The expert will then make his own examination to try to answer the questions: Where? When? How? There are a few simple facts and principles which can help him to fix the primary seat of fire: where it started. Fire normally burns mainly upwards, laterally outwards to a lesser extent and downwards not at all, so he seeks the lowest point of destruction. If the fire has been more or less confined to one part of the building, the primary source will probably also have been exposed longest to the most intense heat, and will therefore show the deepest charring of woodwork and the most severe damage in general (fig. 39). The charring of woodwork is normally deepest on the side whence the fire came, which fact can be used for direction-finding to pin-point the source. (These deductions must however be made with caution: various circumstances—for example, a supply of some especially inflammable material—can cause the hottest part of the fire to develop away from its origin, and draughts and eddies can complicate the charring of woodwork.) What can be learned from any melted metals found? Any part of a fire will melt lead or solder, and the hotter parts of most fires will melt aluminium alloys (melting-point around 650 °C.), but only the centre of an unusually fierce fire will melt copper (M.-P. 1,083 °C.) or even brass (M.-P. 900–1,000 °C.). If there is a piece of furniture such as a desk or chest of drawers at the apparent seat, did the fire start inside or outside this?

Other observations will help to elucidate the general history of the fire. How deeply is the woodwork charred? (The charring of constructional timber increases in depth at an average rate of round about $1\frac{1}{2}$ inches per hour.) Could the fire, from the location of its source, have been smouldering for some time before it was discovered? How dense is the smoke discoloration on window panes and walls in parts of the building not actually destroyed? (Heavy discoloration is evidence of a long slow smouldering period with production of much smoke.) What was the state (open, partly open, shut) of doors and windows? The answers to these questions in conjunction with the witnesses' statements will probably make an estimate of the time of origin and subsequent course of the fire possible. A surprisingly long time from the original cause to the outbreak of obvious fire may have to be postulated—up to many hours—but, as mentioned above, smouldering can be a very slow process.

If, on the other hand, the fire seems to have grown more rapidly than one would expect from the circumstances, the cause of that must be sought. It may indicate the use of an accelerant by an arsonist (see section IV below). However, another possible cause of unexpectedly rapid growth is the extensive modern use of polyurethane foam for upholstery stuffing. This material burns with catastrophic rapidity, producing toxic fumes (see p. 191) and charring all the woodwork of a room within a few minutes. (A less inflammable type has been produced but has not yet been extensively used.) Expanded polystyrene on walls and ceilings also constitutes a serious fire hazard if it has been painted with gloss paint; the combination will drop molten burning masses which spread the fire.

The final, crucial question to be answered is: how did the fire start? If the original source of ignition was simply an accidentally dropped or a maliciously applied light, it is practically certain that no trace of this will remain, but one may be forced to assume it simply by exclusion of all other possible causes. The present writer, for example, once "explained" a fire in a factory stock room by the following considerations: there was no physical evidence of the cause; smoke was seen coming from the building about fifty minutes after the last occupant had left it; near the seat of the fire there were found, protected by some half-burnt stock falling on to it, the remains of some string and packing material (i.e. good smouldering fuel), which was not supposed "officially" to have been there; the seat of the fire was just about in the position where a match or cigarette end would have landed if thrown away in the normal manner by a right-handed person in the act of leaving the building.

If the cause of the fire is an electrical fault, the seat will obviously have to be close to some electrical wiring or fitting. The commonest electrical cause is probably a short-circuit, and it will normally leave evidence of arc-ing and fusing at this point which will survive a fire. A short-circuit may also, however, be caused by the fire, through live wires touching when their insulation has burnt off. For the same reason, finding fuses blown is of no diagnostic significance. It may well be useful, however, to note the time at which any electric clocks stopped.

The writer was once asked to investigate a fire the seat of which was clearly in a room used as a store for physiotherapeutic appliances and containing a panel heater, permanently switched on, fixed to the wall. The fire was noticed by passers-by about 2 hours after the last person had probably left the room. A large number of towels were stored on a shelf above the heater. As a working hypothesis, the cause of the fire was assumed to be towels having been knocked down on to, and covering up, the panel heater. Heaters of this type are safe in that, when properly used with free access of air to their faces, equilibrium between heat supplied and heat radiated and convected away is reached with the surface reaches a temperature of about 60 °C. only. If, however, heat loss is hindered the temperature will rise, possibly to the ignition point of dry fabrics (*cf*. condition (*e*), p. 182). The hypothesis was tested by running an identical heater while it was roughly wrapped in old dusters; the wrapping burst into flames in one hour fifty-five minutes.

In investigating fires in **motor vehicles**, the same principles can be applied. The complete destruction of a motor vehicle by an accidental fire must be counted a rare event. In fact, one American investigator wrote some years ago that it never happens, after he had unsuccessfully tried to fire vehicles by playing a blow-lamp on the carburettors and by similar means. Although his conclusion is certainly rather too sweeping, it is true that a car the whole of which has clearly been sub-jected to intense heat has very probably been soaked in petrol before it was fired. (It has been pointed out, however, that do-it-yourself car builders who use fibre glass are incurring a fire hazard unless they use a type based on a non-inflammable resin.) If the car was soaked in petrol, no physical evidence of this (see p. 189) is likely to be found, however, since such maliciously started fires usually occur in isolated places and have burnt themselves out before the fire brigade arrives. It is important, and usually fairly easy, to discover whether the fire started in front of or behind the dashboard. In the former case, the engine will be severely damaged, with all plastic fittings destroyed and non-ferrous ones possibly melted, and there will probably be evidence of the fire reaching the body through the holes in the bulkhead behind the engine; in the latter case, the engine may show little damage, and there will be evidence of the fire traversing the same route in the opposite direction.

III. SPONTANEOUS COMBUSTION

Certain materials in certain circumstances are liable to catch fire without the action of any external agency, and it is important to discover when this has happened so that malicious firing can be eliminated as a cause.

The key to the possibility of spontaneous ignition is provided by condition (*e*) on p. 182: any spontaneous natural heat-producing process may give rise to a fire if the heat generated cannot be dissipated as fast as it is produced. The commonest processes of this type are oxidation and bacterial action.

The spontaneous oxidation of, for example, phosphorus or pyrophoric iron is well known, and is such a rapid process that a high temperature can be reached even when the heat is freely dissipated—that is, when the bulk of material is small. Other more slowly oxidisable materials will ignite only when present in large bulk—that is, one sufficient effectively to prevent or at least slow down considerably the dissipation of heat. The classic example here is a heap of rags soaked in a "drying" (*i.e.* spontaneously oxidisable) oil such as linseed oil, the slow oxidation of which liberates heat.

Spontaneous ignition by bacterial action is more complicated. All gardeners who have made hot-beds, and anyone who has ever seen a manure heap steam-ing, should know that bacterial action produces heat, and with some materials this can lead to actual ignition. Many materials—esparto grass, oil cake, various seeds and fodders, etc.—are liable to this, but it probably occurs most commonly with hay. One obvious reason for this is that the large mass of a haystack is very effective in preventing the dissipation of heat.

Bacteria will thrive and multiply only in the presence of an adequate supply of moisture, and hay may fire at any time between about two and twelve weeks after stacking if it is stacked too damp. Haystack fires therefore call for scientific investigation, since their occurrence always raises the suspicion of malice or gross negligence.

Just how bacterial action leads to fire is still somewhat obscure: obviously no living organisms can of themselves produce and survive the temperature of actual ignition. It seems, however, to be established that an initial temperature rise due to bacteria or heat-loving moulds can carry over into a further and greater rise produced by purely chemical action. Several mechanisms have been suggested for this, but the most plausible postulates the initial formation of unstable unsaturated compounds which combine with oxygen to form highly reactive peroxides.

When a haystack has been completely destroyed by fire, there is of course no means (other than inference from witnesses' statements, etc.) of discovering how it started. If, however, a spontaneously inflammable stack is examined before it actually ignites, or at least before fire-fighting operations have completely dispersed it, it will show several characteristic features. Malicious or other accidental fires start, naturally, on the outside of the stack; spontaneous ones start inside, and a section of the stack will reveal foci and "flues" of brown or even black overheated hay, which may burst into flames when it is exposed to the air. In addition, hay at the brown stage has a characteristic acrid smell, and is also strongly acid, the acids (mainly lactic and acetic) being presumably derived from the fermentation of carbohydrates. Investigations by Firth and Stuckey at the Preston Forensic Science Laboratory just after the war established that the acidity in this condition varies from about 1 to over 8 per cent. (calculated as lactic acid on the dry weight), depending on the degree of change of the hay. Since the corresponding range for good hay is about 0·5–1·7 per cent., any figure over 2 per cent. can be taken as evidence of liability to spontaneous ignition.

IV. ARSON

The crime of arson may be committed from a variety of motives, of which the commonest are probably the wish to defraud an insurance company, malice towards the owner of the property, an attempt to cover up another crime and pyromania (the uncontrollable urge to enjoy a good blaze). The investigator may suspect arson for a number of reasons, which include the following:

(1) There is no apparent cause, and the normal fire risk is low.

(2) The fire has grown more rapidly than would be expected from the contents of the building. (Conversely, a long smouldering period makes arson prima facie less probable.)

(3) There is a succession of fires on the same premises showing similar features, and/or the same person gives the alarm on each occasion.

(4) The building/contents are insured and the owner or occupier is known to be in financial difficulties.

(5) A small fire has destroyed records or is said to have destroyed money. These reasons are extraneous to the fire itself, and, so far as we are concerned here, their discovery means merely that an especially careful investigation at the scene of the fire along the lines already sketched is necessary. (The investigator should remember, incidentally, when a fire is started to cover up the theft of money or deficiencies in accounts, that the metal strips in Bank of England notes are practically indestructible, and that ledgers, like all books, are very hard to burn completely.)

(6) Two or more fires have broken out simultaneously, or more than one primary seat is discovered subsequently.

(7) Inflammable materials, of a type which one would not expect to find in the premises destroyed, are found at the scene or in the partially burnt debris.

Since the arsonist probably most commonly starts his fire with paper and a match or lighter, evidence of this is most unlikely to be found. As already mentioned, however, this can be assumed only if traces of other methods have been sought and not found. A candle may have been arranged to set fire to kindling when it has burned down and the arsonist is far away; in that case, traces of candle wax may remain beneath the seat of fire and be identifiable by one of the methods described in Chapter 8. If a petrol bomb or "Molotov cocktail" has been used, fragments of the glass bottle should be discoverable and identifiable. Great ingenuity has sometimes been shown in arranging a resistance heater (*e.g.* an electric-iron or immersion-heater element) in a pile of paper or shavings in such a way that it heats up only when a particular switch is quite innocently switched on.

Simultaneous outbreaks, or multiple primary seats, are generally taken for obvious reasons as prima facie evidence of arson. Though this conclusion is usually correct, one must not jump to it. A case is recorded by L. C. Nickolls in which washing on an inside line caught fire; when the line burned through and parted, the burning washing on the two parts started two apparently independent fires. The writer has seen a case in which flame from burning paint on a closed roller shutter, behind which an accidental fire had started, ignited curtains and thereby started a secondary fire on the farther side of a large room, with no fire damage whatever in the intervening space. A spurious appearance of two seats of fire may also sometimes occur where the configuration of the building has caused an eddy of hot gases to produce locally more intense burning, or where flame coming from one side of an interior space has been at first deflected down on to the other side by the roof (as in a reverberatory furnace).

When "foreign" inflammable material is found at the scene or in the debris, laboratory examination will be necessary to identify it. For example, a case is recorded in which the use of old cinema film as kindling was detected primarily through the presence of a relatively high concentration of silver in the debris.

The accelerants most usually encountered in this connection are, however, inflammable liquids such as petrol or kerosene (paraffin oil). If the fire is put out before it has burnt itself out, and if there are any porous or absorbent materials near the seat (*e.g.* cardboard, books, plaster, fabrics, etc.), these may retain a surprising quantity of even quite volatile liquids after being subjected to considerable heat.

Portable "sniffers" incorporating a small hand-pump and a detector such as is used in gas chromatography and sensitive to hydrocarbons have been developed, but traces of petrol, kerosene, paint thinners, etc. are usually detectable in the first instance by their smell—only gas chromatography exceeds the human nose in sensitivity here. For their isolation in the laboratory, and also for that of other volatile combustibles such as alcohol which do not have a pronounced smell, various procedures are possible. The simplest is steam distillation of a fairly large quantity of the suspected debris. Water-immiscible liquids of course simply float on the distillate; with miscible ones, further distillations, possible after saturating the aqueous distillate with salt, are necessary to isolate an identifiable quantity.

Straightforward steam distillation is not really adequate for the isolation of minimal quantities of inflammables and other procedures must be used. Hydrocarbons may be distilled as azeotropes (see Glossary) after the addition of a large quantity of alcohol (*Macoun*'s method) and subsequently, after separation from the distillate by oxidation of the alcohol, examined by gas chromatography. However, amounts of volatile hydrocarbons so small that they can be detected only by the most sensitive tests are probably of no significance in the present context, since they could probably have been derived from the pyrolysis of wood or plastics.

For inflammables which are not steam-volatile (*e.g.* animal or vegetable oils, candle wax, etc.), extraction with a suitable solvent such as petroleum ether is necessary. When a fire has been started with the aid of a pyrotechnic mixture (a very uncommon event, in the writer's experience), the laboratory is likely to be able to help only if the fire-raiser has spilt some at the scene.

It may finally be necessary to compare whatever is recovered in the laboratory with material from a suspect's possession. Inflammable liquids must be freed of water and products derived from the action of the fire; even then, however, the purified product is unlikely to be directly comparable with the control material, for the simple reason that, if it is a mixture such as most hydrocarbon oils are, it will have lost part of its more volatile components. The chemist's best plan is then to evaporate down some of the control material, testing it at various stages to see whether he can duplicate the recovered material. Here, gas chromatography has completely superseded all other methods of testing (see p. 65 and fig. 20). It should be possible by using it to identify the brand and grade of petrol or kerosene, especially if two columns and/or a capillary column (p. 66) are used. Some progress has also been made towards computerising this sort of identification. Linked mass spectrometry (p. 77) may also be possible.

V. FATAL FIRES

A fire involving or resulting in death demands a particularly careful investigation —there may have been foul play, and in any case it is important that the cause shall be discovered. If the fire is a major one, and the death or deaths obviously incidental to it, the investigation will be along the lines already described, the only difference being that the circumstances may demand that no limit at all shall be set to the time and trouble that may be spent on it.

The value of a careful examination of the scene is illustrated by a case in which two children were burned to death in a small caravan, the fire in which had been intense enough to melt the aluminium-alloy sheeting forming its outer walls. There had been a paraffin heater alight in the caravan; it was one of the rectangular upright type in which the front lifts off for access to the burner and chimney. This front was found after the fire buried in the charred debris, with its plastic handle on the under side and practically undamaged by heat; the front must therefore have been lifted off *before* the fire broke out. All the ascertainable circumstances strongly suggested that the children had taken this front off and held a PVC doll over the top of the chimney in order to watch it melting in the heat; the doll had caught fire, and the terrified children had dropped it on to upholstery or some other inflammable surface. It was found by experiment that a PVC doll such as the children had possessed held above the heater chimney caught fire in 10-15 seconds.

A much more common but less publicised type of case is where the (permanent or temporary) sole occupant of a house is found dead after a small fire. In one case, the partly burnt body of a young woman was found in the bedroom of a small terrace house, where a fire had almost destroyed the bed and some of the floor. There was a good deal of blood about, and evidence that someone had tried to put the fire out with water from a bucket. These facts strongly suggested murder, since, if the bucket had been used by the deceased, she ought not to have died, and, if it had not, the other person fell under suspicion. It was eventually established with reasonable certainty that the fire was accidental; the blood was menstrual; and the probable explanation of the mystery of the bucket was that the dead woman had used it in trying to put the fire out and had then been overcome by fumes and collapsed while in the act of opening the window to let the smoke out, after which the fire, not having been properly extinguished, flared up again.

However, the most common pattern of such cases is, in the writer's experience, that the deceased was infirm or under the influence of alcohol or drugs, and had died or lost consciousness from the effects of carbon monoxide produced by the smouldering of upholstery into which a match or cigarette has been dropped. (See p. 122.) In such circumstances one sometimes finds extraordinarily complete combustion of the chair or bed, the patch of floor beneath it and the body, without the room as a whole being very much damaged by the fire. It has been stated that a normal human body can be consumed by the combustion of its own fat.

Deaths in fires are in fact in all circumstances as commonly the result of inhaling toxic gases or fumes as of burning strictly speaking. In addition to the hazard of carbon monoxide from wood or other cellulosic combustibles, many plastics produce toxic gases in burning. PVC produces both carbon monoxide and hydrochloric acid. Polyurethane foam (see p. 185) produces not only a dense paralysing smoke, but also carbon monoxide and a significant amount of highly toxic hydrocyanic acid. Other plastics may turn out to be as dangerous when they have been as thoroughly investigated. Deaths from this cause therefore present a toxicological problem, to solve which the most advanced instrumental methods may be necessary. (See pp. 120–121.)

VI. EXPLOSIONS

Explosives are most familiar to forensic scientists as propellants in firearms; this is discussed in the following chapter. Apart from that, explosives and explosions may demand attention for four other reasons:

(1) Explosives may have to be identified in connection with their theft, illegal possession or nefarious use. This has been dealt with in Chapters 5 and 7.

(2) Unexploded bombs, booby traps, infernal machines and the like may have to be examined and dealt with.

(3) The cause of an unexpected and unexplained explosion may have to be sought.

(4) The circumstances of an explosion may be known, but the nature and construction of the explosive object that caused it may have to be ascertained if possible.

(2) The handling and de-fusing or safely destroying of **unexploded** devices of all sorts is outside the scope of the normal forensic science laboratory and of this book. It is most definitely a job for the expert in the subject (and the expert in this subject has been defined as the one who is still alive). Many of the larger American and Canadian law-enforcement authorities maintain bomb squads as part of their technical police services, commonly separate from but in conjunction with their laboratories. They are staffed by experienced personnel, and equipped with protective clothing and with vehicles fitted with cranes and suitable carrying devices for dealing with live bombs. Most parts of Great Britain have so far been fortunate in not needing this sort of organisation. When they do occur here, problems of this type are outside London normally referred to the nearest Army bomb-disposal unit. In the London area, they are dealt with by "explosives officers" experienced in this work—a method of dealing with the problem which has proved extremely successful.

(3) **Unexpected** and **unexplained explosions** are in most cases accidental rather than criminal. They are therefore usually investigated by specialist investigators rather than the forensic science laboratories, the staffs of which do not normally possess the particular expertise required. As they may, however, be consulted initially, some knowledge of the principles of such an investigation is useful.

Explosions in this category are most commonly either gas or petrol-vapour explosions, or industrial accidents. The first question to be answered is whether the explosion was the deflagration of a dispersed explosive such as a gas-air mixture or the detonation of a high explosive. Gas-air or vapour-air mixtures will explode when their compositions are within certain limits. Some approximate figures (authorities differ as to the precise ones) for these are:

	Explosive limits *(as percentage by volume in air)*
Town gas	4–30 (These figures will vary with the source and composition of the gas.)
Natural gas: see Methane	
Petrol vapour	1·3–6
Butane (Calor gas)	1·5–7·5
Hydrogen	4–74
Methane	5–15

In such explosions (between which and petrol-assisted fires there is no sharp distinction) the pressure is developed relatively slowly (in a time between, say, a millisecond a perceptible fraction of a second), the resulting damage shows no "focus" of greatest intensity (and may even be greater at the periphery than the centre), and the general effect is one of "pushing out" walls, windows, etc. If there were any vents such as open windows the slowly developing pressure is relieved by them and damage to the neighbouring structures lessened. Mixtures of compositions nearer the lower of the above limits give "sharper" explosions, with the least likelihood of fire resulting from them; those nearer the upper limits tend to produce a "whoosh" rather than a true explosion, with the greatest likelihood of fire, and with hydrocarbons to leave a sooty residue.

In the detonation of a high explosive the pressure is developed in a few microseconds, that is, something like 1,000 times more rapidly than in the previous case, and the detonation shock wave travels outward at a supersonic speed, eventually slowing down until at a sufficient distance from the point of explosion it becomes also a simple pressure wave. At the focus, therefore, even the toughest materials such as spring steel are shattered, small fragments are ejected at dangerous velocities and venting near this point does not prevent damage to neighbouring structures.

When the type of explosion has been identified, several other questions remain to be answered. For example, if a high explosive has been detonated, are any identifiable residues recoverable? (Unless the explosive was correctly used in accordance with the manufacturer's instructions, a portion is likely to escape detonation and to be scattered). Does the penetration of wood or other soft material by fragments suggest velocities indicative of a detonation? If the evidence points to a gas or similar explosion, is the damage to walls etc. consistent with the pressures typical of such an explosion? (In the investigation of the notorious Ronan Point disaster in London in 1968, in which a gas leak in a flat in a high-rise block led to an explosion demolishing part of the building, the pressure developed could be estimated from the degree of flattening of some circular biscuit tins in the flat.)

(4) The investigation of the last category of explosions overlaps with the previous one, because the precise cause of the explosion may also initially be unknown, but it is distinguished here because it normally, in the writer's experience, becomes a problem for the forensic scientist. The explosion may have been that of a parcel bomb, booby trap, etc., or it may have been caused by an over-zealous schoolboy experimentalist blowing himself up (as has happened too often and will unfortunately in all probability happen again).

In all such cases, a detailed search of the debris and the surrounding area, however tedious, is an essential first step. Thereafter the scientist must "play it by ear." Explosive residues identifiable by analysis may be found. If a time bomb has contained an alarm clock, recognisable bits of this are certain to be present. If a dry battery was used for detonation, traces of manganese dioxide and of the zinc casing will probably be found. In a case of murder during the war, in which a man in a bath-chair was blown up, fragments of metal were found at the scene; they bore fibres matching the fabrics of his clothing and of the chair cushions and were identifiable as from an anti-tank grenade, and there was other evidence that the murderer had hidden a specially sensitised grenade of this type under the cushions. The writer has had the task of examining the contents of a room on a breakfast table in which a parcel bomb had exploded. Enough fragments of "foreign" wood, small brass hinges, bits of wire etc. were found to show that the device had been contained in a cigar box wired up to explode when the lid was raised. Sufficient fragments of wrapping (even including the stamps and postmark) were also found to suggest a parcel of about the size and shape which the postman remembered delivering. Finally, it is reported from Northern Ireland that the finding of a clothes-peg spring in the debris from a terrorist explosion provided a valuable clue to the mode of construction of a type of bomb used by the I.R.A.

15

FIREARMS

The investigation of shooting cases is often miscalled "ballistics." It has in fact nothing to do with ballistics proper, which is the mathematical study of the flight of projectiles. Nevertheless, the term has probably come to stay and will have to be accepted. "Forensic ballistics" consists of *ad hoc* tests and experiments devised to answer the following questions:

(1) What kind of gun was used to commit the crime?

(2) From what direction, and from how far away, was the shot fired?

(3) What is the condition of the gun? Is it in good working order? Is it liable to accidental discharge? Is it capable of being fired at all?

(4) Has the gun been fired recently?

(5) Were the bullets and/or cartridge cases associated with the crime fired from the gun submitted for examination?

Obviously, the first two questions concern only the result of the shooting; one must try to answer them whether the gun has been found or not. Before describing how the answers are obtained, a few words about firearms in general may be helpful, since the unlawful use of firearms is still a relatively uncommon crime in most parts of Britain, and we are not as a nation familiar with them in peace time.

In the present context, small-arms may be classified as follows:

(1) Rifled weapons:

(a) Rifles:

(i) Air and gas-operated rifles
(ii) ·22 Rifles (miniature rifles)
(iii) Military and sporting rifles.

(b) Single-shot target-practice pistols (usually ·22 calibre).
(c) Revolvers.
(d) Automatic (properly *self-loading*) pistols.
(e) True automatic weapons (machine guns; "Tommy" guns).

(2) Shotguns:

(a) Single-barrel.
(b) Double-barrel.
(c) Repeating and/or self-loading shotguns.

The fundamental difference between shotguns and rifled weapons is of course that the former have a smooth bore and normally fire a charge consisting of a large number of small projectiles (shot), whereas the latter fire a single bullet with each shot, and bear on the interior of the barrel a series of spiral grooves and ridges (known as *lands*) which impart a spin to the bullet, thereby preventing it wobbling or turning over in flight.

The *calibre* of a rifled weapon is the internal diameter of the barrel measured between the surfaces of the lands—·22 [inch], ·38 [inch], 9 millimetres, etc. The calibre of shotguns is frequently designated as such-and-such a number "bore" (or "gauge"); the most popular calibre for sporting guns is probably 12-bore. This is a very old system, and refers to the number of spherical lead balls just fitting the barrel which would together weigh 1 lb. However, the smaller sizes of shotguns are usually described more simply by the internal diameter of the barrel—*e.g.* ·410 [inch].

In all modern guns (except of course air guns—although gas-operated guns in which projectile and propellant cartridges are combined are now available), the bullet or shot, and the propellant, are loaded as one unit—the cartridge. In air rifles, ·22 rifles, and some revolvers plain, hardened lead bullets are used; in other weapons the bullets are jacketed with a hard casing of cupro-nickel or similar metal. The propellant is almost invariably either a nitro-cellulose preparation or else nitro-cellulose gelatinised with nitro-glycerin (cordite, etc.).

When the weapon is cocked—that is, ready to be fired—the *hammer* has been pulled back against a strong spring and is held back by the end of the *sear* resting in a notch known as the *bent* (see fig. 40). The action of pulling the trigger disengages the sear from the bent, and the hammer on flying forward delivers a smart blow on the end of a small push-rod (the *firing-pin*, or striker), the other end of which projects through a small hole in the breech face. Occasionally firing pin and hammer are made in one piece. The ignition cap in the base of the cartridge is a small capsule of soft metal containing a tiny charge of a highly sensitive explosive readily detonated by shock—*e.g.* mercury fulminate or lead azide. The detonation of this *primer* by the firing pin fires the propellant, and the resulting explosion forces the bullet or charge of shot forward through the barrel and (by Newton's Third Law of Motion) simultaneously pushes the cartridge case back with equal force against the breech face.

In some weapons (*e.g.* most revolvers, old shotguns) the hammer is external and can be pulled back independently to cock the gun. In other weapons (so-called "hammerless" guns) the hammer is built in and concealed, and cocking is therefore done by some sort of derived motion; for example, the pulling back of the bolt in a bolt-action weapon. Most shotguns and a few single-shot pistols are "broken" for loading; the weapon is in two parts pivoted together so that the breech can be swung away from the firing mechanism.

Revolvers (see fig. 41) have a rotating cylinder containing several (often six—whence "six-shooter") chambers into which the cartridges are initially loaded by hand, and the rotation of which brings a fresh round into position for the next shot. In single-action revolvers, the rotation is brought about by the action of cocking the hammer; in double-action ones, it is also possible to cock the hammer and rotate the cylinder by pulling the trigger, so that the gun can be emptied by successive trigger pulls.

In **semi-automatic** (or self-loading) weapons ("automatic" pistols—see fig. 41—and modern military rifles), a number of rounds are held in a magazine or clip, from which they are fed by a spring one at a time into the breech. Some mechanical arrangement, commonly worked by the force of the recoil or by gas pressure, after each shot cocks the gun for the next; hence each successive trigger pull fires one shot until the gun is empty. In true **automatic** weapons, a similar arrangement is developed a stage further, so that the recoil both cocks the gun and fires the next shot; hence the gun continues to fire as long as the trigger is kept pressed and there is any ammunition left.

Shotguns are usually single-shot weapons; if they are double-barrelled, there is a separate trigger for each barrel. The cartridge contains, in addition to the propellant and shot, a wad between these to act as a "piston" to push the shot along the barrel, and one or more cardboard discs to keep the shot in the cartridge. Until recently the cartridge almost invariably had a waxed cardboard body and a metal base, but all-plastic cartridges have recently been introduced. Self-loading or "automatic" shotguns (not uncommon in the U.S.A.) have a mechanism similar to that of semi-automatic pistols, and either fire one shot with each trigger pressure without reloading, or have a manually operated pump action, operation of which ejects the spent cartridge and reloads.

We can now return to the list of questions on p. 194.

(1) Where there is a crime but no weapon, the question is urgent: what sort of gun was used? If the bullet is recovered, its shape, weight and diameter will tell us the general type (rifle, pistol, etc.) and calibre of the gun. Some military rifle bullets are of a distinctive shape. It is possible to limit the choice still further by examining the grooves on the bullet left by the lands (p. 195); these may vary, according to the make of the gun, in number, width, direction of twist (that is, right- or left-handed) and pitch (that is, the angle formed with the axis of the bullet).

No such information is of course obtainable if a shotgun was used. Even then, however, there is *some* information to be had. The weighing and measuring of a few pellets will tell us with what size of shot the cartridge was loaded. If the victim received the full charge, then the pellets can be counted by X-raying the body. The size and number of pellets taken together will tell us what the shot load was, which indicates the size of the gun. Some of the individual pellets will be deformed by pressure as the charge passes through the barrel of the gun, so that the finding of such flattened pellets is not necessarily evidence that they have hit anything hard such as bone.

If the bullet is not recovered, then the size of the hole or entry wound it has made will give a rough indication of calibre, though with a considerable margin of error. The composition of the bullet may be discoverable by analysis of tissue from around the entry wound in a dead victim, or of the edges of the entry hole in clothing; various methods (spectrography, atomic absorption, neutron activation, X-ray microanalysis—see Chapter 8) may be used for this.

Cartridge cases, if found, are highly informative. Their shape and size proclaim the type and calibre of the weapon. Revolver and automatic-pistol cartridges differ in the shape of their bases (although caution is necessary here, since ammunition for one type of weapon can sometimes be used in the other). An automatic pistol ejects a cartridge with each shot, whereas with a revolver the empty cartridges remain in the cylinder. Therefore, if no cases are found on a careful search of the scene of the crime, an automatic was in all probability not used, whereas if a case or cases are found a revolver was probably not used.

(2) Whence, and from how far away, was the shot fired?

The question: Whence? rarely allows of more than an approximate answer. If the victim dies and his position at the moment he was struck is known, the track of the bullet(s) through his body as discovered *post mortem* may be revealing. Also, a bullet hitting flesh perpendicularly leaves a circular entry hold whereas the entry hole of a very oblique hit is elliptical. It has recently been reported from California that the marks left by ricochets off car bodies indicate the direction in which the bullet was travelling. If one or more bullets, or part of a charge of shot, miss the victim, then a careful examination of woodwork, fences, trees, the ground, etc., at the scene may yield an indication of direction.

The question of distance is really one of two quite different questions, depending on whether the weapon was a rifled one or a shotgun. In either case, however, although experience can hazard a guess, a reliable answer is possible only when tests can be made with the *actual weapon, and similar ammunition, to that used in the shooting*.

With rifled weapons, there is at very short distances a characteristic series of phenomena: a tearing (often cross-shaped) of the cloth or flesh when the muzzle is actually in contact with it, and at greater distances a circular area of blackening caused by the blast of gas and residues, together sometimes with fragments of unburnt and partially burnt propellant thrown out and adhering to the surface. The blackening may be masked on dark clothing, in which case it can often be revealed clearly by infra-red viewing or photography (fig. 42). In an ingenious method developed in the Federal German Criminal Police Laboratory the residues are transferred on to cellophane and converted to dark-coloured lead sulphide; the cellophane is then rapidly rotated under a scanning device, and this records the integrated optical density produced by the lead sulphide, the distribution around the centre of which is a function of the shooting distance.

Beyond about two or three feet however, none of these effects appear, and it used to be impossible to draw any conclusions about distance (except in the rare accidental event of a bullet turning over at the end of its trajectory—possibly up to several miles for a high-velocity rifle). Within the last few years, however, thanks to the sensitive analytical methods now available, short-range distances measured in yards can be estimated by the detection in the target area of traces of elements such as lead, barium or antimony derived from the primer and propellant. Various methods have been used for this: pressing filter paper wetted with dilute acid on to the area, followed by simple colour spot tests; spectrographic analysis of a concentrate of the area; neutron activation or atomic absorption analysis. S. S. Krishnan (Ontario) has made a very sophisticated use of neutron activation here by using it to analyse concentric circular sections of the target area and formulating an equation connecting the firing distance and the antimony concentration within each section. However, whatever other tests he makes, the expert must first examine the clothing and body for the presence or absence of obvious close-range effects. He must then make tests with the suspected weapon, using if possible ammunition identical in type *and condition* with that used in the crime, to discover at what range a similar effect (if he has found one) is produced, or at what minimum range no visible effects (if he has found none) are discernible.

With shotguns, on the other hand, the estimation of distance, up to the extreme range of the shot, is fairly simple. Practically as soon as the charge leaves the muzzle, it begins to scatter, and it will strike the target as a roughly circular shot pattern, the diameter of which is directly proportional to the distance (and will be less for a given distance with a barrel which is "choked"—that is, slightly constricted in diameter at the muzzle). The distance can therefore be estimated either from the total spread (if this is known), or from the number of shot striking within a given limited area. At short ranges (up to, say, 3–5 yards) the wad travelling with the shot may also leave a mark where it strikes.

Two cases in the writer's experience may be cited. In one, a man fired a shotgun at his wife as she was running away, and it was important to know from what distance. As she had thirteen separate pellet injuries in her legs and buttocks, the distance was easily estimated by test-firing the gun, using cartridges similar to his, at projection diagrams of the relevant portions of the lady's anatomy; on average, thirteen pellets fell within the area of the diagrams at 40 yards. In the other case, a farmer shot and killed a neighbouring farmer's straying horse; he claimed, however, that he had aimed over the horse's head, intending only to frighten it off. Examination of the horse's skin showed that his claim was almost certainly correct: the distribution of pellet holes in the skin indicated a pattern the centre of which was above the horse's head; the farmer had merely underestimated the spread of the shot.

For a similar reason, the likelihood of a charge of shot being lethal also decreases very rapidly with distance. A bullet is as fatal at many hundred yards as at a few feet, and even a ·22 bullet may penetrate flesh at over a mile. On the other hand, whereas a shotgun at very close range is a terrible weapon, blasting a ragged hole big enough to put a fist in or blowing half a skull away, once the shot charge is well spread out (some tens of yards) its effect, with small shot sizes, is likely to be merely painful rather than lethal. The effective range for a given propellant charge depends very much on the size of the shot; the smaller the individual pellets, the greater is their surface in proportion to their weight, and the more rapidly therefore does air resistance reduce their velocity.

(3) What is the condition of the gun? This information may be important in a variety of circumstances. Obviously, a gun cannot have been used to commit a crime unless it could have been fired. A gun in apparently good condition may, for example, be useless as a weapon because the tip of the firing pin has been broken off. The accused in a shooting case may claim that his gun does not work and therefore could not have been used; the truth or falsity of this claim must be tested. More commonly, in an allegedly or apparently accidental shooting, it will be important to decide just how liable to accidental discharge the gun really is. To answer all these questions, the gun must be examined carefully to see whether it can be discharged by a blow or jar when cocked, and if necessary tested with a live or blank round and also dismantled in the search for worn or broken parts.

It is also doubly important in this connection to do what should be a routine in all firearms investigations—measure the trigger pull. This is simply the force which, when applied directly to the trigger of the cocked gun, will just fire it. The following figures are average ones for guns in good condition.

·22 rifle	3–4 lb.
Military rifle	4–7 lb.
Revolver, single action	4–5 lb.
Revolver, double action	10–15 lb.
Automatic pistol	4–8 lb.
Shotgun	4–5 lb.

If the trigger pull is much less than these figures, the gun may be accounted dangerous.

(4) Has the gun been fired recently? The old-timer sheriff smells the muzzle, unless Hollywood has grossly misled us for years. It is true that the gaseous products of a propellant explosion have a characteristic smell which lingers in the gun for some time. The "fouling" of a fired barrel can also be seen on looking through it, and is immediately distinguishable from the smooth polished appearance of a barrel which has been cleaned and oiled. Finally, chemical tests can be made. The barrel can be washed out with hot distilled water and the washings tested for nitrate and nitrite ions, both of which are produced in the combustion of propellants. Very recent use will also, it has been shown, leave a detectable trace of carbon monoxide in the barrel. However, apart from the fact that the latter is bound to disappear fairly quickly, there is no reliable test to tell us precisely when the gun was last fired.

(5) Finally, we come to the crucial question: was the gun submitted for examination that used to commit the crime?

The answer to this depends on the way in which firearms leave their unique characteristics—their tell-tale imprints—on bullets (see figs. 43 and 44) and cartridges fired in them.

The inside of a rifled barrel, and the breech-face of any firearm, are machine-finished surfaces. The fact that such surfaces are never *perfectly* smooth has already been mentioned (p. 19). Therefore a bullet fired through a rifled barrel will show, not only the relatively large-scale grooves formed by the lands, but also a fine pattern of striations corresponding to the "micro-profile" of the inner surface of the barrel. (The matching of striations on individual shot pellets with the interior of a shotgun barrel, generally considered impossible, has also recently been reported by S. S. Krishnan.) Similarly, every detail of the breech-face surface may be imprinted on the relatively soft metal of the cartridge base. (It is important in the subsequent examination to make sure that such apparent imprints were not there *before* firing—that is, are imprints of the machine that stamped out the cartridge base and not of the firearm.) Other events also happen to the cartridge case. An imprint of the end of the firing pin is left on the ignition cap. In guns in which the cartridge is pulled out mechanically by an *extractor*, the claws of this leave marks on the rim of the base. It is not yet known whether similar marks are left on the recently introduced all-plastic shotgun cartridges (p. 196). In automatic pistols, the empty case is thrown out after each shot by recoiling against a hard steel shoulder (or *ejector*) which deflects it out of the gun; this too leaves a mark.

Since the details of all these types of marks are produced by a completely random pattern of minute irregularities, the probability of two different guns having the same pattern is completely negligible, and the marks produced by any given gun can be considered unique. Hence, if the marks on test rounds fired from the suspected gun are identical with those on the crime bullets or cartridge cases, then that gun was used to commit the crime (fig. 43).

There is of course no difficulty in retrieving fired cartridge cases, but it is not so easy to catch bullets in the undamaged condition which is clearly essential. Packed snow, oiled sawdust and blocks of paraffin wax have all been used for this, but a very popular device for this purpose is a long box full of cotton wadding, which, if packed neither too tight nor too loose, stops the bullet even of a high-velocity rifle in a few feet. Opinions are divided among firearms experts whether this may also mark the bullet sufficiently to be objectionable in the subsequent examination. Those (mainly in the U.S.A.) who believe that it may prefer to use a few feet of water to stop their bullets. This may be contained either in a deep vertical tank (which necessitates some special arrangement for the recovery of the bullet from the bottom), or in a horizontal tank which has a waterproof but not bullet-proof membrane at the end together with some sort of mechanical gadgetry to close the end and keep the water in when the membrane has been pierced. In any event, the bullet must not strike the water obliquely, which could deform it and/or cause dangerous ricochets.

After several test rounds have been fired, the first thing is to compare the respective bullets and cartridge cases from successive test rounds with each other, so as to recognise and eliminate any fortuitous and accidental marks on any one. The comparison is normally performed using a comparison microscope such as is described in Chapter 3. One of the test rounds (preferably the first) is then compared in the same way with the corresponding crime material. This is the crucial part of the whole investigation. If there are n lands in the barrel, then of course there are n positions in which the two bullets may be lined up, groove for groove, and n^2 possible groove comparisons, all of which may have to be tried.

There are also several methods of bullet comparison which do not require a comparison microscope. It is possible, though tedious, to use a series of enlarged photographs of the separate grooves (those taken with a scanning electron microscope—p. 82—if it is available are excellent). Flattened-out casts of the whole peripheries made in a suitable flexible plastic may be compared side by side under sufficient magnification. A more recent method is to use a *periphery camera*. This, by projecting the image of a continuously rotating object (the bullet in this case) on to a moving strip of film, produces a single strip photograph of the entire periphery of the object (fig. 44). This method has been so successful that some laboratories use it routinely. An even more recent method is to use a "Talychron" or similar micro-profile recorder (see p. 21), which reproduces the striation pattern in each groove as a magnified trace. Cartridge cases can also be fairly easily compared by means of enlarged photographs taken with identical directions of lighting as oriented using some prominent characteristic mark.

With normal luck, and a good deal of patience, the comparison, however made, will yield definite results fairly quickly, and a suspected weapon can be either cleared or positively indicated as that responsible. This is admittedly a very laborious task if it is one of a large number of "possibles." On one occasion, many years ago, the writer was able to identify a gun as that used to commit a murder after he had examined over 250 similar weapons. (Unfortunately, the gun had been thrown out of a passing car on one of the Thames bridges, and the criminal was never traced.)

Unfortunately, the investigation does not always go so smoothly. A rifled weapon's characteristics are not so immutable as a man's fingerprints. Although it has been demonstrated that the first and the thousandth of successive rounds fired through a clean weapon in good condition can be matched, weapons to be examined are not always clean and free from rust. Secondly, and more frequently, if the crime bullet has struck anything hard, it may be too distorted for any comparison to be made. Lastly, if the gun barrel is very old and worn and if the bullet has a very hard jacket, the marks may be too indefinite for a definite conclusion to be reached.

A few miscellaneous matters remain to be dealt with before we can leave the subject of firearms.

It is sometimes necessary to examine the **hands** of suspects for evidence that they have fired a weapon. The old "paraffin" test once used for this, in which a paraffin-wax cast of the skin was tested for the presence of nitrates, has long been discredited as being quite unreliable. It is however true, as has been demonstrated by photography using micro-second exposures, that in firing some weapons, especially revolvers, smoke and residues are blown back on to the hands of the firers. Reliable tests for detecting these have now been developed. They depend on the detection in hand swabbings, (p. 57) of elements such as lead or barium derived from the propellant or primer. It cannot be said, however, that a positive result from such a test constitutes absolute proof of firing and could in no circumstances have been caused by extraneous contamination. Research is currently in progress on the detection in such swabs of nitrocellulose from the propellant, a substance which is much less likely to have been derived from any other source.

The firearms expert is occasionally asked for an opinion about the **striking energy** of projectiles, either *ad hoc* in connection with a particular investigation, or to decide whether an air-rifle is too powerful to be exempted from licensing under firearms legislation. This quantity varies, according to an elementary law of physics, as the value of mv^2, where m is the mass of the projectile and v its velocity. It is because the velocity appears as its second power in that expression that a light projectile such as a bullet can do so much damage if only it is moving fast enough. (The fastest bullet is not *necessarily*, however, the most destructive. A comparatively slow heavy one, if it is completely stopped by a body or anything else, may in some circumstances do more damage in the process than a fast one which goes right through, since all the energy of the slower, but only a part of the energy of the faster, will have been used up destructively.)

It may therefore be necessary to measure bullet velocities. These may be anything from a few hundred to over 1,500 feet per second. They can be measured in various ways. The simplest is probably to fire the bullet through the periphery of two card discs mounted some distance apart on a rapidly rotating spindle; the second hole will be displaced relative to the first because of the angle through which the discs have rotated in the time spent by the bullet in travelling between them, and the extent of the displacement depends upon the velocity of the bullet. This, however, is a very crude method. A much superior method is to use a *chronograph*. This, in the present context, consists of an electronic microsecond timer aranged to be switched on and off by the passage of the bullet over a measured distance. The switching can be done in various ways—for example, by the rupturing of a conducting membrane, or by the interruption of light beams falling on photo-electric cells. In this way, the velocity can be measured very accurately—with an accurate timer, to probably less than 1 foot per second of the velocity.

Finally, various types of weapons may be submitted for an opinion whether they come within one of the categories of **prohibited** ones. These include sawn-off shotguns, "pen" (American "zip") guns, toy or blank pistols which can easily be converted to fire live ammunition, and tear-gas pistols. The full identification of "tear-gas" (a misnomer, since most lachrymatories are solids) will in the last case be of course a job for a chemist.

16

DOCUMENTS

There are very many reasons why documents may have to be examined in a criminal investigation. The types of examination which may have to be made are also extremely numerous. The subject is also not one which can be treated broadly with a few compendious generalisations. For all of these reasons, any treatment of it which is more than a bare mention cannot offer other than a mass of rather disconnected facts, and only a very superficial sketch of it will be attempted here.

There is also an inevitable and probably desirable tendency for this field to become the exclusive province of the specialist. In America, "document examiners" form a respected and highly skilled body of experts. Also, since cheque frauds are commoner there than here, large fraudulent-cheque files are maintained in their bigger laboratories. Specialisation has not as yet, however, gone so far in Britain, but some has occurred. Although any forensic science laboratory here will probably undertake the simple examination of erasures, alterations and the like, the comparison and identification of handwriting and typewriting, which require a very high degree of specialised expertise, are carried out in only three (other than those of private consultants): the Home Office laboratory in Birmingham (which does the work for most of the English and all the Welsh police forces), the Metropolitan Police Laboratory, and the Laboratory of the Government Chemist.

The necessity for document examinations may arise in, among others, the following circumstances.

(1) The genuineness of a signature may be disputed. In fiction, this occurs most frequently in connection with wills bequeathing large estates; in fact, it arises most frequently in one of two ways: either in connection with stolen and forged or allegedly forged cheques, postal orders and drafts, and the various official forms on which money is paid out against a signature, or because a genuine signature is disclaimed when a deal has "gone sour."

(2) A genuine document may have or appear to have been altered in some way to defraud, or to make it appear that some necessary condition has been complied with. Innumerable examples of this could be given. The sums written on a cheque or I.O.U. may be increased—as, for example, by altering "8" to "80" and "eight"

to "eighty." (This should be impossible with a properly drawn cheque.) The amounts shown on receipts produced by employees in support of a claim for reimbursement of expenses may have been increased. Alternatively, the employees who issue receipts may be able to "fiddle" the carbon copies so that the amount which, according to the record, they have to pay in is less than their actual takings. The date on a document may be altered when it is to someone's advantage to make it appear that it was issued at an earlier or later date than the true one. The number on a "tote" ticket may be altered to that of the winning animal in a particular race. The entries on a stolen car log book or road-fund licence may be altered to fit the thief's vehicle. Time-clock records may be altered to increase the total of hours apparently worked. Something may be added to an agreement which would be to the advantage of the party making the addition.

The above are probably the most frequently occurring circumstances. Others, equally or even more various, but on the whole less frequent, are:

(3) A document may be wholly false or forged. This may be anything from an account for services allegedly rendered or goods supplied, or a receipt produced in support of a claim for reimbursement, to a faked first edition which would be valuable if genuine.

(4) Another type of forged document comprises false paper money and stamps for large amounts (*e.g.* high-denomination insurance stamps).

(5) The authorship of anonymous letters may have to be investigated.

(6) Envelopes which have been through the post may be opened and re-sealed, or may have the name and address altered, in connection with various types of frauds and attempted frauds.

(7) It may be important to show that two pieces of a document were originally one, or that a sheet of paper came from a certain notebook, etc. (This problem, which will not be further discussed in this chapter, is solved by using the same type of simple matching techniques as were described in Chapter 3 in connection with other materials.)

(8) It may be important to decipher partially burnt documents.

(9) Messages in invisible ink may have to be sought or deciphered.

(10) It may be important to link a certain person with a certain piece of writing by other means than handwriting comparison.

Perhaps the most obvious type of link in the last category is provided if blotting paper used to blot the writing has legible traces on it forming an exact facsimile of the blotted writing. However, this sort of link is less likely to be found now that ball-point pens are so nearly universal and blotting paper so little used. Writers of anonymous letters have been convicted in this way from blotting paper taken from their waste-paper baskets. Another type of link occurs if the writing was done with a hard pencil or ball-point pen, and if what was the underlying sheet of paper, which will bear an indented impression of the writing, is found in the person's possession. Such evidence has on several occasions helped to convict murderers. Two examples of this are given later (pp. 211–212).

II. EQUIPMENT

Apart from the occasional chemical tests to be mentioned, most of the document examiner's work consists simply of visual examination and comparison. Other than a good pair of eyes, therefore, he will need:

A large clear flat working space to lay out his material.

Magnifiers of all sorts—simple low-power ones, binocular stereoscopic microscopes giving magnification up to about ×20, and (for the examinaton of paper fibres etc.) ordinary high-power microscopes. For much of his work, a binocular "zoom" microscope, giving variable moderate magnification without changing lenses, is an exceedingly convenient instrument.

A variety of photographic equipment. This will include: (1) a copying camera, preferably mounted on rails, for photographing whole documents. It is convenient to mount those for this on a vertical perforated surface against which they are held by suction, and on which they are illuminated by indirect completely diffuse lighting. (2) Equipment such as is described in the following chapter for macro-photography using a variety of filters and various types of illumination.

An *infra-red* (and possibly also an ultra-violet) *image converter*. These are instruments for making visible the reflectivity of the object under examination to invisible radiations just outside the visible spectrum (see p. 70). Infra-red ones have been available for some time, having been developed primarily for military purposes, and ultra-violet ones have also now been produced. Their principle is that the image is projected on to a surface coated with an electron emitter stimulated by the radiation in question, and the electrons emitted produce on a fluorescent screen an image as "seen" by this radiation.

In a well-equipped laboratory there will probably also be available:

A *comparator* for the simultaneous superimposed viewing of fairly large surfaces. A particularly useful type is a "blink" or "flicking" comparator (such as is used for the checking inspection of printed circuits), in which the two images are exactly superimposed and seen in rapid alternation, which makes any discrepancy between them immediately and plainly obvious.

Unidirectional *"piped light"* using fibre optics.

An *image intensifier* for the examination of very faint writing and marks. A simple semi-transparent (half-silvered) plate may be used for this; if pressed against the document it enhances contrast by multiple reflection. A much more powerful instrument for this purpose is however one incorporating an electronic image-intensifying device such as is used in night-vision telescopes, producing a very large luminosity gain.

Equipment for *soft X-rays*. If the equipment for it is available the very soft so-called "grenz" or "Bucky" radiation of the spectrum region between X-radiation and the far ultra-violet, may be useful.

The uses of all these pieces of equipment will be mentioned in their places.

III. THE EXAMINATION OF THE MATERIAL

Paper money, stamps, etc. Forgery of bank or treasury notes, though a serious, is a rare crime, for the simple reason that it is a very skilled job. The design on a forged note will almost certainly have been reproduced photographically, and is practically certain to show under moderate magnification a coarseness of detail that distinguishes it from the genuine article, and of course the same defects will appear on all forged notes printed from the same plate(s). It is impossible to reproduce a genuine watermark. Simulated ones produced by waxing the paper so as to render it more translucent will probably be detectable by their fluorescence. An analysis of the paper and inks may be necessary, either to show that they are similar to those in the possession of a suspect, or to distinguish them from the genuine; the paper used for banknotes is, needless to say, a very jealously guarded product.

High-denomination insurance stamps are an obviously profitable proposition if the forger can run off several thousand which sell on the black market for perhaps 50p each. It is apparently fairly easy to forge stamps indistinguishable from genuine ones on a casual naked-eye inspection; their detection will depend therefore on paper analysis, fluorescence under ultra-violet (which will usually reveal any difference in the dye used for printing) and, probably, small flaws in the design visible on magnification. Any or all of these may also be used to link the forgeries with materials taken from the forger. Genuine stamps may also be of use in dating documents (p. 211).

Paper. A sheet of paper has a considerable number of properties which can be used to characterise it. Many of these require only simple non-destructive tests for their determination. These include:

Size, and exact shape if not precisely rectangular.
Colour.
Fluorescence (see p. 74); an empirical test, but very characteristic.
Thickness (average of several measurements with a micrometer).
Ruling, if any.
With some papers, the impression of the frame on which the pulp was drained in manufacture ("weave" and "lay").
Watermarks. These, which are thin places in the paper, are easily seen by transmitted light in a clean sheet. A world register of them is published, which enables any watermarked sheet of paper to be traced to its place, and sometimes date, of manufacture. Watermarks obscured by cancellations or printing may be revealed in several ways (to which *D. Graham* of Glasgow has contributed notably). This may be done by using very soft ("grenz"—p. 205) X-rays; by X-raying a sandwich of tin foil, the paper and X-ray film, so that electrons emitted by the tin foil "shadow-graph" the watermark; or by utili-

sing the β-radiation (electrons—see p. 80) emitted by radioactive carbon 14. The detection of simulated watermarks has already been mentioned.

For the examination of the other properties, the paper must be cut or mutilated. These include:

Weight per unit area (after drying to constant weight at a fixed temperature, paper being hygroscopic).

The composition of the water used in manufacture. It has been stated that characteristic impurities in this can be identified using thin-layer chromatography (p. 64).

Sizing and "loading." Practically all papers are sized, for which a variety of substances are used—gelatin, rosin, casein, synthetic resins, etc. There are several simple chemical tests for identifying these. Many papers, especially very cheap writing and glossy ("art") ones, are also loaded with some mineral substance, often kaolin (china clay). This may be identified by a spectrographic or other suitable analysis of the ash. (Chapter 8.)

The dyes used in coloured paper may be identified as described on p. 55.

Nature of the paper fibre. A variety of materials are used in paper making, but 85–90 per cent. of the world's paper is now made from wood pulp; this is divided into "mechanical" and "chemical" types according to the method used to break down the wood. The mechanical is used for newsprint and cheap paper, the chemical for good-quality paper. Straw is used in wrapping papers. The best papers were formerly made from rags, but a pure rag paper is nowadays a scarce and expensive commodity, and is used only for important documents which must be durable and for such special purposes as watercolour painting. Only linen and cotton rags are suitable, and pure rags of these textiles are becoming increasingly scarce; indeed, occasional synthetic fibres can be detected in most modern rag papers. Esparto grass is used extensively in paper for book production. Paper from other parts of the world may contain many different local vegetable fibres—e.g. bamboo or bagasse (sugar-cane residue).

To identify the paper-making materials, a fragment of the paper is completely disintegrated by gentle rubbing or shaking and/or treatment with dilute acid or alkali, and a wet preparation of the separated fibres examined microscopically. Some fibres have very characteristic appearances; wood-pulp fibres often show identifiable micro-anatomical structures characteristic of the woods from which they were derived (cf. Chapter 13). Modern papers may contain quite large amounts of otherwise not particularly common woods, such as oak or birch. Several staining reagents have also been devised; some merely render the fibre structure more easily seen, others (usually solutions containing iodine and a metallic chloride) give different characteristic purple to brown colours with different types of fibre. Finally, fibre counts on stained preparations may be used to determine the percentages of these different types.

Writing implements. In recent years the ball-point pen has become the normal writing implement and has largely displaced the once universal pen-nib. Whether it will in due course itself succumb to the more recent fibre-tip pen remains to be seen. According to a recent count by Mr. R. M. Mitchell, now Director of the Home Office Laboratory in Birmingham (to whom the writer is indebted for the figures), of 1,000 samples of handwriting submitted to him in the early 1970s, 85 per cent. were done with ball-points, 12 per cent. with nibs, just under 2 per cent. with fibre-tips and 1 per cent. with pencil.

The differences between the strokes made with these various implements are obvious and familiar. A nib using liquid ink will normally produce a stroke, especially a downstroke, with darker margins, owing to the nib points loosening the paper fibres and allowing easier penetration of the ink. Ball-points produce lines with a uniform distribution of ink across them and with considerable indentation of the paper. D. A. Black (California) has been able sometimes to identify a ball-point stroke with a particular pen, in cases where the ink has not fully covered the rotating ball, irregularities in which have left characteristic striations. Fibre-tip lines also show a uniform distribution of ink, but with little or no indentation of the paper. They may be streaky if made very quickly, and may show accompanying hair lines produced by outstanding fibres. They may resemble very closely the lines made by a good-quality fairly soft fountain pen. Pencil strokes and those made with "liquid-lead" pencils are superficially indistinguishable, since both consist of graphite; slight magnification will however reveal the difference between a true pencil stroke, in which particles of solid graphite composition have been rubbed off by the paper fibres, and one made by "liquid lead," which is simply a ball-point ink containing colloidal graphite.

Ink. The ink of anything written during the last 30 years or so is likely to be of one of the following types:

Fluid inks (water-based; used with a nib):

Carbon-black ink (Indian ink, waterproof drawing ink).

Iron ink. The basis of most ordinary inks has been for over 1,000 years a solution containing an iron (ferrous) salt and a tannin; on drying and oxidation, complex black ferric gallo-tannates are formed. Since this process is slow, all inks have for over a century also contained a dyestuff (usually blue) in order to give sufficient colour for immediate legibility.

Dyestuff ink. Many blue and all other-coloured inks are of this type; they are essentially dyestuff solutions containing gums, wetting agents, etc.

Quick-drying (alkaline) ink. This type is or was sold under various proprietary names for use in certain fountain pens. Their high alkalinity (pH 11–12) makes them soak quickly into the paper, rendering blotting unnecessary. The colouring matter is usually a copper or vanadium compound.

Pasty (ball-point) *inks*:

The original types of these had a greasy olein base and an oil-soluble dye, but these have been largely replaced by polyethylene glycol formulations containing (usually) a phthalocyanine dye.

Water-based and other inks can be broadly distinguished by their differential solubilities. Water will dissolve some colour out of all water-based inks except very old iron ones. Solvents such as trichlorethylene will dissolve the older type of ball-point inks, but neither the newer type nor water-based inks. A solvent such as alcohol will dissolve both types of ball-point, but not water-based, inks. The colour changes produced by the use of a few simple oxidising and reducing agents suffice to identify the general nature of the colouring matter in a water-based ink. These may be observed under the microscope by spotting a stroke with micro-drops of the reagents. However, Dr. Wilson R. Harrison prefers, as being less disfiguring to the document, to make the tests on tiny discs punched inconspicuously from the centres of strokes with a flat-ended needle.

It will rarely if ever be possible to extract enough dyestuff from an ink-stroke for a full chemical identification. However, most if not all inks contain a mixture of dyes, and the separation of these by thin-layer chromatography (p. 64) or, in some cases, electrophoresis (p. 65), will provide an empirically highly characteristic "spectrum" of coloured spots. If it is available, the porous glass developed by the Corning Glass Works is excellent for such a chromatographic separation.

Erasures and alterations. A false entry on an existing document may be made either by simple alteration of one or more characters, by erasure of the genuine entry and substitution of the false, or by complete over-writing of the original. In the second case, it will be necessary to show that erasure has taken place, to restore the original entry if possible and to show that the false entry differs in some respect from unaltered genuine ones. In the third case, a simple method of revealing the original which has been suggested is to pierce with a needle (using a sharp colour photograph if the original may not be marked) the places where traces of the original ink are visible under magnification, then simply to read the pattern of holes against a light.

Erasures may be either by mechanical removal of the writing or by chemical bleaching of it. Removal of light pencil by india-rubber may be practically undetectable on direct examination, but may be revealed by dusting the paper with a powder which adheres to areas where traces of rubber remain; graphite can be used, but is messy, and fluorescent powders unnoticeable in ordinary lighting have been developed to replace it. Most india-rubber erasers also contain sulphur, so that areas of erasure may be shown up by contact for some time with a chemically clean silver plate, which will be stained by the formation of brown silver sulphide. If any traces of pencil writing remain, they can occasionally be revealed, or even made legible, by the use of an image-intensifier, or by infra-red viewing or photography (pp. 205 and 222), since paper fibres are fairly transparent to infra-red whereas the residual graphite particles entangled in them are opaque. More vigorous mechanical erasure (for example, with a typewriter eraser, or by simple scraping) will almost certainly be detectable under low-power magnification by the disturbance of the paper fibres which it leaves.

Chemical erasure is in general possible only with iron and dyestuff inks. "Ink eradicators" are usually acid oxidising solutions which bleach dyes and dissolve iron salts. It is practically impossible to use them without leaving some trace, even if only from wetting the paper surface. The electrical conductivity of the paper in the erased areas will also be altered by the residual salts present. More simply, however, examination under ultra-violet will probably reveal the erasure as a patch of altered fluorescence. It may also render the erased writing visible, especially if it was done with an iron ink; traces of iron salts left in the paper quench its fluorescence, and bleached strokes show as a faint pattern of diminished fluorescence (*cf.* fig. 45). Iron-ink writing can sometimes also be restored chemically—but attempts to do so may stain the whole document disastrously.

Any new, false entry, whether it replaces erased matter or is a simple alteration (*e.g.* "1" to "7" or "six" to "sixty") is unlikely to have been made with the same writing material as the genuine original, and some difference in shade or appearance will almost certainly be visible under magnification. Visually undetectable or barely detectable differences may be revealed or enhanced, as the case may be, by infra-red viewing or photography, by infra-red luminescence (p. 223) or by photography through a suitable filter. Viewing through a dichroic filter (*i.e.* one transmitting two quite different regions of the spectrum) may also differentiate apparently identical ink colours. Awkward stroke junctions and cramped spacing are also causes for suspicion.

It is sometimes important in distinguishing the genuine from the false to discover the *order* in which crossing strokes were made. For example, if lines forming respectively part of the text of a document and part of its signature intersect, and if it can be shown that the signature stroke was there first, that part of the text is prima facie false. This question of stroke order is often a very difficult one, and has been the subject of much investigation. No general criteria have, however, been discovered, and each case must be considered on its own, mainly in the light of the writing material(s) used. With liquid inks, a stroke crossing a fold in the paper will show a diffusion of ink along this if made after it, and where two strokes cross the ink of the later may run out along the earlier. With pencil, ball-point and typewriting, and with any of these in conjunction with ink, the determination of order is more difficult and may be impossible. The actual appearance may be quite misleading. The deposition of a thin film of metallic gold by vacuum sputtering may sometimes provide the answer.

When strokes cross, the upper one was obviously made later; however, even when they do not, it may be possible to discover in other ways the order in which they were made, provided that the time-gap is long enough. Most water-based inks, once they are dry, continue to change slowly. Some become less soluble, so that less colour is extractable by a pressed-on damp filter paper. Iron inks undergo a complex series of changes: the solubility decreases, and the ink, which has at first darkened by oxidation, fades after a time measured in years or even centuries to a brownish-yellow colour. Iron inks also contain small amounts of chloride and sulphate ions which, over a period of years, migrate into the surrounding paper or into facing sheets in contact with the writing and can be detected there by simple chemical tests. Since the older of two strokes will show more ion diffusion, such tests will distinguish between the ages if both were made with the same ink on the same document, or on identical documents which have been stored under the same conditions.

Absolute dating. Tests such as we have just mentioned are always useless for *absolute* dating, since the results obtained vary widely and unpredictably according to the paper, ink and conditions of storage. It may however be possible to assign absolute limits to the age of a document from the evidence of its own contents or materials. It must obviously have been completed before any date on it known to be genuine, and it cannot have been completed before its materials, or stamps etc. on it, were first available. The document laboratory must therefore have an extensive knowledge of the history of paper and inks, and of the dates at which various designs of adhesive stamps were introduced. Some stamps are also even more narrowly dated by watermarks in their paper; it has been found possible to reveal these even in affixed stamps by using one of the X-ray methods described above under "Paper."

A document is of course proved to be a forgery if it incorporates materials not available till after its purported date of issue. Two examples of this may be cited. The first is the famous series of investigations published by J. Carter and J. Pollard in 1934 into the authenticity of certain nineteenth-century first editions much treasured by bibliophiles. Most of these had been "discovered" by one, Thomas Wise, who died in 1937 worth £138,000. Many of them bore dates before 1850, yet Carter and Pollard found that the paper on which they were printed contained esparto grass, first introduced in 1860 or 1861. Similarly, a whole series dated 1842–73 were printed on paper containing chemical wood pulp, first used in 1874. The other example is a more recent one. In 1967 eleven bound notebooks of what was alleged to be Mussolini's private diary kept during the 1920s were offered for sale, the price asked being £245,000. Examination by various types of expert failed to provide conclusive evidence one way or the other of their genuineness, and they were finally submitted to Dr. Julius Grant (London). He, from his own personal professional knowledge of paper-making in Italy during the period in question, was able to decide the issue. The volume for 1925 was written on paper containing 40 per cent. of straw pulp, which was not made in Italy before 1937, and microscopic examination of the paper excluded the only other possible sources from which bleached straw might have come before that date. Forgery was therefore proved, and eventually admitted.

Indented and blotted writing. The occasional importance of deciphering and/or matching these was mentioned on p. 204. Two examples may be quoted of the evidential value of indented writing. One is the so-called Southampton garage murder in 1928, in which, by an investigation starting six weeks after the murder because the body had lain undiscovered all that time, the murderer was traced partly through indentations on a receipt book which demonstrated that he had had business dealings with the victim and had been defrauding him. The other example is a case which occurred in one of the Home Counties shortly before the war. A farmer's daughter had, by a man G, an illegitimate child, who was boarded out with a foster mother. G was clearly anxious to escape from his obligation to support the child, and eventually came forward with a story, in support of which he produced a letter, that he had been approached by a couple who wanted to adopt the baby. Arrangements for the adoption were made and a rendezvous with the adopting parents agreed, but at this G turned up alone with another letter in which "they" (who did not in fact exist) apologised that they could not come and asked that the child be entrusted to him to bring to them. When the child's murdered body was found on the following day, a search of G's place of residence was made, and in it was found a writing pad bearing on its top sheet the indented text of the second letter from the "adopting parents." G was convicted of the murder.

Indented impressions may be deciphered simply by using a narrow beam of very oblique light, which shows them up in the same way that car headlamps show up faint undulations on a tarmac surface. Such a beam can be produced by a narrow slit in front of the light, but the completely unidirectional "piped light" possible with modern fibre optics is probably better. It is usually however much easier to read them in that way than to photograph them. Since the paper is rarely if ever perfectly flat, the optimum angles of illumination for different parts of it will be different; this is easily provided for in reading by moving the light, but is impracticable in photography. One method of photography which has been successful on occasion is to prepare a positive transparency of the same contrast as the negative and sufficiently out-of-focus to obliterate the details of the writing while retaining the broad general differences in illumination between the different parts, and to mask the negative with this in printing, thus allowing the indentation details sharply rendered in the negative to be recorded in a contrasty print.

Other methods of revealing indented writing have also been used successfully (though they involve marking the document). One (with glossy paper) is to rub a dark paste into the surface and remove the surplus with adhesive plaster, leaving the paste only in the indentations; the writing then appears dark-on-light on the paper surface, and light-on-dark on the plaster. The other method (*D. Graham*) is to cover the paper surface with lead dust and roll off the surplus with an inflated toy balloon; the lead-filled indentations may then be revealed by X-rays. This method can be used with any type of paper, which may also be printed on, making it impossible clearly to see the indentations with oblique light.

Charred documents. Examination of these was important during the war, and may sometimes be necessary even in peace-time. For example, an attempt may have been made to destroy an incriminating document by fire, or in connection with an insurance claim it may be suspected that the charred papers produced are not what they are said to be.

If the paper is merely "toasted," writing done with pencil or with most inks except pure dye ones, typewriting and printing can sometimes be rendered legible by infra-red viewing or photography. If the paper is completely carbonised, the problem is much more difficult, not the least difficulty being the manipulation of the brittle charred sheets or, even worse, the separation of the leaves of a charred book. One possible solution is to strengthen the charred paper by impregnation with a suitable flexible plastic and then to rely on faint differences in reflectivity for the decipherment of the writing or printing on it. Other methods of decipherment have included: enhancement of the faint differences by treatment with chloral hydrate; differential imbibition of a fluorescent oil; treatment with silver nitrate solution, which deposits silver on the writing-line traces. (It is uncertain whether this last effect is due to straightforward reduction or to the photochemical decomposition of silver chloride produced by the interaction with traces of chloride from the ink.) None of these methods is universally applicable, and this type of examination is inevitably still subject to much trial-and-error.

IV. HANDWRITING

Handwriting examinations most commonly have to be made to decide if possible whether:

(1) a particular signature is forged, or

(2) two passages were or were not written by the same person.

These two questions are not entirely independent. Although it is often possible to show that an isolated signature is a forgery, the answer to question (1) may also involve a comparative examination to decide who could not and who could have written it.

Question (1) is by far the simpler of the two if a mere decision as to genuineness is all that is required. (We are not concerned here of course with the case in which the forger writes a fictitious name in his normal handwriting, since there will then be no *internal* evidence susceptible of scientific examination.) A real signature may be forged either by (1) copying or (2) tracing. Copying requires skill or patience or both. With a degree of the former which is fortunately rare, the forgery may indeed be undetectable. More commonly the copier, possibly after several "dummy runs," tries in effect to copy his genuine model by *drawing* it; this inevitably produces a hesitant and irregular line, with frequent pen lifts (as the forger stops after each letter to survey his handiwork), which is quite different from the free-flowing line of a genuine signature. It goes without saying, also, that the successful copy-forger must be at least as good a penman as the true author of the signature; the smooth, even and well-graded lines of good writing are something that only another good writer can imitate.

A traced forgery may be done either directly by superimposition of the sheets against a light, or via an intermediate tracing-paper or carbon-paper stage. In either case, the forgery will again betray a hesitancy and irregularity of line due to the laborious operation of tracing. In the latter, indentations or traces of pencil or of carbon-paper pigment may also be visible under magnification beside or around the ink strokes. In addition, if the genuine original from which the tracing was made is available, it and the forgery may show such a degree of identity in conformation and spacing as to be in itself proof of forgery, since no one ever does or can write two signatures identical to this degree.

The general examination and comparison of handwriting is a much larger and more complex subject. The factors which determine the appearance of a piece of handwriting are:

(1) the style which the writer was taught as a child;
(2) the personal idiosyncratic characteristics of the writer;
(3) the extraneous factors operative at the time of writing.

These last may be subdivided into:

(a) the fortuitous ones—whether the writer was hurried or unhurried, fresh or tired, comfortable or uncomfortable, and (though this is less important) the writing materials used, and whether these were of the writer's accustomed type;

(b) whether or not the writer was trying to disguise his handwriting.

It is the business of the handwriting examiner to isolate and distinguish the effects of these three sets of causes. Broadly speaking, this task involves an analytical appreciation of the recurrent or characteristic features of the piece of writing under examination, and of the differences between that piece and the handwritings of different people. A scientific appraisal of these factors will then enable him to decide whether or not two pieces of writing were certainly, probably or possibly, as the case may be, written by the same person.

The examiner must therefore first collect all the control material he can get, preferably written at various times under various circumstances, and if possible including some written with and on the same materials as the suspected document. Although he cannot have too much, a valid opinion can be based on very little if some sufficiently distinctive characteristic appears. He is then ready for the analysis of this material. He will note characteristics such as: letter slope; an upward or downward trend of the lines of writing; word, letter and line spacing; the ratio of the heights of small to large or capital letters; the positions relative to their parent letters of the dots of i's and the bars of t's; the presence or absence, and the length if present, of initial and terminal strokes to words; pen lifts (whether the writer frequently lifts his pen in the middle of a word or, alternatively, runs words together); whether the pen strokes are smooth-flowing or irregular and tremulous; whether, if an ordinary nib has been used, the shading differentiation between upward and downward strokes is slight or pronounced. He will then go on to consider the formations of individual letters; taking first all the small a's, then the small b's and so on, and working similarly through the capital letters if the passage is long enough to have a representative collection of these.

He will of course start with simple though careful visual examination (aided, if the writing is very faint, by image intensification with one of the methods mentioned on p. 205). At this stage, he may find it helpful to make rough sketches of any salient features. However, it will obviously make the examination easier if the whole document is photographed (preferably at rather over natural size) and the separate letters cut out and grouped together. In any case, this procedure will be necessary to prepare the analytical charts of letter formation which form an essential part of the presentation of handwriting evidence.

The recognition of mere style characteristics (the first class of factors above) will have come during the preliminary examination, but at the stage he has now reached the examiner will be able to identify the writer's unique characteristics (the second class of factors) and to distinguish them from the accidental variations of form (the third class of factors) which all handwriting shows. It may safely be said that no two specimens of the same letter will be absolutely identical, and specimens made under different conditions of writing may show wide random differences. Any characteristics, however, which appear in all or nearly all specimens, and especially those which persistently appear in spite of different conditions, may confidently be taken as personal. Examples are: an unusually large or small number of pen lifts; a tendency to dot i's well to the right or to the left; open tops on closed letters (a, o, etc.); n's made like v's, or v's like n's; the use of small eyelets or closed loops in places where the stroke has to be reversed (in writing a's, g's, o's, p's, etc.). These are only a few of the almost innumerable possible examples.

It is this sort of examination which may enable the examiner to pronounce with confidence that two passages of superficially dissimilar handwriting were written by the same person, or alternatively that two superficially similar passages were not. Whatever words the writer is using, their actual formation and that of their constituent letters, once the writer is past the childhood stage of learning to write, are a process not under, or even amenable to, conscious control. Anyone who is trying to disguise his handwriting will find it practically impossible, in a passage of any length, to prevent some of his personal writing characteristics appearing, of the use of which he is probably unconscious anyway. Even if he alters his letter design, he will tend to make the new design with the same sort of pen motions as characterise his normal writing.

For a similar reason, though the examiner's task is easier if he knows the language in which the passage is written, this is not essential. However, if the writing is hurried or careless, he may even if the script is one with which he is familiar need a typed transcript prepared by someone who knows the language well, since he cannot, as he can with his own language, identify malformed letters by their context. He can also fruitfully apply the same methods even to writing in an unfamiliar script (e.g. Arabic, if he is English-speaking). To do so he must first of course find out, if the script is an alphabetic one, which characters or groups of characters represent letters and words, so that he may recognise the

features to be compared. The same basic principles have however been successfully applied even to ideographic writing such as Chinese.

For example, in connection with a recent investigation into the disappearance
of a married Pakistani woman living in southern England, it was important to
discover the authorship of several letters written in Urdu; one of these, pur-
portedly from a certain Mr. S. and produced by the suspects, made an allegation
explaining her disappearance. Urdu is written in an Arabic script, the form of
each letter varies according to its place in the word, and no capitals are used. In
spite of these difficulties, the English examiner was able to demonstrate clearly
that: the Urdu handwritings of the three original suspects were clearly distinguishable; none of them had written the vitally important letters, including that
from "Mr. S." (who, there was every reason to suppose, was fictitious); the
handwriting of that letter, and that of a previously unsuspected younger brother
of the missing woman's husband, showed no significant differences and so many
points of similarity that it could be concluded that he had written it. In reaching
that conclusion the examiner had first to identify the letters and words in the
Urdu documents. For this, a translator was supplied with Xerox copies of the
letters (*i.e.* documents) and asked to mark off each word and to write in a Roman
alphabet transliteration and the English translation. Each separate letter (*i.e.*
written character) could then be identified with the aid of an Urdu dictionary
and alphabet. Forty-five Pakistani volunteers were also asked to write in Urdu
each of 25 key words given to them. This last step enabled the examiner to collect
sufficient material to study the variability of Urdu handwriting and to base a
valid opinion on the characteristics present in the questioned writing.

To return to the usual cases involving only the examiner's own language,
attempts have been made to reduce this sort of analysis to an exact numerical
science by marking the features of the writing as they are examined on a "points
system." The idea has also been suggested of making a statistical analysis of the
frequencies with which certain characteristics occur, and storing these in a
computer memory, so that on the basis of the characteristics present any piece
of writing can be given a "coefficient of significance." So far, however, none of
these ideas has progressed beyond the pipe-dream stage.

Finally, handwriting examination, as it has been described, has no connection
with *graphology*. This is the study of handwriting for the elucidation of personal
characteristics and psychological traits. Most document examiners are sceptical
of its claims and consider it a pseudo-science.

V. TYPEWRITING

The occasions on which it has to be proved that two specimens of typewriting
were or were not done on one machine are common in fiction and not uncommon
in fact. The first recorded case of this (*c.* 1893) by Sherlock Holmes in *A Case
of Identity*, is an instance of the already-mentioned foresight of Sir Arthur Conan
Doyle. More recently, many people will remember the case of Alger Hiss, who
was convicted in the U.S.A. in 1950 for passing information to the Communists,

his guilt being established partly by expert testimony that the documents passed had been typed on a machine admittedly used by Mrs. Hiss for her private letters.

The factors which determine the appearance of a typed passage are:

(1) The make and date of the machine. At one time, each manufacturer used his individual letter designs and some changed theirs from time to time. Nowadays (unfortunately for the examiner) a few large specialist firms supply many manufacturers with a limited number of type-face designs. The inter-letter and inter-line spacing are also characteristics of the machine.

(2) The state of the machine. The features due to this can be subdivided into:

(*a*) Constant, or at least very slowly changing, features—mainly broken or misaligned letters.

(*b*) Temporary features, due to things such as the age of the ribbon and the amount of dirt in the type.

(3) The way in which the machine is used. Unskilled typing may lead to displaced letters, imperfectly formed capitals, etc.

The examination of typewriting can therefore be sharply divided into (1) the examination of the document by itself to discover the make and model of machine on which it was typed (a part of the examination which has no parallel in handwriting examination), and (2) comparison, if a particular machine is suspected, to discover whether the document was in fact typed on it.

For the first of these tasks, the examiner must have available a complete reference collection of all the type faces now or formerly used by all the typewriter manufacturers. These must also be *classified* in some way. There is no universally accepted system of classification here, but the invention or choice of that finally adopted will probably rest, as with blood-group systems (*cf.* p. 15), on the criterion of *discriminatory power*: the primary classifying characteristics chosen will be those which most sharply divide all type faces into roughly equal groups. For the final identification, many characteristics, especially of certain letters, are available. These include, among others: the ratios of capital and lower-case letter heights; the angles of the stroke intersections in letters such as v or w; the presence or absence of serifs; the symmetry or asymmetry, on either side of the upright, of the cross bar in letters such as f or t; the construction of multiform letters and figures—whether a's have short or long loops, g's tails or closed lower loops, 4s are closed or open, etc. By transferring all the noted characteristics to punched cards, one for each make and model of machine, that used for any unknown piece of typing can be rapidly identified, or at least limited to a small number of possibles. The computerisation of this sort of information may also be on its way.

The examiner will tackle the second task—the identification of the particular machine—much as he does with handwriting; he will by a process of analysis distinguish between those features which are permanent or at least long-lasting characteristics of a particular machine (*e.g.* broken letters), those which are due to the temporary condition of the machine and its ribbon and those which can be ascribed to the way in which it has been used. He must at the same time, however, guard against certain pitfalls into which inexperience might have led him; to take only one example, a missing serif may be due to a broken letter, but, unless it is seen to occur whenever this letter appears, it could be due to a pitted roller surface having prevented this part of the letter from marking the paper.

An obvious step at this stage is to type on the suspected machine a facsimile of the passage under examination for comparison with it. This comparison is much easier and more certain if a "flicking" or "blink" comparator (p. 205) is available; it has indeed been authoritatively stated that this apparatus will distinguish between two identical passages typed on two machines of the same make and model, which can differ only in minute variations in letter alignment.

The ink, if enough may be removed from the document, can also be compared with that in the suspected ribbon by thin-layer chromatography (p. 64).

How far this comparison can be carried depends on circumstances. At one extreme, two pieces of typing done by the same typist very close to each other in time will agree in respect of all of the classes of feature listed above; at the other, two pieces done by different typists at widely separated times may be so different that the machine will only be identifiable, if at all, by a very detailed analytical examination.

Modern developments in typewriter technology have unfortunately created difficulties for the examiner. Electric typewriters will not show user characteristics. Still worse, from the present point of view, are the recently introduced electric machines in which the type is mounted, not on type bars, but on a single rotatable replaceable ball, which is not subject as bars are to alignment variations. The problems posed here are being vigorously tackled, especially in the U.S.A.; how far they will be soluble remains to be seen.

17

PHOTOGRAPHY

Photography is a tool useful at many stages of crime detection. References to some of its uses have been scattered throughout this book, but it will be convenient to give a brief coherent account of these in this chapter.

The purposes for which it is used are, briefly:

(1) Routine recording. This includes the photography of prisoners and of fingerprints, the photocopying of documents, photolithographic reproduction of material for circulation, etc. All this is everyday police work, and will not be further considered here.

(2) The provision of permanent pictorial records, for reference at later stages in the investigation, and/or to show to the courts the appearance of scenes and subjects which they cannot by the nature of things see for themselves. This use may be subdivided into:

(a) The photography of scenes of crime, road accidents, etc. This again is a routine job for the photographic departments maintained by all police forces. However, the writer, before dismissing this aspect of the subject, would like to pay a tribute in passing to the ordinary, unsung, rarely praised police photographer, who must be ready to turn out in all weathers at any time of the day or night, and produce, with complete confidence that they will be successful (since he will not have a second opportunity), acceptable photographs of what are often extremely difficult subjects. The standard of work which the best of them achieve in these circumstances is superb.

(b) The photography of exhibits received in the laboratory before their appearance is altered by subsequent work on them, and of laboratory tests the results of which are essentially visual but which cannot, or cannot conveniently, be demonstrated in court. As far as laboratory practice is concerned, this overlaps with

(3) The use of photography as a primary tool, to show effects that only it can reveal. At one time the most important use in this category was infra-red photography, but this has been overtaken by modern developments in image converters (p. 205). There are still however a few things which photography can do better than the eye; they will be referred to in their places below.

To be able to tackle every job that may prove necessary, something like the following range of equipment will be necessary:

A conventional camera for straightforward photography at scales of reproduction up to natural size. Almost any professional camera on a really stable adjustable stand is perfectly suitable.

A camera which has a long bellows extension (up to, say, 20 inches for a 5 inch × 4 inch format) and which can be fitted with a variety of short-focus interchangeable lenses (with focal lengths ranging from, say, 1 inch to 6 inches for the size mentioned). This combination serves for photography at, say, 1 to 20 times natural size ("macrophotography"). One of the modern monorail technical cameras would be suitable.

Photomicrographic equipment. This may be anything from a simple extension body and plate holder to fit into the microscope draw tube, to a complete horizontal or vertical photomicrographic unit; the more complex and expensive, the more versatile.

A variety of light sources, including: floodlights; sources giving a highly concentrated beam (*i.e.* spotlights or microscope lamps, which are in effect miniature spotlights); rigidly unidirectional fibre-optics "piped light"; sources giving extremely uniform shadowless illumination over a small area. (The last requirement is probably best met by a ring illuminator, in which a series of small lamps, shielded from the lens, is arranged annularly around the lens axis.)

Sources of infra-red and filtered ultra-violet radiation.

A very complete range of light filters transmitting various broad and narrow spectral regions, and a polarising screen.

A variety of sensitive materials, of different speeds, contrasts and spectral sensitivity ranges.

Most laboratory photographic jobs are "one-off"; in many of them much trial-and-error is necessary, with development and inspection of each exposure before the next is attempted; needle-sharp definition, and sometimes dimensional stability in the material, are essential. For all these reasons, most photographers in this field prefer to use individual plates (or sheet films if dimensional stability is not important) in a fairly large format. There are however some who prefer even for all laboratory work the 35-millimetre format so universally popular today.

The specialised types of photographic equipment required for document examination and for firearms work have already been mentioned in their places (pp. 205 and 201 respectively).

There is also a considerable potential use in forensic science for *Polaroid* equipment and material, with which, as is well known, a finished print can be produced on the spot. Polaroid photography can be particularly valuable at a scene of crime, and can also sometimes usefully replace in laboratory notes sketches of the material examined. It has also been much used for quick permanent records of chromatographic, electrophoretic and similar tests.

A good deal of straightforward record work is required in the laboratory. It may for example be desirable to record the presence and position of a flake of paint on a jemmy, or of hairs on a weapon, before these are removed for laboratory examination. It is sometimes also more convenient to photograph the matching of broken edges, of tools and marks, etc., than to attempt to demonstrate the actual fit or match in court. This type of photography demands chiefly careful adjustment of the lighting to show the significant feature(s) as clearly as possible, and an intelligent choice of sensitive material of the most suitable contrast range and spectral sensitivity. Where the precise shape of, for example, a housebreaking implement is important, a useful technique (which comes from the Los Angeles laboratory) is to photograph it with back lighting; this outlines the shape as an illuminated rim, which may be combined for effective demonstration with a photograph of a mark allegedly made with the instrument.

If colour material is not available (see below), some experimentation with panchromatic materials and a variety of contrast filters may be necessary for the best results in black-and-white. For example, a speck of green paint and a red object to which it is adhering may well in a "straight" record be reproduced as the same tone of grey, rendering the speck practically invisible in the picture; a filter must therefore be chosen which makes the speck appear either much lighter (*i.e.* a green or minus red filter) or much darker (*i.e.* a red or minus green filter) than its background.

A point to be remembered in this connection is that it is often easy with yellows and reds to filter out the colour completely, so that the coloured object photographs as white, whereas this is rarely if ever possible with blues and greens. This is because the properties of dyes and pigments are such that a colour at the yellow-red end of the spectrum can be both strong and saturated (*i.e.* loosely, pure), whereas a strong green or blue is unsaturated and therefore, unless very pale, contains a high proportion of neutral grey, which component cannot of course be filtered out.

Though it might reasonably be supposed that photography by light in any part of the visible spectrum could only be used to record something already perceptible by the eye, this is in practice not so; photography still has a place here as a primary tool. There are two reasons for this. One lies in the difference between the spectral sensitivity responses of the eye and of photographic emulsions. The eye is most sensitive to a yellow-green colour and least sensitive to the ends of the spectrum; all emulsions, on the other hand, are most sensitive to blue, and panchromatic ones are also highly sensitive to red and less sensitive to green. The eye and an emulsion therefore "see" the same colour differently. The other reason is that the eye's response to light is instantaneous, whereas that of the emulsion is cumulative. In a dim light, a dark-adapted eye sees all that it is going to see at once; in photography, dimness of illumination can up to a point be fully compensated* by increasing the exposure time, and it is therefore possible to take a picture in such circumstances showing more than the

---

* That this sort of compensation is possible only within limits is due to the phenomenon of *reciprocity failure*. Over a wide range of light intensities the response of photographic emulsions is proportional to (intensity × time of exposure): if the intensity is reduced to, say, one tenth of its original value, exactly the same result is obtained by making the exposure ten times as long. However, with *very* high or *very* low light intensities this proportionality breaks down: if the intensity were reduced to, say, one thousandth, more than 1,000 times the exposure would be needed for the same result.

eye could ever see. In consequence, a filter transmitting only a narrow region of the spectrum may well (especially if it is a blue or red one—see above) transmit too little light for vision unless the illumination is impracticably intense, though photography through such a filter is perfectly possible.

In this type of photography it is usually much easier to support and arrange the object(s) to be photographed if they are laid on a horizontal surface than if they have to be supported in any other position. A vertical camera position is usually therefore most convenient; it is essential if a specimen has to be photographed under water, as is sometimes the case; it also makes it possible to produce a completely uniform, shadow-free background by supporting the object on a sheet of glass.

For macrophotography at over natural size, the same general considerations apply, with one or two additional ones as well. Lighting is usually fairly critical. It is therefore best, in order to make as much room as possible for experiment with it, to make the lens-object distance a maximum, which is done by using the longest-focus lens which gives the magnification required with the maximum available camera extension. When highly directional lighting is used—for example, in the reproduction of shallow tool marks, faint striations and the like—the resulting brightness range of the subject is very great, so that a material with a long exposure range (scale of gradation) must be used.

For certain subjects which are, or may be, transient, such as re-developed erased numbers (Chapter 5), it is important to have the camera set up and ready before the final operation on the object to be photographed.

Photomicrography is not so frequently useful as might be supposed. It is sometimes desirable to record the matching of scratch marks, bullets, etc., in a comparator or comparison microscope (Chapters 3 and 15), where the magnification is around $\times 20$ to $\times 50$, but with work needing high magnifications (say $\times 100$ to $\times 1,000$) what is seen through the microscope is significant only to the expert's trained eye, and a photograph of it would be meaningless to a court of scientific laymen. There are, however, justifiable exceptions to this rule—for example, when several obviously different types of diatom occur in a safe ballast and in dust from a suspect's clothing (*cf.* p. 42). Photography at the enormous magnifications possible with the scanning electron microscope may also sometimes provide a convincing demonstration (*cf.* p. 83 and fig. 7).

Invisible radiations. Considerable use is made in the laboratory of radiations outside the visible spectrum—infra-red and ultra-violet (see p. 70 and fig. 45).

Infra-red photography is used mainly for: document examinations (Chapter 16); revealing stencilled and such-like identification marks in cases where the obliterating medium happens to be transparent to infra-red; revealing powder blackening etc. (fig. 42) on dark fabrics. It requires: a source of infra-red radiation; a filter transmitting infra-red but opaque to ordinary light; infra-red-sensitive material. The second and third of these requirements can be obtained from the leading manufacturers. The first may be a special infra-red lamp, but an ordinary metal-filament bulb is also an adequate source, since it emits over 90 per cent. of its energy as infra-red and heat. Focusing presents a problem here, since, as photographic lenses are not corrected for infra-red, the correct focusing position will be slightly different from that for visible light, and cannot of course be seen, infra-red being by definition invisible. The simplest solution is to use the largest lens aperture for focusing and a very small one for the photography, relying on the depth of focus for an acceptably sharp picture. A better solution is to use an infra-red image converter constructed to fit the camera back with the infra-red-sensitive surface exactly in the focal plane.

As already mentioned, however, infra-red photography is no longer an essential primary tool, because the quality of the image produced by a good modern image converter is so high that visual examination with one will reveal as much as a photograph can. In general, therefore, infra-red photography is now used mainly for the production of permanent records. Also, unfortunately, it appears to be no longer possible to obtain, in this country at least, the very contrasty infra-red materials formerly available and so desirable for the recording of very faint details.

"Straight" *ultra-violet* photography (which means, when glass lenses are used, photography using the approximate wavelength range 360–400 nm.) is easy. All photographic emulsions are very sensitive to these wavelengths, and the only special equipment required is a source of filtered ultra-violet radiation (normally a mercury-in-quartz arc with a Wood's glass filter). It is in fact rarely used; it can, however, be helpful on occasion, by differentiating between surfaces with otherwise indistinguishable reflective properties. For example, of the two common white pigments titanium dioxide and zinc oxide, the former has a high ultra-violet reflectivity and photographs white, while the latter does not reflect ultra-violet and therefore photographs black.

Ultra-violet radiation is much more commonly utilised for its property of stimulating visible *fluorescence*. The photography of this differs from its visual examination in that, photographic emulsions being as already mentioned unlike the eye very sensitive to ultra-violet, unchanged reflected ultra-violet must not be allowed to enter the camera, where it would completely "swamp" the much fainter fluorescence. With that proviso, however, the photography is not difficult using the arrangement shown diagrammatically in fig. 46. If the fluorescence is very faint, the exposures may be very long, running into minutes or even tens of minutes.

Although "fluorescence" is generally used to mean absorption of ultra-violet and emission of visible light, it is as already mentioned (p. 75) strictly speaking and more generally the emission of any wavelength longer than that absorbed. It would for example be quite easy to photograph fluorescence at longer ultra-violet wavelengths (say 360–400 nm.—roughly the region transmitted by glass) stimulated by shorter (*e.g.* the 254 nm. mercury line); the writer does not know of this method having been used in forensic science, but it would seem to be worth a trial. However, another type of fluorescence which is now well-tried and has proved valuable is the so-called *infra-red luminescence*. In this, the absorbed radiation is in the (visible) blue-green part of the spectrum and the re-emitted in the (invisible) infra-red. The object is therefore illuminated by blue-green light from which all infra-red has been filtered out (a liquid filter of copper sulphate solution serves), and examined through an image-converter or photographed after filtering out all reflected visible light.

This technique is particularly useful in document examinations, revealing some otherwise undetectable faded writing and differences between superficially similar inks (fig. 47); this application was pioneered in the U.S.A. The intensity of the emitted infra-red is always very faint; as in all fluorescence photography, long exposures are necessary, and visual examination requires very high-intensity illumination (of the order of 1,000 watts).

For some purposes, the ingenuity of the photographer may profitably be taxed to devise ways of demonstrating fits and matches by means of *superimposed transparencies* or of *double exposures*. The former can be effective with footwear and footprints, or with tools and toolmarks. A now classic use of the latter is the superimposition by double exposure on one plate of a skull which is to be identified and an enlargement of a photographic head taken during life of the deceased person whose skull it is presumed to be. This technique was probably first used in the famous Ruxton case (1935), in which some dismembered remains found in Scotland were eventually identified as those of two women missing in Lancashire. A piece of equipment for this very purpose was some years ago devised in Germany; it has an optical bench with the skull mounted at one end and a camera at the other, and in between a series of frames for lining up and adjusting the comparison photographs to be used.

On many occasions **colour photography** is undoubtedly much superior to black-and-white. Where the purpose of the photograph is to demonstrate something which, visually, depends on a colour difference, it is obviously better to do so by a natural-seeming colour photograph than by a possibly misleading black-and-white differentiation based on the use of contrast filters (p. 221). However, although their use is increasing, colour processes are less widely used in this field than their superiority would seem to justify. Reversal transparencies are easily made but are necessarily unique copies and are not easily shown to a court. Negative-positive colour prints are admirable for production in court but have certain disadvantages from the forensic photographer's point of view: they take considerably longer to make; it is quite a critical operation to ensure that a set of prints are exactly identical in colour balance, which of course is essential when different prints from the same negative are being examined by judge, jury and opposing counsel; and, of course, the fact that the prints must legally be the work of the photographer witness excludes the use of any commercial colour-print service. However, recent advances in the technology of colour photography are rapidly removing the first two of these disadvantages, and its use in this field is increasing.

Finally, it must be obvious that handwork of any sort, even simple spotting, is completely taboo on photographs used in evidence. To adapt a well-known legal maxim, not only must the photograph be unfaked, it must be clearly manifest that there could not possibly have been any faking. "Faking" means here of course handwork; shading during enlargement and similar "dodges" are not only permissible but sometimes essential if a recognisable picture is to be produced; the criterion is whether or not everything in the final picture is a representation of the original image formed by the camera lens. The photographer must therefore be a clean worker and deft craftsman.

18

THE SCIENTIST IN THE WITNESS BOX

The justification and climax of the forensic scientist's work is his appearance in court as an expert witness. In practice, of course, this point may never be reached: if his evidence points inescapably to guilt, the defendant may plead guilty, and often does in minor cases; his examination may lead to the clearing of a suspect, so that no charge is preferred; or he may find nothing of value to either side and consequently not be called as a witness. The British expert used to spend much more of his time in the witness box than his counterparts elsewhere did. He used to have to appear in person, sometimes at least twice (for committal and trial), in every contested case, whereas in most European countries agreed expert evidence can be accepted by the courts without the expert appearing in person, and in the U.S.A. the defence frequently "stipulates"—that is, indicates that it accepts the expert's report and does not insist that he be called. Now, however, in this country also, since the Criminal Justice Act 1967 came into force, the expert is called to give evidence only when his presence is specifically demanded—that is, when his evidence is crucially important, or when its further elucidation or his cross-examination is deemed necessary.

Assuming, however, that the expert does appear in the witness box, his evidence will be based on a report which he has already submitted on the examination he has made. He will give first the bare facts as he ascertained them, then in most cases his opinion as to the significance of these facts. In this respect expert evidence differs from that of the ordinary witness of fact, who is not normally allowed to express his opinions. The expert is, however, not only allowed but expected to do so. For example: the facts ascertained by him are consistent (but no more) with the vehicles in question having collided; or, there are so many independent pieces of evidence pointing to the vehicles having been in violent contact that he is satisfied that they were, and in his opinion no other explanation of the facts is tenable.

What the courts require of the expert may be summed up as: impartiality, reliability, clarity, relevancy. A forensic science service which is to command credence and respect must obviously be, and be known to be, completely objective and impartial. This obligation has always been clearly recognised and honoured in British laboratories, and the writer has no reason to believe that that is not also true of other countries. To establish his reliability the expert must make the court feel that he is a man of absolute integrity, that his opinions have been formed with scrupulous care and that, if he says something is a fact, every possible precaution to avoid error has been taken. For the remaining requirements, he must remember that, on his own subject, he is probably much better informed than anyone else in the court; he must therefore eschew unnecessary technical jargon and must carefully avoid giving the impression that he is trying to "blind them with science." He must stick to the point in his answers and avoid explanatory lecturettes unless he is asked for them.

It may be suggested to him that he is mistaken; that of course is a possibility which he must always admit, but it is then open to him to draw attention politely to the length of his experience and to the number of confirmatory tests which he has (or should have) made before he testifies to anything factual—reliability again. He must of course admit at once the possibility of another expert forming a different opinion from the same facts, but he should modestly but firmly stick to his own; if he cannot honestly do so, he should not have expressed it in the first place. If the witness is a senior and experienced man in his own profession, it can also happen that some previously published statement of his own which seems to be at variance with what he is now saying in the witness box is quoted against him; a famous medical expert in that situation made the classic reply: "Medicine advances with the times, and I endeavour to keep pace with its progress."

What the expert must not do is "get himself out on a limb"; it is fatal to his specific evidence in particular and damaging to his reputation in general to go any further than his findings warrant. If he is not sure of something, or simply does not know, he should say so. He must not of course in the factual part of his evidence depart by even a hair's breadth from the strict truth, but, when he is asked to interpret this, he is usually bound to offer shaded or qualified opinions; at this stage he will find that what he says will command more respect if he underplays rather than overplays his hand.

The main cause of any genuine difficulty in which the conscientious and experienced expert witness may find himself is the different mental attitudes of lawyers and scientists. In many years' experience in the witness box, the writer has come to the conclusion that lawyers think of science as a body of facts which, once established, are embodied for evermore in the corpus of knowledge. Science is not of course in the least like that. For the scientist, the true business of science is the formulation and testing of hypotheses about the physical world. The testing involves finding out facts, and he accepts provisionally that hypothesis which seems, on a balance of probability, to fit them. They themselves are only a means to an end.

Now, although it is true that most scientific expert evidence deals with quite elementary facts ascertained by the disciplines of science, it is this fundamentally different approach to the value of facts which produces these differences in mental attitudes. Lawyers tend, in the writer's experience, to approach scientific matters with suspicion, and he believes that he has observed this reaction even in the most eminent and brilliant of them. In fact, the scientist's attitude to his science is much more like the lawyer's to his case than the latter seems to realise. The lawyer accepts the hypothesis of guilt as proved "beyond reasonable doubt," and the scientist similarly accepts his hypothesis as provisionally established, if in both cases all the ascertainable facts are consistent, and none wholly inconsistent, with them.

The modern view of some philosophers of science is (following Professor Karl Popper) that no hypothesis can ever be *proved* in strict logic; it can always at any time be *disproved* by the discovery of a fact inconsistent with it, but in the absence of any such facts all that we can logically do is to accept it as provisionally established, more or less firmly according to the amount and reliability of the information tending to demonstrate its truth. This situation seems, to the writer at least, very much like that which a jury faces when they are directed to arrive at a verdict. It is certainly that facing the forensic scientist in his laboratory. If the hypothesis has been formulated that this jemmy was used to commit this housebreaking, then one single fact—such as that it is the wrong size for the mark left in the window frame—may suffice to disprove the hypothesis; on the other hand, it can never be proved with logical finality that no other jemmy could have been used; at the best, there may be such a body of facts—matching of scratch marks, coincidence of unusual paints and so forth—tending to establish the truth of the hypothesis that the only practically tenable conclusion is that the hypothesis is proved "beyond all reasonable doubt."

There remains the difficulty that the law's "reasonable doubt" is not a quantifiable concept, whereas the scientist is always anxious where possible to give numerical expression to the probability that his hypothesis is true. There are signs, however, that this division is being bridged. The courts, at least in Britain, have for some time now happily accepted numerical data about blood-group distribution as relevant and assimilable evidence, and some forward-looking lawyers on both sides of the Atlantic have been considering ways in which the reaching of just decisions might be helped by probability calculations. What does "reasonable doubt" mean, they have been asking, in terms of the probability that the hypothesis of guilt is true? And how does one calculate such a probability? Can one assign a statistical "weight" to a particular piece of evidence? Work such as that of Parker on hair analysis (p. 173) may be a signpost to the way in which these questions can be answered and in which the proof of guilt will some day be approached.

FURTHER READING

The following suggestions do *not* constitute a complete bibliography of the subject (the compilation of which would be in any case a daunting if not impossible task). Also, no attempt whatsoever has been made to meet the needs of the practising forensic scientist; they are adequately met by the existing methods for the dissemination of scientific information, with the operation of which he is assumed to be familiar. The following section contains rather:

(1) A reasonably complete list of English-language, and a few other, books and periodicals specifically devoted to the subject, except for some either now quite out-of-date or purely popular in their approach.

(2) References, which it is hoped will be useful both to the tyro forensic scientist and to the professionally interested but scientifically untrained reader, to starting points for further reading in those parts of the field which fall rather outside the range normally covered by the literature of science or the law.

BOOKS ON FORENSIC SCIENCE

These fall into three categories: (1) Books addressed to a popular readership but of possible interest to the more serious reader because of the illustrative cases described; (2) Books for the police officer or other *user* of forensic science, telling him what it is and what it can do for him; (3) Manuals for the practising forensic scientist.

Examples of the first category are: *Science and the Detection of Crime*, by C. R. M. Cuthbert, who was for a number of years police liaison officer in the Metropolitan Police Laboratory (Hutchinson, London, 1958); *A Scientist Turns to Crime*, by J. B. Firth, a former director of the Home Office North-Western Forensic Science Laboratory and for long a leading expert on fire investigations (William Kimber, London, 1960); *Expert Witness*, by the present writer (John Long, London, 1972; in the U.S.A., *Scotland Yard Scientist*, Taplinger Publishing Co., New York, 1973).

The second and third categories cannot be clearly separated, since some books span both. The following is, to the best of the writer's knowledge, a fairly complete list (with the qualification mentioned above).

Forensic Chemistry and Scientific Criminal Investigation. A. Lucas (Arnold, London, 1945). For the scientist. Out-of-date, but worth reading for its appreciation of general principles.
Forensic Science and Laboratory Techniques. Ralph F. Turner (Charles C. Thomas, Springfield, Ill., and Blackwell Scientific Publications, Oxford, 1949).
Crime Investigation. Paul L. Kirk (Interscience Publishers, New York, 1953, reprinted 1960). For the scientist. The writer was in his lifetime a senior figure in forensic science and professor of the subject at Berkeley University. The book

is now rather out-of-date and is not, in the present writer's opinion, very conveniently arranged.

The Scientific Investigation of Crime. L. C. Nickolls (Butterworth, London, 1956). A manual for the forensic scientist. Now inevitably out-of-date in many parts. By a former director of the Metropolitan Police Laboratory, a writer of encyclopedic knowledge and immense experience.

Scientific Investigation and Physical Evidence. Leland V. Jones (Charles C. Thomas, Springfield, Ill., 1959). Good on marks, physical fits, etc.—the rest rather cursory. For the investigating officer rather than the scientist on the whole.

Manuel de Police Scientifique (in French). Jean Gayet (Payot, Paris, 1961). Of limited scope, but deals in some detail with fingerprints, contact traces generally, firearms, fires and explosions, handwriting and typewriting comparison, counterfeit money.

Modern Critimal Investigation. Harry Söderman and John J. O'Connell, revised by Charles E. O'Hara (Funk and Wagnalls, New York, 1962). A revision of the original authors' *An Introduction to Criminalistics* (1952). Primarily for the investigating officer.

Criminal Investigation. Hans Gross, 5th edition revised by Richard Leofric Jackson (Sweet & Maxwell, London, 1962). A classic, once the detective's Bible, first published in 1906. For the investigating officer, but has much to say about the role of science in his work. The present editor is a former Assistant Commissioner of the Metropolitan Police C.I.D.

Methods of Forensic Science (Interscience Publishers, New York). An ambitious multi-volume and multi-author work intended to be the definitive textbook for practising forensic scientists. Four volumes appeared between 1962 and 1965, the first two edited by Dr. Frank Lundquist (Denmark) and the last two by Dr. A. S. Curry (England), but the series then stopped. Each topic is dealt with by an appropriate expert; some of the contributions are disappointing, but most are good and some are very good.

Scientific Evidence for Police Officers. James R. Richardson (W. H. Anderson Co., Cincinnati, 1963). By a lawyer and from a legal point of view.

The Scientific Investigator. R. O. Arther (Charles C. Thomas, Springfield, Ill., 1965). For the policeman; there is a large section on the polygraph ("lie detector").

Techniques of Crime Scene Investigation. Arne Svensson and Otto Wendel, translated from the Swedish by Jan Beck, edited by J. D. Nicol (Elsevier Publishing Co., New York, 1965). A revised and enlarged edition of the same authors' *Crime Detection* (Cleaver-Hume Press, London, 1955). A compendious textbook for the investigating officer.

The Crime Laboratory: Case Studies of Scientific Criminal Investigation. James W. Osterburg (Indiana University Press, Bloomington and London, 1968). A large book for the investigating officer; contains a wealth of examples of marks, scratches, physical fits, footprints, etc.

Criminal Investigation and Physical Evidence Handbook. Staff of State of Wisconsin Crime Laboratory (Department of Justice, State of Wisconsin, 1968). A first-rate brief guide for the police officer submitting material to the laboratory in all types of crime

Fundamentals of Criminal Investigation. Charles E. O'Hara (Charles C. Thomas,

Springfield, Ill., 2nd edition 1970). For the investigating officer, with ample reference to the laboratory's function.

The Criminologist. Edited by Nigel Morland (Wolfe Publishing Ltd., London, 1971). A collection of reprints of articles from the journal of the same name (see below), some of these being of scientific interest.

An Introduction to Criminalistics. James W. Osterburg (Indiana University Press, Bloomington and London, 1972). A revised version of a book first published by Messrs. Macmillan in 1949.

Parts of the subject are also treated in the standard textbooks of forensic medicine (*e.g.* those by Sydney Smith and by Glaister, which are frequently revised and have passed through numerous editions). The numerous more recent smaller textbooks of the subject—most of the leading forensic pathologists have written at least one each—tend to reflect the pressures of an ever-expanding medical curriculum, and to be purely medical, omitting most of the toxicology and all details of laboratory methods.

The classic English language authority in this field is *Taylor's Principles and Practice of Medical Jurisprudence* (12th edition, revised by Professor Keith Simpson and collaborators; Churchill Livingstone, Edinburgh and London; two volumes, 1965). *Gradwohl's Legal Medicine* (2nd edition, revised by the late Professor Francis E. Camps; John Wright, Bristol, 1968) is a rather splendidly produced British revision of a former American rival.

JOURNALS

Journal of the Forensic Science Society (published by the Society). Contains original papers for a scientific readership; good abstracts section.

Medicine, Science and the Law (the journal of the British Academy of Forensic Sciences; published by John Wright & Sons, Bristol). Mainly medical and legal, but contains some original scientific papers; also review articles.

Journal of Forensic Sciences (the journal of the American Academy of Forensic Sciences). Original papers for the professionally concerned reader; covers the whole field.

Forensic Science (a new journal incorporating the former South African *Journal of Forensic Medicine*; published by Elsevier Sequoia S.A., Lausanne). Original papers for the professionally concerned reader. Proposes to cover the whole field, but the first issues have dealt mainly with medical topics.

Journal of Criminal Law, Criminology and Police Science (published for the North-Western School of Law by Williams and Wilkins Co., Baltimore, Md.). Contains a small but useful scientific section; the "science" of "police science" includes a good deal of psychology and sociology. Excellent abstracts section.

Australian Journal of Forensic Sciences (published for the Australian Academy of Forensic Sciences by The Law Book Publishing Co., Sydney). A small journal; general and review articles; no scientific papers.

Journal of the Canadian Society of Forensic Science (published by the Society in Ottawa). Contains scientific papers covering the whole field.

Journal of the Indian Academy of Forensic Science (published in Calcutta). Appears to cover the whole field, but has proved difficult to obtain in the West.

Medico-Legal Journal (the journal of the Medico-Legal Society, London). No purely scientific papers, but contains articles of general interest in the field—accounts of unusual cases, etc.

The Criminologist (Forensic Publishing Co., London). For the interested general reader, but often contains articles of scientific interest taken from less easily accessible sources.

All of the above journals are in English, and most appear quarterly.

Médicine Légale et Dommage Corporel (in French; published by J.-P. Baillière, Paris; formerly *Annales de Médicine Légale*). Original research papers for the professional reader; primarily medical, but also covers immunology, toxicology, etc.

Zeitschrift für Rechtsmedizin and Journal of Legal Medicine (contents in either German or English; published by Springer Verlag, Berlin and Heidelberg, and by J. F. Bergmann, Munich; formerly *Deutsche Zeitschrift für die gesamte gerichtliche Medizin*). Original research papers for the professional reader; primarily medical, but also covers immunology, toxicology, drink-and-driving studies, etc.

Kriminalistik und forensische Wissenschaften (in German; published from the Humboldt University, Berlin; the medico-legal journal for Communist Europe). Original papers for the professional reader, mainly immunology and toxicology; also criminology and penology from a Communist point of view.

Archiv für Kriminologie (in German; published by Georg Schmidt, Lübeck). Criminology, police methods and forensic science.

Kriminalistik (in German; published by Verlag für kriminalistische Fachliteratur, Hamburg). Primarily a police journal, but contains occasional articles on the more non-technical parts of forensic science such as document examination.

LABORATORY ORGANISATION

Crime Laboratory by Paul L. Kirk and L. W. Bradford (Charles C. Thomas, Springfield, Ill., 1965).

"The Administration of a Forensic Science Laboratory" by Robert F. Borkenstein, in *Methods of Forensic Science*, Vol. 3 (1964), p. 151.

Both of these are informed discussions of the subject by very experienced authors, although the present writer does not agree with all of the opinions expressed in them.

MARKS, SCRATCHES AND PHYSICAL FITS

A monograph specifically on footprint comparison is *Footwear Evidence* by John Reginald Abbott (Charles C. Thomas, Springfield, Ill., 1964).

ROAD ACCIDENTS

For the role of tyre failures in accidents, and the investigation of tyre damage in general, see R. J. Grogan (*Journal of the Forensic Science Society* Vol. 9 (1969), p. 13, and Vol. 12 (1972), p. 285). See also P. D. B. Clarke (*ibid.* Vol. 12 (1972),

p. 559). For the calculation of speeds see C. K. Riler (*Journal of Criminal Law, Criminology and Police Science* (1967), Vol. 58, p. 119).

GEMMOLOGY

"The Role of Gemmology" by Robert Webster (*Medicine, Science and the Law* (1972), Vol. 12, p. 31) is an excellent short review of the subject. The following are standard textbooks covering every aspect of it: *Gem Testing* by B. W. Anderson (Butterworth & Co., London, 8th edition 1971); *Gemstones* by G. F. Herbert Smith, revised by F. C. Coles Phillips (Chapman & Hall, London, 14th edition 1972); *Gems: their Sources, Description and Identification* by Robert Webster (Butterworth & Co., London, 2nd revised edition 1972). The last-mentioned author's *The Gemmologist's Compendium* is a small handbook packed with useful information. A more specialised work is *Diamonds* by E. Bruton (N. A. G. Press, London, 1970).

ALCOHOL AND ROAD TRAFFIC

The literature of this subject is widely scattered in numerous scientific journals, research reports, etc. The most important of these sources are cited in *Drink, Drugs and Driving*, by H. J. Walls and A. R. Brownlie (Sweet & Maxwell, London, 1970), which covers, but in greater detail, the same ground as the scientific parts of Chapter 9, and deals fully with the English and Scottish law on the subject up to 1969. The clinical aspect is dealt with shortly, readably and authoritatively in *The Drinking Driver* (British Medical Association, 1965). Much valuable material bearing on the subject is published in the U.S.A. by the National Safety Council (425 North Michigan Avenue, Chicago, Ill., 60611). The only journal wholly devoted to the subject is *Blutalkohol* (in German), published by Verlag Deutsche Polizei, Hamburg. An excellent recent monograph on a closely allied specific topic is *Drugs and Driving* by Gerald Milner (S. Karger, Basel and Australasian Drug Information Services Pty. Ltd., Sydney; distributed in U.K. by John Wiley & Sons Ltd., Chichester, 1972).

TOXICOLOGY AND DRUG IDENTIFICATION

This is technically a most extensively documented subject. *Poisons*, by F. Bodin and C. F. Cheinisse, translated by Harold Oldroyd (World University Library paperback; Weidenfeld & Nicolson, London, 1970), is a useful little background book, though not unnaturally with a French "slant." *Toxicology of Drugs and Chemicals*, by William B. Deichmann and Horace W. Gerarde (Academic Press, New York and London, 1969), should be a useful source of information about any particular poison, consisting as it does of an alphabetically arranged short encyclopedia of poisonous substances and their properties.

Two books specifically about the hallucinatory drugs and their effects are: *Drugs of Hallucination* by Sidney Cohen (Secker & Warburg, London, 1965) and *The Varieties of Psychedelic Experience* by R. E. L. Masters and Jean Houston (Anthony Blond, London, 1967).

IDENTIFICATION

The official textbook on the Henry fingerprint system is *The Fingerprint System at Scotland Yard*, by F. R. Cherrill (H.M.S.O., 1954).

An interesting account of a murder case in Scotland, in which crucial evidence was provided by the matching of the accused's teeth with bite marks on the victim's body, is given in a multi-author monograph forming the whole of Vol. 8, part 4, of the *Journal of the Forensic Science Society* (1968).

There is a vast literature on blood and bloodstain grouping, but almost all of it is highly technical. A monograph on the subject written specifically for the lawyer by A. R. Brownlie appeared as Vol. 5, part 3 of the *Journal of the Forensic Science Society* (1965); it cannot of course take account of more recent scientific advances, and recent legislation, especially the Family Law Reform Act 1969, has also made it out-of-date in some legal respects. An excellent account of the present British law on the subject will be found in "The Use of Blood Tests in the Pursuit of Truth," by Mary Hayes (*Law Quarterly Review* (1971), Vol. 87, p. 86). The American use of blood grouping in paternity tests is fully dealt with in *Blood Grouping Tests: Medicolegal Uses*, by Leon Sussman (Charles C. Thomas, Springfield, Ill., 1968); the book contains a good deal of technical information on the inheritance of groups within the most important systems.

FIRES AND EXPLOSIONS

Fire Investigation, by Paul L. Kirk (John Wiley, New York, London, Sydney and Toronto, 1969) gives a fairly complete and well-balanced account of the subject, while assuming little or no scientific background.

The illegal use of explosives (other than in connection with safe-blowing) is dealt with briefly but authoritatively in *Explosives and Home-Made Bombs*, by J. C. Stoffel (Charles C. Thomas, Springfield, Ill., 1962).

FIREARMS

The limited field of firearms is fairly intensively documented. *The Identification of Firearms and Forensic Ballistics*, by Sir Gerald Burrard (1st, British, edition, Herbert Jenkins, London, 1951; 2nd, American, edition, A. S. Barnes & Co., New York, 1962); *Firearms Investigation, Identification and Evidence*, by Julian S. Hatcher, Frank J. Jury and Jac Weller (The Stackpole Company, Harrisburg, Penn., 1957); *Hatcher's Notebook*, by Julian S. Hatcher (ibid., 1962) are all excellent. An excellent paperback, *Firearms and Ammunition Fact Book*, was published in 1964 by the National Rifle Association, Washington, D.C. The Stackpole Company also publishes an excellent and detailed series of books by W. H. B. Smith on the various types of small arms. The last word on the subject is probably the encyclopedic *Firearms Identification*, by J. Howard Matthews (2 volumes; University of Wisconsin Press, 1962). More recently a bibliography of the subject has been produced as a pamphlet by the International Criminal Police Organisation: *Identification of Firearms and Ammunition* (Interpol, Paris, 1970).

DOCUMENTS

Questioned Documents, by Albert S. Osborn (American; 2nd edition 1929), was for many years the standard reference work in this field, and even yet cannot be considered quite superseded. More recent compendious textbooks in English are: *The Scientific Examination of Documents* by Ordway Hilton (Callaghan & Co., Chicago, 1956); *Evidential Documents* by J. V. P. Conway (Charles C. Thomas, Springfield, Ill., 1959); *Suspect Documents: their Scientific Examination* by Wilson R. Harrison (Sweet & Maxwell, London, 1958). *Forgery Detection* (Sweet & Maxwell, 1964), also by Dr. Harrison, who was for many years the leading British authority in this field, is a small book addressed specifically to the non-expert and containing much practical good advice.

PHOTOGRAPHY

There are a number of books dealing with photography in law enforcement, though not specifically with laboratory photography. The largest of these is the immense three-volume *Photographic Evidence*, by Charles C. Scott (West Publishing Co., St. Paul, Minn., 2nd edition 1969). Two other American books are: *Photographic Evidence: the Preparation and Use of Photographs in Civil and Criminal Cases*, by S. G. Ehrlich and Leland V. Jones (Maclaren & Sons, London, 1967) and *Modern Photography for Police and Firemen*, by Sam J. Sansone (W. H. Anderson, Cincinnati, Ohio, 1971). A British one is: *Police Photography*, by H. Pountney (Elsevier Publishing Co., London, 1971).

Messrs. Kodak publish an excellent series of booklets on various aspects of photography in connection with law enforcement. The papers presented at a meeting of the Forensic Science Society on "Forensic Photography" are reproduced in Vol. 4, nos. 2 and 3 (1963 and 1964) of the Society's *Journal*. Other useful information will be found in the articles "Crime Photography," "Evidence by Photographs," "Forgery Detection" and "Police Photography" in *The Focal Encyclopedia of Photography* (Focal Press, London, 1965). Finally a modest little new journal specifically devoted to this topic has appeared: *Forensic Photography* (quarterly from Forensic Photography, P.O. Box 18, Bognor Regis, Sussex).

THE SCIENTIST IN THE WITNESS BOX

An interesting account of a colloquium on "The Expert Witness" appears in the *Journal of the Forensic Science Society* (1961), Vol. 2, p. 19. The misunderstanding which arises between lawyers and scientists has been discussed by the present writer in an article in *The Criminal Law Review* (1971, p. 458), where reference will be found to other discussions of the evidential use of statistical probabilities. The paper's hypothetical statistics have been criticised, but, right or wrong, should provide something to think about.

GLOSSARY

Words in CAPITALS are defined elsewhere in the glossary.

Adsorption. The process whereby the surface of a solid may attract and hold firmly the molecules of another gaseous, liquid or dissolved substance. The most effective adsorbents are therefore finely divided and/or porous, so that their surface area is large in relation to their gross bulk.

Alcohol. One of a class of chemical compounds containing a *hydroxyl* RADICAL (one oxygen and one hydrogen atom) attached to an open carbon-atom skeleton. The best known is *ethanol* (or ethyl alcohol), the alcohol present in intoxicating liquors. Another is *methanol* (methyl alcohol; wood alcohol).

Aliquot. A precisely known proportional part, from the analysis of which the composition of the whole can be calculated.

Allele. See p. 141.

Allelomorph. See p. 141.

Alveoli. The ultimate tiny air spaces in the lungs through the walls of which gases and vapours are exchanged between the breath and the blood.

Anaerobic. Of organisms which can live, or processes which can occur, in the absence of air (oxygen).

Angiosperms. Plants the seeds of which are enclosed in an ovary; synonymous for practical purposes with *flowering plants*. One of the two sub-divisions of *seed plants* (*cf.* GYMNOSPERMS).

Anion. See ION.

Aromatic. A technical term of organic chemistry, applied to compounds in which the carbon-atoms skeletons form closed rings having a certain type of inter-atomic bonding, and of which *benzene* is the prototype.

Asymptotic. Mathematically, of a line to which another continually approaches without ever meeting it. Loosely and by analogy, of a continued gradual approach without actual meeting.

Autoradiography. A method of showing radio-activity, or radio-active sites, in an object by allowing it to act on a piece of X-ray film in contact with it.

Axis (of a lens). The line joining the centres of the spheres of which the glass surfaces of the lens are parts; the line about which the lens is circularly symmetrical.

Azeotrope. A mixture of liquids of a composition such that it has a constant boiling-point lower or higher than that of any other mixture of the same components (*cf.* EUTECTIC), and hence distils without change of composition.

Bast fibres. Fibres occurring beneath the bark or outer layer of plant stems; some (flax, jute, hemp, etc.) are used in making fabrics or cordage.

Bio-assay. The estimation of the amount or potency of a drug or other physiologically active substance by its action on a suitable living organism.

Birefringence. The property whereby some fibres, natural crystals and certain constituents of living tissues have two *refractive indices* (see p. 69), and so split a ray of light passing through them into two (*cf.* isotropic).

Buffer. A solution of salts, etc., so formulated that the effects of adding small quantities of acid or alkali are neutralised, and such additions do not change the P_H.

Catalysis, Catalyst. A catalyst is any substance which promotes a chemical reaction by its presence without itself being used up in the reaction. This effect is called *catalysis*.

Cation. See ION.

c.c. See METRIC UNITS.

Centimetre. See METRIC UNITS.

Centrifuge. An instrument for rapidly separating the constituents of a suspension of a solid in a liquid, or of one liquid in another with which it is immiscible, (*e.g.* blood, milk, muddy water) by whirling it round in a suitable container, so that separation by centrifugal force is much faster than it would be by gravity alone.

Chain reaction. A reaction (often explosively rapid) in which the energy liberated by the reaction of the first few molecules serves to "trigger off" the reaction of others, and so on progressively until all of the available material has reacted.

Chromatography. See p. 63.

Chromosomes. See p. 140.

Collimate. A collimator is an optical arrangement using slits or the like to produce or isolate parallel rays from a divergent beam.

Colloid. Substances of large MOLECULAR WEIGHT, such as starches, gums and proteins, which form amorphous solids and dissolve or disperse in water to form "gooey" solutions.

Conchoidal. A conchoidal fracture is one resulting in a smooth, generally curved and sometimes slightly fluted surface, as with glass or pitch.

Contractions. See METRIC UNITS.

Depth of focus. The limits of distance within which the image is acceptably sharp on either side of the optimum focusing position for a lens.

Dialysis. A process whereby substances having small molecules or IONS (*e.g.* most salts) can be separated from a solution also containing COLLOIDS by allowing them to diffuse into water through the pores of a membrane (frequently cellophane) too fine for the colloids to pass through.

Diatoms. Various species of minute single-celled water-living organisms with silica "skeletons" which show a fine structure characteristic of the species.

Electrolysis. See ION.

Electron beam. See p. 81.

Electrophoresis. See p. 65.

Emulsion (photographic). The thin gelatin coating on a photographic plate or film which carries the light-sensitive compounds forming the image after exposure and development.

Endothermic. Of a chemical reaction which absorbs heat.

Enzymes. The constituents of living matter which act as CATALYSTS for the chemical processes of life.

Esters. A class of compounds each formed by the combination of an ALCOHOL and an acid. They have two-word names, the first word indicating the alcohol and the second the acid—*e.g. ethyl acetate*. Usually liquids with a strong, characteristic, often fragrant, smell. However, *fats* (p. 56) are also esters.

Eutectic. The melting- or freezing-point of any element or compound is lowered by the presence of another in solution. Hence if two substances A and B are miscible in all proportions, the melting-point of A is progressively lowered by the increasing addition of B, and similarly that of B by A. An A–B mixture of some particular composition will therefore have a minimum melting-point: this is the *eutectic* mixture. There may also be eutectic mixtures of more than two components. (*cf.* AZEOTROPE).

Exothermic. Of a chemical reaction which produces heat.

Eyepiece. In microscopy, the compound lens nearest the eye; usually interchangeable according to the degree of magnification required.

Fluorescence. See p. 74.

Focal length. The distance, for a lens or concave mirror, between its centre (or *nodal point* for a compound lens such as that of a camera or microscope) and the point at which parallel rays of light entering it are brought to a focus. For a lens, it depends upon the *refractive index* (see p. 69) of the glass(es) and the curvatures of the surfaces.

γ. Greek *gamma*. An obsolescent contraction for *microgram*. γ-radiation is very short-wave radiation produced by radioactive substances. (See p. 78).

Gas chromatography. See p. 65.

Gel. A technical and more strictly delimited term for "jelly"; the state of a COLLOID such as starch or gelatin which has swollen and softened by the absorption of water (*cf.* IMBIBITION).

G.L.C. Contraction for *gas-liquid chromatography*: see p. 65.

Gram; gramme. See METRIC UNITS.

Gymnosperms. Plants the seeds of which are naked, the best-known examples being the coniferous trees (*cf.* ANGIOSPERMS).

Half-life. See p. 80.

Heterozygous. See p. 141.

Homologous. In chemistry, a homologous series is one of organic compounds each member of which differs from its predecessor by possessing one more carbon atom and associated hydrogen atoms; *e.g.* the ALCOHOLS methanol, ethanol, propanol, butanol, etc.

Homozygous. See p. 141.

Hydrate. A SALT which contains water in loose chemical combination.

Hydrolysis. Decomposition of a compound into two or more simpler ones by the action and addition of water. This may require the action of heat, acids, alkalis, ENZYMES etc.

Hyperglycaemia. The condition in which the blood-glucose (blood-sugar) level is above the normal limits.

Hypoglycaemia. The condition in which the blood-glucose level is below the normal limits.

Ignition. Has the technical meaning in chemistry of heating to a high temperature. The substance ignited may be incombustible and may not actually burn.

Imbibition. The softening and swelling of a gelatinous material by the absorption of water.

Immunology. The study of the reactions of living organisms to the introduction into their bodies of foreign substances of biological origin which provoke an *immune reaction* (*e.g.* immunisation by vaccination is such a reaction). *Immunoserology* is the study of immune reactions occurring in or associated with the blood serum; many of the reactions used in blood grouping are of this type.

Infra-red. See p. 70.

Interference. In optics (the study of light) an effect due to light behaving as a wave motion, so that if the "troughs" of one set of waves coincide with the "crests" of another, the waves will cancel each other out and the light will be extinguished. With white light, interference can lead to the production of colours by the extinguishing of some parts of the spectrum (*e.g.* the colours of an oil film on water).

Internal standard. Certain methods of analysis which are primarily qualitative (*e.g.* gas chromatography—p. 65; emission spectrography—p. 70) can be made quantitative by the addition to the mixture to be analysed of a known amount of a component not originally present—*i.e.* an *internal standard*. The ratio of the magnitudes of the effects produced by any original component and by the internal standard can then be used to measure the amount of the former.

Ion. An ion is an atom or molecule which, by losing or gaining one or more electrons, has acquired an electric charge. Gases may be ionised, and soluble salts, acids and bases exist in solution as positive and negative ions. Hence the passage of an electric current through such a solution (*electrolysis*) causes the negative ions (*anions*) to move to the positive electrode (*anode*) and the positive ions (*cations* or, occasionally, *kations*) to the negative electrode (*cathode*).

Ion-exchange resin. A resinous compound so formulated that it will remove selected ions from a solution by an exchange of these with ions present in its own substance.

Isotonic saline. A solution of salt having the same *osmotic pressure* as tissue fluids, in which cells will therefore neither swell through water passing in by osmosis, nor shrink by it passing out.

Isotope. An atom consists of a *nucleus* of *protons* and *neutrons* surrounded by as many electrons as there are protons in the nucleus. This number—the *atomic number*—determines the chemical properties of the atom (*i.e.* its identity as an element). Elements composed of atoms having the same atomic numbers but different numbers of neutrons in the nucleus are chemically identical and are known as *isotopes*. They can be separated by very small differences in their physical properties. There is no inherent connection between the phenomenon of radio-activity and the existence of isotopes, but the terms are often associated because of the theoretical interest and technical importance of artificially made radio-active isotopes of non-radio-active elements.

Isotropic. Having identical optical properties in all directions through the material (*cf.* BIREFRINGENCE).

Kilogram. See METRIC UNITS.

λ. Greek *lambda*. Commonly used to designate *wavelength*.

Labile. Of a substance which is inherently unstable and therefore liable to decompose or disappear on keeping.

Laser (from *Light Amplification by Stimulated Emission Radiation*). An electrical/optical device for producing a *coherent* parallel beam of light—that is, one in which the light waves are all in phase. Such a beam can be made much more precisely narrow and parallel than can one of ordinary light.

Litre. See METRIC UNITS.

μ. Greek *mu* (pronounced "mew"). Commonly used to designate *refractive index*. See also METRIC UNITS.

Metabolism. The system of chemical reactions in a living organism which are essential to, and occur during, life. The substances produced by these reactions are known as *metabolites*. Hence drugs administered may, after undergoing reactions in the body, be excreted or recovered as their metabolites.

Metalloids. Certain elements (*e.g.* arsenic, antimony) which are intermediate between metals and non-metals in their properties. Commonly, the element is metallic in appearance and in some of its physical properties in the solid pure state, but behaves as a non-metal when in chemical combination.

Metric units. The following units are commonly used in the sciences. Accepted contractions are shown in brackets.

Length

    Centimetre (cm.) $1/100$ of a *metre*; approximately $= 0\cdot4$ inch.

    Millimetre (mm.) $1/10$ of a centimetre.

    Micron ⎫
    Millimicron ⎬ See p. 69, footnote.
    Nanometre ⎭

    Ångstrom unit (Å or A.U.). See p. 78.

Volume

    Cubic centimetre (c.c.) Formerly used in medicine and chemistry; now superseded by the MILLILITRE.

    Litre (l.) Originally defined as 1,000 cubic centimetres. 1 litre = approximately 35 fluid ounces or $1\frac{3}{4}$ British pints.

    Millilitre (ml.) $1/1,000$ of a litre. Approximately = 20 average drops. Commonly referred to by chemists as "mil."

Weight (more correctly, *Mass*)

    Gram, Gramme (g.; sometimes, but incorrectly, gm.) Originally defined as the weight of 1 c.c. of water at 4 °C. Approximately = 15 grains or 1/28 of an ounce avoirdupois. Three aspirin tablets weigh approximately 1 gram.

    Kilogram (kg.) 1,000 grams. About 2·2 pounds.

The following prefixes are used for fractions of the basic units:

    Milli- (m). $1/1,000$ (Unit $\times$ 10^{-3}).

    Micro- (μ). $1/1,000,000$ (Unit $\times$ 10^{-6}).

    Nano- (n or mμ). $11,000,000,000$ (Unit $\times$ 10^{-9}).

    Pico- (μμ). $11,000,000,000,000$ (Unit $\times$ 10^{-12}).

Molecular weight. A number proportional to the weight of a molecule, on a scale in which the relative weight 16 is arbitrarily assigned to the oxygen atom.

Monomer. A compound, usually liquid, the molecules of which readily react with each other to form a solid *polymer*. Many polymers are technically useful as plastics, synthetic fibres, etc.

n. Commonly used to designate *refractive index*.

Nano-. See METRIC UNITS.

Neoprene. A synthetic rubber made by the polymerisation of the appropriate MONOMER.

Nicol prism. A slab of BIREFRINGENT material cut so that one of the rays emerging from it is POLARISED.

Normal saline. Another term for ISOTONIC SALINE.

Objective. In *photography*, a rather formal term for the camera lens. In *microscopy*, the compound lens nearest the object under examination, and therefore usually at the lower end of the microscope barrel. The shorter the FOCAL LENGTH of the objective, the higher the magnification produced, and the less the distance between the objective and the object. With very short focal lengths, this distance must for technical reasons be filled with a medium having a higher refractive index than air; an oil is normally used for this—hence *oil-immersion objective* (or *lens*).

Olein. The ESTER of oleic acid and the ALCOHOL glycerol (glycerin). One of the chief constituents of non-drying fats and oils.

Optical activity. See RACEMIC.

Organoleptic. Of testing or identification by means of the senses—commonly smell or taste.

Oxidation. A chemical reaction which results in the production from an element of a compound with oxygen, or in the transformation of a compound into another containing more oxygen or (which is chemically equivalent) less hydrogen; also increasing the electron deficit of a SALT-forming positive ION.

Parameter. A measurable quantity which can have any magnitude but the magnitude of which in a specific case constitutes an identifying characteristic; *e.g.* the length of a piece of string, or the cylinder capacity of a motor car.

Partition coefficient. When two immiscible liquids are shaken together and any dissolved substance soluble in both is present, its concentrations in the two liquids after separation depend on a PARAMETER known as the *partition coefficient*.

pH. See p. 67.

Pharmacognosy. The identification of plant materials used in pharmacy by means of their microscopic appearance.

Phase. In chemistry, "any homogeneous and physically distinct part of a system which is separated from the other parts of the system by definite bounding surfaces" (Samuel Glasstone, *Textbook of Physical Chemistry*). For example, gin-and-tonic is a one-phase system; oil and vinegar a two-phase; ice, water and water vapour a three-phase. All solutions and gases are one-phase systems. In a typical rock, there are as many phases as there are separate crystalline minerals.

Phase contrast. A type of microscopy in which a transparent object is made more visible by arranging for INTERFERENCE to occur between rays which have, and those which have not, passed through the object.

Photons. According to the *quantum theory* any electromagnetic radiation can behave either as a wave motion or as a stream of discrete *quanta* of energy. Photon is the name applied to a quantum of light or other radiant energy of very short wavelength.

Photosynthesis. A synthetic (*i.e.* building-up) reaction which uses energy reaching the reactants as light (*e.g.* the production in sunlight of chlorophyll, the green colouring matter of plants).

Pico-. See METRIC UNITS.

Pipette. A pointed glass tube for delivering small volumes of liquid. The type used in chemistry delivers an accurately known volume from a graduation mark. The type used in bacteriology, blood grouping, etc., is not graduated and delivers a roughly-known volume, or a chosen number of drops, by compression of a rubber teat.

Plasma. The liquid part of the blood, in which the cells are suspended. *Cf.* SERUM.

Polarisation, polarised light. The mathematical physics of light considered as a wave motion makes it necessary to assume that the displacement which constitutes each wave is randomly in all directions perpendicular to the direction in which the light is travelling. After passage through certain materials, or reflection in certain circumstances, the light behaves as if the displacement was then in one direction (plane) only; it is then *polarised*. The properties of polarised light make it valuable as an illuminant for microscopy in certain circumstances.

Polyethylene glycol. One of a class of compounds having a long chain of hydrogen-bearing carbon atoms and a hydroxyl RADICAL at each end. They are liquid or waxy, soluble in both water and organic solvents, and used as lubricants, wetting agents, the stationary phase in gas chromatography, etc.

Polyphasic. Containing or consisting of more than one PHASE.

Polymer, polymerisation. See MONOMER.

Proteolytic. Of ENZYMES, mostly derived from the digestive juices, which CATALYSE the chemical breakdown of proteins to simpler compounds.

Pyrolysis. Breaking down by heat of complex into simper compounds.

Racemic. If the molecule of an organic compound has no plane of symmetry, the compound is *optically active*—*i.e.* a solution of it "twists" the plane of POLARISATION of polarised light in one direction or the other, according to whether it is the *dextro* (*d*) or mirror-image *laevo* (*l*) form. A mixture of the two forms in equal proportions is optically inactive and is known as *racemic*.

Radical (also radicle). In chemistry, any sub-molecular grouping of atoms which occurs as a constant recognisable entity in a variety of different compounds; (*e.g.* the hydroxyl radical in ALCOHOLS).

Radiochemistry. The branch of chemistry concerned with the manipulation of radio-active substances, with which special techniques and precautions are necessary.

Rare earth elements. A group of rare elements closely similar in their chemical properties and forming highly infusible (*i.e.* "earth"-like) oxides. The best-known member is *cerium*, the oxide of which was used in gas mantles.

Recorder. An instrument for amplifying very small potential (voltage) fluctuations, and displaying these as a continuous graph on a roll of paper. Used therefore as the recording instrument in any analytical method in which the "signal" is or can be converted to an electric potential—*e.g.* gas chromatography.

Reduction. The opposite of OXIDATION (*q.v.*)—*i.e.* the removal of oxygen or addition of hydrogen, or decreasing the electron deficit of a positive ION.

Refractive index. (Designated *n* or μ; the two symbols do not stand for exactly the same thing, but the difference can be ignored here.) See p. 69. It determines the amount of deviation which a ray of light undergoes on passing across the boundary between that substance and another (normally air).

Refractometer. See p. 69.

Saline. Often used loosely for ISOTONIC SALINE, *q.v.*

Salt. A compound of positive IONS (normally of a metallic element) and negative ions of an acid (e.g. *sodium chloride, copper sulphate*). All true salts are crystalline, the crystals consisting of an ordered *lattice* of the two sorts of ions. Most salts are also soluble in water, and are present in solution largely or wholly as ions, not as molecules.

Saturation (of colour). A *saturated* colour is one which can be exactly matched by a pure colour of the spectrum, or by a mixture of spectrum red and violet. To match an *unsaturated* colour, white or a neutral tint must be added to the spectrum colour.

Serology, serum. The *serum* is the liquid remaining after all solid and clottable constituents of blood have been removed. Often used loosely for PLASMA. *Serology* is the study of the reactions and properties of serum. See also IMMUNOLOGY.

Spectrograph, spectroscope. See p. 70.

Spectrophotometer. See p. 72.

Standard deviation. If a measurement or analysis is repeated several times, the results will not, because of inevitable small experimental errors, be exactly the same in every case. The *standard deviation* is a quantity which is calculated from their individual departures from their mean value, and which measures their "scatter"—the extent to which they collectively depart from the mean, and presumed, correct value. It can then also be used to predict the probable accuracy of another measurement or analysis made by the same operator using the same method.

Super-cooled liquid. Strictly, a liquid cooled below its freezing-point without having solidified, this being possible in certain circumstances. Loosely, a glass or glass-like substance which merely softens on heating and for which there is at no temperature a sharp change from the solid to the liquid state.

Temperature scales.
  For conversion:
  °F to °C: Subtract 32 and multiply by 5/9.
  °C to °F: Multiply by 9/5 and add 32.

Thermocouple. Temperature-measuring device which depends on the fact that, in a closed circuit containing two identical junctions between different metals, if the junctions are at different temperatures a current flows in the circuit. In practice, one junction is kept at a low constant temperature (o °C—melting ice) and the other is exposed to the unknown temperature. The electric potential then produced is then proportional to, and can be used to measure, that temperature.

Thermoplastic. Of plastics which soften on heating and harden on cooling, this process being repeatable as desired (*e.g.* Perspex).

Thermosetting. Of plastics which harden irreversibly on heating (*e.g.* Bakelite).

Titration. The analytical operation of adding a reagent until a reaction is complete and measuring the volume so added.

T.L.C. Contraction for *thin-layer chromatography*. (See p. 64.)

Ultra-violet. See p. 70.

Units (and contractions). See METRIC UNITS.

Vapour pressure. The gas pressure, normally expressed in barometric units (equivalent *millimetres of mercury*), of the vapour above the surface of a liquid. It rises with temperature, and is equal to the atmospheric pressure at the boiling-point of the liquid.

V.P.C. Contraction for *Vapour-phase chromatography* (See p. 65).

v/v. Contraction for *volume/volume*. (See below.)

Wave number. A number inversely proportional to the wavelength of a radiation, and therefore proportional to the *frequency*. Commonly used instead of wavelength in specifying infra-red radiation used in spectrophotometry. (See p. 74.)

w/v. Contraction for *weight/volume*.

w/w. Contraction for *weight/weight*.

The last two entries (together with v/v—see above) are all used following figures referring to the concentrations of solutions. For example, if a solution of alcohol in water is:

"5 per cent. v/v," it contains 5 millilitres of alcohol per 100 millilitres of solution;

"5 per cent. w/v," it contains 5 grams of alcohol per 100 millilitres of solution;

"5 per cent. w/w," it contains 5 grams of alcohol per 100 grams of solution.

Obviously, when the solute (in this case alcohol) and the solvent (in this case water) have different densities, then these "5 per cent." concentrations will all be different.

X-ray crystallography. See p. 78.

INDEX

Proper names appear in *italics*, unless they form part of a recognised technical term (*e.g.* Stokes' Law).

As this is not a text-book of toxicology, the numerous drugs and poisons mentioned in Chapter 10 have been indexed only if they are well known, representative or mentioned several times.

n: reference is to a footnote on the page in question.